a dictionary of
contemporary
GERMANY

TRISTAM CARRINGTON-WINDO & KATRIN KOHL

Hodder & Stoughton

A MEMBER OF THE HODDER HEADLINE GROUP

British Library Cataloguing in Publication Data

A catalogue record is available from the British Library

ISBN 0 340 65518 6

First published 1996
Impression number 10   9   8   7   6   5   4   3   2   1
Year   2001   2000   1999   1998   1997   1996

Typeset by Wearset, Boldon, Tyne and Wear.
Printed in Great Britain for Hodder & Stoughton Educational, a division of
Hodder Headline Plc, 338 Euston Road, London NW1 3BH by Redwood Books.

For Alice and Eliot

Foreword

A Dictionary of Contemporary Germany has over 2,000 entries providing explanations of terms and abbreviations used in the contemporary German press, and gives information about institutions and personalities in German public life. The dictionary is intended for students of German and other readers who require information on Germany of the kind that an educated person living in Germany would tend to be familiar with. Particular emphasis has been placed on terms connected with national and local government and education. In view of the federal nature and history of Germany, the dictionary highlights regional differences in all aspects of culture and public life. The economic importance of Germany is reflected in the entries on major companies, trade fairs and business concepts.

The dictionary cannot lay claim to being comprehensive in any systematic sense. Entries have been selected on the basis that they provide important information on contemporary German life. Occasionally more off-beat entries are included that give peripheral detail, such as that for the town SWAKOPMUND in Namibia, a remnant of Germany's colonial aspirations. Words that pose no particular linguistic or conceptual problem for the English user have normally not been included (e.g. *Schule* is not given, but GYMNASIUM is; however, UNIVERSITÄT is given because it needs to be distinguished from HOCHSCHULE). Usefulness has been the guiding principle rather than systematic inclusiveness. A severe limitation is of course the exclusion of information on Austria and Switzerland, and especially the artificial wedge driven between German, Austrian and Swiss culture. Institutions and concepts relating to the GDR have been excluded unless they continue to play an active part in contemporary life in the united Germany. Personalities have been limited to those who are alive at the time of going to press, and in the case of politicians normally those in office, although in some cases information on other personalities may be found under a more general heading (e.g. Hitler under DRITTES REICH).

The arrangement of the keywords is alphabetical. Where they consist of more than one word, the second (and third...) word is treated separately, so the following keywords would be found in this order:

DEUTSCH-POLNISCHER GRENZVERTRAG

DEUTSCHE LUFTHANSA AG

DEUTSCHER FILMPREIS

DEUTSCHES ARZNEIBUCH

Each word in small capital letters within an entry refers the reader to another keyword. Abbreviations are given as keywords with cross references to the full form, where the explanation will be found. Where the abbreviated form is the official designation, the details are given there (e.g. BMW AG). We have aimed to avoid sending the reader on a 'dictionary-go-round' from a capitalised cross-reference within one entry to a keyword that in turn refers on, but occasionally this has proved unavoidable where officialese would fail to reflect common usage, as with a reference to the broadcasting corporation ZDF, where the explanation is in fact under the full form ZWEITES DEUTSCHES FERNSEHEN. Towns with populations under 200,000 inhabitants have been included only in special cases (e.g. capitals of the Länder, UNESCO world heritage sites). Universities are preceded by the town or city in which they are located (e.g. BERLIN, FREIE UNIVERSITÄT). Placenames, organisations and institutions that are now historical are in italics (e.g. kingdom of *Württemberg*), except when they refer to a keyword and are in small capitals (e.g. SCHLESIEN). The German form of towns, organisations and political entities has normally been used (e.g. Sachsen, München, Potsdamer Abkommen, Land, Regierender Bürgermeister).

Population, membership and circulation figures are based on a variety of contemporary sources, including information supplied direct by towns, companies, etc. They have been given in round figures and are of course subject to fluctuation.

We should like to express our gratitude to the many towns and organisations in Germany who have provided information for this book. We also wish to thank the colleagues and friends who have helped in its compilation, and particularly Gordon Townsend for his practical support. Thanks are due especially to Günter Kohl (Ass. jur.), who read many of the entries and supplied invaluable information on political and legal subjects.

Our aim in writing this dictionary is to provide readers of German with a snapshot of life in contemporary Germany and a tool for accessing sources about Germany. The authors have made every effort to ensure that the information is accurate but welcome any corrections or suggestions from readers.

Tristam Carrington-Windo
Katrin Kohl
Oxford, April 1996

About the authors

Tristam Carrington-Windo worked as an editor of biographical reference works in Germany for three years. He is now a scientific and technical translator who has worked in the German market since 1980. He has published German language courses and is a visiting lecturer at the University of Westminster.

Katrin Kohl is a Faculty Lecturer in German at the University of Oxford and Fellow in German at Jesus College, Oxford. She has published multi-media German language courses with the BBC as well as books and articles on German language and literature.

The authors have jointly published *Deutsches Business Magazin* (Hodder & Stoughton, 1991) and *German means Business* (BBC, 1993).

AA See: *AUSWÄRTIGES AMT*

AACHEN (AIX-LA-CHAPELLE)

The most westerly city in Germany is situated in NORDRHEIN-WESTFALEN close to the Belgian and Dutch borders (dialling code 02 41, postal area code 52...). Aachen has played an important role in Germany's history: after 794 it became the principal seat of the Emperor Charlemagne (Karl der Große), and German kings were crowned in the cathedral between 936 and 1531. The city's magnificent cathedral with its DOMSCHATZKAMMER has been made a UNESCO world heritage site. Aachen's annual Karlsfest is held on 31 January each year in honour of Charlemagne, an international equestrian competition is held at the beginning of June, and the Stadtfest with theatre, music and pantomime takes place in September.

The city has a population of some 255,000 with a total student population of around 46,000 (1 UNIVERSITÄT and 3 other HOCHSCHULEN) and about 13% foreigners (26% Turkish). A coalition between the SPD and BÜNDNIS 90/DIE GRÜNEN has been running the city on a slim majority since 1989. Industries include paper, food and drink, chemicals, mining and electrical engineering. Important companies include Zentis, Lindt, Sprüngli, PHILIPS and Uniroyal with products such as tyres, chocolates, jam and the famous Aachener Printen (long, spicy Christmas biscuits).

AACHEN, RHEINISCH-WESTFÄLISCHE TECHNISCHE HOCHSCHULE

University in NORDRHEIN-WESTFALEN founded in 1880 and teaching some 36,000 students. The Rheinisch-Westfälische Technische Hochschule has a strong reputation in engineering and has faculties of science, architecture, civil engineering and surveying, mechanical engineering, mining and metallurgy and geology, electrical engineering, arts, economics, medicine.

AACHENER REVIER
The coalmining area around AACHEN.

ABB See: *ASEA BROWN BOVERI AG*

ABENDGYMNASIUM
A GYMNASIUM offering evening courses leading to ABITUR. These institutions are part of the ZWEITER BILDUNGSWEG and are only open to individuals in employment who have completed a BERUFS-AUSBILDUNG. See also: KOLLEG

ABENDREALSCHULE
A REALSCHULE offering courses leading to the REALSCHULAB-SCHLUSS. These institutions are part of the ZWEITER BILDUNGSWEG and are only open to individuals in employment.

ABENDSCHULE
An evening school providing general and vocational courses for the ZWEITER BILDUNGSWEG. These schools are only open to people in employment and are financed by a particular sector of industry or a local authority.

ABENDZEITUNG (MÜNCHEN)
Regional daily newspaper established in 1948 and published by the Verlag der Abendzeitung in MÜNCHEN. The *Abendzeitung* is published in the evening and is distributed throughout BAYERN with a circulation of 205,000.

ABFINDUNG
One-off redundancy payment as compensation for loss of employment. Redundancy payments in Germany are generally negotiated by the appropriate GEWERKSCHAFT and tend to be on the generous side.

ABGEORDNETENHAUS
The BERLIN equivalent of a LANDTAG (LANDESPARLAMENT). See also: BÜRGERSCHAFT

ABGEORDNETER

Elected member of the BUNDESTAG or a LANDTAG. *Artikel* 38 of the GRUNDGESETZ states that a *Bundestagsabgeordneter* (MITGLIED DES BUNDESTAGES) has to vote according to his or her conscience. Any citizen of the BUNDESREPUBLIK DEUTSCHLAND is eligible for election as an *Abgeordneter* or *Abgeordnete* provided that they have attained the age of 18 years on the day of the election and have had German nationality for a period of at least one year. See also: FRAKTIONSZWANG

ABITUR

The *Abitur* (or *Abi* for short) is the final examination taken by pupils in a GYMNASIUM at the age of 19/20, or by mature students following the ZWEITER BILDUNGSWEG. The ABITURZEUGNIS entitles students to study at a university.

Assessment for the *Abitur* is based on coursework in the 22 GRUNDKURSE and eight LEISTUNGSKURSE taken in the last two years at the *Gymnasium* (classes 12 and 13) and the results of the final examination in four subjects (2 *Leistungsfächer*, 2 *Grundkursfächer*). The *Abitur* result is expressed in terms of a traditional grading scale running from 1 to 6 that is in turn related to a complex point system. The grades used are: 1 (*sehr gut*, 13–15 points), 2 (*gut*, 10–12 points), 3 (*befriedigend*, 7–9 points), 4 (*ausreichend*, 4–6 points), 5 (*mangelhaft*, 1–3 points), 6 (*ungenügend*, 0 points).

Each of the 22 *Grundkurse* is worth a maximum of 15 points (maximum total 330 points). The two *Leistungskurse* taken in the final *Halbjahr* are each worth a maximum of 15 points, while the other six *Leistungskurse* are counted double, giving a maximum of 210 points for the eight *Leistungskurse*. A maximum of 300 points are awarded for the *Abitur* examination (including a component of 60 points for course assessment during the final *Halbjahr*). The final result is then computed by converting the point score obtained for the *Grundkurse*, *Leistungskurse* and final examination (maximum of 840 attainable points) to a NOTENDURCHSCHNITT on the scale of 1 to 6. The pass mark is 280 points or grade 4.0.

The *Abitur* is generally taken after 13 years at school.

Education is under the jurisdiction of the LÄNDER and consequently there are slight variations in the *Abitur* according to the
Land, e.g. in some NEUE BUNDESLÄNDER the *Abitur* is taken after
12 years at school. See also: HOCHSCHULREIFE; NUMERUS CLAUSUS;
KULTURHOHEIT DER LÄNDER

ABITURIENT
School-leaver completing a course of study at a GYMNASIUM with
the ABITUR as a university entrance qualification.

ABITURZEUGNIS
Certificate awarded to a pupil on successfully passing the ABITUR
examination.

ABONNEMENT
Many households in Germany subscribe to a daily newspaper
with an *Abonnement*. The German press has always relied on
subscriptions for finance, since they ensure that newpaper publishers have a regular income. People also subscribe to magazines by *Abonnement*.

ABSCHLUSSPRÜFUNG
Final examination taken by a pupil or student at a school, BERUFS-
SCHULE, HOCHSCHULE or other educational institution. Passing the
exam qualifies the candidate for entrance to a particular type of
school, or for taking up a particular AUSBILDUNG, STUDIUM or
Beruf.

Abschlußprüfung also refers to the statutory annual audit carried out in AKTIENGESELLSCHAFTEN and certain GMBHS by a
WIRTSCHAFTSPRÜFER.

ABSCHLUSSZEUGNIS
Certificate issued to a pupil or student following successful completion of a course or stage of education.

ABTREIBUNG See: *SCHWANGERSCHAFTSABBRUCH*

ACHTERNBUSCH, HERBERT (1938–)
Bavarian writer and film director. His work explores the experiences of the individual in society. His films – written, produced,
directed and acted in by Achternbusch – regularly break social

taboos, and the religious controversy surrounding his film *Das Gespenst* (1982) led to the withdrawal of a grant by the BUNDESIN-NENMINISTERIUM. Other films include *Das Andechser Gefühl* (1975), *Das letzte Loch* (1981), *Heilt Hitler* (1986), *I know the way to the Hofbräuhaus* (1991), *Ich bin da, ich bin da* (1992) and *Ab nach Tibet!* (1993).

ADAC See: *ALLGEMEINER DEUTSCHER AUTOMOBIL-CLUB*

ADAC MOTORWELT
Motoring magazine and Germany's biggest monthly with a circulation of 11.8 million. It is the membership magazine of the ALL-GEMEINER DEUTSCHER AUTOMOBIL-CLUB and covers all types of motoring issues. It is published by ADAC Verlag in MÜNCHEN.

ADN See: *ddp/ADN ALLGEMEINER DEUTSCHER NACHRICHTENDIENST GmbH*

ADORF, MARIO (1930–   )
Stage and film actor who started his career in 1954 and has lived and worked in Italy since the 1960s. Adorf has played in more than 70 films including SCHLÖNDORFF/TROTTA's *Die verlorene Ehre der Katharina Blum* (1975), Schlöndorff's *Die Blechtrommel* (1979) and Fassbinder's *Lola* (1981). He starred as the retired executive Peter Bellheim in the hugely successful four-part TV crime series *Der große Bellheim* (1993).

AEG AG
Electricals company founded in 1883, focusing on rail systems, microelectronics, diesel engines, power engineering and automation. The company ran into difficulties in the early 1980s and was taken over by DAIMLER-BENZ in 1985. Company headquarters are in FRANKFURT AM MAIN. AEG has some 45,000 employees.

AG See: *AKTIENGESELLSCHAFT*

AGB See: *ALLGEMEINE GESCHÄFTSBEDINGUNGEN*

AGFA-GEVAERT-GRUPPE
Photographic company, now a wholly-owned subsidiary of

BAYER. Company headquarters are in Leverkusen (NORDRHEIN-WESTFALEN). Agfa-Gevaert has some 23,000 employees.

AGIV-AG
General engineering company founded in 1881, with interests in machinery and electronics, energy, construction, transport and logistics. Company headquarters are in FRANKFURT AM MAIN. Agiv has some 41,000 employees.

AKADEMIE DER WISSENSCHAFTEN See: *KONFERENZ DER DEUTSCHEN AKADEMIEN DER WISSENSCHAFTEN*

AKADEMISCHES AUSLANDSAMT
Institution at each HOCHSCHULE to promote international contacts at university level and provide support for foreign students.

AKADEMISCHES VIERTEL
The 'academic 15 minutes' at the beginning of a lecture at a *wissenschaftliche* HOCHSCHULE. Traditionally a lecture scheduled for 9.00 will begin *cum tempore* at 9.15. A lecture *sine tempore* would begin at 9.00 on the dot.

AKTIENGESELLSCHAFT (AG)
A publicly owned company with a stock-market listing. Shares (*Aktien*) in the Aktiengesellschaft are bought and sold on the stock exchange. The VORSTAND is responsible for running the company and reports to the AUFSICHTSRAT, which is made up of representatives of shareholders and employees. See also: GESELLSCHAFT MIT BESCHRÄNKTER HAFTUNG

AKTIONÄR
Person holding shares in an AKTIENGESELLSCHAFT.

AKTIONSKUNST
Installation art that is generally executed outside the studio. Joseph Beuys was one of the first exponents of this art form concentrating on art as an event; for example, he had himself taken across the Rhine in a dug-out canoe. The pinnacle of installation art in Germany was the wrapping of the REICHSTAG by husband-and-wife team CHRISTO in 1995, which attracted some 5 million visitors.

ALDI EINKAUF GmbH & CO KG
Discount supermarket chain with over 2,000 outlets concentrating on a small number of products at knock-down prices. Headquarters of Germany's biggest food retailer are in Mülheim (NORDRHEIN-WESTFALEN). The company's success derives not least from its formula of just-in-time delivery, fast turnover and astute investment.

ALEXANDER VON HUMBOLDT STIFTUNG
Foundation established in 1925 and based in BONN. It provides some 500 scholarships annually to young academics from abroad to carry out post-doctoral research in all disciplines at universities in Germany. It also awards research grants to German academics to carry out post-doctoral research abroad.

ALEXANDERPLATZ
Large square at the centre of BERLIN (in the former east) with a distinguished history. It was named after the Russian Czar Alexander I and was canonised in Alfred Döblin's novel *Berlin Alexanderplatz* (1929), turned into a 14-part film epic by Rainer Werner Fassbinder (1980). Revolutionaries set up barricades there during Germany's two revolutions in 1848 and 1918, and in the bloodless revolution of 1989 a million people flocked to the *Alex* on 4 November 1989 shortly before the Wall was breached on 9 November. The enormous *Fernsehturm* and the *Weltzeituhr* are landmarks of the square's recent DDR past.

ALLERHEILIGEN
All Saints' Day on 1 November honours all the Christian saints and is a public holiday in predominantly Catholic LÄNDER (BADEN-WÜRTTEMBERG, BAYERN, NORDRHEIN-WESTFALEN, RHEINLAND-PFALZ and SAARLAND).

ALLFINANZ
The provision of a full range of financial services under one roof by an insurance company or bank – including insurance, banking, share dealing, etc.

ALLGÄU
Area including parts of BAYERN, BADEN-WÜRTTEMBERG and

Austria, and renowned for its beautiful mountainous scenery. The Allgäu is partly mountainous and also encompasses the Voralpenland leading up to the Alpen. It extends from the BODENSEE in the west to the river Lech in the east, with lush hills of the Voralpenland giving way to the spectacular Allgäuer Alpen in the south.

ALLGEMEINE GESCHÄFTSBEDINGUNGEN (AGB)
The general terms and conditions of business that regulate the relationship between the parties to a contract. They are generally laid down by the association covering a particular industry or service or by individual companies, and cover matters such as delivery, payment and insurance.

ALLGEMEINE HOCHSCHULREIFE See: *HOCHSCHUL-REIFE*

ALLGEMEINE ORTSKRANKENKASSEN (AOK)
Public health-insurance organisations originating in the 1880s as part of Bismarck's social programme. The Allgemeine Ortskrankenkassen provide statutory health insurance for all individuals living within a particular area (KREIS, STADT) who are obliged to take out mandatory health insurance unless they join an alternative scheme (e.g. ERSATZKASSE, BETRIEBSKRANKENKASSE). In 1996 the AOKs received a challenge to their memberships when other health-insurance organisations were permitted to accept members who did not belong to their traditional clientele (e.g. trade, professional, company scheme). See also: KRANKENKASSEN

ALLGEMEINER DEUTSCHER AUTOMOBIL-CLUB (ADAC)
Germany's largest automobile club with a membership of nearly 13 million. The organisation represents the interests of the motorist and rallying, and is a powerful force at BUND level, having successfully lobbied – alongside the automobile industry – for unrestricted speeds on the AUTOBAHN for many years.

ALLGEMEINER DEUTSCHER NACHRICHTENDIENST
See: *ddp/ADN ALLGEMEINER DEUTSCHER NACH-RICHTENDIENST GmbH*

ALLGEMEINER STUDENTENAUSSCHUSS (AStA)

The autonomous student executive body that represents the STU-DENTENSCHAFT at HOCHSCHULEN (except BADEN-WÜRTTEMBERG and BAYERN, where independent *Allgemeine Studentenausschüsse* have been abolished). Students' interests are represented on bodies convened for the university as a whole. The VORSTAND is elected by the *Studentenparlament* and appoints REFERENTEN for particular areas. See also: VERFASSTE STUDENTENSCHAFT

ALLIANZ AG HOLDING

Europe's biggest insurance group founded in 1890, a household name in Germany with its advertising slogan '*Hoffentlich Allianz versichert*'. Group headquarters are in MÜNCHEN. Allianz has some 67,000 employees.

ALLIANZ FÜR DEUTSCHLAND

Electoral grouping formed in the DDR for the elections to the VOLKSKAMMER in March 1990. It was composed of the CDU, DSU and DEMOKRATISCHER AUFBRUCH. The grouping stood for a rapid move towards reunification and institution of LÄNDER in the DDR and won the election, taking 47.79% of the votes cast. See also: MERKEL, ANGELA

ALLZUSTÄNDIGKEIT

The general competence that the GRUNDGESETZ guarantees to local authorities (GEMEINDEN, KREISE). They have the right to per-form functions at a local level except for duties that have been assigned to a higher authority or functions that are expressly prohibited.

ALMSICK, FRANZISKA VAN (1978–   )

Germany's most successful female swimmer trained in East Germany from the age of seven. At the Barcelona Olympic Games in 1992 she won two bronze and two silver medals and took six European titles in 1993. At the European champi-onships in Wien in 1995 '*Gold-Franzi*' won five gold medals and was nominated *Sportlerin des Jahres* in the same year despite a controversial comment about National Socialism in an interview earlier in the year. She has concluded a number of lucrative sponsorship contracts.

ALPEN See: *BAYERISCHE ALPEN*

ALTANA AG
Holding company with interests in pharmaceuticals, Milupa baby foods and chemicals, founded in 1977. Company headquarters are in Bad Homburg (HESSEN). Altana has some 10,000 employees.

ALTE BUNDESLÄNDER
The old LÄNDER in the west of Germany that constituted the old West Germany (BUNDESREPUBLIK) before reunification. They are BADEN-WÜRTTEMBERG, BAYERN, BERLIN, BREMEN, HAMBURG, HESSEN, NIEDERSACHSEN, NORDRHEIN-WESTFALEN, RHEINLAND-PFALZ, SAAR-LAND, SCHLESWIG-HOLSTEIN.

ALTERNATIVMEDIZIN
A landmark judgement by the BUNDESGERICHTSHOF during a hearing concerning wood preservatives in 1995 permitted judges to take theories from 'alternative medicine' into account when reaching a judgement. See also: SCHULMEDIZIN

ÄLTESTENRAT
The body in the BUNDESTAG that sets the agenda of the Bundestag and its standing committees (BUNDESTAGSAUSSCHÜSSE), takes decisions on all internal administrative issues and nominates the chairpersons for the standing committees. Members of the Ältestenrat are the BUNDESTAGSPRÄSIDENT and his/her representatives (*Stellvertreter*) and 23 members drawn from all the FRAKTIONEN. In addition, any *Gruppe* in the Bundestag is represented by one member. See also: SÜSSMUTH, RITA

ALTMARK
Rural region in SACHSEN-ANHALT that was the first tract of Slav land to be taken over in the quest for eastern territory at the beginning of the Middle Ages.

ALTSTADT
The old part of a town or city, in some cases still surrounded by a city wall. Many *Altstadtviertel* suffered heavy destruction during the Second World War, notably DRESDEN, MAINZ and HAMBURG. Some of the *Altstadtviertel* were meticulously reconstructed after

the war, others rebuilt in a utilitarian 1950s-style architecture with perhaps a few important buildings being restored. In the DDR the tendency was to sweep away the old with the desire to construct a new socialist state and this is particularly marked in the centre of the former East BERLIN and in CHEMNITZ with its Soviet-style buildings and gaping thoroughfares.

AMBIENTE

Up-market lifestyle magazine established in 1980 and published eight times a year in MÜNCHEN by Globus Verlag. *Ambiente* has a circulation of 64,000 and caters for high earners with an interest in interior design and culture.

AMPEL-KOALITION

Coalition between the SPD, FDP and BÜNDNIS 90/DIE GRÜNEN, so called because of the red, yellow and green colours of the parties resembling a set of traffic lights. BRANDENBURG was ruled by an *Ampel-Koalition* after the 1990 elections, which was replaced by an SPD government in 1994. The *Ampel-Koalition* in BREMEN collapsed early in 1995. See also: REGENBOGEN-KOALITION

AMT

An *Amt* is a government institution, department or office with a particular area of responsibility (e.g. AUSWÄRTIGES AMT, EINWOHNER-MELDEAMT, GRUNDBUCHAMT, LANDRATSAMT). *Amt* may also refer to a particular post (area of responsibility), usually of a BEAMTER.

In some LÄNDER (SCHLESWIG-HOLSTEIN, NORDRHEIN-WESTFALEN, SAARLAND) an *Amt* is an intermediate tier of local government comprising a number of GEMEINDEN. The *Amt* forms a unit of government between the Gemeinde and the KREIS and carries out functions in its own right, duties delegated to it by the Land, and functions assigned voluntarily to it by individual Gemeinden.

AMTSBÜRGERMEISTER

Honorary position in NORDRHEIN-WESTFALEN held by the chairperson of the AMT.

AMTSDIREKTOR

The most senior BEAMTER of an AMT in NORDRHEIN-WESTFALEN,

carrying out executive duties. The equivalent of the HAUPTVER-
WALTUNGSBEAMTER in most other LÄNDER.

AMTSGERICHT
The lowest court of law in Germany, which is empowered to deal
with civil claims not exceeding DM 10,000, tenancy cases and
maintenance claims. Criminal cases involving offences that carry
a fixed fine or a maximum of four years' imprisonment can also
be tried in this court. The Amtsgericht can enforce judgements,
deal with bankruptcy proceedings, auctions, probate, and cases
involving guardianship, and the Amtsgericht is also responsible
for maintaining the GRUNDBUCH. Civil cases are normally heard
by one *Richter* or a *Rechtspfleger* (registrar). Criminal cases are
heard either by one *Richter*, or for more serious offences, by a
Schöffengericht consisting of one BERUFSRICHTER and two
Schöffen (EHRENAMTLICHE RICHTER). Appeals against rulings of the
Amtsgericht are generally heard by the LANDGERICHT.

AMTSLEITER
The head of a BEZIRK IN Hamburg.

AMTSORDNUNG See: *GEMEINDEORDNUNG*

AMTSVORSTEHER
The most senior BEAMTER of an AMT in SCHLESWIG-HOLSTEIN and
SAARLAND, carrying out executive duties. The equivalent of the
HAUPTVERWALTUNGSBEAMTER in most other LÄNDER.

ANALYTICA (INTERNATIONALE FACHMESSE FÜR BIOCHEMISCHE UND INSTRUMENTELLE ANALYTIK, DIAGNOSTIK UND LABORTECHNIK)
The 'International Trade Fair for Biochemical and Instrumental
Analysis, Diagnostics and Laboratory Technology' is a trade fair
for instrument manufacturers and the biotechnology industry
and is held in MÜNCHEN every two years with around 32,000 visitors.

ANARCHO-SIEDLUNG CONNEWITZ
Squatters' settlement in Connewitz (LEIPZIG) formed at the time
of the WENDE by punks, anarchists and idealists occupying rows of
old houses to prevent them from being torn down and to experi-

ment with alternative lifestyles. There have been numerous clashes between the squatters and the police but the city now wants to regularise the situation by officially allowing the squatters to occupy 15 houses.

ANDREAE-NORIS ZAHN AG
Pharmaceuticals wholesaler founded in 1841. Company headquarters are in FRANKFURT AM MAIN. Andreae-Noris has some 3,300 employees.

ANGA VERBAND PRIVATER NETZBETREIBER – SATELLITEN- UND KABELKOMMUNIKATION – e.V.
An interest group of private network-operators that aims to develop and improve the reception of radio signals and introduce interaction communications services using privately operated broadband cable networks.

ANGELERNTER ARBEITER
Person who has completed at least three months of training to carry out their job but who has not participated in an apprenticeship scheme. See also: ARBEITER

ANGESTELLTER
White-collar worker receiving a fixed monthly salary paid directly into their bank account. An *Angestellter* may work in the private sector or as an ÖFFENTLICHER BEDIENSTETER without the special legal status of a BEAMTER in the public sector. *Angestellte* in the ALTE BUNDESLÄNDER have special rights as far as holiday, social benefits and period of notice are concerned.

ANUGA COLOGNE – WORLD FOOD MARKET
The 'World Food Market' for food, beverages, food-processing technology, fittings and furnishings is a trade fair for the hotel and catering industry held in KÖLN every two years with nearly 200,000 visitors.

ANWALT See: *RECHTSANWALT, STAATSANWALT-SCHAFT*

ANZEIGE See: *STRAFANZEIGE*

AOK See: *ALLGEMEINE ORTSKRANKENKASSEN*

APO See: *AUSSERPARLAMENTARISCHE OPPOSITION*

ARAL AG
The oil company with the biggest network of service stations in Germany (more than 2,600), founded in 1926. Company head-quarters are in BOCHUM. Aral has some 1,800 employees.

ARBEITER
General term for someone who works, but generally used for a manual or blue-collar worker who carries out physical work with his or her hands. There is a general trend for the number of *Arbeiter* to decline and the number of ANGESTELLTE to increase. A change in the status of *Arbeiter* is also underway in which they are becoming more like *Angestellte* (e.g. paid monthly by bank transfer).

ARBEITGEBER
A company or person who employs others to carry out pre-scribed tasks in return for a salary or wage. See also: ARBEIT-NEHMER

ARBEITGEBERANTEIL
The employer's contribution to the statutory SOZIAL-VERSICHERUNG, in which the ARBEITGEBER pays 50% of the contri-bution for ARBEITSLOSENVERSICHERUNG, KRANKENVERSICHERUNG, RENTENVERSICHERUNG. The newly introduced PFLEGEVERSICHERUNG (1995) is effectively being financed by the ARBEITNEHMER. See also: ARBEITNEHMERANTEIL

ARBEITGEBERVERBAND
An employers' association representing the interests of employ-ers from a particular sector. The *Arbeitgeberverbände* for a par-ticular sector have a FACHSPITZENVERBAND that lobbies for the interests of the sector at the level of the BUND. At LAND level there is a *Landesvereinigung* that represents all the employers' organisations of that Land. The *Arbeitgeberverbände* carry out annual pay negotiations for a particular sector with the GEWERK-

SCHAFTEN. The aims of the *Arbeitgeberverbände* are to promote entrepreneurial values, private ownership and wages policies for the overall benefit of the particular sector.

ARBEITNEHMER
An individual who works for an ARBEITGEBER in return for a LOHN or GEHALT. Employees include ARBEITER, ANGESTELLTE and AUSZUBILDENDE. Judges, BEAMTE and representatives of legal entities such as companies are not classified as *Arbeitnehmer*.

ARBEITNEHMERANTEIL
The employee's contribution to the statutory SOZIALVERSICHERUNG, in which the ARBEITNEHMER pays 50% of the contribution for ARBEITSLOSENVERSICHERUNG, KRANKENVERSICHERUNG, RENTENVERSICHERUNG. The ARBEITGEBER deducts the contributions from the employee's BRUTTOLOHN and then pays the money to the insurance funds. The newly introduced PFLEGEVERSICHERUNG (1995) is financed in the same way, but *Arbeitnehmer* have had to give up a public holiday (BUSS- UND BETTAG/PFINGSTMONTAG) so that in effect they are carrying the cost of the insurance; in SACHSEN, *Arbeitnehmer* pay the full cost, as abolition of a public holiday was rejected by the CDU. See also: ARBEITGEBERANTEIL

ARBEITNEHMERERFINDUNG
Patentable invention by an ARBEITNEHMER. A distinction is made between DIENSTERFINDUNGEN and FREIE ERFINDUNGEN.

ARBEITNEHMERPAUSCHBETRAG
The annual tax allowance of DM 2,000 introduced on 1 January 1990 to replace the *Arbeitnehmerfreibetrag*. It is normally deducted from income derived from employment prior to deduction of EINKOMMENSTEUER and LOHNSTEUER and is intended to cover costs incurred by the employee including WERBUNGSKOSTEN. The allowance is under review and may be reduced to DM 1,000.

ARBEITNEHMERVERBAND See: *GEWERKSCHAFT*

ARBEITSAMT
A local office of the BUNDESANSTALT FÜR ARBEIT, which acts as a job centre providing job-seekers with advice on careers, employment opportunities and vocational training. The office also deals with claims for KURZARBEITERGELD, SCHLECHTWETTERGELD, ARBEITS-

LOSENGELD and ARBEITSLOSENHILFE, and the *Familienkasse* deals with claims for KINDERGELD.

ARBEITSBESCHEINIGUNG
Certificate provided by the ARBEITGEBER when an ARBEITNEHMER leaves a firm, giving details of the type of work, length of service, amount of remuneration and the reason for leaving the employment. This certificate has to be presented to the ARBEITSAMT in order to obtain ARBEITSLOSENGELD or ARBEITSLOSENHILFE. See also: ARBEITSZEUGNIS

ARBEITSDIREKTOR
Member of the AUFSICHTSRAT elected to represent the employees' interests on the VORSTAND. See also: BETRIEBSVERFASSUNGSGESETZ; MITBESTIMMUNG

ARBEITSERLAUBNIS
Work permit required by all foreign nationals taking up work in Germany apart from EU nationals and stateless foreigners.

ARBEITSGEMEINSCHAFT DER ÖFFENTLICH-RECHTLICHEN RUNDFUNKANSTALTEN DER BUNDESREPUBLIK DEUTSCHLAND (ARD)
Public broadcasting organisation formed in 1950 on the basis of cooperation between the regional broadcasting corporations set up after 1945 in each LAND. Latterly it has been joined by SENDER FREIES BERLIN, MITTELDEUTSCHER RUNDFUNK and OSTDEUTSCHER RUNDFUNK. The two national broadcasting stations DEUTSCHE WELLE and DEUTSCHLANDRADIO are also members of the ARD. The LANDESRUNDFUNK- UND FERNSEHANSTALTEN transmit radio programmes and regional TV programmes (DRITTES PROGRAMM). The ARD runs the main German public TV channel known officially as Deutsches Fernsehen but commonly called ERSTES PROGRAMM. In 1986 the ARD joined forces with the Schweizerische Radio- und Fernsehgesellschaft to transmit the satellite programme EINS PLUS. Company headquarters are in KÖLN and ARD has some 23,000 employees.

ARBEITSGERICHT
The court of first instance for settling labour disputes between

ARBEITNEHMER and ARBEITGEBER, between *Arbeitnehmer*, and between unions and management, and also cases related to the BETRIEBSVERFASSUNGSGESETZ and TARIFVERTRÄGE. The court is made up of a BERUFSRICHTER as chairperson and two EHREN-AMTLICHE RICHTER (one *Arbeitnehmer*, one *Arbeitgeber*). The court settling this type of dispute in the NEUE BUNDESLÄNDER is known as the KREISGERICHT. See also: BUNDESARBEITSGERICHT; LANDESARBEITSGERICHT

ARBEITSGRUPPE
Work group or working party set up to carry out a specific task or function. Students often work and learn together in informal *Arbeitsgruppen* of three or four to overcome the impersonal nature of university life and lack of small teaching groups in Germany.

ARBEITSLOHN See: *LOHN*

ARBEITSLOSENGELD
Unemployment benefit paid by the ARBEITSAMT to all individuals who are unemployed and have been in work paying contributions to the ARBEITSLOSENVERSICHERUNG for at least 360 days over the previous three years and who are available for work. The period of time for which unemployment benefit is payable varies between 78 and 312 days according to length of service. Benefit is payable for up to 832 days after the age of 54. 60% of the previous net pay is payable, or 67% if an unemployed person has at least one child. *Arbeitslosengeld* is an area of state welfare that is subject to wide-ranging discussion concerning reduction of benefit payable and the period of eligibility. See also: ARBEITSLOSEN-HILFE

ARBEITSLOSENHILFE
A safety net not dependent on contributions and financed from taxation for the long-term unemployed who are no longer entitled to ARBEITSLOSENGELD or for unemployed persons who have not paid enough contributions to qualify for *Arbeitslosengeld*. The financial resources of applicants must be below a certain threshold. *Arbeitslosenhilfe* is payable for a maximum of one year and is 53% of net pay or 57% of net pay in the case of

unemployed people with at least one child. Like *Arbeitslosengeld* this safety net is being looked at carefully with a view to introducing measures restricting this benefit.

ARBEITSLOSENVERSICHERUNG

The part of the SOZIALVERSICHERUNG paid to cover the risk of unemployment. It is payable by all ARBEITER and ANGESTELLTE whether they are working or undergoing training for 18 or more hours a week. See also: ARBEITSLOSENGELD; KONKURSAUSFALLGELD; KURZARBEITERGELD; SCHLECHTWETTERGELD

ARBEITSMORAL

The Calvinistic work ethic that powered Germany's WIRTSCHAFTSWUNDER is rumoured to be in decline in the mid-1990s. Nowadays, the older generation complain that concern with leisure is taking over. See also: FREIZEIT

ARBEITSPLATZ

The place where work is carried out. Also used in a broader sense to mean job and employment. With around 4.5 million unemployed and one in three people out of work in east Germany, *Arbeitsplätze* are high on the political agenda. Some 1.2 million industrial jobs were lost between 1991 and 1995.

ARBEITSRICHTER

Judge active in an ARBEITSGERICHT or LANDESARBEITSGERICHT, or in the BUNDESARBEITSGERICHT.

ARBEITSZEUGNIS

The reference provided by an ARBEITGEBER to an ARBEITNEHMER or AUSZUBILDENDER at the end of the employment or period of training. An *einfaches Zeugnis* gives details of the type of work and length of employment. A *qualifiziertes Zeugnis* is provided for an *Auszubildender* or in other cases at the request of the *Arbeitnehmer* and gives an assessment of the conduct and performance of the employee. Details of unfavourable incidents or mistakes are not permitted, and comments on personality traits have to be geared to the type of work involved (e.g. honesty for a bank clerk). Any information on health or behaviour outside

work should only be included on the request of the employee.
See also: ARBEITSBESCHEINIGUNG

ARCHITEKTUR & WOHNEN
Magazine published twice a month specialising in architecture
and design. It has a circulation of 68,000 and is published in HAM-
BURG by JAHRESZEITEN VERLAG.

ARD See: *ARBEITSGEMEINSCHAFT DER ÖFFENTLICH-RECHTLICHEN RUNDFUNKANSTALTEN DER BUNDESREPUBLIK DEUTSCHLAND*

ART
Consumer art magazine published monthly in HAMBURG with a
circulation of 76,000. It is an exclusive art magazine published by
GRUNER + JAHR and appeals to a well-to-do under-fifties readership.

ARTE – DER EUROPÄISCHE KULTURKANAL
European TV channel set up in 1992 by ARD, ZDF and the French
broadcaster La Sept-ARTE. It is based in Strasbourg and
Baden-Baden (BADEN-WÜRTTEMBERG) and transmits a range of
cultural programmes.

ÄRZTEKAMMER
Professional organisation for doctors of medicine at LAND level.
All doctors have to belong to the *Ärztekammer.*

ASD See: *AXEL-SPRINGER-INLAND-DIENST*

ASEA BROWN BOVERI AG (ABB)
Electricity generation and distribution company founded in 1988
as a member of the ABB group with head office in
Zürich/Switzerland. Company headquarters are in MANNHEIM.
Asea Brown Boveri has some 35,000 employees.

ASKO DEUTSCHE KAUFHAUS AG
Food retailer founded in 1972. Asko has nearly 1,000 food retail
outlets as well as DIY and fashion stores. Company headquarters are in SAARBRÜCKEN. Asko has some 66,000 employees.

AStA See: *ALLGEMEINER STUDENTENAUSSCHUSS*

ASYLANT

A seeker of asylum under *Artikel* 16 *Paragraph (§)* 2 of the
GRUNDGESETZ. Germany still has the most liberal asylum laws in
Europe, but during the 1980s the government and the population
at large came to the conclusion that many of the asylum-seekers
were economic migrants seeking a better life in Germany's affluent society. Asylum-seekers are now only accepted for a hearing
under *Artikel* 16 *§2* of the Grundgesetz if they arrive by ship or
plane from a country that is not regarded as safe or secure, and
the number of applicants for asylum has been reduced drastically. Asylum-seekers are housed in camps or hostels for up to
three years while their cases are being heard. During this time
they receive an allowance for food and clothing, are provided with
accommodation and are allowed to work after a year. Asylum-
seekers awaiting a hearing have been victims of a number of
attacks by right-wing extremists in the 1990s. See also: ASYLRECHT

ASYLBERECHTIGTER

An individual recognised as having the right of asylum in
Germany. See also: BUNDESAMT FÜR DIE ANERKENNUNG AUSLÄNDI-
SCHER FLÜCHTLINGE

ASYLBEWERBER See: *ASYLANT*

ASYLBEWERBERHEIM

Hostel where asylum-seekers are housed prior to their case
being heard.

ASYLRECHT

A desire to redress the persecution of the Jews under Hitler's
Nazi regime gave Germany the most liberal legislation on asylum in Europe. Under *Artikel* 16 *Paragraph (§)* 2 of the
GRUNDGESETZ, an individual arriving on German soil is granted
the right to a proper investigation into their claim that they
would risk persecution if they returned to their country of origin.
However, the influx of refugees in the 1980s brought pressure to
bear on the government to modify the country's open-house policy, resulting in *Artikel* 16a (1993). It confirms the right of asylum

for all foreigners who are being persecuted in their country of origin (*politisch Verfolgte*) but excludes those who arrive in Germany from an EU state or from any other country deemed to be free from political persecution.

AUDI AG
Manufacturer of executive automobiles, founded in 1969 and a wholly-owned subsidiary of VOLKSWAGEN. Company headquarters are in Ingolstadt (BAYERN). Audi has some 32,000 employees.

AUDIO
Popular weekly hi-fi magazine published in STUTTGART with a circulation of some 80,000.

AUF EINEN BLICK
Germany's biggest selling weekly TV listings guide, founded in 1983 and published in HAMBURG by BAUER VERLAG. It has a circulation of 2.5 million and includes topical features as well as a programme guide.

AUFBAUSTUDIUM
A further course of study taken at a HOCHSCHULE following completion of the first degree. The *Aufbaustudium* is taken in the context of continuing education in another field of study or further specialisation within the same branch of knowledge.

AUFENTHALT
A place of temporary residence within Germany for a German citizen.

AUFSICHTSRAT
The supervisory board in the two-tier board structure present in AKTIENGESELLSCHAFTEN (and some other types of company). The *Aufsichtsrat* is appointed by the AKTIONÄRE and must have three, nine or 21 members depending on the size of the company, and a third of the members must be elected in a secret ballot by the ARBEITNEHMER. In companies that fall under the *Mitbestimmungsgesetz* of 1951 and 1976, the composition of the *Aufsichtsrat* must conform to those requirements. The *Aufsichtsrat* appoints the VORSTAND. The annual accounts (*Jahresabschluß*) and annual report (*Geschäftsbericht*) are audited by an independent

WIRTSCHAFTSPRÜFER. The auditor's report (*Prüfungsbericht*) together with the *Jahresabschluß* and *Geschäftsbericht* are submitted to the *Aufsichtsrat* by the *Vorstand*. The *Aufsichtsrat* adopts the annual accounts and recommends them to the *Hauptversammlung* for acceptance at the end of each financial year. See also: MITBESTIMMUNG

AUFTRAGSVERWALTUNG

The delegation of functions laid down in certain BUNDESGESETZE by the BUND to the LÄNDER (e.g. management of the AUTOBAHN network). Similarly certain functions are delegated by the Länder to the KREISE or GEMEINDEN. *Auftragsangelegenheiten* carried out by the Kreise or Gemeinden include registration of births, marriages and deaths, and issuing of passports. See also: SELBSTVERWALTUNG; STANDESAMT

AUGSBURG

The administrative centre for the Bavarian REGIERUNGSBEZIRK of Schwaben, Augsburg is situated in BAYERN at the confluence of the river Lech and the Wertach (dialling code 0821, postal area code 86...). Augsburg has been the seat of a Catholic bishop since 739 (granted a charter in 1156) and in the FUGGEREI boasts the world's oldest social housing for the poor. Augsburg's colourful WEIHNACHTSMARKT starts with a pageant, and a unique Friedensfest is held every summer to celebrate the end of the Thirty Years' War.

The city has a population of some 263,000 with a total student population of around 18,000 (1 UNIVERSITÄT and 1 FACHHOCHSCHULE) and about 17% foreigners (37% Turkish). The CSU has been running the city as the strongest party since 1990, although lack of an absolute majority has necessitated the support of other parties. Industries include heavy and precision engineering, aeroplane construction, welding machinery, computers, paper and textiles. Important companies include MAN, DASA, Kuka and AT & T. See also: ROMANTISCHE STRASSE; SCHWABEN

AUGSBURG, UNIVERSITÄT

University in BAYERN founded in 1970 and teaching some 15,000 students. The Universität Augsburg has faculties of Catholic theology, economics and social sciences, law, philosophy (arts), natural sciences.

AUGSBURGER ALLGEMEINE
This daily newspaper was established in 1945 and is published daily in AUGSBURG by Presse Druck Verlags GmbH with a circulation of 367,000.

AUGSTEIN, RUDOLF (1923–)
Journalist and publisher who founded news magazine DER SPIEGEL in 1947 and remains HERAUSGEBER of the weekly news magazine and co-owner of the SPIEGEL-VERLAG. Augstein was highly critical of Adenauer's post-war governments and briefly served as a MITGLIED DES BUNDESTAGES for the FDP in 1972–1973. He pioneered investigative journalism in Germany and his arrest during the SPIEGEL-AFFÄRE proved a test of the effectiveness of West German democracy.

AUSBILDENDER
Person (or organisation) providing training for the AUSZUBILDEN-DER, and previously known as the *Lehrherr*. The BERUFS-BILDUNGSGESETZ lays down rights and obligations for the *Ausbildender*, who has to ensure that the trainee acquires the necessary skills and knowledge. The trainer also has to ensure that trainees are only required to carry out tasks in accordance with the aim of their training and their physical strength. The trainer has to pay trainees in accordance with the TARIFVERTRÄGE in force, and the trainees have to be released to attend classes at the BERUFSSCHULE. At the end of training, the trainer has to issue a certificate. If the *Ausbildender* lacks the requisite vocational qualifications, the training function must be delegated to an AUS-BILDER.

AUSBILDER
A person authorised by the AUSBILDENDER to carry out the BERUFS-AUSBILDUNG of AUSZUBILDENDE. This person must be suitably qualified and approved for the task.

AUSBILDUNGSBERUF
A vocation or trade recognised by the German government in

accordance with the BERUFSBILDUNGSGESETZ. There are more than 300 registered *Ausbildungsberufe* in Germany.

AUSBILDUNGSORDNUNG

This prescribes the conditions for a BERUFSAUSBILDUNG recognised in accordance with the BERUFSBILDUNGSGESETZ. The *Ausbildungsordnung* includes a description of the AUSBILDUNGSBERUFE, specifies the length of training, describes the practical skills and theoretical knowledge that should form part of the training, lays down a framework for the training, and stipulates the requirements for examinations.

AUSBILDUNGSVERGÜTUNG

The remuneration paid by the AUSBILDENDER to the AUSZUBILDENDER. It is paid monthly including periods at the BERUFSSCHULE and examinations, and is based on the age of the trainee and the stage reached in training.

AUSCHWITZ-LÜGE

Denial of the holocaust in the Nazi concentration camps. In 1994 the BUNDESVERFASSUNGSGERICHT rejected a claim (*Verfassungsbeschwerde*) by the right-wing NPD that such a denial was permissible under the GRUNDGESETZ *(freie Meinungsäußerung)*. Also in 1994 the BUNDESTAG passed a law that made denial of mass murder under National Socialism a criminal offence with up to three years' imprisonment. See also: HISTORIKERSTREIT

AUSFALLZEIT

Period during which an employee does not have to pay contributions to the RENTENVERSICHERUNG but which still count towards pension entitlement. Such periods include incapacity due to illness or accident, pregnancy, unemployment and training.

AUSGABE

The edition of a book, newspaper or magazine. Newspapers in Germany have regional editions with a local section for a particular area.

AUSLÄNDER

A term that covers all people in Germany with non-German nationality. Foreign workers, known euphemistically as GASTAR-

BEITER, were welcomed during the 1950s and 1960s to meet the demands of German industry and the shortfall in the labour market. As unemployment took hold in the 1970s and 1980s, resentment against *Ausländer* increased and this was exacerbated by reunification in 1989.

The GRUNDGESETZ grants citizenship to refugees and VERTRIEBENE, or their spouses or descendants, from the territories within the borders of the German REICH on 31 December 1937. They are thus not regarded as foreigners or *Ausländer*.

AUSLÄNDERFEINDLICHKEIT

Xenophobic hostility to foreigners and antisemitism have come to the fore again in Germany during the 1990s with racial abuse, isolated serious attacks on foreigners resulting in death, and desecration of Jewish cemeteries and monuments. The massive unemployment accompanying the collapse of east German industry made ASYLANTEN and AUSLÄNDER in general the target of racially motivated attacks and abuse with slogans such as '*Ausländer raus*'.

AUSSCHUSS See: *BUNDESTAGSAUSSCHUSS*

AUSSENMINISTER See: *BUNDESMINISTER DES AUSWÄRTIGEN*

AUSSENWIRTSCHAFTSGESETZ (AWG)

Law passed in 1961 that guarantees Germany's commitment to free trade in goods, services and capital with other countries. The commitment to free trade has been fundamental to Germany's economic success.

AUSSERPARLAMENTARISCHE OPPOSITION (APO)

The loose-knit opposition movement that came into being in the BRD in 1966. The movement was composed of left-wing students and some trade-union groups that promoted opposition to the establishment from outside official channels in the BUNDESTAG. The GROSSE KOALITION formed in 1966 between the CDU/CSU and SPD had brought about a weakening of parliamentary opposition, and the APO saw radical protest as the only effective way of achieving political and social change. The movement was anti-authoritarian, opposed the concentration of the media and called for reform of the system of higher education.

Following the attempted murder of left-wing activist Rudi Dutschke, two years of protest culminated in a campaign against the SPRINGER VERLAG in 1968 and the protests against the NOTSTANDSGESETZE that May. See also: ROTE-ARMEE-FRAKTION

AUSSIEDLER
Ethnic Germans who lived in eastern Europe and are returning to Germany now that the borders have been thrown open. They often speak an antiquated form of German and find it difficult to adjust to the modern Germany. Each LAND takes a quota, and the *Aussiedler* receive full unemployment benefits, German-language courses and training in order to help them to become established in modern German society. The German government is trying to stem the exodus of ethnic Germans from Russia and other eastern countries by providing support in their adopted country with cultural centres, German television and German teachers.

AUSSTELLUNGS- UND MESSE-GmbH DES BÖRSEN-VEREINS DES DEUTSCHEN BUCHHANDELS
A subsidiary of the BÖRSENVEREIN DES DEUTSCHEN BUCHHANDELS E.V. that organises the world-famous FRANKFURTER BUCHMESSE each October.

AUSWÄRTIGES AMT (AA)
The federal ministry with responsibility for foreign affairs. See also: BUNDESMINISTER DES AUSWÄRTIGEN

AUSZUBILDENDER
A trainee on a vocational course for an AUSBILDUNGSBERUF, previously known as a LEHRLING and frequently shortened to *Azubi*. The rights and obligations of *Auszubildende* are laid down in the BERUFSBILDUNGSGESETZ. Trainees are obliged to work towards achieving training goals and they are subject to the authority of the AUSBILDENDER and other authorised instructors.

AUTO – DER DEUTSCHE STRASSENVERKEHR
Fortnightly motoring magazine established in 1990 and published in BERLIN with a circulation of 353,000. It is a general

motoring magazine and carries technical reports, articles on travel and news on cars.

AUTO/STRASSENVERKEHR

This is a motoring magazine for east Germany, offering advice and value for money. It was established in 1990 and is published fortnightly in STUTTGART with a circulation of 360,000.

AUTOBAHN

Germany has Europe's most extensive motorway network with more than 10,000 km. of *Autobahn*. The first motorway was opened in 1932 between BONN and KÖLN, and by the end of the war a network of 2,100 km. had been completed. The motorway network is owned by the BUND, and the *Autobahnpolizei* patrol the highways. The country's powerful car lobby has ensured that there is no overall speed limit, but speed restrictions are imposed on parts of the motorways in some LÄNDER, and recommended speeds are signposted in places, over and beyond the generally recommended speed limit of 130 km./h. Many of the motorways have only two lanes, which can lead to long traffic jams (*Staus*). Germany's motorways are not for the faint-hearted as speeds over 200 km./h. are not unusual. See also: AUFTRAGSVERWALTUNG

AUTOBILD

Weekly motoring magazine published by SPRINGER VERLAG in HAMBURG with a circulation of 866,000. It was established in 1986 and has national coverage, appealing mainly to male readers with articles on all aspects of motoring and supplements on caravans and mobile homes.

AVA ALLGEMEINE HANDELSGESELLSCHAFT DER VERBRAUCHER AG

Wholesale and retail company founded in 1975, with a majority shareholding owned by EDEKA ZENTRALE. Company headquarters are in BIELEFELD. AVA has some 25,000 employees.

AVIGNON, JIM (1966–   )

Pioneer of a new form of pop art and self-styled as Germany's craziest painter. He combines art with TECHNO music and shocked

DOCUMENTA visitors in the early 1990s by destroying his own pictures pronouncing that his work was not for eternity.

AWG See: *AUSSENWIRTSCHAFTSGESETZ*

AXEL-SPRINGER-INLAND-DIENST (ASD)
Press agency founded by publishing tycoon Axel Springer in 1969, based in HAMBURG. See also: SPRINGER VERLAG

AZUBI See: *AUSZUBILDENDER*

BA See: *BUNDESANSTALT FÜR ARBEIT*

BAADER-MEINHOF-GRUPPE

A left-wing group which was part of the ROTE-ARMEE-FRAKTION (RAF) that resorted to terrorism after the student protests of 1968. The leaders were Andreas Baader, Gudrun Ensslin and Ulrike Meinhof, and the group carried out bomb attacks and bank robberies before the three leaders were arrested in 1972. They were sentenced to life imprisonment in 1977 after long-drawn-out trials that were accompanied by further terrorist activity and commanded considerable publicity. Meinhof had meanwhile committed suicide in prison (Stuttgart-Stammheim) in 1976, and the deaths of Baader and Ensslin immediately following the RAF hijack of a Lufthansa jet to Mogadishu (Somalia) in October 1977 were also attributed to suicide by the authorities.

BADEN-WÜRTTEMBERG

Baden-Württemberg is a FLÄCHENSTAAT covering an area of 35,751 sq. km., with a population of some 10.2 million. The LANDTAG (LANDESPARLAMENT) enacts legislation and comprises 146 members elected every five years, with the next election in 2001. The Landtag elects the MINISTERPRÄSIDENT, head of the Regierung des Landes Baden-Württemberg, which holds executive powers. The Ministerpräsident appoints the ministers with responsibility for individual portfolios. Baden-Württemberg has four REGIERUNGSBEZIRKE divided into nine STADTKREISE and 35 KREISE. The LANDESHAUPTSTADT is STUTTGART. Baden-Württemberg was formed in 1952 from three LÄNDER created by the American and French occupying powers on the territory of the grand duchy of *Baden* and the kingdom of *Württemberg*.

A mild climate and fertile soil make Baden-Württemberg a premier area for the cultivation of fruit and wine while the

Swabian characteristics of thrift and hard work have turned it into a highly industrialised area. Stuttgart is an automobile metropolis with the headquarters of DAIMLER-BENZ and PORSCHE, and other industrial giants such as BOSCH also have their headquarters there. Further industrial centres include Heilbronn, KARLSRUHE, MANNHEIM and Ulm. The SCHWARZWALD is traditionally a centre for the clockmaking industry, and the tradition of precision engineering has continued throughout Baden-Württemberg in the fields of automotive engineering, electronics and optics, as well as other industries such as jewellery in Pforzheim. Small and medium-sized companies flourish supplying the big multinationals located in and around Stuttgart. Germany's oldest university is in Heidelberg, and Karlsruhe is the seat of the BUNDESGERICHTSHOF and the BUNDESVERFASSUNGSGERICHT. Baden-Württemberg has some of Germany's most impressive landscapes including the Schwarzwald, the lush fruit-growing areas around the BODENSEE, and the Schwäbische Alb. Baden-Württemberg was ruled by coalition governments up to 1972 when the CDU was able to form a majority government that was returned to power for the next 20 years. The Land was ruled by a coalition between the CDU and SPD from 1992 to 1996, and since then has been governed by a coalition between the CDU and the FDP. See also: LAND; LANDESREGIERUNG; SCHWABEN; TEUFEL, ERWIN

BADENWERK AG
Electricity generation and distribution company founded in 1921. Company headquarters are in KARLSRUHE. Badenwerk has some 3,800 employees.

BADISCHE NEUESTE NACHRICHTEN
Daily newspaper established in 1946 and distributed in KARLSRUHE and the surrounding area with a circulation of 165,000.

BADISCHES LANDESMUSEUM
Housed in the former baroque *Schloß* in KARLSRUHE devastated during the Second World War, the museum has prehistoric and classical collections, a Renaissance gallery, a unique collection of Turkish exhibits captured in the seventeenth century and a spectacular collection of JUGENDSTIL art and artefacts.

BAEDEKER GmbH, VERLAG KARL
Founded in 1827, Baedeker is based near STUTTGART and publishes the famous Baedeker series of travel guides, now running under the imprint *Baedekers Allianz-Taschenbuch-Reiseführer.*

BAföG See: *BUNDESAUSBILDUNGSFÖRDERUNGS-GESETZ*

BAG See: *BUNDESARBEITSGERICHT*

BAGGER, HARTMUT (1938–   )
Soldier and general, he entered the BUNDESWEHR in 1958 and went on to become a brigade and divisional commander in 1984 and 1992. In 1994 he was appointed *Heeresinspekteur* and in 1996 he became GENERALINSPEKTEUR DER BUNDESWEHR.

BAHNPOLIZEI See: *BUNDESGRENZSCHUTZ*

BAHNREFORM
Reform of the railways carried out in 1993, which paved the way for the two state railway companies DEUTSCHE BUNDESBAHN and DEUTSCHE REICHSBAHN to be amalgamated into a single public company, the DEUTSCHE BAHN AG, on 1 January 1994.

BAHRO, RUDOLF (1935–   )
Journalist, philosopher and a prominent Marxist critic of the DDR regime who had joined the SED at the age of 16 and became deputy editor-in-chief of official student magazine *Forum* (FDJ) in 1965–1967. Removed from his post for publishing a play by Volker BRAUN, he then worked in a rubber factory and continued writing in secret on a critique of the Communist system, *Die Alternative. Zur Kritik des real existierenden Sozialismus* (1977). He was arrested in 1977 and condemned to eight years' imprisonment for treason but was released in 1979 and emigrated to the BRD, where he was a member of DIE GRÜNEN in 1980–1985. He returned to east BERLIN soon after the fall of the BERLINER MAUER and cooperated with CDU politician Kurt BIEDENKOPF in setting up an organic farming project at Pommritz (SACHSEN). The unconventional Bahro remains an enigma for the west German establishment but was recently elected a member of the New York Academy of Sciences.

BAIRISCH

An *oberdeutsche Mundart* spoken in BAYERN and also Austria. The independently minded Bavarians maintain that it is not a dialect of German but a language in its own right. It has its own grammatical structure – the imperfect tense is a foreign concept – a rolled 'r' and vowels that differ strikingly from those of HOCHDEUTSCH. '*Oans, zwoa, gsuffa*' ('*eins, zwei, gesoffen*') heard at many a beer festival illustrates both the Bavarian propensity for beer and gives an indication of why '*Zuagroasde*' ('*Zugereiste*') from the north have difficulty in understanding the language spoken south of the WEISSWURSTÄQUATOR.

BAK See: *BARMER ERSATZKASSE*

BAKred See: *BUNDESAUFSICHTSAMT FÜR DAS KREDITWESEN*

BAMBERG

The ALTSTADT in this beautiful town in FRANKEN has been made a UNESCO world heritage site.

BAMBERG, OTTO-FRIEDRICH-UNIVERSITÄT

University in BAYERN founded in 1947 and teaching some 8,000 students. The Otto-Friedrich-Universität Bamberg has faculties of Catholic theology, education and philosophy and psychology, languages and literature, history and earth sciences, social and economic sciences.

BARMER ERSATZKASSE (BAK)

The biggest ERSATZKASSE in terms of number of members, based in Barmen (WUPPERTAL). It has a tradition of being oriented towards ANGESTELLTE.

BARSCHEL-AFFÄRE

In 1987, Uwe Barschel, the CDU MINISTERPRÄSIDENT of SCHLESWIG-HOLSTEIN, was accused of running a smear campaign against his SPD opponent, Björn ENGHOLM, during the run-up to the election for the LANDTAG. Barschel later committed suicide in Switzerland, and the affair brought down Engholm in May 1993 when it was discovered that he had misled the Landtag committee investigating the affair after the election. He claimed to have heard about the campaign on the night of the election on 13 September 1987 but it transpired that his lawyer had informed him about it on 7 September.

BASELITZ, GEORG (1938–   )

Neo-expressionist painter and sculptor (real name Hans-Georg Kern). He studied in West BERLIN in 1957–1964 and returned there as a professor in 1983–1988. He was accused of pornography by the authorities in the early 1960s because of his picture *Die große Nacht im Eimer* (1962/1963). His canvasses are monumental and he has painted his subjects upside down since 1969. He has also been producing wooden sculptures since 1980.

BASF AG

One of Germany's big three chemical companies, founded in 1952. BASF produces a wide range of products including chemicals, plastics, fibres, paints and retail products such as cassette tapes and diskettes. Company headquarters are in LUDWIGSHAFEN. BASF has some 106,000 employees.

BAU (INTERNATIONALE FACHMESSE FÜR BAUSTOFFE, BAUSYSTEME, BAUERNEUERUNG)

The 'International Trade Fair for Building Materials, Building Systems, Building Renovation' is a trade fair for the construction industry held in MÜNCHEN every two years with around 170,000 visitors.

BAU-FACHMESSE LEIPZIG

The 'Construction Trade Fair Leipzig' for building materials, fittings and machinery is a trade fair for the construction industry held in LEIPZIG every two years with around 100,000 visitors.

BAUAUFSICHTSAMT

The office responsible for granting building permission and ensuring that building regulations are complied with.

BAUER VERLAG GmbH, HEINRICH

Publishing company founded in 1875, publishing Germany's biggest-selling TV listings magazine AUF EINEN BLICK. Company headquarters are in HAMBURG. Bauer Verlag has some 7,000 employees.

BAUHERR
The person or entity that concludes a contract with a construction company to carry out a building project. The *Bauherr* decides on the design of the building, bears the risk and provides the financial resources necessary for construction.

BAUHERRNMODELL
A model for the financing of construction projects in which the actual costs of construction are kept separate from expenses that are immediately deductible. This model can provide considerable tax advantages that increase with the proportion of debt used to finance the project.

BAUORDNUNGSAMT See: *BAUAUFSICHTSAMT*

BAUSCH, PINA (1940–)
Ballet dancer and choreographer who trained in ESSEN and New York and founded the Wuppertaler Tanztheater in 1973. She is an exponent of modern dance, and her innovative productions combine facets of mime, dance, theatre and circus. Performances on a stage littered with obstructions and mimes of sexual acts have attracted considerable attention and often rave reviews from the critics both in Germany and abroad. Her productions include *Iphigenie auf Tauris* (1974), *Victor* (1986) and *Tanzabend I* (1993).

BAUSPARKASSE
Savings institution set up for the purpose of saving to buy a house or building land by means of a BAUSPARVERTRAG.

BAUSPARVERTRAG
Savings agreement between a saver and a BAUSPARKASSE for a specific sum towards the purchase or construction of a house. The agreement attracts tax advantages, and ARBEITNEHMER can gain an additional benefit from the ARBEITGEBER in the form of VERMÖGENSBILDUNG. See also: EIGENHEIM

BAV See: *BUNDESAUFSICHTSAMT FÜR DAS VERSICHERUNGSWESEN*

BAYER AG

One of Germany's big three chemical companies, founded in 1951. The company produces more than 6,000 products ranging from plastics and paint to pharmaceuticals. Company headquarters are in Leverkusen (NORDRHEIN-WESTFALEN). Bayer has some 147,000 employees.

BAYERISCHE ALPEN

The Alps in OBERBAYERN stretch along the Austrian border with the well-loved Zugspitze as the tallest peak. The Bayerische Alpen are home to some of the most enduring of German stereotypes – *Lederhosen, Dirndl,* cow bells, picturesque villages. These are part of a rich culture and sense of identity that manifests itself in colourful local festivals, devout Catholicism and fierce independence.

BAYERISCHE GRENZPOLIZEI See: *GRENZPOLIZEI, BAYERISCHE*

BAYERISCHE HYPOTHEKEN- UND WECHSEL-BANK AG

One of the two big REGIONALBANKEN, founded in 1835 and with branches in all major cities. Company headquarters are in MÜNCHEN. Hypo-Bank has some 15,000 employees.

BAYERISCHE MOTORENWERKE AG See: *BMW AG*

BAYERISCHE STAATSBIBLIOTHEK

The Bavarian state library in MÜNCHEN was founded in 1558. It holds nearly 6.5 million volumes and 600,000 microforms, as well as manuscripts, maps, journals and musical scores. The library is a deposit library for BAYERN.

BAYERISCHE STAATSGEMÄLDESAMMLUNGEN

The Bavarian state galleries include the Alte Pinakothek (14th to 18th century European painting, including the world's most important collection of the German School), Neue Pinakothek (18th and 19th century European painting and sculpture), Staatsgalerie moderner Kunst (20th century European and American art), Schack Galerie (19th century German art), all in MÜNCHEN, and art galleries in over a dozen provincial towns in BAYERN.

BAYERISCHE VEREINSBANK AG
One of the two big REGIONALBANKEN, founded in 1869 and with branches in all major cities. Company headquarters are in MÜNCHEN. Bayerische Vereinsbank has some 14,000 employees.

BAYERISCHER RUNDFUNK (BR)
Regional public-service radio and TV broadcasting corporation based in MÜNCHEN and broadcasting principally to BAYERN. Bayerischer Rundfunk is a member of the ARD. See also: LAN-DESRUNDFUNK- UND FERNSEHANSTALTEN

BAYERISCHER WALD
A relatively poor region of BAYERN that is mountainous and densely wooded. It has remained a backwater as a result of its lack of industry and natural resources, and its proximity to former Communist borders. The Bayerischer Wald national park was created in 1970 and has been declared a world biosphere reserve by UNESCO.

BAYERN, FREISTAAT
The 'Free State of Bavaria' is Germany's largest FLÄCHENSTAAT covering an area of 70,547 sq. km., with a population of some 11.9 million. The LANDTAG (LANDESPARLAMENT) enacts legislation and comprises 204 members elected every four years, with the next election in autumn 1998. The Landtag elects the MINISTER-PRÄSIDENT, head of the Bayerische Staatsregierung, which holds executive powers. The Ministerpräsident appoints the ministers with responsibility for individual portfolios, and it is the only LAND to have a non-executive body called the SENAT, which has an advisory role and comprises 60 members. Bayern has seven REGIE-RUNGSBEZIRKE comprising 25 KREISFREIE STÄDTE and 71 KREISE. The LANDESHAUPTSTADT is MÜNCHEN.

Bayern has a long history as an independent kingdom ruled by the WITTELSBACH dynasty, being re-formed as a Land in the BRD by the American military government in 1945. It is predominantly rural and largely Catholic, with industrial centres in AUGS-BURG, Ingolstadt, München, NÜRNBERG and Regensburg. The headquarters of electronics giant SIEMENS, automobile manufacturer BMW (Bayerische Motorenwerke) and insurer ALLIANZ are all located in München, and the city boasts a large trade-fair complex. Nürnberg is home to mail-order company QUELLE and to the biggest annual toy fair in the world. Bayern is a centre for brewing (over 700 breweries at the last count), electronics and automobile manufacturing, and other industries include engineering, aerospace, textiles, glass and porcelain.

Bayern is a spectacular recreational area with the Alps (including the Zugspitze, Germany's highest mountain), lakes, rivers, the BAYERISCHER WALD, the hills of the Voralpenland, König Ludwig II's fairytale castles, and picturesque towns on the ROMANTISCHE STRASSE (Dinkelsbühl, Rothenburg ob der Tauber, WÜRZBURG). Bayern is overwhelmingly conservative, and the right-wing CSU has almost exclusively governed the state since the Second World War, with the SPD predominantly governing the city of München. See also: LAND; LANDESREGIERUNG; STOIBER, EDMUND

BAYERN MÜNCHEN, FC
FC Bayern München is Munich's outstandingly successful football team that has won the BUNDESLIGA twelve times since it was started up in 1964 and has supplied numerous players for the national team *(Nationalelf)*. See also: BECKENBAUER, FRANZ

BAYERNKURIER
The CSU's party newspaper published weekly was established in 1950 and is distributed in BAYERN with a circulation of about 155,000.

BAYERNPARTEI (BP)
Party formed in 1947 with extreme federalist aims and represented in the LANDTAG in BAYERN until 1966. The party appealed to strongly rural elements in Bayern but now only has about 1,400 members.

BAYERNWERK AG
Electricity generation and distribution company founded in 1921 providing electricity in BAYERN and the new LÄNDER. Company headquarters are in MÜNCHEN. Bayernwerk has some 15,000 employees and is almost wholly owned by VIAG.

BAYREUTH, UNIVERSITÄT
University in BAYERN founded in 1972 and teaching some 9,000

students. The Universität Bayreuth has departments of mathematics and physics, biology and chemistry and geosciences, law and economics, languages and literature, cultural studies.

BAYWA AG
Agricultural trading company founded in 1923. Company headquarters are in MÜNCHEN. BayWa has some 12,000 employees.

BDA See: *BUNDESVEREINIGUNG DER DEUTSCHEN ARBEITGEBERVERBÄNDE e.V.*

BDSG See: *BUNDESDATENSCHUTZGESETZ*

BDZV See: *BUNDESVERBAND DEUTSCHER ZEITUNGS-VERLEGER e.V.*

BEAMTER
Public official with special legal status. The relationship between the *Beamter* or *Beamtin* and the BUND/LAND (*'öffentlich-rechtliches Dienst- und Treueverhältnis'*) precludes strike action and demands restraint in political acitivities but also confers considerable privileges. *Beamte* are found in all areas of government and public service (e.g. teachers). Judges and soldiers are not covered by the *Bundesbeamtengesetz* but have similar status. The career structure for *Beamte* has four levels: *einfacher Dienst, mittlerer Dienst, gehobener Dienst* and *höherer Dienst* according to qualifications and other criteria. See also: ÖFFENTLICHER DIENST

BECHER, BERND (1931–   ) and HILLA (1934–   )
Husband-and-wife team of photographers focusing on industrial subjects. Their photographs of industrial buildings brought documentary photography to Germany and they later turned to water towers and half-timbered houses (*Fachwerkhäuser*) as subjects. In 1990 they were awarded the *Goldener Löwe* at the Venice Biennale.

BECK, KURT (1949–   )
SPD politician who has been a member of the LANDTAG in RHEIN-LAND-PFALZ since 1979. He was chairman of the SPD-FRAKTION in the Landtag in 1991–1993 and has been MINISTERPRÄSIDENT of a coalition between the SPD and FDP since 1994.

BECKENBAUER, FRANZ (1945–   )
Germany's football hero who played for BAYERN MÜNCHEN and for the German national team that was runner-up in the 1966 World Cup, European champion in 1972 and winner of the World Cup in 1974. Between 1965 and 1977 he played for Germany more than 100 times. From 1984–1990 he was trainer of the national team that was runner-up for the World Cup in 1986 and winner of the World Cup in 1990. Beckenbauer was appointed trainer with Bayern München in 1994.

BECKER, BORIS (1967–   )
German tennis player who shot to fame at the age of 17 when he won the Wimbledon men's singles in 1985 as the first German and youngest player to do so. Since then he has been Wimbledon champion three times.

BECKER, GÜNTER (1924–   )
Composer who founded the *Gruppe MHz* in 1969, which is dedicated to music with electronic instruments.

BECKER, JUREK (1937–   )
Writer who spent part of his childhood in Nazi concentration camps, lived in East BERLIN from 1945 and studied philosophy there in 1957–1960. He was a member of the SED until his expulsion in 1976 following his protest against the expatriation of Wolf BIERMANN, and he then moved to West Berlin. His novels show the individual from a tragi-comic perspective. *Jakob der Lügner* (1969) with its poignant portrayal of life in the ghetto brought his first big success, other works include *Der Boxer* (1976), *Bronsteins Kinder* (1986) and *Amanda herzlos* (1992). He has also written film scripts, notably for the TV series *Liebling – Kreuzberg* (1986).

BECKER, JÜRGEN (1932–   )
Writer and journalist who was a member of GRUPPE 47 and was director of radio plays at DEUTSCHLANDFUNK in 1974–1993. He has himself written radio plays (e.g. *Die Abwesenden*, 1983) and experiments with prose and poetry that transcends conventional genres. Jürgen Becker was awarded the HEINRICH-BÖLL-PREIS in 1994. Collections include *Phasen* (1960, with *Typogramme* by

Wolf VOSTELL), *Ränder* (1968), *Die Türe zum Meer* (1983) and *Foxtrott im Erfurter Stadion* (1993).

BEDNORZ, JOHANNES GEORG (1950–   )

Mineralogist who received the Nobel Prize for physics in 1987 (with K.A. Müller) for the discovery of superconduction at high temperatures on ceramic metal oxides.

BEFÄHIGUNG ZUM RICHTERAMT

Eligibility to hold office as a judge, which is obtained by passing the ZWEITES STAATSEXAMEN in law. It is a prerequisite for becoming a RICHTER, RECHTSANWALT, STAATSANWALT or NOTAR.

BEHNISCH, GÜNTER (1922–   )

Architect known for his introduction of industrially pre-fabricated elements to German architecture and tent-like roof designs. He was appointed professor at the TECHNISCHE HOCHSCHULE DARMSTADT in 1967 and was head of planning for the Olympic complex designed by Frei OTTO at the 1972 Games in MÜNCHEN.

BEHÖRDE

A general term referring to any government or local authority at the level of BUND, LAND, KREIS or GEMEINDE.

BEHREND, SIEGFRIED (1933–   )

Classical guitarist integrating elements of folk music in his style. He studied in BERLIN in 1949–1952 and gave his first public performance in 1952. He has been giving international performances outside Europe since 1963. His compositions include *Xenographie* (1969).

BEIERSDORF AG

Health-care and pharmaceuticals company founded in 1882. Company headquarters are in HAMBURG. Beiersdorf has some 17,000 employees.

BEIGEORDNETER

A member of a local council elected by a GEMEINDEVERTRETUNG to serve as an official in a GEMEINDE. The position may be that of a full-time BEAMTER as a deputy to the HAUPTVERWALTUNGSBEAMTER or may be honorary. See also: MAGISTRATSVERFASSUNG

BELLA

Weekly magazine for young women, with articles on fashion, cosmetics and diet. It was established in 1977 and is published in HAMBURG by BAUER VERLAG. Although not ranking as one of the top women's weeklies, it has a respectable circulation of 663,000.

BEREITSCHAFTSPOLIZEI

Special police units in each LAND that provide support for the SCHUTZPOLIZEI and KRIMINALPOLIZEI and are deployed if the security of the BUND or Land is under threat, e.g. during demonstrations. These units are also responsible for training new recruits to the police.

BERGHAUS, RUTH (1927–   )

Dancer, choreographer and opera director who was INTENDANTIN at the BERLINER ENSEMBLE in 1971–1977 and since 1977 director at the Deutsche Staatsoper BERLIN. Berghaus has been criticised for her cooperation with the SED but she is in demand internationally and her unconventional productions have generated controversy and admiration.

BERGISCHES LAND

Once the duchy of *Berg*, this area became an important industrial centre and is now in NORDRHEIN-WESTFALEN. It is a wooded, hilly region and important towns include DÜSSELDORF, KREFELD, Leverkusen, MÖNCHENGLADBACH, SOLINGEN and WUPPERTAL. See also: RHEINISCH-WESTFÄLISCHES INDUSTRIEGEBIET

BERGWACHT

The mountain rescue service in BAYERN, BADEN-WÜRTTEMBERG and HESSEN. In Bayern it is part of the Bayerisches Rotes Kreuz and elsewhere part of the DEUTSCHES ROTES KREUZ.

BERLIN (LAND)

After the Second World War, Berlin formed an island within the Soviet zone of occupation and was divided into four sectors (American, British, French, Soviet), and in 1948 the city became divided politically into East and West Berlin. West Berlin became a LAND of the BRD in 1950 but was not constitutionally part of West Germany, with sovereignty being vested in the

three Western powers; Berlin members of the BUNDESTAG and
BUNDESRAT did not have full voting rights. East Berlin became the
capital of the DDR and in 1961 the DDR government built the
BERLINER MAUER around West Berlin to prevent the exodus of
East Germans to the West. Berlin was reunited in 1990 following
the collapse of East Germany's Communist regime to become a
fully-fledged Land.

Berlin is a STADTSTAAT covering an area of 889 sq. km., with a
population of nearly 3.5 million. The ABGEORDNETENHAUS (LAN-
DESPARLAMENT) enacts legislation and has 241 members elected
every five years, with the next election in autumn 2000. The
Abgeordnetenhaus elects the REGIERENDER BÜRGERMEISTER, head
of the SENAT (LANDESREGIERUNG), which holds executive powers.
The SENATOREN with responsibility for individual portfolios are
appointed by the Regierender Bürgermeister. Electronics giant
SIEMENS was founded here in the nineteenth century, and electronics and engineering remain Berlin's main industries with
other industries including chemicals, and food and drink. Berlin
has a left-wing tradition and West Berlin had an SPD government
throughout the post-war years until 1981, apart from two years in
the 1950s. However, since 1991 a CDU/SPD coalition has governed
the city under Eberhard DIEPGEN, and the 1995 elections left the
SPD with the lowest percentage of votes cast since 1945. Berlin
is Germany's most populous city and the country's biggest industrial centre. See also: BERLIN (STADT); LAND

BERLIN (STADT)

Capital of Germany since reunification on 3 October 1990 and a
STADTSTAAT in its own right (as such it is the LANDESHAUPTSTADT of
LAND BERLIN). Berlin is situated at the heart of Europe and straddles the rivers Havel, Spree and Panke (dialling code 0 30, postal
area code 10..., 11... and 12...). It is a city of contrasts with
monumental architecture (PERGAMONMUSEUM), reminders of terri-
ble destruction (KAISER-WILHELM-GEDÄCHTNISKIRCHE), dilapidated
buildings from a bygone age (Prenzlauer Berg), icons of a new
era (POTSDAMER PLATZ), spacious parks (Tiergarten), woodlands
(Grunewald) and extensive lakes with sandy beaches (Wannsee).

Founded only in the thirteenth century (charter in 1237), the city rose to become the capital of PREUSSEN and then Germany. After the fall of the DRITTES REICH, Berlin was divided and the BERLINER MAUER became a symbol of the cold-war struggle between Communism and capitalism. The Berlin Wall was breached on 9 November 1989, and dismantling of the Wall commenced in January 1990. Berlin was finally reunited on 3 October 1990 when the DDR formally acceded to the GRUNDGE-SETZ. The first joint elections for the united city since 1946 were held on 2 December 1990 and the seat of the German government is due to transfer from BONN to Berlin by the year 2000. Berlin has long been a centre of culture and the tradition continues with political cabaret, opera, the Berliner Philharmoniker, museums, the Internationale Filmfestspiele Berlin, the Theatertreffen in May and an annual jazz festival. Shopping is epitomised by the KURFÜRSTENDAMM and the emporium KaDeWe.

The city has a population of some 3.47 million with a total student population of around 150,000 (3 UNIVERSITÄTEN and 14 other HOCHSCHULEN) and about 12% foreigners (33% Turkish); it is said to be the biggest Turkish city outside Istanbul. A coalition between the CDU and SPD has been running the city since 1991. Berlin is now Germany's largest industrial city and its industries include electrical engineering, machinery, chemicals, food processing and vehicle construction. Important companies include SIEMENS, ABB and SCHERING. The 'ICC Berlin' is the world's largest conference centre, and the city's trade-fair complex hosts trade fairs such as GRÜNE WOCHE (International Green Week), ILA-BERLIN-BRANDENBURG (aerospace), the INTERNATIONALE TOURISMUS-BÖRSE (tourism) and the INTERNATIONALE FUNKAUSSTELLUNG (audio and video). See also: BERLIN (LAND)

BERLIN, FREIE UNIVERSITÄT

University in BERLIN (former west Berlin) founded in 1948 and teaching some 55,000 students. The Freie Universität Berlin has departments of medicine, dentistry, veterinary medicine, law, economics and business studies, philosophy and social sciences, communication, education, history, classics and archaeology, political science, German language and literature, modern lan-

guages and literature, mathematics, physics, chemistry, pharmacy, biology, geosciences.

BERLIN, HUMBOLDT-UNIVERSITÄT ZU
University in BERLIN founded in 1810 and teaching some 25,000
students. Berlin's traditional university is in east Berlin and now
has nearly 250 professors from west Germany alongside 165 professors from the east. The Humboldt-Universität zu Berlin has
departments of medicine, law, economics, theology, social sciences, education, rehabilitation, philosophy and history, cultural
studies, languages and literature, Asian and African studies,
mathematics, physics, electronics, computer science, biology,
chemistry, psychology, pharmacology, geography, agriculture.

BERLIN, TECHNISCHE UNIVERSITÄT
University in BERLIN founded in 1946 and teaching some 38,000
students. The Technische Universität Berlin has departments of
communication and history, education, mathematics, physics,
chemistry, process and environmental engineering and materials
science, environment and society, architecture, civil engineering
and applied earth sciences, transport and applied mechanics,
mechanical and production engineering, electrical engineering,
computer science, economics and management, food science and
biotechnology.

BERLINALE
A film festival held in BERLIN every summer at which the film
prize *Goldener Berliner Bär* is presented.

BERLINER ENSEMBLE
Theatre company founded in East BERLIN in 1949 by Bertolt
Brecht and Helene Weigel. Brecht here experimented with 'epic
theatre' in a wide range of productions of his own plays and
adaptions of Shakespeare and others. Since 1954 the Berliner
Ensemble has occupied the Theater am Schiffbauerdamm, and
in 1992 it was transformed into a GMBH run by a group including
dramatist Heiner Müller, producers Peter ZADEK and Peter
PALITZSCH, and later actress Eva MATTES; from 1995 Heiner Müller
had control of the company until his death in January 1996,

which was a severe loss to the Ensemble. The actor and producer Martin Wuttke was appointed INTENDANT in 1996.

BERLINER KRAFT- UND LICHT (BEWAG)-AG
Electricity generation and distribution company with headquarters in BERLIN. BEWAG has some 11,000 employees.

BERLINER MAUER
The Communist government in the DDR ordered the erection of a wall around West BERLIN on 13 August 1961 as an economic barrier to prevent the exodus of skilled labour and professionals to the West. The *Berliner Mauer* was built in subsequent months and became a potent symbol of the enduring split between the two Germanies. When the Wall was breached on 9 November 1989 it became symbolic of the reunification of the two parts of Germany.

BERLINER MORGENPOST
Newspaper founded in 1898 and published every day including Sunday. It has an average circulation of 186,000 and is distributed in BERLIN and the surrounding suburbs. This is a respected quality newspaper with national and regional news.

BERLINER TESTAMENT
A joint will where each spouse leaves their estate to the other absolutely. On the death of the surviving spouse, the residual estate passes to a third party, usually the joint children.

BERLINER ZEITUNG
Daily newspaper with a circulation of 235,000 published in BERLIN. It was established in the Russian sector of Berlin in 1945 and was run by the SED as one of East Germany's more digestible papers. It is now owned by GRUNER +JAHR.

BERLINERISCH
The language of the Bundeshauptstadt is the brash '*Berliner Schnauze*' – epitomised in the assertion '*Den ha' ick aba de Meinung jesacht*' ('*Dem habe ich aber die Meinung gesagt*') – 'I gave him a piece of my mind'. Characteristics of *Berlinerisch* by comparison with HOCHDEUTSCH are 'k' for 'ch' (e.g. *ick* for *ich*), 'e' for 'ei' and 'o' for 'an' (e.g. *keen* for *kein* and *ooch* for *auch*), 'p'

for 'pf' (e.g. *Appel* for *Apfel*), 't' for 's' (e.g. *dat* for *das*) and 'j' for 'g' (e.g. *jut* for *gut*).

BERTELSMANN AG
The world's biggest publishing and entertainment group, founded in 1971. The group has interests in publishing and press, printing and distribution, and entertainment (broadcasting, film, music). Bertelsmann has a majority holding in publisher GRUNER + JAHR, a stake in TV channel RTL and an interest in TV channel VOX through its subsidiary UFA. Company headquarters are in Gütersloh (NORDRHEIN-WESTFALEN). Bertelsmann has some 24,000 employees.

BERUFLICHE BILDUNG
The system of vocational training comprising BERUFSAUSBILDUNG, BERUFLICHE FORTBILDUNG and BERUFLICHE UMSCHULUNG.

BERUFLICHE FORTBILDUNG
Further training that develops the knowledge and skills necessary in an AUSBILDUNGSBERUF or takes account of technical innovations.

BERUFLICHE UMSCHULUNG
A second training undertaken in order to enter a different profession because of unemployment in popular vocations or because a vocation has ceased to exist.

BERUFSAUFBAUSCHULE
Educational institutions in the ZWEITER BILDUNGSWEG that prepare pupils for the FACHSCHULREIFE. The HAUPTSCHULABSCHLUSS is the entrance requirement and students may study here during their BERUFSAUSBILDUNG or while they are working.

BERUFSAUSBILDUNG
Germany has a structured system of vocational training in which the knowledge and skills required for a particular AUSBILDUNGS-BERUF are imparted. The normal age of apprentices is between 15/16 and 19, though an increasing number of 19–year-olds who have taken the ABITUR are entering vocational training. Training lasts two to three years and trainees with *Abitur* can cut the length of their training by six months to a year. The apprentice-

ship is based on a twin-track system (DUALES SYSTEM) of practical, on-the-job training in the workplace and theoretical tuition at BERUFSSCHULEN, where AUSZUBILDENDE receive specialist teaching and study general subjects. Large companies have their own training workshops, and in smaller companies practical training takes place on-the-job. Apprentices sign a LEHRVERTRAG approved by the local chamber of commerce and receive a wage which increases annually.

Vocational training is organised mainly by the local INDUSTRIE-UND HANDELSKAMMERN (to which all companies must belong) and HANDWERKSKAMMERN, which set examinations and ensure that companies and businesses can provide suitable training with qualified instructors. *Auszubildende* are examined by a committee made up of representatives of the ARBEITGEBER, ARBEITNEHMER and *Berufsschulen*. The curriculum for training courses is laid down in the AUSBILDUNGSORDNUNG drawn up by the appropriate ministry and is based on proposals by industrial associations, ARBEITGEBERVERBÄNDE and the GEWERKSCHAFTEN. There are more than 300 registered trades and vocations in Germany ranging from hairdresser to dental technician and car mechanic. See also: AUSBILDENDER; AUSZUBILDENDER

BERUFSBILDUNGSGESETZ
The law regulating the part of the BERUFSAUSBILDUNG carried out within the company or trade. It does not regulate training carried out in the public services. This law lays down the framework within which the training takes place and specifies the duties and obligations of the AUSBILDENDER and the AUSZUBILDENDER.

BERUFSFACHSCHULE
A school that prepares pupils for a vocational training (BERUFS-AUSBILDUNG), the entrance requirement being a HAUPTSCHULAB-SCHLUSS. The course of study generally lasts two years and the leaving certificate (ABSCHLUSSZEUGNIS) qualifies pupils to study at the FACHOBERSCHULE.

BERUFSGENOSSENSCHAFTEN
Trade associations providing statutory UNFALLVERSICHERUNG. This insurance is taken out by enterprises for their employees. These

organisations are responsible for the prevention of accidents at work and for providing rehabilitation and pensions for employees who have suffered industrial injury or pensions for their surviving dependants.

BERUFSRICHTER
Professional judge who has the BEFÄHIGUNG ZUM RICHTERAMT. Judges are generally appointed to the office for life. See also: EHRENAMTLICHER RICHTER

BERUFSSCHULE
A vocational training college providing specialist teaching and general education for AUSZUBILDENDE. Attendance is obligatory for two days a week, or for blocks of several weeks at a time, throughout two or three years of training. Trainees receive an ABSCHLUSSZEUGNIS at the end of their training detailing their grades and achievements. Attendance at the *Berufsschule* is also compulsory for all young people under the age of 18 who are not attending any other school.

BERUFSSOLDAT
Professional soldier serving in the BUNDESWEHR.

BERUFSVERBAND
Professional association of members of the same profession to promote the interests of that profession.

BESCHLEUNIGTES VERFAHREN
Expedited proceedings that a STAATSANWALT can apply for if the facts surrounding a criminal case are straightforward and it does not involve a sentence of more than one year's imprisonment.

BESOLDUNG
Remuneration paid to BEAMTE, judges and soldiers. See also: ENTGELT

BETRIEBSKRANKENKASSE
A PFLICHTKRANKENKASSE for all the ARBEITNEHMER in a company with at least 450 employees.

BETRIEBSRAT
A works council which is legally obliged to act in accordance

with the company's well-being. ARBEITNEHMER in companies with a workforce of five or more full-time workers are legally entitled to set up a *Betriebsrat*.

BETRIEBSVERFASSUNGSGESETZ

The Industrial Constitution Act of 1952 stipulated that in an AKTIENGESELLSCHAFT, the employees should elect a third of the AUFSICHTSRAT. This regulation still holds for *Aktiengesellschaften* with up to 2,000 employees, and other companies with 500 to 2,000 employees. The coal and steel industry forms an exception: since 1951 companies with more than 1,000 employees have had PARITÄT between the AKTIONÄRE and the ARBEITNEHMER on the *Aufsichtsrat*, with an additional neutral member agreed by both sides. The *Aufsichtsrat* also elects an ARBEITSDIREKTOR to represent the interests of the *Arbeitnehmer* on the VORSTAND.

The unions have been keen to extend this model to other sectors, but have had to be content with the *Mitbestimmungsgesetz* of 1976. This law gives the two sides *Parität* in companies with more than 2,000 employees, but the chairperson, who is elected by the *Aktionäre*, has the casting vote. See also: MITBESTIMMUNG

BEWAG See: *BERLINER KRAFT- UND LICHT (BEWAG)-AG*

BEYER, FRANK (1932–   )

Theatre producer and film director from the former DDR. He was a director in the DEFA film studios in 1958–1966, director at the Staatsschauspiel in DRESDEN and was appointed director at the Gorki-Theater in East BERLIN in 1969. His films include *Nackt unter Wölfen* (1962, after the novel by B. Apitz) and *Jakob der Lügner* (1974, after the novel by Jurek BECKER). The film *Spur der Steine* (1965/1966) about contemporary society in the DDR was banned by the authorities and could not be shown until 1990.

BEZIRK

A general term referring to a district. In BERLIN and HAMBURG a Bezirk is an administrative district, with a BEZIRKSBÜRGERMEISTER in Berlin and an AMTSLEITER appointed by the SENAT in Hamburg. In BAYERN, Bezirk refers to a GEMEINDEVERBAND.

The LÄNDER formed in the DDR after the war were soon broken up by the East German government into smaller administrative units called *Bezirke* (14) in an effort to deprive the population of a sense of identity and make the country easier to control.

BEZIRKSBÜRGERMEISTER
The head of a BEZIRK in BERLIN.

BFH See: *BUNDESFINANZHOF*

BGB See: *BÜRGERLICHES GESETZBUCH*

BGBl See: *BUNDESGESETZBLATT*

BGH See: *BUNDESGERICHTSHOF*

BGS See: *BUNDESGRENZSCHUTZ*

BIBB See: *BUNDESINSTITUT FÜR BERUFSBILDUNG*

BIBLIOTHEK FÜR ZEITGESCHICHTE
Germany's foremost library of contemporary history in STUTTGART. The Bibliothek für Zeitgeschichte was founded in 1915 as the *Weltkriegsbücherei* and was re-established in 1948. It specialises in contemporary history and political science with particular emphasis on the two world wars and twentieth-century military history. The library has some 300,000 volumes, together with collections of maps, leaflets, photographs and posters.

BIEDENKOPF, KURT HANS (1930–   )
Lawyer and CDU politician. He pursued a career in academia and industry and was GENERALSEKRETÄR of the CDU in 1973–1977. Biedenkopf was a member of the BUNDESTAG in 1976–1980 and was re-elected in 1987. He was a member of the LANDTAG in NORD-RHEIN-WESTFALEN in 1980–1987 and has been MINISTERPRÄSIDENT of SACHSEN since 1990.

BIELEFELD
Bielefeld is situated on the edge of the TEUTOBURGER WALD in NORDRHEIN-WESTFALEN (dialling code 05 21, postal area code 33…). The city was founded by the Ravensburg counts (charter

in 1214) and flourished as a centre for the linen trade. Bielefeld's annual Leineweber-Markt at the end of May brings street theatre, concerts and traditional displays to the town, and tournaments and a medieval fair come to the castle for the Sparrenburgfest in July.

The city has a population of some 324,900 with a total student population of around 25,400 (1 UNIVERSITÄT and 4 other HOCHSCHULEN) and about 15% foreigners (37% Turkish). A coalition between the SPD and BÜNDNIS 90/DIE GRÜNEN has been running the city since 1994. Industries include textiles, engineering, food, printing, chemicals and pharmaceuticals. Products include clothing, household appliances and cosmetics.

BIELEFELD, UNIVERSITÄT

University in NORDRHEIN-WESTFALEN founded in 1969 and teaching some 19,000 students. The Universität Bielefeld has faculties of law, sociology, education, history and philosophy, linguistics and literature, mathematics, economics, physics, biology, chemistry, psychology and sports science, theology and arts, geography, technology.

BIELEFELDER KATALOG JAZZ

Established in 1952, this compendium is published twice a year and gives a comprehensive survey of jazz recordings.

BIERMANN, WOLF (1936–   )

Writer of satirical songs and poems (real name Karl-Wolf Biermann) who was born in HAMBURG but moved to the DDR in 1953. His work was socialist in nature but was critical of the party and the BERLINER MAUER. He fell foul of the STAATSSICHERHEITSDIENST during the 1960s and was expelled from the SED in 1963. Publication of his works was banned and for a time he was not allowed to perform in public, although he had a big following in the West. Biermann was finally stripped of his DDR citizenship in 1976 when performing in West Germany, an act which caused a crisis among the DDR intelligentsia and an international outrage. He was active in the German ecology and peace movement and has contributed extensively to the debate about the DDR since the WENDE. Biermann was awarded the

GEORG-BÜCHNER-PREIS in 1991 and the HEINE-PREIS in 1993. His works include *Die Drahtharfe* (1965), *Deutschland ein Wintermärchen* (1972), *Der Friedensclown* (1977) and *Klartexte im Getümmel – Dreizehn Jahre im Westen* (1990).

BIKE

This magazine reflects Germany's enduring love affair with cycling and in particular mountain bikes. The ten issues every year give enthusiasts the latest news on bikes and cycling. It has a circulation of 139,000 and is published in BIELEFELD.

BILD AM SONNTAG

The Sunday edition of BILD ZEITUNG, published by the SPRINGER VERLAG with a circulation of some 2.7 million. It is a tabloid covering general news and also has a supplement with articles on travel, the home, health and beauty, and pets.

BILD DER FRAU

Weekly women's magazine published every Monday by the SPRINGER VERLAG. It has a circulation of two million and covers the classic women's topics of cookery, fashion and the home, as well as current affairs.

BILD DER WISSENSCHAFT

Glossy general science magazine founded in 1964 and published at the end of every month in STUTTGART by the Deutsche Verlags-Anstalt. It has articles on science and technology right across the spectrum, focusing in particular on popular science and everyday applications. This magazine appeals mainly to men with a general interest in science who are decision-makers and opinion leaders in the upper-income bracket. It has a relatively high circulation of 127,000, reflecting the high level of interest in science and technology in the country.

BILD + FUNK

Weekly TV guide published every Friday. It was established as a radio guide in 1927. It has a circulation of 668,000 and mainly appeals to the under-fifties in the middle-income bracket. As well as being a programme and leisure guide, *Bild + Funk* reports on celebrities and new TV series, and has film reviews and general articles on family entertainment.

BILD ZEITUNG

Far and away Germany's biggest selling daily newspaper (ÜBER-REGIONALE ZEITUNG) with a circulation of 4.5 million. It is also Europe's biggest selling tabloid. *Bild* was founded in 1952 and is owned by the SPRINGER VERLAG in HAMBURG. It pursues an assertive populist, right-wing agenda. The paper is famous for its lurid headlines and pursuit of scoops and sensation. Heinrich Böll based his novel *Die verlorene Ehre der Katharina Blum* (1974) on the paper's ruthless hounding of individuals. See also: WALLRAFF, GÜNTER

BILDUNGSWESEN

The educational system including schools, vocational training in BERUFSSCHULEN and tertiary education in HOCHSCHULEN.

BILDWOCHE

Radio and TV guide with general articles for women. It has a circulation of 457,000 and is published by the SPRINGER VERLAG. The magazine section has articles on the stars and ordinary people, and anyone who likes puzzles will find plenty to do.

BILFINGER + BERGER BAU AG

Construction company founded in 1880. Company headquarters are in MANNHEIM. Bilfinger has some some 47,000 employees.

BINNIG, GERD (1947–   )

Physicist who received the Nobel Prize for physics in 1987 (with E. Ruska and H. Roher) for inventing the scanning tunnelling microscope that allows individual atoms to be identified on the surfaces of conducting or semiconducting materials.

BISKY, LOTHAR (1941–   )

Professor and PDS politician. He was REKTOR of the Hochschule für Film und Fernsehen (POTSDAM) in 1987–1989. Bisky is a member of the LANDTAG in BRANDENBURG and has been chairman of the PARTEI DES DEMOKRATISCHEN SOZIALISMUS since 1993.

BK See: *BUNDESKANZLERAMT*

BKA See: *BUNDESKRIMINALAMT*

BKartA See: *BUNDESKARTELLAMT*

BLITZ ILLU
Weekly magazine for the youth market with a circulation of 564,000.

BLÜM, NORBERT (1935–   )
CDU politician who trained as a toolmaker and then studied at university and took a doctorate in philosophy. He has been a member of the *Bundesvorstand* of the CDU since 1969 and a member of the BUNDESTAG since 1983. In 1987 he became chairman of the CDU in NORDRHEIN-WESTFALEN. Blüm has been BUNDESMINISTER FÜR ARBEIT UND SOZIALORDNUNG since 1982 and is the longest-serving member of the KOHL government apart from Helmut Kohl himself.

BLUMENBERG, HANS (1920–   )
Philosopher and writer who explores metaphor, fictionality and myth in his work, which includes *Paradigmen zu einer Metaphorologie* (1960) and *Die Lesbarkeit der Welt* (1981).

BM See: *BUNDESMINISTER; BUNDESMINISTERIUM; BÜRGERMEISTER*

BMA See: *BUNDESMINISTER[IUM] FÜR ARBEIT UND SOZIALORDNUNG*

BMBau See: *BUNDESMINISTER[IUM] FÜR RAUMORDNUNG, BAUWESEN UND STÄDTEBAU*

BMBWFT See: *BUNDESMINISTER[IUM] FÜR BILDUNG, WISSENSCHAFT, FORSCHUNG UND TECHNOLOGIE*

BMF See: *BUNDESMINISTER[IUM] DER FINANZEN*

BMFSFJ See: *BUNDESMINISTER[IUM] FÜR FAMILIE, SENIOREN, FRAUEN UND JUGEND*

BMG See: *BUNDESMINISTER[IUM] FÜR GESUNDHEIT*

BMI See: *BUNDESMINISTER[IUM] DES INNERN*

BMJ See: *BUNDESMINSTER[IUM] DER JUSTIZ*

BML See: *BUNDESMINISTER[IUM] FÜR ERNÄHRUNG, LANDWIRTSCHAFT UND FORSTEN*

BMPT See: *BUNDESMINISTER[IUM] FÜR POST UND TELEKOMMUNIKATION*

BMU See: *BUNDESMINISTER[IUM] FÜR UMWELT, NATURSCHUTZ UND REAKTORSICHERHEIT*

BMV See: *BUNDESMINISTER[IUM] FÜR VERKEHR*

BMVg See: *BUNDESMINISTER[IUM] DER VERTEIDIGUNG*

BMW AG
Luxury car and motorbike manufacturer founded in 1916 as an aircraft company, turning to automobile production in 1922. Company headquarters are in MÜNCHEN and include a museum of the motorcar. BMW has some 109,000 employees.

BMWi See: *BUNDESMINISTER[IUM] FÜR WIRTSCHAFT*

BMZ See: *BUNDESMINISTER[IUM] FÜR WIRTSCHAFTLICHE ZUSAMMENARBEIT*

BND See: *BUNDESNACHRICHTENDIENST*

BOCHUM
Bochum is situated in NORDRHEIN-WESTFALEN between ESSEN and DORTMUND at the heart of the RUHRGEBIET (dialling code 02 34, postal area code 44...). Bochum received a charter as a market town in 1321, and during the industrial revolution rose to become one of the leading towns in the Ruhrgebiet, based on coalmining and the iron and steel industry. The Propsteikirche was the city's only historic building to emerge from the destruction of the Second World War. The city's architecture now is starkly modern, epitomised by the utilitarian RUHR-UNIVERSITÄT. Bochum has a drama school and is one of Germany's main centres for theatre.

The city has a population of some 408,000 with a total student population of around 45,000 (1 UNIVERSITÄT and 4 other

HOCHSCHULEN) and about 9% foreigners (40% Turkish). The SPD runs the city and has been in office since 1946. Bochum's economy has undergone massive restructuring since the closure of many coalmines, and the city's biggest employer now is the General Motors European subsidary Opel. Other industries include iron and steel, electrical engineering, with products such as televisions and cars.

BOCHUM, RUHR-UNIVERSITÄT
New university in NORDRHEIN-WESTFALEN with a modern, concrete campus, founded in 1961 and teaching some 38,000 students. The Ruhr-Universität Bochum has faculties of Protestant theology, Catholic theology, philosophy and pedagogy and journalism, history, philology, law, economics, social sciences, East Asian studies, sports science, psychology, mechanical engineering, civil engineering, electrical engineering, mathematics, physics and astronomy, geosciences, chemistry, biology, medicine.

BODENSEE
Lake Constance lies on the border between Germany and Switzerland, with the easternmost area around Bregenz belonging to Austria. The Rhine flows through Germany's biggest lake, which is also known as the *Schwäbisches Meer*. It is popular especially with people in SCHWABEN as a holiday resort and its favourable climate – subtropical in places (Insel Mainau) – makes it a prime area for growing fruit. The town of Friedrichshafen (BADEN-WÜRTTEMBERG) on the Bodensee was the birthplace of the Zeppelin dirigibles.

BOHL, FRIEDRICH (1945–   )
Lawyer and CDU politician who served as a member of the LANDTAG in HESSEN in 1970–1980, becoming a MITGLIED DES BUNDESTAGES in 1980. Since 1991 he has been MINISTER IM BUNDESKANZLERAMT.

BÖHM, KARLHEINZ (1928–   )
Film actor who first came to prominence in *Sissi* (1955–1957) and whose films include several by Fassbinder: *Fontane Effi Briest* (1974), *Martha* (TV 1974, cinema release 1994), *Mutter Küsters' Fahrt zum Himmel* (1976). Television appearances include the series *Die Laurents* (1981). With money from TV programme

WETTEN, DASS ...? in 1981 he established the foundation Menschen für Menschen for the relief of famine in Africa and has worked to combat poverty and hunger in Ethiopian refugee camps, writing the book *Nagaya. Ein Dorf in Äthiopien* (1987) and the autobiography *Mein Weg* (1991).

BONN

The capital of the BRD from 1949 to 3 October 1990, Bonn is situated in NORDRHEIN-WESTFALEN on the river Rhine (dialling code 02 28, postal area code 53...). It will remain the seat of government until power is transferred to BERLIN by the year 2000, although the BUNDESRAT and a number of ministries (e.g. BUNDESMINIS-TERIUM DER VERTEIDIGUNG and BUNDESMINISTERIUM FÜR BILDUNG, WISSENSCHAFT, FORSCHUNG UND TECHNOLOGIE) will continue to be in Bonn. The BUNDESTAG, the BUNDESREGIERUNG, the majority of the BUNDESMINISTERIEN and many federal institutions will be moving to Berlin. However, there will also be exchange traffic in that a number of federal institutions will be moving from Berlin to Bonn (e.g. BUNDESKARTELLAMT). The BUNDESRECHNUNGSHOF is being moved from FRANKFURT to Bonn.

Bonn started life in Roman times as a river crossing and went on to become a Roman fortification on the Rhine as *Castra Bonnensia*. The city was the residence of the archbishops of KÖLN between 1238 and 1794, when it became a state in its own right. The city was also the birthplace of Ludwig van Beethoven and now has an international Beethoven festival every three years. Following the Napoleonic wars, Bonn became part of PREUSSEN in 1815. A quiet residential town for the wealthy in the nineteenth century, Bonn was an unlikely choice as West Germany's provisional capital in 1949. Looked down on as the 'BUNDESDORF' by more impressive cities, it seemed in danger of returning to its existence as a sleepy RHEINLAND town when the government moves out and the embassies and diplomatic missions leave. In fact, however, there are plans for Bonn to retain two-thirds of ministry jobs and the government has committed considerable resources to retaining Bonn's role as an important administrative centre and centre for scientific research.

The city currently has a population of some 313,000 with a

total student population of around 37,000 (1 UNIVERSITÄT and 2 other HOCHSCHULEN) and about 13% foreigners (15% Turkish). A coalition between the SPD and BÜNDNIS 90/DIE GRÜNEN has been running the city since 1994. Because of Bonn's status as a residential town for the rich, the city actively discouraged development during the industrial revolution with the result that only light industry developed, manufacturing products such as aluminium, sweets, cosmetics, organs and flags. The city's biggest employers are the government and service industries revolving around Bonn's diplomatic status.

BONN, RHEINISCHE FRIEDRICH-WILHELMS-UNIVERSITÄT
University in NORDRHEIN-WESTFALEN founded in 1786 and teaching some 38,000 students. The Rheinische Friedrich-Wilhelms-Universität Bonn has faculties of Protestant theology, Catholic theology, law and economics, medicine, philosophy, mathematics and natural sciences, agriculture, education.

BONNER RUNDSCHAU
Daily newspaper established in 1946 and distributed in the RHEINLAND with a circulation of 61,000.

BOOT DÜSSELDORF
'International Boat Show' – a trade fair for boats, water sports, fishing and accessories held in DÜSSELDORF annually with over 400,000 visitors.

BORCHERT, JOCHEN (1940–   )
Farmer and CDU politician who has been a member of the BUNDESTAG since 1981. He was appointed BUNDESMINISTER FÜR ERNÄHRUNG, LANDWIRTSCHAFT UND FORSTEN in 1993.

BÖRSE
There are eight stock exchanges in Germany: BERLIN, BREMEN, STUTTGART, FRANKFURT AM MAIN, DÜSSELDORF, HAMBURG, HANNOVER and MÜNCHEN, with Frankfurt having by far the biggest turnover.

BÖRSEN ZEITUNG
This is the official journal of the eight BÖRSEN in Germany.

Established in 1952, it is published daily in FRANKFURT AM MAIN and has a reputation for reliable financial reporting.

BÖRSENVEREIN DES DEUTSCHEN BUCHHANDELS e.V.

An organisation of publishers and booksellers founded in 1825 in LEIPZIG. After the Second World War it was reconstituted in FRANKFURT AM MAIN to form the umbrella organisation for publishers, booksellers and book dealers. Its organisations at LAND level represent members' interests in discussions with government authorities, carry out negotiations for wage agreements and advance the members with information and training events. In 1991 the *Börsenvereine* in Frankfurt and Leipzig merged, establishing headquarters in Frankfurt and an office in Leipzig. See also: AUSSTELLUNGS- UND MESSE-GMBH DES BÖRSENVEREINS DES DEUTSCHEN BUCHHANDELS; FRIEDENSPREIS DES BÖRSENVEREINS DES DEUTSCHEN BUCHHANDELS

BOSCH GmbH, ROBERT

Electricals giant producing spark plugs to power drills, founded in 1886. Company headquarters are in STUTTGART. Bosch has some 156,000 employees.

BÖTSCH, WOLFGANG (1938–   )

Lawyer and CSU politician who has been a member of the BUNDESTAG since 1976. In 1989–1993 he was chairman of the CSU-FRAKTION in the BUNDESTAG and was appointed BUNDESMINISTER FÜR POST UND TELEKOMMUNIKATION in 1993.

BOULEVARDPRESSE

Tabloid newspapers with characteristic sensational headlines and news items, carrying lots of photographs and relatively little copy, for example BILD ZEITUNG. One means of distribution in towns is via newspaper dispensers on the pavement, with a slot for payment.

BP See: *BAYERNPARTEI; DEUTSCHE BP HOLDING AG*

BPA See: *PRESSE- UND INFORMATIONSAMT DER BUNDESREGIERUNG*

Bpatg See: *BUNDESPATENTGERICHT*

BR See: *BAYERISCHER RUNDFUNK*

BRACHER, KARL DIETRICH (1922–   )

Historian and political scientist who was professor in BONN (RHEINISCHE FRIEDRICH-WILHELMS-UNIVERSITÄT) in 1959–1987. He was chairman of the *Beirat* of the INSTITUT FÜR ZEITGESCHICHTE in 1980–1988. He has written extensively on National Socialism and shaped the development of political science in the BRD based on democratic principles. His works include *Die Auflösung der Weimarer Republik* (1955), *Die deutsche Diktatur* (1969) and *Die totalitäre Erfahrung* (1987).

BRANDENBURG

Brandenburg is a FLÄCHENSTAAT covering an area of 29,481 sq. km. with a population of some 2.5 million. The LANDTAG (LANDESPARLAMENT) enacts legislation and comprises 88 members elected every four years, with the next election in autumn 1999. The Landtag elects the MINISTERPRÄSIDENT, head of the Regierung des Landes Brandenburg, which holds executive powers. The Ministerpräsident appoints the ministers with responsibility for individual portfolios. Brandenburg is divided into four KREISFREIE STÄDTE and 14 KREISE. The LANDESHAUPTSTADT is POTSDAM. The LAND Brandenburg in the former DDR (historically an Electorate with territory in modern Germany and Poland, and the core of the *Königreich* PREUSSEN) was formed in 1990 based on the borders of the former province in *Preussen* west of the ODER-NEISSE-LINIE. The people are overwhelmingly Protestant.

Brandenburg is a region of farmland, forest and lakes and the most important industries are agriculture and forestry. The Land has few areas of dense population without the city of BERLIN, and industrial production is concentrated around the outskirts of the city including Potsdam. Other industrial areas are Brandenburg, Cottbus, Eisenhüttenstadt and Frankfurt an der Oder with industries including iron and steel, heavy engineering, lignite production with vast open-cast mines, chemicals and textiles. These industries have suffered massive cutbacks since the WENDE with iron, steel and textiles shedding over three-quarters of their workforce. Cottbus hosted the Bundesgartenschau with over 2 million visitors in 1995. DAIMLER-BENZ is investing heavily in a new truck manufacturing facility at Ludwigsfelde south of Berlin, BASF is spending hundreds of millions updating the chemical plant at Schwarzheide, and the tourist industry is exploiting the leisure potential of the lakes and forests. The SPREEWALD is Brandenburg's most beautiful landscape, populated mainly by the SORBEN. The city of Potsdam with its royal palace has been intrinsically bound up with the development of *Preussen* and has been at the epicentre of modern German history. Following reunification, Brandenburg was ruled by a coalition between the SPD, FDP and BÜNDNIS 90/DIE GRÜNEN but the SPD gained an absolute majority in 1994. See also: LAND; LANDESREGIERUNG; STOLPE, MANFRED

BRANDENBURGER TOR
A series of arches finished in 1791 as a monumental gateway leading into the city of BERLIN. The refurbished *Quadriga* – a horse-drawn chariot – atop the gate was originally intended as a symbol of peace, but after the Second World War the gate instead came to symbolise the unity of imperial Germany and triumphalism tainted by militarism. When the BERLINER MAUER was breached in November 1989 the gate was the scene of euphoric celebrations, necessitating extensive restoration work. Following the bloodless revolution in the DDR, it has come to symbolise unity in peace.

BRAUN, VOLKER (1939–   )
Writer who studied philosophy at LEIPZIG after working as a printer and construction worker, and then worked at the BERLINER ENSEMBLE. Braun's writing during the DDR years was concerned with socialist society and while showing commitment to socialism, it was strongly critical of conditions in the DDR. His poetry collections include *Gegen die symmetrische Welt* (1974) and *Training des aufrechten Gangs* (1979), prose works include *Unvollendete Geschichte* (1975) and *Hinze-Kunze Roman* (1985), and dramas include *Die Kipper* (1966/1972), Die *Übergangsgesellschaft* (1987) and *Böhmen am Meer* (1992).

BRAUN AG
Manufacturer of domestic electrical appliances founded in 1921. Company headquarters are in Kronberg (HESSEN) and Braun went public in 1961. Braun has some 8,000 employees.

BRAUNSCHWEIG
Braunschweig is situated in NIEDERSACHSEN on the river Oker (dialling code 05 31, postal area code 38...). In the twelfth century, Braunschweig was the residence of Heinrich der Löwe and it went on to become an important commercial centre and home to one of Germany's oldest technical universities, the Collegium Carolinum founded in 1745. The city hosts a festival of modern chamber music in November and a medieval market is held in early summer.

The city has a population of some 252,000 with a total student population of around 18,000 (1 TECHNISCHE UNIVERSITÄT and 3 other HOCHSCHULEN) and about 7% foreigners (41% Turkish). A coalition between the SPD, FDP and BÜNDNIS 90/DIE GRÜNEN has been running the city since 1991. Braunschweig is an international centre for scientific research and is home to the PHYSIKALISCH-TECHNISCHE BUNDESANSTALT. The city's industries include electrical engineering, vehicles, electronics and food, with products such as pianos, computers and gingerbread. Important companies include VOLKSWAGEN and SIEMENS.

BRAUNSCHWEIG, TECHNISCHE UNIVERSITÄT CAROLO-WILHELMINA ZU
One of Germany's oldest technical universities was founded in 1745 as the Collegium Carolinum and became established as a centre for technical studies in 1835, acquiring university status in 1968. The university is in NIEDERSACHSEN and teaches some 16,000 students. The Technische Universität Carolo-Wilhelmina zu Braunschweig has departments of mathematics and computer science and economics, physics and geosciences, chemistry and pharmacology and biosciences, architecture, construction engineering, mechanical engineering, electrical engineering, philosophy and social sciences, education.

BRAVO

A weekly magazine for teenagers with a circulation of 1.3 million. Established in 1956, *Bravo* serves up a diet of pop music, sport and youth culture for 12–18 year-olds.

BRAVO GIRL

The complement to BRAVO, catering for young girls. Published every fortnight with a circulation of some 790,000, the magazine has articles on fashion, lifestyle and entertainment.

BRD See: *BUNDESREPUBLIK DEUTSCHLAND*

BREMEN, FREIE HANSESTADT (LAND)

The STADTSTAAT Bremen is Germany's smallest LAND, covering an area of 404 sq. km. and with a population of some 682,000. The BÜRGERSCHAFT (LANDESPARLAMENT) of the Freie Hansestadt Bremen enacts legislation and has 100 members elected every four years, with the next election in spring 1999. The SENAT (LANDESREGIERUNG) holds executive powers and the SENATOREN are elected by the Bürgerschaft. Two of the senators are elected BÜRGERMEISTER and one of the mayors is simultaneously Präsident des Senats (SENATSPRÄSIDENT).

The Land Bremen was created in 1947 by the American military government and comprises the LANDESHAUPTSTADT Bremen (550,000) and Bremerhaven (131,000), separated by territory belonging to NIEDERSACHSEN. Bremerhaven was founded in 1827 as Bremen's deep-water harbour and is now Germany's busiest fishing port, with the world's biggest container terminal. Trade and shipbuilding have been Bremen's main industries since the time of the *Hanse*, but following contraction of the shipbuilding industry, other important industries also include aerospace, electronics, and food and drink. Bremen has a reputation for political radicalism, and the ecology movement gained its first seats in a *Landesparlament* in 1979 (Bremer Grüne Liste), going on to become an important force in national politics. The SPD held power continually from 1947 until 1991 when elections removed the SPD majority. The Land was then ruled by an AMPEL-KOALITION with the FDP and DIE GRÜNEN, which broke up early in 1995.

After the 1995 elections a GROSSE KOALITION between the SPD and CDU was formed. See also: BREMEN (STADT); LAND; SCHERF, HENNING

BREMEN (STADT)

The 'Free Hanseatic City' of Bremen is both a city and a STADTSTAAT, and as such it is the LANDESHAUPTSTADT of the LAND BREMEN. The city is situated on the river Weser (dialling code 04 21, postal area code 28. . .). The city state is Germany's second oldest political entity. A bishopric was created in 787 and the city joined the Hanseatic League in 1358. For much of its history the city has been ruled by its merchants. This set it apart from the myriad of principalities that made up the rest of Germany, and Bremen has been known as the Freie Hansestadt Bremen since 1815. The Eiswette is held annually on 6 January and a Freimarkt starts off with a procession in October.

The city has a population of some 550,000 with a total student population of about 25,000 (1 UNIVERSITÄT and 3 other HOCHSCHULEN) and about 12% foreigners (38% Turkish). A coalition between the SPD and CDU has been running the city since 1995. Bremen is Germany's second largest port after HAMBURG and is an important shipbuilding centre. Other industries include engineering, electronics, and processing coffee and tea. The city is also one of Germany's big beer cities and exports Beck's beer. The university founded in 1971 marked a departure from traditional German universities, in line with the city's reputation as a centre for radical ideas. See also: BREMEN (LAND)

BREMEN, UNIVERSITÄT

University in BREMEN founded in 1971 with a new type of multidisciplinary curriculum and a more relaxed staff/student relationship. It has a reputation for being left-wing and there were a number of clashes between police and students in the 1970s and early 1980s. The Universität Bremen teaches some 18,000 students and has departments of physics, biology and chemistry, mathematics and computer science, geosciences, law, economics, sociology and geography and history and politics, religious studies, languages and literature, psychology, education and sport.

BREMER VULKAN VERBUND AG
Shipbuilding, transport and distribution company founded in 1893. The headquarters of Germany's biggest shipbuilding company are in BREMEN. Bremer Vulkan has some 25,000 employees.

BRETH, ANDREA (1952–   )
Theatre producer influenced by film whose productions are characterised by their precision and adherence to the original text. Her productions include Lessing's *Emilia Galotti* (1980), Garcia Lorca's *Bernarda Albas Haus* (1984), Shakespeare's *Was ihr wollt* (1989) and Kleist's *Der zerbrochene Krug* (1991).

BRIEFWAHL
Postal vote that voters can apply for before an election if they are not going to be in their electoral district to cast their vote on election day or if they will be otherwise unable to attend in person. The voter sends in the WAHLSCHEIN and STIMMZETTEL to the local election officer in a sealed envelope.

BRIGITTE
Women's magazine published fortnightly in HAMBURG by GRUNER + JAHR with a circulation of around one million.

BROKDORF
A small community in SCHLESWIG-HOLSTEIN with a large nuclear plant. Construction of the nuclear plant started in 1976, and the plant was the site of a massive confrontation between demonstrators and police. Court action halted construction but work began again in 1982 and was completed in 1986.

BRÜDER-GRIMM-MUSEUM
Schloß Bellevue in KASSEL is home to a museum dedicated to the Grimm brothers. It holds a collection of work by the three brothers Jacob, Wilhelm and Ludwig Emil Grimm including paintings, letters, drawings, etchings and an annotated manuscript of the famous *Märchen*.

BRÜHL
The two castles Augustusburg and the Jagdschloß Falkenlust in Brühl (NORDRHEIN-WESTFALEN) have been made a UNESCO world heritage site.

BRUNSWICK See: *BRAUNSCHWEIG*

BRUTTOLOHN
The gross wage before any deductions for tax or SOZIALVER-
SICHERUNG have been made.

BSG See: *BUNDESSOZIALGERICHT*

BUBIS, IGNATZ (1927–   )
Prominent member of the Jewish community who was impris-
oned by the Nazis in a concentration camp and returned to
FRANKFURT after the Second World War. A controversial property dealer who was responsible for some of the high-rise development in Frankfurt. He became a politician with the FDP and
was elected chairman of the ZENTRALRAT DER JUDEN in Germany
in 1992. In the wake of acts of violence directed towards Jews
and foreigners in Germany he has called for laws on racism to be
strictly applied, while seeking dialogue with political opponents.

BUCHHEIM, LOTHAR-GÜNTHER (1918–   )
Writer, publisher, photographer and painter who studied art
before founding an art-book publishing house in the 1950s. His
novel *Das Boot* (1973) was based on his wartime experiences
and brought him fame when it was made into an internationally
successful feature film in 1981. He has also written *Der
Luxusliner* (1980) and the autobiographical *Sächsische Heimat*
(1991).

BÜLOW, VICCO VON See: *LORIOT*

BUND
The central state or federation in Germany compared with the
regional political entities, each of which is referred to as a LAND.
The Bund is the first of two tiers of state government, the Land
being the second level. The GRUNDGESETZ clearly prescribes distinct functions for the Bund and the Länder. For example, the
Bund is responsible for defence while each Land is responsible
for provision of education. See also: BUNDESRECHT

BUNDESAMT
Authority directly below a BUNDESMINISTERIUM in charge of a clearly defined area of responsibility throughout the BUND.

BUNDESAMT FÜR ANERKENNUNG AUSLÄNDISCHER FLÜCHTLINGE
The federal office that deals with applications from asylum-seekers and refugees from abroad and decides whether they should be recognised as ASYLBERECHTIGTE. The office is part of the BUNDESMINISTERIUM DES INNERN.

BUNDESANSTALT
An institution at the level of the BUND directly under the supervision of a BUNDESMINISTERIUM and charged with administration or research for a particular area.

BUNDESANSTALT FÜR ARBEIT (BA)
The federal authority for matching job seekers with employment vacancies. The agency was founded in 1927 and is based in KASSEL. It also administers unemployment insurance, vocational training and continuing training. See also: ARBEITSAMT

BUNDESANSTALT FÜR POST UND TELEKOMMUNIKATION
A holding company for the government's shares in the three public companies created in the POSTREFORM II from the old DEUTSCHE BUNDESPOST. See also: DEUTSCHE POST AG; DEUTSCHE POSTBANK AG; DEUTSCHE TELEKOM AG

BUNDESANWALT
A STAATSANWALT who is a member of the staatsANWALTSCHAFT at the BUNDESGERICHTSHOF. In certain cases a Bundesanwalt may appear before an OBERLANDESGERICHT.

BUNDESARBEITSGERICHT (BAG)
The court of appeal in points of law (*Revision*) for settling labour disputes between ARBEITNEHMER and ARBEITGEBER, between *Arbeitnehmer*, between unions and management, and in cases related to the BETRIEBSVERFASSUNGSGESETZ. The court is made up of a BERUFSRICHTER as chairperson, two other *Berufsrichter* and two EHRENAMTLICHE RICHTER (one *Arbeitnehmer*, one

Arbeitgeber). The court was established in 1953 and is due to move from NÜRNBERG to ERFURT.

BUNDESARBEITSMINISTERIUM See: *BUNDESMINI-STERIUM FÜR ARBEIT UND SOZIALORDNUNG*

BUNDESARCHIV
Germany's central archive was founded in 1952 and is based in Koblenz (RHEINLAND-PFALZ). It is part of the BUNDESMINISTERIUM DES INNERN and is responsible for preserving for posterity certain categories of government and official documents, and other documentation of national and contemporary importance. It has nearly a quarter of a million metres of shelving, housing documents from the REICH, the BRD and the DDR, 1.6 million volumes and collections of feature films, documentaries, newsreels, private papers, maps, photographs, technical drawings, political posters, etc.

BUNDESÄRZTEKAMMER
The umbrella organisation for all the LANDESÄRZTEKAMMERN.

BUNDESAUFSICHTSAMT FÜR DAS KREDITWESEN (BAKred)
The federal banking watchdog is based in BERLIN and is under the authority of the BUNDESMINISTERIUM DER FINANZEN. The authority ensures that banks comply with the banking regulations and takes action to remedy circumstances that threaten the funds held by banks, endanger the liquidity of the banking system or pose a threat to the economy. The authority cooperates closely with the DEUTSCHE BUNDESBANK.

BUNDESAUFSICHTSAMT FÜR DAS VERSICHERUNGSWESEN (BAV)
The federal watchdog for the insurance industry is based in BERLIN and is under the authority of the BUNDESMINISTERIUM der FINANZEN. The authority regulates insurance companies, protects consumers and endeavours to prevent insolvency in insurers.

BUNDESAUSBILDUNGSFÖRDERUNGSGESETZ (BAföG)
Law regulating the provision of grants and loans to students undergoing vocational training, further and tertiary education.

Students at HOCHSCHULEN receive BAföG (means-tested) as part loan, part grant.

BUNDESBANK See: *DEUTSCHE BUNDESBANK*

BUNDESDATENSCHUTZGESETZ (BDSG)
The data protection law came into effect in 1990 and restricted the dissemination of personal data processed by the BUND and by private companies. *Landesdatenschutzgesetze* apply to public authorities in the individual LÄNDER. See also: DATENSCHUTZ; DATENSCHUTZBEAUFTRAGTER

BUNDESDORF
The 'Federal Village' – a derogatory term applied to BONN by inhabitants of Germany's larger cities indicating its origins as a small residential town on the Rhine. Konrad Adenauer, first BUNDESKANZLER of the BRD, favoured the choice of Bonn as the provisional capital of the new West Germany (he was himself from the neighbouring city of KÖLN), and Bonn triumphed over FRANKFURT AM MAIN as the only other contender. Bonn lost out to BERLIN when the BUNDESTAG voted by a narrow majority on 20 June 1991 to reinstate Berlin as the seat of power in the new Germany.

BUNDESFILMPREIS See: *DEUTSCHER FILMPREIS*

BUNDESFINANZHOF (BFH)
The highest court for settling disputes concerning tax law. The court was established in 1950 and is based in MÜNCHEN.

BUNDESFINANZMINISTER See: *BUNDESMINISTER DER FINANZEN*

BUNDESGERICHTSHOF (BGH)
The highest court for civil and criminal proceedings. The court was established in 1950 and is based in KARLSRUHE. The Bundesgerichtshof only hears appeals on points of law (Revisionen) concerning judgements made by the OBERLANDES-GERICHTE and in some cases by the LANDGERICHTE.

BUNDESGESETZ
A federal law is passed by the BUNDESTAG after three readings. It

is referred to the relevant BUNDESTAGSAUSSCHUSS once and in many cases has to receive the approval of the BUNDESRAT. See also: BUNDESRECHT

BUNDESGESETZBLATT (BGBl)

The official gazette for the *Gesetze* and RECHTSVERORDNUNGEN of the BRD. The BGBl is issued by the BUNDESMINISTERIUM DER JUSTIZ, and the first issue in 1949 contained the GRUNDGESETZ.

BUNDESGRENZSCHUTZ (BGS)

The border police comes under the jurisdiction of the BUND and is part of the BUNDESMINISTERIUM DES INNERN. This special police force was originally set up to monitor and guard the national borders of the new BUNDESREPUBLIK, but following the wave of terrorism at the beginning of the 1970s, the powers of the *Bundesgrenzschutz* were extended to cover the protection of official buildings housing important government departments such as the BUNDESKANZLERAMT. The *Bundesgrenzschutz* is permitted to operate within 30 km. of the border in peacetime, and throughout the country in times of war or civil unrest. In 1992 the functions of the railway police (*Bahnpolizei*) and security on board civilian aircraft were brought under the umbrella of the *Bundesgrenzschutz*. This police force also provides support for the LÄNDER during demonstrations, large sporting events and state visits. See also: GRENZPOLIZEI, BAYERISCHE

BUNDESINNENMINISTERIUM See: *BUNDES-MINISTERIUM DES INNERN*

BUNDESINSTITUT

An institute at the level of the BUND engaged primarily in research in a specified subject area.

BUNDESINSTITUT FÜR BERUFSBILDUNG (BIBB)

The institute for vocational training is based in BERLIN and is responsible for directing national policy on vocational training.

BUNDESKANZLER

The Bundeskanzler is head of the BUNDESREGIERUNG and need not be a member of the BUNDESTAG. A candidate is put forward by the BUNDESPRÄSIDENT for approval and is then elected by the

Bundestag normally for a period of four years. If the candidate fails to gain a majority of all Bundestag members, the Bundestag has 14 days in which to elect a Bundeskanzler. If the Bundestag fails to elect a Bundeskanzler within this period, another vote is held and the candidate with the majority is elected. If the elected candidate has the majority, the Bundespräsident has to appoint this candidate within seven days. If the candidate fails to obtain a majority of all Bundestag members, the Bundespräsident can still appoint the candidate within the statutory seven days or dissolve the Bundestag, with fresh national elections automatically following within a period of 60 days. See also: BUNDESREPUBLIK DEUTSCHLAND; KONSTRUKTIVES MISSTRAUENSVOTUM

BUNDESKANZLERAMT (BK)
The central office of the BUNDESKANZLER is responsible for planning, control and coordination of the Kanzler's duties and functions. It is responsible for carrying out the preparatory work to enable his policies to be put into action.

BUNDESKARTELLAMT (BKartA)
The federal cartel office is based in BERLIN and is under the auspices of the BUNDESMINISTERIUM FÜR WIRTSCHAFT. The office produces a report every two years on its activities and developments in the field of anti-trust over the previous two years.

BUNDESKRIMINALAMT
The central organisation for combating crime is based in WIESBADEN and is answerable to the BUNDESMINISTER DES INNERN. It is responsible for coordinating activities between BUND and LÄNDER. The individual LANDESKRIMINALÄMTER are independent, and the Bundeskriminalamt coordinates their activities when criminals operate over the borders of the individual Länder or internationally.

BUNDESLAND See: *LAND*

BUNDESLIGA
The top league in several German sports, notably football.

BUNDESMINISTER (BM)

A minister in the BUNDESREGIERUNG at the head of one of the BUNDESMINISTERIEN.

BUNDESMINISTER DER FINANZEN (BMF)

The minister responsible for financial affairs. This post has been held by CSU politician Theo WAIGEL since 1989. See also: BUNDESMINISTERIUM DER FINANZEN

BUNDESMINISTER DER JUSTIZ (BMJ)

The minister responsible for law and order. This post has been held by FDP politician Edzard SCHMIDT-JORTZIG since January 1996. See also: BUNDESMINISTERIUM DER JUSTIZ

BUNDESMINISTER DER VERTEIDIGUNG (BMVg)

The minister responsible for defence. This post has been held by CDU politician Volker RÜHE since 1992. See also: BUNDESMINISTERIUM DER VERTEIDIGUNG

BUNDESMINISTER DES AUSWÄRTIGEN

The minister responsible for foreign affairs. This post has been held by FDP politician Klaus KINKEL since 1992. See also: AUSWÄRTIGES AMT

BUNDESMINISTER DES INNERN (BMI)

The minister responsible for internal affairs. This post has been held by CDU politician Manfred KANTHER since 1993. See also: BUNDESMINISTERIUM DES INNERN

BUNDESMINISTER FÜR ARBEIT UND SOZIALORDNUNG (BMA)

The minister responsible for employment and social affairs. The post has been held by CDU politician Norbert BLÜM since 1982. See also: BUNDESMINISTERIUM FÜR ARBEIT UND SOZIALORDNUNG

BUNDESMINISTER FÜR BILDUNG, WISSENSCHAFT, FORSCHUNG UND TECHNOLOGIE (BMBWFT)

The minister responsible for education, science, research and technology. This post has been held by CDU politician Jürgen RÜTTGERS since 1994. See also: BUNDESMINISTERIUM FÜR BILDUNG, WISSENSCHAFT, FORSCHUNG UND TECHNOLOGIE

BUNDESMINISTER FÜR ERNÄHRUNG, LANDWIRTSCHAFT UND FORSTEN (BML)

The minister responsible for food, agriculture, forestry and fisheries. This post has been held by CDU politician Jochen BORCHERT since 1993. See also: BUNDESMINISTERIUM FÜR ERNÄHRUNG, LANDWIRTSCHAFT UND FORSTEN

BUNDESMINISTER FÜR FAMILIE, SENIOREN, FRAUEN UND JUGEND (BMFSFJ)

The minister responsible for family affairs, senior citizens, women and young people. This post has been held by CDU politician Claudia NOLTE since 1994. See also: BUNDESMINISTERIUM FÜR FAMILIE, SENIOREN, FRAUEN UND JUGEND

BUNDESMINISTER FÜR GESUNDHEIT (BMG)

The minister responsible for health. This post has been held by CSU politician Horst SEEHOFER since 1992. See also: BUNDESMINISTERIUM FÜR GESUNDHEIT

BUNDESMINISTER FÜR POST UND TELEKOMMUNIKATION (BMPT)

The minister responsible for post and telecommunications. This post has been held by CSU politician Wolfgang BÖTSCH since 1993. See also: BUNDESMINISTERIUM FÜR POST UND TELEKOMMUNIKATION

BUNDESMINISTER FÜR RAUMORDNUNG, BAUWESEN UND STÄDTEBAU (BMBau)

The minister responsible for planning, construction and urban development. This post has been held by CDU politician Klaus TÖPFER since 1994. See also: BUNDESMINISTERIUM FÜR RAUMORDNUNG, BAUWESEN UND STÄDTEBAU

BUNDESMINISTER FÜR UMWELT, NATURSCHUTZ UND REAKTORSICHERHEIT (BMU)

The minister responsible for environmental protection and reactor safety. This post has been held by CDU politician Angela MERKEL since 1994. See also: BUNDESMINISTERIUM FÜR UMWELT, NATURSCHUTZ UND REAKTORSICHERHEIT

BUNDESMINISTER FÜR VERKEHR (BMV)

The minister responsible for transport. This post has been held

by CDU politician Matthias WISSMANN since 1993. See also: BUN-
DESMINISTERIUM FÜR VERKEHR

BUNDESMINISTER FÜR WIRTSCHAFT (BMWi)

The minister responsible for economic affairs. This post has been
held by FDP politician Günter REXRODT since 1993. See also: BUN-
DESMINISTERIUM FÜR WIRTSCHAFT

BUNDESMINISTER FÜR WIRTSCHAFTLICHE ZUSAMMENARBEIT (BMZ)

The minister responsible for economic cooperation. This post
has been held by CSU politician Carl-Dieter SPRANGER since 1991.
See also: BUNDESMINISTERIUM FÜR WIRTSCHAFTLICHE ZUSAMMENARBEIT

BUNDESMINISTERIUM (BM)

The BRD has 16 federal ministries.

BUNDESMINISTERIUM DER FINANZEN (BMF)

This ministry has responsibility for setting the federal budget and
is the highest authority for fiscal and tax affairs. It regulates the
financial affairs between the BUND and the LÄNDER and is responsible for making financial settlements relating to the Second
World War and for ensuring that tax revenues are distributed
evenly between the Länder. The BMF is also responsible for the
government's monetary policy and matters relating to currency
and credit, without infringing the independent responsibilities of
the DEUTSCHE BUNDESBANK.

BUNDESMINISTERIUM DER JUSTIZ (BMJ)

This ministry is responsible for legislation relating to the administration of justice and the federal legal system. It examines draft
legislation from other ministries to ensure that it conforms with
the requirements of the constitution and legal system. The BMJ
oversees the appointment of judges to the BUNDESVERFASSUNGS-
GERICHT and to the other supreme federal courts.

BUNDESMINISTERIUM DER VERTEIDIGUNG (BMVg)

This ministry is responsible for defence, and the BUNDESMINISTER
DER VERTEIDIGUNG has responsibility for the BUNDESWEHR.

BUNDESMINISTERIUM DES INNERN (BMI)

This ministry is responsible for internal affairs. The BMI bears responsibility for constitutional law, and for organising civil defence. The legal framework regulating public administration, sport, the media, statistics, welfare, planning and local government all come under the umbrella of the BMI.

BUNDESMINISTERIUM FÜR ARBEIT UND SOZIALORDNUNG (BMA)

This ministry is responsible for employment and social affairs, and takes responsibility for labour laws regulating employees' rights at work, industrial safety, job creation, and the payment of unemployment and welfare benefits; the BMA also bears responsibility for the welfare of war disabled and war widows and dependants. It also regulates the use of technology in medicine and hospitals, and controls the legal framework governing the fees charged by doctors and health-care workers.

BUNDESMINISTERIUM FÜR BILDUNG, WISSENSCHAFT, FORSCHUNG UND TECHNOLOGIE (BMBWFT)

This ministry has the task of promoting research and development, and is responsible for planning education and educational research. It also has the task of promoting education and training and ensuring that the legal framework for tertiary education is in place. The BMBWFT also coordinates basic research and promotes technology development, information technology, research into nuclear power and Germany's space programme. See also: KULTURHOHEIT DER LÄNDER

BUNDESMINISTERIUM FÜR ERNÄHRUNG, LANDWIRTSCHAFT UND FORSTEN (BML)

This ministry is responsible for all aspects of government policy relating to food, agriculture, forestry and fisheries.

BUNDESMINISTERIUM FÜR FAMILIE, SENIOREN, FRAUEN UND JUGEND (BMFSFJ)

This ministry is responsible for matters concerning the family, senior citizens, women and young people. It covers marriage and family law, welfare and legislation governing KINDERGELD.

BUNDESMINISTERIUM FÜR GESUNDHEIT (BMG)

The ministry of health is responsible for health and health insurance (KRANKENVERSICHERUNG). The ministry has responsibility for both human and veterinary medicine, governs the licensing of pharmaceutical products and regulates the pharmacy sector, and deals with matters relating to consumer protection and food safety.

BUNDESMINISTERIUM FÜR POST UND TELEKOMMUNIKATION (BMPT)

The ministry for post and telecommunications is divided up into the three sectors *Postdienst*, *Postbank* and *Telekom*. The ministry is due to be disbanded at the end of 1997 in accordance with the privatisation of post and telecommunications services. Regulation of the industry will then be under the auspices of the BUNDESMINISTERIUM FÜR WIRTSCHAFT. See also: POSTREFORM

BUNDESMINISTERIUM FÜR RAUMORDNUNG, BAUWESEN UND STÄDTEBAU (BMBau)

The ministry for planning, construction and urban development is responsible for housing, new towns and construction for civil defence.

BUNDESMINISTERIUM FÜR UMWELT, NATURSCHUTZ UND REAKTORSICHERHEIT (BMU)

This ministry is responsible for the nuclear industry including reactor safety. It is also responsible for the environment and the protection of natural resources.

BUNDESMINISTERIUM FÜR VERKEHR (BMV)

The ministry of transport is responsible for all matters relating to roads, railways, inland waterways, maritime and air traffic. It also oversees construction of roads and inland waterways, and runs the meteorological service.

BUNDESMINISTERIUM FÜR WIRTSCHAFT (BMWi)

This ministry is responsible for economic policy and administration and also takes care of economic cooperation with the European states.

BUNDESMINISTERIUM FÜR WIRTSCHAFTLICHE ZUSAMMENARBEIT (BMZ)

This ministry is responsible for economic cooperation with foreign countries including the developing countries. It develops and implements policy, runs aid programmes and coordinates aid to the developing countries, and arranges technical aid programmes.

BUNDESNACHRICHTENDIENST (BND)

The German intelligence service was founded in 1956 and is based at Pullach near MÜNCHEN. The service is entrusted with gathering and analysing secret political, military, commercial, scientific and technical intelligence from abroad. In 1994, the government achieved a consensus with the SPD and voted to increase the powers of the intelligence service to help it in the fight against organised crime. See also: PORZNER, KONRAD

BUNDESPATENTAMT See: *DEUTSCHES PATENTAMT*

BUNDESPATENTGERICHT (BPatG)

The federal patent court was founded in 1961 and is based in MÜNCHEN. It decides on disputes relating to the granting of patents by the DEUTSCHES PATENTAMT.

BUNDESPOSTMINISTERIUM See: *BUNDESMINISTERIUM FÜR POST UND TELEKOMMUNIKATION*

BUNDESPRÄSIDENT

The president of the Federal Republic is elected by the BUNDESVERSAMMLUNG. Any German citizen who has the right to vote for the BUNDESTAG elections and has reached the age of 40 is eligible to become Bundespräsident. The period of office lasts five years and a president may be re-elected for another five years to follow on immediately from the first five years. The election by the Bundesversammlung must take place within 30 days of the presidential office being vacant and election is by a simple majority. If no majority is obtained in two elections, the candidate with the most votes cast is elected.

The president is very much a figurehead and is not allowed by law to play any part in the government of the BUND or any of the

LÄNDER. He (or she – though there has as yet been no female incumbent) is the legal representative of the German people and signs agreements with foreign powers in the name of the state. The president proposes a candidate for BUNDESKANZLER to the Bundestag and appoints and dismisses BUNDESMINISTER according to the advice of the Bundeskanzler. He appoints and dismisses judges, civil servants and officers (commissioned and non-commissioned) in the BUNDESWEHR. The president has a number of other powers including the right to pardon criminals.

The non-executive office of Bundespräsident reflects Germany's recent troubled history. However, a strong personality can exert considerable personal influence over events by taking a principled stance above the hurly-burly of party-political feuding. See also: BUNDESREPUBLIK DEUTSCHLAND

BUNDESRAT

The second chamber of Germany's parliamentary structure, comprising representatives of the LÄNDER. Germany has a federal system and is divided into 16 Länder, including the three STADT-STAATEN of BERLIN, BREMEN and HAMBURG. Each Land is represented at national level in the Bundesrat with three to six votes (depending on the population of the Land). The members of the Bundesrat are appointed by each landesregierung and must cast their votes in a block. Bills affecting central interests of the Länder that have been passed by the elected assembly (BUNDESTAG) have to be passed by the Bundesrat before they become law. The Bundesrat only has a right of objection in the case of other legislation and the Bundestag can overrule. Any proposed changes to the GRUNDGESETZ require a two-thirds majority in the Bundesrat.

BUNDESRECHNUNGSHOF (BRH)

The federal audit office was founded in 1950 as a control on the BUNDESREGIERUNG and the BUNDESTAG. It is based in FRANKFURT AM MAIN and is due to move to BONN by the year 2000. The Bundesrechnungshof acts independently of the Bundesregierung and is responsible for examining the expenditure and income of the BUND.

BUNDESRECHT

The GRUNDGESETZ defines the extent to which the BUND has powers of jurisdiction that take precedence over the powers of the LÄNDER (*'Bundesrecht bricht Landesrecht'*, *Artikel* 31, GG). In certain areas (foreign affairs, defence, monetary policy) the Bund has the exclusive right to legislate (*ausschließliche Gesetzgebungskompetenz*) and the Länder may only pass laws in these areas if expressly permitted. In other areas, the Länder may enact legislation if the Bund chooses not to make use of its right to legislate (*konkurrierende Gesetzgebungskompetenz*) and the Bund should refrain from legislating unless legislation at federal level is necessary; such areas in which the Bund has made use of its right to legislate are BÜRGERLICHES RECHT, Arbeitsrecht and SOZIALVERSICHERUNG. HOCHSCHULEN and the press are areas where the Bund has jurisdiction to enact framework legislation (*Rahmengesetze*) laying down general principles within which the Länder are empowered to enact their own detailed legislation. The BUNDESVERFASSUNGSGERICHT decides in cases of disagreement between the Bund and Länder over their powers of jurisdiction.

BUNDESREGIERUNG

The federal government in Germany comprising the BUNDESKANZLER and the BUNDESMINISTER. They are responsible for policy and answer to the BUNDESTAG for the actions of the government.

BUNDESREPUBLIK DEUTSCHLAND (BRD)

The Federal Republic of Germany was founded in May 1949. The GRUNDGESETZ, the 'provisional' constitution of this part of the divided Germany, was drawn up by the *Parlamentarischer Rat* convened in BONN on 1 September 1948; this comprised 65 delegates from the LANDTAGE of the LÄNDER in the Western zones of occupation. The Grundgesetz was approved by the council on 8 May 1949 and was proclaimed on 23 May 1949. The first elections to the BUNDESTAG were held on 14 August 1949. The Grundgesetz created a federal structure that gave substantial powers to the Länder and drastically reduced the power of the *Präsident* by comparison with his role in the WEIMARER REPUBLIK.

Elections to the Bundestag were to be held every four years with a FÜNFPROZENTKLAUSEL as a means of avoiding the political fragmentation which had dogged the Weimarer Republik. The BUNDESVERFASSUNGSGERICHT was established to guarantee human rights and the Grundgesetz expressly prohibited any party that was contrary to democratic principles.

The first elections resulted in a CDU/CSU and FDP coalition government under Konrad Adenauer, who played a major role in drawing up the Grundgesetz and is viewed as the founding father of the BRD, steering it carefully through the first decade and a half of democracy. He was BUNDESKANZLER from 1949–1963 (and also BUNDESMINISTER DES AUSWÄRTIGEN 1951–1955) and retired from public life in 1963. His strong personality was instrumental in establishing the Bundesrepublik and restoring West German sovereignty in 1955 through the DEUTSCHLANDVERTRAG. Adenauer worked closely with the Western powers to ensure that West Germany became part of the Western European Union (1955) and a member of NATO (1955). In 1955 he established diplomatic relations with the Soviet Union and negotiated the return of all remaining German prisoners of war. The first units of the BUNDESWEHR were formed in 1956.

The WIRTSCHAFTSWUNDER that continued throughout the 1950s and beyond ensured that German industry was able to lay the economic foundations for a prosperous and stable democracy. The concept of MITBESTIMMUNG was enshrined in law in 1952 and was one of the foundations that allowed the SOZIALE MARKTWIRTSCHAFT to thrive. The BRD became a member of the European Coal and Steel Community in April 1951 and the Treaty of Rome established the European Economic Community in 1957 with West Germany a founder member.

The building of the BERLINER MAUER in 1961 seemed to mark the end of any prospect of a reunited Germany. The coalition government between the CDU/CSU and the FDP collapsed in 1962 in the wake of the SPIEGEL-AFFÄRE as West Germany faced up to its first real test of democracy, and a new government took over without CSU leader Franz Joseph Strauß. A GROSSE KOALITION was formed in 1966 between the CDU/CSU and the SPD to deal with the problems of economic recession, but the lack of real parliamentary opposition generated considerable unrest and the formation of an AUSSERPARLAMENTARISCHE OPPOSITION.

Elections in 1969 ushered in the SPD/FDP coalition which governed from 1969–1982. The first SPD Bundeskanzler Willy Brandt embarked on a policy of OSTPOLITIK and rapprochement with the Eastern bloc and the DDR in particular. Brandt resigned in 1974 when an aide was found to be a DDR spy, and Helmut SCHMIDT (a pragmatist on the right of the SPD) became Bundeskanzler. He continued Brandt's *Ostpolitik* and ensured that West Germany came through a period of destabilizing terrorist activity by the ROTE-ARMEE-FRAKTION without democracy being endangered. Schmidt embraced NATO's twin-track option on the deployment of medium-range nuclear weapons, but was beset by mounting economic problems. The ecology movement gained the first seats in a LANDTAGSWAHL in 1979 (BREMEN) and Schmidt's government experienced increasing criticism from his own party on environmental issues and defence.

Schmidt resigned after a KONSTRUKTIVES MISSTRAUENSVOTUM in 1982 following withdrawal of FDP support, and Helmut KOHL formed a coalition government between the CDU/CSU and the FDP. Kohl was confirmed in office with a clear majority by an election in 1983 and has gone on to win elections in 1987, 1990 and 1994. After the Berlin Wall was breached on 9 November 1989 and the subsequent collapse of the DDR, Kohl was widely seen as the architect of the successful reunification of Germany. Border restrictions between the two countries were lifted on 1 July 1990 and simultaneously the WIRTSCHAFTS- UND WÄHRUNGS-UNION introduced the D-mark to the DDR. The EINIGUNGSVER-TRAG on 31 August 1990 paved the way for the integration of the DDR into the BRD and the ZWEI-PLUS-VIER-VERTRAG restored full sovereignty to the Bundesrepublik on 12 September 1990. Germany was formally reunited on 3 October of the same year and all-German elections to the Bundestag in December 1990 confirmed the Kohl coalition between the CDU/CSU and FDP in a landslide victory.

The cost of reunification was seriously underestimated and billions were poured into revitalizing east German industry and infrastructure and support for the unemployed. Unpopular tax increases in 1991 brought defeat for the CDU in LANDTAG elections while high unemployment and recession led to an increase in the popularity of the right wing in the form of the REPUBLIKANER. Unemployment and immigration became the issues of the moment and the early 1990s saw a rash of brutal racist attacks on AUSLÄNDER, particularly in the east. Germany at the heart of the European Union (*Europäische Union*) is the central theme of the late 1990s as western Europe struggles to come to terms with the re-emergence of the nation state in eastern Europe.

Bundespräsidenten: Theodor Heuss (CDU, 1949–1959), Heinrich Lübke (CDU, 1959–1969), Gustav W. Heinemann (SPD, 1969–1974), Walter Scheel (FDP, 1974–1979), Karl Carstens (CDU, 1979–1984), Richard Freiherr von WEIZSÄCKER (CDU, 1984–1994), Roman HERZOG (CDU, since 1994).

Bundeskanzler: Konrad Adenauer (CDU, 1949–1963), Ludwig Erhard (CDU, 1963–1966), Kurt Georg Kiesinger (CDU, 1966–1969), Willy Brandt (SPD, 1969–1974), Helmut Schmidt (SPD, 1974–1982), Helmut Kohl (CDU, since 1982).

See also: DEUTSCHE DEMOKRATISCHE REPUBLIK; DRITTES REICH

BUNDESRUNDFUNKANSTALTEN
There are only two public-service broadcasting stations founded on federal legislation: DEUTSCHE WELLE is funded by the BUND and DEUTSCHLANDRADIO is funded by Bund and LÄNDER. They are both members of the ARD.

BUNDESSOZIALGERICHT (BSG)
The highest court for settling matters relating to welfare law. It was founded in 1953 and is based in KASSEL.

BUNDESSTRASSEN
The network of trunk roads throughout the BRD, e.g. B12. The responsibility for maintaining the *Bundesstraßen* is delegated to the LÄNDER.

BUNDESTAG
The legislative assembly of the BRD is elected every four years, with the next election in 1998. The Bundestag is responsible for federal legislation (BUNDESGESETZE) and the election of the BUN-

DESKANZLER. The BUNDESREGIERUNG is answerable to the Bundestag. There are 656 MITGLIEDER DES BUNDESTAGES, half of which are elected directly by ERSTSTIMMEN and half of which are elected by proportional representation through ZWEITSTIMMEN. The number of ABGEORDNETE may be higher if one or more parties gain ÜBERHANGMANDATE. The Bundestag elected on 16 October 1994 has 672 *Abgeordnete*: CDU/CSU 294 (244/50), SPD 252, BÜNDNIS 90/DIE GRÜNEN 49, FDP 47, PDS 30.

The Bundestag is rather a formal affair with little of the cut and thrust of a lively debating chamber (partly due to a semi-circular arrangement of the seating) despite attempts to loosen up proceedings. Even the election of *Abgeordnete* from DIE GRÜNEN at the beginning of the 1980s, who brought with them informal clothing and sat doing their knitting during speeches, made little impact on the formality of the Bundestag. See also: BUNDESRAT; BUNDESTAGSWAHL; FRAKTION; FÜNFPROZENTKLAUSEL

BUNDESTAGSABGEORDNETER See: *MITGLIED DES BUNDESTAGES*

BUNDESTAGSAUSSCHUSS
A standing committee of the BUNDESTAG which considers each bill once during its passage through the Bundestag. The Bundestag elected in 1994 has 22 *Bundestagsausschüsse* with between 17 and 41 members, roughly along the lines of the BUNDESMINISTERIEN (e.g. Auswärtiger Ausschuß, Innenausschuß, Haushaltsausschuß). The number of members from each party is allocated according to the size of the fraktion and the committees are reconstituted after each election.

BUNDESTAGSFRAKTION See: *FRAKTION*

BUNDESTAGSPRÄSIDENT
The highest office in the BUNDESTAG and chair of the ÄLTESTENRAT. The post is generally occupied by a member of the largest FRAKTION, even if that party does not form the government. See also: SÜSSMUTH, RITA

BUNDESTAGSWAHL
The elections for the BUNDESTAG that are held every four years.

MITGLIEDER DES BUNDESTAGES are elected by a complex combination (*Mischwahl*) of proportional representation (*Verhältniswahl*) and direct elections (*Mehrheitswahl*). Germany is divided into 328 WAHLKREISE in which direct candidates stand and are elected by a direct majority (ERSTSTIMME). Voters use their ZWEITSTIMME to select the LANDESLISTE of a particular party. It is thus possible to vote for two different parties simultaneously, although the *Zweitstimmen* hold the key to final percentages and therefore to the number of MANDATE for each party in the Bundestag. Elections are always held on a Sunday to ensure that voters are free to cast their votes. See also: FÜNFPROZENTKLAUSEL; ÜBERHANGMANDAT

BUNDESVERBAND
Because of the federal organisation in Germany, associations of like-minded people or organisations will tend to have a LANDESVERBAND at LAND level and an umbrella organisation or *Bundesverband* at the level of the BUND.

BUNDESVERBAND DER DEUTSCHEN VOLKSBANKEN UND RAIFFEISENBANKEN e.V.
The federal association of VOLKSBANKEN and RAIFFEISENBANKEN (KREDITGENOSSENSCHAFTEN) was formed in 1972 and is based in BONN. This umbrella organisation provides members with legal, tax and economic advice. The association carries out public-relations work for the cooperative movement and provides administrative support.

BUNDESVERBAND DEUTSCHER ZEITUNGSVERLEGER e.V. (BDZV)
The federal association of German newspaper publishers represents the interests of newspaper publishers. The LÄNDER have their own associations under the umbrella of the national association.

BUNDESVEREINIGUNG DER DEUTSCHEN ARBEITGEBERVERBÄNDE e.V. (BDA)
The federation of German employers' associations was founded in 1949 and is based in KÖLN. The federation has 16 associations at LAND level and 46 associations for specific industrial or profes-

sional sectors. The federation is an interest group with the aim of promoting the social and political interests of private-sector companies to the government, the unions and the public which extend beyond the scope of a particular economic or industrial sector.

BUNDESVEREINIGUNG DER KOMMUNALEN SPITZENVERBÄNDE

Federal association based in KÖLN that represents the interests of the associations of local authorities at federal level. See also: DEUTSCHER LANDKREISTAG; DEUTSCHER STÄDTE- UND GEMEINDEBUND; DEUTSCHER STÄDTETAG

BUNDESVERFASSUNGSGERICHT (BVerfG, BVG)

The supreme legal body in Germany for settling issues and disputes relating to the constitution (GRUNDGESETZ). The court was established in 1951 and is based in KARLSRUHE. It has two SENATE, each comprising eight judges. See also: LIMBACH, JUTTA

BUNDESVERSAMMLUNG

The function of the Bundesversammlung is to elect the BUNDESPRÄSIDENT. It consists of the MITGLIEDER DES BUNDESTAGES and an equal number of delegates elected by the LANDESPARLAMENTE. The Bundespräsident has to be elected by an absolute majority.

BUNDESVERWALTUNGSGERICHT (BVerwG)

The highest court for the settlement of disputes relating to administrative law. It was established in 1952 and is based in BERLIN.

BUNDESWEHR

The armed forces of Germany that come under the direction of the BUNDESMINISTERIUM DER VERTEIDIGUNG. The Bundeswehr is divided up into the HEER, the LUFTWAFFE and the MARINE. Following the Second World War the Bundeswehr came into being in 1955/1956, requiring changes to the GRUNDGESETZ. It was initially a voluntary force, compulsory conscription being introduced in 1956. The length of military service is currently 10 months, and BERUFSSOLDATEN sign up for up to 15 years.

The Bundeswehr was conceived as a defensive army, with the

Grundgesetz precluding military deployment abroad. The armed forces of the DDR were disbanded with reunification on 3 October 1990, and a programme of massive reduction in strength has been implemented since then. Before reunification the Bundeswehr had 490,000 service personnel under arms while by 1995 its strength had been reduced to 370,000, with hundreds of tanks and planes being scrapped. Germany has been a member of NATO since 1973 and provides the biggest military contribution of all European countries. Following reunification there has been pressure for Germany to assume a more active role in the world, and Germany started by participating in humanitarian and support operations for peace-keeping missions abroad. In July 1994 the BUNDESVERFASSUNGSGERICHT laid down a historic judgement that paved the way for the participation of the German armed forces in combat and peace-keeping missions, provided each case has the specific approval of the BUNDESTAG.

BUNDESWIRTSCHAFTSMINISTER See:
BUNDESMINISTER FÜR WIRTSCHAFT

BUNDESZENTRALREGISTER
The central register of criminal convictions and certain other information held by the GENERALBUNDESANWALT. See also: FÜHRUNGSZEUGNIS

BÜNDNIS 90/DIE GRÜNEN
An amalgamation of the Green parties of the former DDR and those of the BRD. After the bloodless revolution in November 1989, Bündnis 90 was formed from a number of civil rights movements in the DDR. A Grüne Partei was also formed in the DDR and these two parties joined together in the elections following reunification to form Bündnis 90/Grüne which gained eight MANDATE in the 1990 all-German elections. This marriage of convenience broke up in 1991, and in 1993 Bündnis 90 joined forces with the DIE GRÜNEN from west Germany to form Bündnis 90/Die Grünen. This party passed the five percent barrier in the 1994 elections to gain 49 *Mandate* and become the third biggest party in the BUNDESTAG. Bündnis 90/Die Grünen originated in the rising concern for ecological issues, and stands for social justice

and an equitable distribution of wealth and resources. The party is committed to grass-roots participation in the democratic process. See also: DIE GRÜNEN; FUNDI; REALO

BUNTE

Published by BURDA, *Bunte* was established in 1954 and is published in MÜNCHEN every Thursday with a circulation of 779,000. A women's magazine covering a wide range of issues from the lives of celebrities and ordinary people to the environment and technology.

BURDA GmbH & CO KG

Publishing house with a string of women's and lifestyle magazines. Company headquarters are in MÜNCHEN. Burda has some 5,000 employees.

BURDA MODEN

A fashion magazine founded in 1949 and published monthly with a circulation of 414,000. It is reputedly the most widely distributed fashion magazine in the world and covers all aspects of fashion, including sewing patterns, but also articles on gardening, health, travel, etc.

BÜRGERANTRAG

A petition that must be supported by a specified percentage of the electorate in a local community. This form of petition is permitted under the legislation in some LÄNDER, for example BADEN-WÜRTTEMBERG, and allows the local community to express its views on a particular issue and to demand action. Provided that the petition is legal, the local authorities must deal with the matter within a period of three months.

BÜRGERBEGEHREN

A request to a GEMEINDERAT in BADEN-WÜRTTEMBERG to carry out a BÜRGERENTSCHEID.

BÜRGERENTSCHEID

A decision taken by the electorate on a matter of importance in the local affairs of the community in BADEN-WÜRTTEMBERG. The decision is reached by means of a referendum which may have been initiated by the electorate or by the GEMEINDERAT. The result of the referendum is binding on the Gemeinderat. See also: BÜRGERBEGEHREN

BÜRGERHAUS

A type of house seen in the ALTSTADT of many of Germany's older towns and cities. The *Bürgerhaus* came into being in the early Middle Ages and was used by the citizen to house his family and to carry out his business.

BÜRGERINITIATIVE

Citizens' action group that is made up of like-minded members of the electorate without any formal affiliation to a particular political party or interest group or organisation. *Bürgerinitiativen* are formed to bring pressure to bear on the authorities to achieve a particular aim supported by the members. The first *Bürgerinitiativen* were formed at the end of the 1960s, and there are now many thousands of such groups addressing issues related to planning, traffic, the environment etc. Many *Bürgerinitiativen* are related to environmental issues and these started to influence local, regional and national politics at the end of the 1970s in the form of Green groupings such as the Grüne Liste, Bunte Liste, Grün-Alternative-Liste. The regional groupings developed into a new political force as DIE GRÜNEN in 1980 and have presented the electorate with an alternative to the traditional political parties.

BÜRGERLICHES GESETZBUCH (BGB)

The German civil code, contained in five volumes. The code was introduced on the first day of the twentieth century, and following suspension in the DDR it was re-introduced for the NEUE BUNDESLÄNDER with reunification on 3 October 1990. The law governing the application of the civil code has been amended to take account of the introduction of the code into the LÄNDER of the former DDR.

The five volumes of the Bürgerliches Gesetzbuch cover general principles of civil law, debt, property, family and inheritance. Although the original intention was to cover all areas of PRIVATRECHT (civil law) with the exception of commercial law, some areas of law remain outside the civil code (e.g. insurance law, copyright). Other areas have remained the province of legislation in individual Länder (e.g. fishing, forestry and hunting rights, which are partly subject to ÖFFENTLICHES RECHT anyway).

BÜRGERLICHES RECHT

The civil code used in Germany and laid down in the BÜRGERLICHES GESETZBUCH. See also: PRIVATRECHT

BÜRGERMEISTER (BM)

The role and powers of the mayor vary in the different LÄNDER and the position may be honorary (*ehrenamtlich*) or full-time (*hauptamtlich*) with a varying burden of executive duties; some Bürgermeister may have the status of BEAMTE. In southern Germany the Bürgermeister is elected by the electorate for a period of office lasting five or six years and is both the chairman and chief executive of the GEMEINDERAT or STADTRAT. In NORDRHEIN-WESTFALEN and NIEDERSACHSEN the Bürgermeister is honorary and is elected by the council for a shorter term of office as chairperson of the Gemeinderat or Stadtrat. In the city states of BERLIN, BREMEN and HAMBURG the head of the city is also head of the Land government and as such is the equivalent of the MINISTERPRÄSIDENT in other Länder. The term Bürgermeister used on its own in these three Länder refers to the deputy head of government. See also: STADTSTAAT

BÜRGERMEISTER, EHRENAMTLICHER

The position of honorary mayor with no executive functions held by the chairperson of the GEMEINDERAT or STADTRAT in NORDRHEIN-WESTFALEN and NIEDERSACHSEN.

BÜRGERMEISTER, ERSTER

The official title of a mayor in BAYERN. The Erster Bürgermeister in HAMBURG is the chairperson of the SENAT and head of the city; this position therefore fulfils the dual roles of MINISTERPRÄSIDENT in other LÄNDER and mayor in large cities.

BÜRGERMEISTER, HAUPTAMTLICHER

A full-time mayor who may be RATSVORSITZENDER and HAUPTVERWALTUNGSBEAMTER in BADEN-WÜRTTEMBERG, BAYERN, RHEINLAND-

PFALZ and SAARLAND or a HAUPTVERWALTUNGSBEAMTER in HESSEN and SCHLESWIG-HOLSTEIN.

BÜRGERMEISTER, REGIERENDER

The Regierender Bürgermeister in BERLIN is the chairperson of the SENAT and head of the city. The position therefore fulfils the dual roles of MINISTERPRÄSIDENT in other LÄNDER and mayor in large cities.

BÜRGERMEISTER UND SENATSPRÄSIDENT

The Bürgermeister und Senatspräsident is the chairperson of the SENAT and head of the city in BREMEN. The position therefore fulfils the dual roles of MINISTERPRÄSIDENT in other LÄNDER and mayor in large cities.

BÜRGERMEISTERAMT See: *RATHAUS*

BÜRGERMEISTERVERFASSUNG

A type of local-authority constitution applicable in RHEINLAND-PFALZ, SAARLAND, and GEMEINDEN in SCHLESWIG-HOLSTEIN. The BÜRGERMEISTER is elected by the GEMEINDEVERTRETUNG (in towns STADTRAT); the Bürgermeister carries out executive and administrative duties with the support of the BEIGEORDNETE. See also: MAGISTRATSVERFASSUNG; NORDDEUTSCHE RATSVERFASSUNG; SÜDDEUTSCHE RATSVERFASSUNG

BÜRGERSCHAFT

The official title of the STADTRAT in LÜBECK, and the equivalent of a LANDTAG in HAMBURG and BREMEN. *Bürgerschaft* also refers to the electorate entitled to vote in local-government or national elections.

BURSCHENSCHAFTEN See: *STUDENTISCHE VERBINDUNGEN*

BUSS- UND BETTAG

The day of repentance and prayer on the third Wednesday of November, a public holiday in SACHSEN. *Buß- und Bettag* used to be a general public holiday but it was abolished in 1994 (with the exception of Sachsen) to pay for the new PFLEGEVERSICHERUNG.

Re-introduction of this public holiday is under discussion in BAYERN.

BVerfG See: *BUNDESVERFASSUNGSGERICHT*

BVerwG See: *BUNDESVERWALTUNGSGERICHT*

BVG See: *BUNDESVERFASSUNGSGERICHT*

BVR See: *BUNDESVERBAND DER DEUTSCHEN VOLKSBANKEN UND RAIFFEISENBANKEN e.V.*

BZ
Long-established daily tabloid providing regional and national news and covering BERLIN and the surrounding region with a circulation of 307,000. This tabloid was founded in 1876 and is published by ULLSTEIN VERLAG (owned by SPRINGER VERLAG).

BZ AM SONNTAG
Sunday tabloid established in 1992 with a circulation of 140,000. It is published by ULLSTEIN VERLAG and is circulated in BERLIN and the surrounding region.

C & A MODE & CO
Value-for-money fashion retailer with nearly 200 stores. Company headquarters are in DÜSSELDORF.

CAPITAL (OST)
Capital appears in a special edition for east Germany, established in 1991. This is published by GRUNER + JAHR in HAMBURG and has a circulation of 46,000. The magazine addresses the needs and requirements of a new business environment and is aimed at senior executives.

CAPITAL (WEST)
Established in 1956 at the height of the German WIRTSCHAFTSWUNDER, *Capital* is the leading German monthly for business and finance. It is aimed at decision-makers in industry and is particularly popular with middle management. *Capital* is published monthly by GRUNER + JAHR in HAMBURG and has a circulation of 259,000.

CARINA
Monthly women's magazine established in 1977 with a circulation of 231,000. It targets young women aged between 18 and 34 and has articles on fashion, beauty, cooking and sewing. This magazine reflects the pre-eminence of German publishers in the European women's magazine market and is published in Dutch, Italian and Spanish as well as in German.

CARL-ZEISS-STIFTUNG
Foundation owning Carl Zeiss, precision engineering and optical instruments manufacturer. Head office is in Heidenheim. Carl Zeiss has some 33,000 employees. An agreement between BADEN-WÜRTTEMBERG and THÜRINGEN opened the way for the Carl-

Zeiss-Stiftungen Heidenheim (Baden-Württemberg) and Jena (Thüringen) to be amalgamated.

CDU See: *CHRISTLICH-DEMOKRATISCHE UNION*

CeBIT (WELT-CENTRUM BÜRO, INFORMATION, TELEKOMMUNIKATION)

The 'World Center for Office, Information and Telecommunications Technology' is a trade fair for office equipment and communication, networks, IT and telecommunications held in HANNOVER annually with around 700,000 visitors.

Centre0

Centre0 is a massive 70,000 sq. m. out-of-town shopping centre owned by METRO in the RUHRGEBIET city of OBERHAUSEN (opening autumn 1996). Strict controls have been imposed on the development of green-field shopping centres in west Germany, and the effect of this centre on local shops and businesses will be closely followed. Development of out-of-town shopping centres in east Germany has proceeded at a rapid pace, with LEIPZIG and HALLE alone having 14 centres with 400,000 sq. m. in 1995 and another 360,000 sq. m. due to open in 1997/98.

CGB See: *CHRISTLICHER GEWERKSCHAFTSBUND DEUTSCHLANDS*

CHAOS-TAGE

Generally peaceful annual meeting of punks held in the centre of HANNOVER at the beginning of August since 1982. After clashes with the police in 1994, efforts on the part of the authorities to move the festival outside the town in 1995 failed due to the lack of an organisational structure among the punks themselves. Chaos-Tage 95 ended in riots between punks and police with nearly 500 people injured, numerous cases of arson and a supermarket ransacked.

CHEFREDAKTEUR

The editor of a newspaper or magazine who is responsible for the overall content of the publication. The *Chefredakteur* will often write the LEITARTIKEL and is seen as broadly representing the views of the newspaper or magazine. See also: HERAUSGEBER

CHEMNITZ
Chemnitz is situated in SACHSEN in the ERZGEBIRGE (dialling code
03 71, postal area code 09. . .). The city was founded in 1170 and
rose to become a centre for the textile industry in Saxony.
Industrial development during the nineteenth century made the
city a focal point for the German labour movement. After the
Second World War the city was renamed and called *Karl-Marx-
Stadt* between 1953 and 1990. The city has a Mozart festival in
early summer and a festival of theatre and music in the autumn.
It was rebuilt modelled on Soviet styles and retains a Russian
feel even with today's heavy traffic.

The city has a population of some 273,000 with a student population of around 5,000 (1 UNIVERSITÄT) and about 2% foreigners.
The SPD has been running the city as the strongest party since
1994, although lack of an absolute majority has necessitated the
support of other parties. The traditional industries of textiles and
engineering continue to dominate this industrial centre but the
city is now diversifying into microelectronics. Products include
machine tools and textile machinery.

CHEMNITZ-ZWICKAU, TECHNISCHE UNIVERSITÄT
University in SACHSEN founded in 1836 and teaching some 6,000
students. The Technische Universität Chemnitz-Zwickau has
faculties of electrical engineering, mathematics, mechanical engineering, information science, economics, philosophy (arts).

CHRISTI HIMMELFAHRT
Ascension day is a public holiday throughout Germany and
always falls on a Thursday, 40 days after Easter.

CHRISTKINDLMARKT See: *WEIHNACHTSMARKT*

CHRISTLICH-DEMOKRATISCHE UNION (CDU)
The CDU was formed in 1945 as a grouping of regional parties
based on Christian principles. The CDU in the Soviet zone was
completely under the control of the SED from 1948 to 1989. In the
Western zones the party developed to form a right-of-centre
national party operating in all the LÄNDER except BAYERN, which
had its own party, the CSU. The CDU adopted the concept of a
SOZIALE MARKTWIRTSCHAFT advocated by Ludwig Erhard and

pursued Konrad Adenauer's policies of integration with the Western powers. Elections in 1949 returned the CDU to power in the first BUNDESTAG in coalition with the CSU and the FDP, and Adenauer led the party to victory at elections in 1953 and 1957 with the continuation of the coalition. The CDU lost ground in the 1961 election and a GROSSE KOALITION was formed in 1966–1969 between the CDU/CSU and the SPD. The CDU was voted out of office in 1969 and began a period of opposition until the FDP's withdrawal of support from the SPD/FDP coalition enabled Helmut KOHL to form a coalition between the CDU/CSU and FDP. This coalition was confirmed in office in the 1983 elections and in three subsequent elections in 1987, 1990 and 1994.

After the collapse of Communism, the CDU in East Germany formed the electoral grouping ALLIANZ FÜR DEUTSCHLAND and as the strongest party formed the government under Lothar de Maizière following elections on 18 March 1990. On reunification the CDU in the DDR was merged with the Western CDU at the beginning of October 1990. In the 1994 elections the CDU/CSU polled 41.5% of the votes across Germany and obtained 294 MANDATE in the BUNDESTAG.

The CDU is committed to conservative principles, with an emphasis on a free-market economy, private ownership, individual freedom and integration of Germany in Europe.

Parteivorsitzende: Konrad Adenauer (1950–1966), Ludwig Erhard (1966–1967), Kurt Georg Kiesinger (1967–1971), Rainer Barzel (1971–1973), Helmut Kohl (since 1973).

CHRISTLICH-SOZIALE UNION (CSU)

The party was formed in BAYERN in 1946 as a party based on conservative Christian principles. The party only fields candidates in Bayern and forms a FRAKTION in the BUNDESTAG with the CDU. The CSU has been the strongest party in the LANDTAG since the Second World War and has ruled Bayern continuously with the exception of a short period in the mid-1950s, forming a majority government there since 1966. The CSU was led by the controversial politician Franz Josef Strauß from 1961 until his death in

1988, and since then has been led by Theo WAIGEL. The weekly
BAYERNKURIER is the party newspaper.

The CSU is on the right wing of the CDU/CSU block with a
Catholic base and strong support in Bayern's rural heartlands.

CHRISTLICHER GEWERKSCHAFTSBUND DEUTSCHLANDS (CGB)

Small union based on confessional allegiance with around
300,000 members.

CHRISTO

Title of the husband-and-wife team that wrapped the REICHSTAG
in 100,000 sq. m. of silvery polypropylene fabric (*Der verhüllte
Reichstag/The Wrapped Reichstag*) for two weeks in the summer
(23 June to 6 July) of 1995 and the installation was visited by five
million people in two weeks. Together with his wife Jeanne
Claude – who refrains from establishing an individual artistic
identity – the American-Bulgarian artist Christo Javacheff
(1935–) thereby realised a project conceived some 24 years
previously. After the polypropylene wrapping was removed on 6
July, work began on modifying the Reichstag in accordance with
the plans of British architect Sir Norman Foster for its new role
in a reunited Germany.

CLASSIC See: *D2–NETZ*

CLAUSTHAL, TECHNISCHE UNIVERSITÄT

University in Clausthal-Zellerfeld (NIEDERSACHSEN) in the HARZ. It
was founded in 1775 as a school of mining (university status
1968) and teaches some 3,500 students. The Technische
Universität Clausthal has departments of mathematics and natural sciences and computer science, physics, chemistry, geology
and geophysics and mineralogy, mining, metallurgy and materials science, mechanical and process engineering.

COCA COLA GmbH

Subsidiary of American soft-drinks company, founded in 1929.
Company headquarters are in ESSEN. Coca Cola GmbH has some
14,000 employees.

COHN-BENDIT, MARC DANIEL (1945–   )

German citizen who rose to prominence in 1968 as one of the leaders of the student movement in Paris which provoked the May events. He was expelled from France and refused entry for ten years. He then became involved in the student movement in Germany and was associated with Rudi Dutschke. He has been a member of DIE GRÜNEN since 1984 and was elected to the STADT-RAT in FRANKFURT AM MAIN in 1989, where he advocates coopera-tion with the SPD. His writings include *Wir haben sie so geliebt, die Revolution* (1987) and *1968: Die letzte Revolution, die noch nichts vom Ozonloch wußte* (1988). See also: AUSSERPARLAMEN-TARISCHE OPPOSITION

COLANI, LUIGI (1928–   )

Versatile German designer of industrial objects ranging from aeroplanes to toilet bowls, famed for his aerodynamic lines and with offices from BREMEN to Panama and Japan. His interests now focus on design that is in tune with nature.

COLOGNE See: *KÖLN*

COMMERZBANK AG

The third of the 'big three' German banks, founded in 1870 and a full-service UNIVERSALBANK. Company headquarters are in FRANKFURT AM MAIN. Commerzbank has some 26,000 employees.

CONSTRUCTEC HANNOVER (INTERNATIONALE FACHMESSE FÜR TECHNISCHE GEBÄUDESYSTEME, BAUTECHNIK UND ARCHITEKTUR)

The 'International Trade Fair for Building Services, Construc-tion and Architecture' is a trade fair for the construction indus-try held in HANNOVER annually with around 17,000 visitors.

CONTINENTAL AG

Rubber and chemicals company founded in 1871 and manufac-turing car tyres and accessories. Company headquarters are in HANNOVER. Continental has some 49,000 employees.

COTTBUS, BRANDENBURGISCHE TECHNISCHE UNIVERSITÄT

University in BRANDENBURG founded in 1991 and teaching some

2,500 students. The Brandenburgische Technische Universität Cottbus has faculties of mathematics and physics and information science, architecture and civil engineering, mechanical engineering and electrical engineering and industrial engineering, environmental science and process engineering.

CSU See: *CHRISTLICH-SOZIALE UNION*

D-ZUG See: *SCHNELLZUG*

D1–NETZ
Cellular telephone network operated by DEUTSCHE TELEKOM subsidiary DETEMOBIL. The network offers a business service *ProTel* and a private service *Telly.*

D2–NETZ
Cellular telephone network operated by Mannesmann Mobilfunk GmbH based in DÜSSELDORF. The network offers a business service *Classic* and a private service *Fun.* See also: MANNESMANN AG

DA See: *DEMOKRATISCHER AUFBRUCH*

DAAD See: *DEUTSCHER AKADEMISCHER AUSTAUSCHDIENST e.V.*

DAB See: *DEUTSCHE AUSGLEICHSBANK; DEUTSCHES ARZNEIBUCH*

DAG See: *DEUTSCHE ANGESTELLTEN-GEWERKSCHAFT*

DAIMLER-BENZ AG
Arms to automobiles industrial conglomerate with a broad range of high-tech engineering products from cars and aircraft to turbines and consumer electronics. The company took over a clutch of famous names in the mid-1980s including Dornier (aerospace), MTU (turbines) and AEG (electrical goods). It also rescued Airbus manufacturer Messerschmidt-Bölkow-Blohm (MBB) by taking a majority stake and forming DAIMLER-BENZ AEROSPACE AG. In early 1996 it withdrew financial support for Dutch aircraft-maker Fokker. Company headquarters are in

STUTTGART with a big new centre planned for POTSDAMER PLATZ. Daimler-Benz has some 330,000 employees. The attempt to turn an automobile manufacturer into a high-tech conglomerate halved the share price between 1987 and 1995 and resulted in massive redundancies and works closures at DASA. At the centenary AGM in May 1996 Jürgen SCHREMPP announced there would be no dividend after the biggest losses in German company history.

DAIMLER-BENZ AEROSPACE AG (DASA)
Aircraft manufacturer founded in 1989 as Deutsche Aerospace AG when DAIMLER-BENZ took over MBB, owners of Deutsche-Airbus. The company was renamed at the beginning of 1995 and company headquarters are in MÜNCHEN. Daimler-Benz Aerospace has some 75,000 employees.

DAK See: *DEUTSCHE ANGESTELLTEN-KRANKENKASSE*

DARBOVEN, HANNE (1941–   )
Conceptual artist whose art uses numbers (generally dates) and words to present her view of time in visual form. Her works include *Ein Jahrhundert* (1971–1975) comprising 402 files with number sequences, hand-written *Wiederaufschreibungen* of literary works such as Homer's *Odyssee*, personal *Geschichtsbücher* and the collage *Vier Jahreszeiten* (1981).

DARMSTADT, TECHNISCHE HOCHSCHULE
University in HESSEN founded in 1836 (university status 1895) and teaching some 18,000 students. The Technische Hochschule Darmstadt has departments of law and economics, history and social sciences, education and psychology and sports science, mathematics, physics, mechanics, chemistry, biology, geosciences and geography, surveying, architecture, civil engineering, mechanical engineering, electrical engineering, control and data technology, computer science, materials science.

DAS HAUS
Magazine with a circulation of some 2.2 million published by BURDA. The magazine deals with buying a property and with home improvements and redesigning home and garden.

DAS NEUE
Women's magazine catering for young women managing home, family and career. It was established in 1983 and is published weekly by BAUER VERLAG in HAMBURG. *Das Neue* has a circulation of 467,000 and reports on radio and TV celebrities and gives advice on home, beauty, travel, etc.

DASA See: *DAIMLER-BENZ AEROSPACE AG*

DATENSCHUTZ
The rights protecting the dissemination of data on private citizens. *Artikel 2 Paragraph (§)* 1 of the GRUNDGESETZ forms the legal basis for this protection by giving every citizen the right to the free development of their personality (*freie Entfaltung der Persönlichkeit*). Data protection was brought up to date for the age of the computer by the BUNDESDATENSCHUTZGESETZ that came into effect in 1991, prohibiting the processing and use of personal data unless expressly authorised by law or approved by the person concerned. Citizens have the right of access to information about data held on them on computer, the right to amend data, the right to block data that is not justifiable and the right to have data erased if it has been illegally stored.

DATENSCHUTZBEAUFTRAGTER
A data-protection officer has to be appointed by any company with five employees or more processing personal data automatically, to ensure compliance with data-protection regulations.

DAV See: *DEUTSCHER ALPENVEREIN e.V.; DEUTSCHER ANWALTVEREIN e.V.*

DB AG See: *DEUTSCHE BAHN AG*

DBB See: *DEUTSCHER BEAMTENBUND*

DBP (DEUTSCHE BUNDESPOST) See: *DEUTSCHE POST AG*

DBV See: *DEUTSCHER BAUERNVERBAND e.V.*

DCV See: *DEUTSCHER CARITASVERBAND e.V.*

ddp/ADN ALLGEMEINER DEUTSCHER NACHRICHTENDIENST GmbH

The Deutscher Depeschen-Dienst (ddp) was a German-language news agency founded in 1971 and based in BONN. Following the collapse of the DDR it bought up the former East German Allgemeiner Deutscher Nachrichtendienst (ADN) from the TREUHANDANSTALT. The Allgemeiner Deutscher Nachrichtendienst used to be the news agency of the DDR in East BERLIN. It was founded in 1946 and acted as the official mouthpiece of the East German government and the SED. The new agency ddp/ADN Allgemeiner Deutscher Nachrichtendienst GmbH was founded as a GMBH in June 1990 and is based in Berlin with an office in Bonn. The agency specialises in news from the NEUE BUNDESLÄN-DER and countries of the former Eastern bloc.

DDR   See: *DEUTSCHE DEMOKRATISCHE REPUBLIK*

DEA-MINERALÖL AG

Oil company wholly owned by RWE-DEA AG (owned by RWE AG). Company headquarters are in HAMBURG. DEA has some 3,200 employees.

DEFA

DEFA – short for Deutsche Film AG – was the first film company to be formed in Germany following the Second World War, being granted a licence at Babelsberg (POTSDAM), in the Soviet zone. Following an illustrious pre-war history as UFA, producing films such as F. Lang's *Metropolis* and J. v. Sternberg's *Der blaue Engel* with Marlene Dietrich, the DEFA film studios became the centre of the East German film industry but fell on less propitious times when the BERLINER MAUER came down. The Babelsberg Studiotour seeks to recreate the mystique of past glories.

DEGENHARDT, FRANZ JOSEF (1931–   )

Writer, singer and lawyer who calls himself *Väterchen Franz* and gained a following in the 1960s with his contemporary ballads criticising society, particularly the Vietnam War and the NOT-STANDSGESETZE. His songs follow in the French chanson tradition and took on a sharper edge during the 1970s. He has recorded many collections of ballads and songs including *Spiel nicht mit den Schmuddelkindern* (1965), *Mit aufrechtem Gang* (1975) and *Der Wind hat sich gedreht im Lande* (1979). He has also written a number of novels including *Zündschnüre* (1973), *Die Abholzung* (1985) and *August Heinrich Hoffmann, genannt von Fallersleben* (1991).

DEGUSSA AG

Precious metals, chemicals and pharmaceuticals group founded in 1873 (as the Deutsche Gold- und Silber-Scheideanstalt). Degussa is involved in cutting and refining precious metals (including mercury) and non-precious metals, and producing metal and chemical products. Company headquarters are in FRANKFURT AM MAIN. Degussa has some 27,000 employees.

DEHMELT, HANS-GEORG (1922–   )

German-born physicist awarded the Nobel Prize for physics in 1989 (with W. Paul and N.F. Ramsey) for development work on atomic spectroscopy.

DEISENHOFER, JOHANN (1943–   )

Physicist who was awarded the Nobel Prize for chemistry in 1988 (with R. HUBER and H. MICHEL) for determining the structure of a photosynthetic reaction centre using X-ray diffraction techniques. He worked at the Max-Planck-Institut für Biochemie (MÜNCHEN) in 1971–1988 and has been professor at the University of Texas since 1988.

DEKAN

The head or dean of a FAKULTÄT or FACHBEREICH appointed from the body of PROFESSOREN.

DEMOKRATIE JETZT (DJ)

A democracy movement centred on the Church and founded in the early autumn of 1989. It played a significant role in the introduction of democracy in the DDR and merged with BÜNDNIS 90 in 1991. See also: BÜNDNIS 90/DIE GRÜNEN

DEMOKRATISCHER AUFBRUCH (DA)

A political party founded in the DDR in December 1989 shortly after the fall of the BERLINER MAUER following an initiative started by the Church in the previous July. The party joined forces with the CDU-Ost and DSU in the elections to the VOLKSKAMMER in March 1990 to form the ALLIANZ FÜR DEUTSCHLAND. The party later joined the CDU-Ost and was integrated in the western CDU after reunification in October 1990.

DENKMALPFLEGE
The protection of the cultural heritage in Germany is regulated by legislation at BUND and LAND level, and the protection of buildings and monuments is the responsibility of the Land. Each Land has a LANDESAMT FÜR DENKMALPFLEGE that is directly responsible to the KULTUSMINISTERIUM of the Land.

DENKMALSCHUTZ See: *DENKMALPFLEGE*

DER FEINSCHMECKER
Distinctly up-market monthly bought by gourmets with a taste for epicurean perfection, sophisticated lifestyle and travel. It has a circulation of 60,000 and provides readers with reviews of new hotels and restaurants, and the latest in gastronomy.

DER SPIEGEL
The doyen of investigative journalism in Germany, *Der Spiegel* is a news magazine read by intellectuals, politicians and business people to find out about current affairs and the latest scandals. *Der Spiegel* was established in 1947 and is published weekly by founder Rudolf AUGSTEIN in HAMBURG, with a circulation of some one million. Over the years this liberal news magazine has unearthed some major scandals involving top politicians and businesses, including 'Neue Heimat' and the 'Flick Affäre'. The probing journalism of the news magazine put Germany's fledgling democracy to the test in the SPIEGEL-AFFÄRE. A major competitor FOCUS was established in 1993.

DESY See: *DEUTSCHES ELEKTRONEN-SYNCHROTRON*

DeTeMOBIL DEUTSCHE TELEKOM MOBILFUNK GmbH
Subsidiary of DEUTSCHE TELEKOM founded in 1993. DeTeMobil operates the D1–NETZ cellular telephone network and introduced the SCALL radio-paging service in 1994. Company headquarters are in BONN and DeTeMobil has some 4,000 employees.

DEUBAU (DEUTSCHE BAUFACHMESSE INTERNATIONAL)

'German Building Fair International' – a trade fair for construction materials, sanitation, heating and environmental technology held in ESSEN every two years with around 130,000 visitors.

DEUTSCH-POLNISCHER GRENZVERTRAG

The treaty signed following German reunification on 14 November 1990 by Germany and Poland confirming the ODER-NEISSE-LINIE as an inviolable border. Both sides committed themselves to maintaining the territorial integrity of the other and promised not to make territorial claims on each other.

DEUTSCH-POLNISCHER NACHBARSCHAFTSVERTRAG

An agreement between Germany and Poland signed in 1991 to guarantee the rights of the POLENDEUTSCHE to follow their own religion and to maintain their cultural heritage and language.

DEUTSCH-TSCHECHOSLOWAKISCHER NACHBARSCHAFTSVERTRAG

An agreement between Germany and the former Czechoslovakia signed in 1992 relinquishing the rights of the SUDETENDEUTSCHE to reinstatement and compensation for property confiscated at the end of the Second World War.

DEUTSCHE AKADEMIE FÜR SPRACHE UND DICHTUNG

An association of writers, linguists and scholars dedicated to the German language and literature. The academy is based in Darmstadt (HESSEN) and was founded in 1949. The prestigious GEORG-BÜCHNER-PREIS is awarded annually by the academy.

DEUTSCHE ANGESTELLTEN-GEWERKSCHAFT (DAG)

Trade union with some 520,000 members representing white-collar workers in clerical, technical and administrative employment. The union is based in HAMBURG and was founded in 1949. The DAG rejected the principle of one union for each industry and insisted that white-collar workers in banking, insurance, the public services etc. should be represented by a separate union. The union takes part in the collective-bargaining process but is not a member of the DEUTSCHER GEWERKSCHAFTSBUND. See also: GEWERKSCHAFT

DEUTSCHE ANGESTELLTEN-KRANKENKASSE (DAK)
Health-insurance fund based in HAMBURG and the second biggest ERSATZKASSE in Germany.

DEUTSCHE AUSGLEICHSBANK (DtA-Bank) (DAB)
A bank set up by the BUND in 1986 to replace the *Lastenausgleichsbank*. The bank finances measures implemented by the Bund to promote the economy mainly in the MITTELSTAND and the FREIE BERUFE, to fund social programmes, environmental protection measures and to assist people affected by the Second World War as well as other groups of people in need such as homeless foreigners and refugees. The bank is under the joint responsibility of the BUNDESMINISTER DES INNERN and the BUNDESMINISTER DER FINANZEN. See also: LASTENAUSGLEICH; ÖFFENTLICH-RECHTLICHE KREDITINSTITUTE

DEUTSCHE BABCOCK AG
Power engineering and machinery construction company founded in 1898. Company headquarters are in OBERHAUSEN. Deutsche Babcock has some 35,000 employees.

DEUTSCHE BAHN AG (DB AG)
Following the BAHNREFORM, the assets of the DEUTSCHE BUNDESBAHN and the DEUTSCHE REICHSBAHN were merged on 1 January 1994 to form a public company, the DEUTSCHE BAHN AG, with all the shares being held by the BUND. Company headquarters are in BERLIN with administration being based in FRANKFURT AM MAIN. The Deutsche Bahn AG has some 357,000 employees. Full privatisation is envisaged by the year 2002 with the Deutsche Bahn AG being split into four different companies.

DEUTSCHE BANK AG
The biggest of the 'big three' German banks. The bank was originally founded in 1870 in BERLIN and its headquarters are now in FRANKFURT AM MAIN. It is a full-service UNIVERSALBANK. Deutsche Bank has some 73,000 employees. The bank handles over 20%

of Germany's foreign trade and holds shares in many German companies including DAIMLER-BENZ.

DEUTSCHE BAUFACHMESSE INTERNATIONAL
See: *DEUBAU*

DEUTSCHE BIBLIOGRAPHIE
The national bibliography of books published in German has been produced by the DEUTSCHE BIBLIOTHEK since 1953.

DEUTSCHE BIBLIOTHEK
The German national deposit library that was formed in 1990 from an amalgamation of the Deutsche Bibliothek in FRANKFURT AM MAIN, the DEUTSCHE BÜCHEREI in LEIPZIG and the Deutsches Musikarchiv in BERLIN. The headquarters of 'Die Deutsche Bibliothek, Frankfurt am Main und Leipzig' are in Frankfurt. The Deutsche Bibliothek in Frankfurt was founded in 1947 and has over 5.5 million volumes and some 100,000 periodicals published since 1945.

DEUTSCHE BP HOLDING AG
Oil company founded in 1904 with more than 1,400 service stations in Germany. BP claims to have built Europe's biggest petrol station just outside DRESDEN. Company headquarters are in HAMBURG. BP has some 2,400 employees.

DEUTSCHE BÜCHEREI
The Deutsche Bücherei was founded in LEIPZIG in 1912. It has been a national deposit library since 1913 and with over 7.5 million volumes is the largest collection of German-language works in the world. The history of books is documented in the Deutsches Buch- und Schriftmuseum within the Deutsche Bücherei. See also: DEUTSCHE BIBLIOTHEK

DEUTSCHE BUNDESBAHN See: *DEUTSCHE BAHN AG*

DEUTSCHE BUNDESBANK
Germany's powerful central bank with the exclusive right to issue banknotes. The Bundesbank regulates the money supply and the amount of credit available to the economy. The headquarters are at FRANKFURT AM MAIN and the bank was founded in

1957. It has a president, a vice-president and up to six directors as well as the presidents of each of the LANDESZENTRALBANKEN. The central bank is widely respected for independence from government interference, for its enviable record of combating inflation, and for setting the parameters for a thriving economy. See also: TIETMEYER, HANS

DEUTSCHE BUNDESPOST (DBP) See: *DEUTSCHE POST AG*

DEUTSCHE DEMOKRATISCHE REPUBLIK (DDR)
The Deutsche Demokratische Republik was formed from the Soviet occupation zone. Soon after the unconditional surrender of Germany in May 1945, the Russians brought in members of the KOMMUNISTISCHE PARTEI DEUTSCHLANDS trained in the Soviet Union and under the leadership of Walter Ulbricht. Four political parties were licensed in the Soviet zone: Kommunistische Partei Deutschlands (KPD), SOZIALDEMOKRATISCHE PARTEI DEUTSCH-LANDS (SPD), *Christlich-Demokratische Union Deutschlands* (CDU) and *Liberal-Demokratische Partei Deutschland* (LDPD). The Soviet zone was quickly divided up into *Länder* and the military authorities commenced the dismantling of industry. In April 1946 the KPD was forcibly merged with the SPD in the Soviet zone to form the SOZIALISTISCHE EINHEITSPARTEI DEUTSCHLANDS (SED). By 1948 this party had become a Soviet-style Stalinist party dominated by Communists and the SED instigated the formation of two more parties in 1948, the *National-Demokratische Partei Deutschlands* (NDPD) and the *Demokratische Bauernpartei* to integrate disaffected groups within the system. By this time a major programme of nationalisation was in progress, a land reform was being carried out and all political parties were being directed by the SED, effectively precluding any form of democratic rule. The Soviet Union removed much industrial machinery and equipment in the form of reparations and carried out a radical programme of denazification.

In the West, the *Bizone* was formed on 1 January 1947 (fusing the American and British zones of occupation) and a *Wirtschaftsrat* on 25 June 1947. The Soviet zone established a centralised executive, the *Deutsche Wirtschaftskommission*, on

14 June 1947. In December 1947 the SED set up the *Deutscher Volkskongreß* that in turn constituted the *Deutscher Volksrat* in March 1948. The WÄHRUNGSREFORM (20 June 1948) in the three Western zones was followed by a hastily introduced reform in the Soviet zone and BERLIN. When the Allies responded by introducing the D-mark into the Western sectors of the city the Soviet Union closed off all the roads and waterways between the Western zones and Berlin on the night of 23 June 1948. The blockade of Berlin lasted from 24 June 1948 until 12 May 1949, with the Berlin airlift continuing until September 1949. It cemented the resolve of the Western powers to establish a West German state to counter Communism and the BRD was formally established on 23 May 1949.

The DDR was established on 7 October 1949 when the *Volksrat* approved a constitution which vested power in a VOLKSKAMMER where the different political parties and mass organisations represented were allocated a certain number of seats with the SED in overall control. Elections to the *Volkskammer* in 1950 presented the electorate with a unified list incorporating all the parties and organisations in the *Volkskammer* under the leadership of the SED. The first government (*Ministerrat*) was led by Otto Grotewohl (*Ministerpräsident* and former SPD leader in Berlin) but although it contained representatives from other parties, the SED under Walter Ulbricht (*Generalsekretär*) remained dominant and the government took its orders from the Soviet military administration, with Wilhelm Pieck as first head of state (*Präsident*).

The five *Länder* in the DDR were abolished in 1952 and replaced by smaller *Bezirke* to facilitate centralized control. Stalin's offer of a neutral united Germany in 1952 was rejected out of hand by Konrad Adenauer and the West. The widespread protest strikes by construction workers in East Berlin against an increase in work quotas on 17 June 1953 spread to other cities and were put down by Russian troops. This effectively ended any hopes of reunification and the 1950s saw a push for industrialisation, the collectivisation of agriculture and nationalisation of smaller businesses. In 1955 the Soviet Union recognized the sovereignty of the DDR, which became a member of the newly established Warsaw Pact with the formation of a *Nationale Volksarmee* in 1956. Throughout the 1950s there was a steady drain of skilled labour to the West across the open border in Berlin. On 13 August 1961 the border between East and West Berlin was sealed at 1.00 am and an hour later workers started putting up barbed wire and erecting barriers. Over the coming months a permanent BERLINER MAUER was constructed to prevent the exodus of DDR citizens to the more prosperous West.

In 1963 the SED introduced a *Neues ökonomisches System der Planung und Leitung* which provided for a certain amount of decentralised decision-making and introduced limited incentives for skilled workers. The 1960s saw the citizens of the DDR making the best of their situation. The economy gradually picked up to become the strongest economy in the Warsaw Pact and East Germany rose to become (on paper at least) one of the top ten industrial nations. In 1970 the Soviet Union guaranteed access for civilian traffic and goods between the BRD and West Berlin, and from 1969 Willy Brandt's OSTPOLITIK initiated a gradual improvement in relations between the two German states after Erich Honecker had replaced hardline Walter Ulbricht as SED leader in 1971. The international community finally accepted the existence of two Germanys when they became full members of the United Nations in September 1973.

The STAATSSICHERHEITSDIENST ensured that East Germans toed the party line, and East Germany turned out to be the staunchest of the Soviet Union's Communist allies. Honecker's government gave the populace some access to the consumer goods that they desired and irksome travel restrictions between the two states were slightly eased. All in all, the citizens of the DDR enjoyed a comfortable if unspectacular standard of living in comparison with their Communist neighbours and the country's superb sportsmen and women brought honour and self-respect to their country. The culmination of the new relationship between the two Germanys was Erich Honecker's visit to the BRD in 1987 when he was received by BUNDESKANZLER KOHL with the trappings accorded to other heads of state.

Real power in the DDR resided in the *Ministerrat* with ultimate power being held by the politburo of the SED. The

Staatsrat was a ceremonial council as a figurehead for the state and the *Volkskammer* remained a rubber-stamp organization that rarely met. The reforms in the Soviet Union under Mikhail Gorbachev in the late 1980s left the elderly leadership of the DDR isolated and out of touch and the mass demonstrations in the autumn of 1989 brought about a more or less bloodless revolution leading to the WENDE. When the borders were effectively thrown open on 9 November 1989 the repressed population were satisfied with nothing less than complete overthrow of a bankrupt system. On 13 November the Volkskammer voted moderate Communist Hans Modrow head of the *Ministerrat* and he led a coalition government of the DDR parties. The leading role of the SED was expunged from the constitution on 1 December 1989 by the *Volkskammer.* Party functionary Egon Krenz was swept aside on 6 December 1989 after he attempted to introduce too little too late, the SED rapidly transformed itself into the PARTEI DES DEMOKRATISCHEN SOZIALISMUS, and a number of new parties and electoral groupings sprang up including: ALLIANZ FÜR DEUTSCHLAND, BÜNDNIS 90, DEMOKRATIE JETZT, DEMOKRATISCHER AUFBRUCH, DEUTSCHE FORUMPARTEI, DEUTSCHE SOZIALE UNION, Grüne, NEUES FORUM. Elections on 18 March 1990 returned Lothar de Maizière (CDU in the Allianz für Deutschland) as head of a government with a clear mandate to negotiate rapid reunification, which ensued on 3 October 1990.

Ministerpräsidenten (*Ministerratsvorsitzende*): Otto Grotewohl (SED, 1949–1964), Willi Stoph (SED, 1964–1973), Horst Sindermann (SED, 1973–1976), Willi Stoph (SED, 1976–1989), Hans Modrow (SED, 13 Nov. 1989–Mar. 1990), Lothar de Maizière (CDU-Ost, Mar.–Oct. 1990).

Parteichefs der SED: Wilhelm Pieck and Otto Grotewohl (SED-*Vorsitzende,* 1946–1954), Walter Ulbricht (SED-*Generalsekretär,* 1950–1953; SED-*1. Sekretär* 1953–1971), Erich Honecker (SED-*1. Sekretär,* 1971–1976; SED-*Generalsekretär* 1976–1989), Egon Krenz (SED-*Generalsekretär,* 18 Oct. 1989–8 Dec. 1989), Gregor Gysi (SED-*Vorsitzender,* party name changed to *Sozialistische Einheitspartei Deutschlands – Partei des demokratischen Sozialismus* (SED-PDS) on 15 Dec. 1989 and then on 4 Feb. 1990 to Partei des Demokratischen Sozialismus).

Staatsoberhäupter: Wilhelm Pieck (SED, DDR-*Präsident*, 1949–1960), Walter Ulbricht (SED, DDR-*Staatsratsvorsitzender*, 1960–1973), Willi Stoph (SED, DDR-*Staatsratsvorsitzender*, 1973–1976), Erich Honecker (SED, DDR-*Staatsratsvorsitzender*, 1976–1989), Egon Krenz (SED, DDR-*Staatsratsvorsitzender* Oct. 1989–Dec. 1989), Manfred Gerlach (LDPD, *amtierender* DDR-*Staatsratsvorsitzender* Dec. 1989–Mar. 1990), Sabine Bergmann-Pohl (CDU-Ost, *amtierendes* DDR-*Staatsoberhaupt*, Mar. 1990–2 Oct. 1990).

See also: BUNDESREPUBLIK DEUTSCHLAND; DRITTES REICH

DEUTSCHE FORSCHUNGSANSTALT FÜR LUFT- UND RAUMFAHRT e.V. (DLR)

Aerospace research institute founded in 1951 and based in KÖLN.

DEUTSCHE FORSCHUNGSGEMEINSCHAFT e.V. (DFG)

Organisation founded in 1951 that promotes research in Germany and fosters international cooperation. HOCHSCHULEN, research institutes and organisations and learned societies are members of the DFG. It provides financial support for research activities in the arts, sciences and technology, and finances research facilities in institutes of higher education. The DFG also advises LAND and BUND on matters relating to research and academic policy.

DEUTSCHE GENOSSENSCHAFTSBANK   See: *DG BANK*

DEUTSCHE GIROZENTRALE (DGZ)

Central giro institution for the SPARKASSEN but dealing with the regional *Girozentralen*. The bank manages the reserves of the *Girozentralen*, runs the giro system and arranges loans to local authorities. See also: DEUTSCHER SPARKASSEN- UND GIROVERBAND; LANDESBANKEN

DEUTSCHE GOLD- UND SILBER-SCHEIDEANSTALT   See: *DEGUSSA*

DEUTSCHE KOMMUNALBANK   See: *DEUTSCHE GIROZENTRALE*

DEUTSCHE KOMMUNISTISCHE PARTEI (DKP)

A revamped Communist party formed in the BRD in 1968 in the

wake of student unrest, replacing the KOMMUNISTISCHE PARTEI DEUTSCHLANDS that had been banned in 1956. The new party had no stated commitment to the revolutionary overthrow of society but has never gained any real electoral successes. The DKP has around 6,000 members.

DEUTSCHE LANDWIRTSCHAFTS-GESELLSCHAFT (DLG)

An association of agricultural producers and scientists to promote the development of agriculture in Germany. The association is responsible for awarding the DEUTSCHES WEINSIEGEL.

DEUTSCHE LUFTHANSA AG (DLH)

The German national airline founded in 1953. Part of the company was floated on the stock market but some 35% of the share capital is held by the BUND. Company headquarters are in KÖLN and Lufthansa has some 58,000 employees.

DEUTSCHE MARK (DM)

The national currency introduced by the Western Allies on 20 June 1948 and on 24 June in West BERLIN to replace the *Reichsmark* (WÄHRUNGSREFORM). The *D-Mark* was introduced in the DDR on 1 July 1990 following the WIRTSCHAFTS- UND WÄHRUNGS-UNION between the two countries.

DEUTSCHE MUNDARTEN

There are many dialects spoken in Germany. They are broadly divided into *niederdeutsche Mundarten* (PLATTDEUTSCH), *westmitteldeutsche Mundarten* (e.g. HESSISCH), *ostmitteldeutsche Mundarten* (e.g. SÄCHSISCH) and *oberdeutsche Mundarten* (e.g. SCHWÄBISCH, BAIRISCH). Dialect is widely used not only at home but also in public life and prominent politicians may take pride in their regional accent. See also: HOCHDEUTSCH

DEUTSCHE OSTGEBIETE

The eastern territories within the 1937 borders of the German REICH that were annexed by the Soviet Union and Poland at the end of the Second World War. These territories were east of the river Oder, comprising OSTPREUSSEN, WESTPREUSSEN, and the parts of the Prussian provinces of *Brandenburg, Pommern, Sachsen* and *Schlesien* that were east of the ODER-NEISSE-LINIE. The POTSDAMER ABKOMMEN assigned these territories to Poland and the Soviet Union, and it was agreed that the German population would be transferred west of the Oder-Neiße-Linie. The western boundary of Poland was finally confirmed in the DEUTSCH-POLNI-SCHER GRENZVERTRAG signed between Germany and Poland establishing this line as the easternmost border of German territory. See also: MEMELLAND; ZWEI-PLUS-VIER-VERTRAG

DEUTSCHE PFANDBRIEFANSTALT

The most important public-sector mortgage bank provides finance for housing construction and urban development. The bank is based in BERLIN and WIESBADEN.

DEUTSCHE POST AG (DP)

The POSTREFORM II converted the state-run postal service into an AKTIENGESELLSCHAFT. The government's shares will be held by the BUNDESANSTALT FÜR POST UND TELEKOMMUNIKATION until privatisation is complete. The government has plans for opening up the postal service to competition. Delivery of direct advertising mail was opened up to private companies at the beginning of 1995. Deutsche Post is working to improve services to meet competition from the private sector and now offers next-day delivery for parcels up to distances of 550 km. and next-day delivery for the INFOBRIEF service. The introduction of 99 letter centres by 1999 is intended to speed up the delivery of letters. Company headquarters are in BONN and Deutsche Post has some 340,000 employees.

DEUTSCHE POSTBANK AG

The POSTREFORM II converted the state-run postal banking service into an AKTIENGESELLSCHAFT. The government's shares will be held by the BUNDESANSTALT FÜR POST UND TELEKOMMUNIKATION until 1998. The Postbank is now providing services other than the traditional giro and savings accounts and has been offering private customers credit up to DM 50,000 and a share-dealing service since mid-1995. Deutsche Postbank has the biggest branch network in Germany, with some 20,000 outlets at postal-service counters.

DEUTSCHE POSTGEWERKSCHAFT (DPG)

Trade union with 530,000 members representing workers in the postal services.

DEUTSCHE PRESSE-AGENTUR See: *dpa DEUTSCHE PRESSE-AGENTUR GmbH*

DEUTSCHE REICHSBAHN See: *DEUTSCHE BAHN AG*

DEUTSCHE SHELL AG
Oil company with over 1,700 service stations in Germany. Company headquarters are in HAMBURG. Deutsche Shell has some 2,900 employees.

DEUTSCHE SIEDLUNGS- UND LANDESRENTENBANK (DSL BANK)
The bank was set up by the BUND to provide government subsidies to agriculture. It has now moved into commercial banking and 48% of the shares have been sold off to the public. See also: ÖFFENTLICH-RECHTLICHE KREDITINSTITUTE

DEUTSCHE SOZIALE UNION (DSU)
A party based on Christian principles and founded in 1990 from conservative opposition groups in the DDR. It received support from the CSU and joined the ALLIANZ FÜR DEUTSCHLAND for the March 1990 elections. The party did badly in the elections in October 1990 and in the later LANDTAGSWAHLEN, and became irrelevant.

DEUTSCHE SPORTHOCHSCHULE KÖLN
Sports university in NORDRHEIN-WESTFALEN founded in 1920 in BERLIN and relocated to KÖLN in 1947, teaching some 6,000 students.

DEUTSCHE TELEKOM AG
The POSTREFORM II converted the state-run telecommunications service into an AKTIENGESELLSCHAFT. The government's shares will be held by the BUNDESANSTALT FÜR POST UND TELEKOMMUNIKATION until the world's biggest privatisation is completed. The first tranche of Telekom shares is being sold off in 1996 when share-dealing on the FRANKFURT stock market will commence, with two-thirds of the shares remaining in government hands. The second tranche is planned for 1998 and completion of the privatisation is expected in the year 2000. Company headquarters are in BONN. Deutsche Telekom employs some 225,000 and envisages what is

probably the world's biggest employee share-ownership programme with around 130,000 employees purchasing an estimated
one billion marks worth of shares when the company is privatised.

DEUTSCHE UNILEVER AG

Food manufacturing company founded in 1930. Company headquarters are in HAMBURG. Deutsche Unilever has some 24,000
employees.

DEUTSCHE VERKEHRSWACHT e.V. (DVW)

The federal organisation for the prevention of road accidents
and the improvement of road safety. It provides advice to the
relevant authorities and runs hard-hitting advertising campaigns
to promote responsible driving. It develops individual campaigns
targeted at all age groups from small children to the elderly, carries out cycling-proficiency training and trains SCHÜLERLOTSEN.

DEUTSCHE VOLKSUNION (DVU)

An extreme right-wing party founded in 1987.

DEUTSCHE WEINSTRASSE

Germany's oldest officially designated tourist route (1936) leading tourists through the vineyards of RHEINLAND-PFALZ from
Bockenheim to the Deutsches Weintor at Schweigen on the
French border. The climate verges on subtropical in places, permitting the cultivation of lemons.

DEUTSCHE WELLE RADIO & TV (DW)

Public-service national radio station based in KÖLN. Prior to
reunification the purpose of the radio station Deutsche Welle
was to broadcast a comprehensive profile of news, life and culture in West Germany to the two German states and to the outside world. Following reunification the station incorporated the
American station RIAS Berlin (Fernsehen) and the foreign-
language sections of Deutschlandfunk (the remainder of which is
now part of DEUTSCHLANDRADIO). The station continues to be
financed by the BUND. Deutsche Welle transmits programmes in
German and other languages. There are plans afoot to transfer
the only radio station directly under the auspices of the BUND to
BONN.

DEUTSCHE WERTARBEIT

The concept *Deutsche Wertarbeit* emphasises high skilling levels and the hard-wearing and reliable nature of the products of German craftsmanship. Quality consciousness among German customers increases the incentives for German manufacturers to produce top-quality goods. German companies are justifiably proud of being able to use the quality of German goods as an advertisement, though the older generation – as anywhere else – grumble about the declining work ethic and complain that things are not what they used to be.

DEUTSCHER AKADEMISCHER AUSTAUSCHDIENST e.V. (DAAD)

An independent organisation of institutions of higher education. The DAAD is based in BONN and is responsible for arranging international exchanges of scholars and students. The DAAD also runs an extensive programme providing foreign institutions of higher education with German LEKTOREN.

DEUTSCHER ALPENVEREIN e.V. (DAV)

German alpine club founded in 1869 and dedicated to promoting mountain walking and climbing.

DEUTSCHER ANWALTVEREIN e.V. (DAV)

The German lawyers' society was re-established in 1947 with headquarters in BONN. The society upholds the professional and economic interests of lawyers.

DEUTSCHER BAUERNVERBAND e.V. (DBV)

A voluntary association of agricultural producers that maintains a neutral stance on politics and religion. It is the umbrella organisation for the agricultural industry and advises members on economic and political matters. The association lobbies federal authorities on matters affecting agriculture and maintains international contacts with similar associations in other countries.

DEUTSCHER BEAMTENBUND (DBB)

Union with about 1.1 million members representing civil servants. The state and civil servants have long had a special relationship whereby civil servants have no right to strike in exchange for special privileges. The status of BEAMTER is highly sought-after but workers in the private sector tend to regard *Beamte* as having a cushy job.

DEUTSCHER CARITASVERBAND e.V. (DCV)

The Catholic charity organisation in Germany with headquarters in Freiburg im Breisgau (BADEN-WÜRTTEMBERG). It carries out all types of charitable and social work in hospitals, special homes and many other places. The DCV has nearly 200,000 full-time employees and over half a million voluntary helpers.

DEUTSCHER DEPESCHEN-DIENST See: *ddp/ADN ALL-GEMEINER DEUTSCHER NACHRICHTENDIENST GmbH*

DEUTSCHER ENTWICKLUNGSDIENST (DED)

A development agency founded in 1963 and based in BERLIN. The agency provides state and private organisations with specialists for development aid programmes abroad.

DEUTSCHER FILMPREIS

Annual awards (*Filmbänder in Gold/Silber*) for films and achievements of individual actors, directors, etc. The jury consists of figures from public life, especially the arts.

DEUTSCHER FUSSBALLBUND (DFB)

The German football association was founded in 1900 and is based at FRANKFURT AM MAIN. It is the biggest sports body in Germany and is responsible for representing the interests of football at federal level.

DEUTSCHER GENOSSENSCHAFTS- UND RAIFFEISENVERBAND e.V. (DGRV)

The umbrella organisation for the cooperative movement is based in BONN. It promotes the common interests of its members and lobbies at the level of the BUND on economic, legal and tax issues that affect cooperatives.

DEUTSCHER GEWERKSCHAFTSBUND (DGB)

The German Trade Union Federation is Germany's biggest trade union organisation. The DGB is the umbrella organisation for 13 unions representing blue-collar workers, white-collar workers and government employees in Germany. The organisation was formed in 1949 with the aim of creating an independent trade union movement as a guard against industrial upheaval, and this was achieved with lack of demarcation as one of the guiding principles. The DGB is based in DÜSSELDORF and has a total of around 9.3 million members.

Dieter SCHULTE has been head (*Vorsitzender*) of the DGB since 1994. The *Bundesvorstand* is made up of the chairpersons of 13 unions and the nine members of the executive elected by the *Bundeskongreß* that meets every three years. The *Bundesvorstand* represents the DGB but is bound by the resolutions of the *Bundeskongreß* and the *Bundesausschuß*. The *Bundesausschuß* comprises 100 members drawn from the individual unions, the *Bundesvorstand* and regional chairpersons (*Landesbezirksvorsitzende*). The DGB publishes a number of journals and finances a research institute for economics and social science (Wirtschafts- und Sozialwissenschaftliches Institut des Deutschen Gewerkschaftsbundes GmbH). See also: GE-WERKSCHAFT

DEUTSCHER HANDWERKSKAMMERTAG (DHKT)
The umbrella organisation for the HANDWERKSKAMMERN in Germany, based in BONN.

DEUTSCHER INDUSTRIE- UND HANDELSTAG (DIHT)
The umbrella organisation for all the INDUSTRIE- UND HANDELS-KAMMERN in Germany. It was founded in 1861 and is based in BONN. The organisation ensures cooperation between the individual chambers, safeguards the interests of trade and industry at the level of the BUND, and represents German industry abroad.

DEUTSCHER JOURNALISTEN-VERBAND (DJV)
The union of German journalists was founded in 1948 and has around 27,000 members. The purpose of the DJV is to promote the interests of professional journalists.

DEUTSCHER JUGENDLITERATURPREIS
A prize for youth literature financed by the BUNDESMINISTERIUM FÜR FAMILIE, SENIOREN, FRAUEN UND JUGEND and awarded annually

by a jury. It was founded in 1956 as the *Deutscher Jugend-buchpreis* and was renamed in 1980. Award-winners include Michael Ende (1961), Reiner KUNZE (1971) and JANOSCH (1979).

DEUTSCHER KÜNSTLERBUND e.V.

The German association of artists is based in BERLIN and holds an annual exhibition of contemporary art.

DEUTSCHER LANDKREISTAG

The national association of KREISE. The association lobbies for the interests of Kreise in any new legislation and carries out pub-lic-relations exercises.

DEUTSCHER LEHRERVERBAND (DLV)

The umbrella organisation for all teachers' associations was founded in 1969 and is based in BONN.

DEUTSCHER PRESSERAT

The German press council was founded in 1956 by the publish-ers' and journalists' associations to provide self-regulation for the industry. It is based in Bad Godesberg, a suburb of BONN, and is made up of ten publishers from the newspaper and magazine sectors, ten journalists also from these sectors, and two or three other members elected by the two sides. The purpose of the council was to ensure that the press remained independent after the Nazi excesses.

DEUTSCHER RICHTERBUND (DRB)

The umbrella organisation for all associations of judges and pub-lic prosecutors. The organisation aims to sponsor legislation, promote the rule of law and preserve the independence of the judiciary.

DEUTSCHER SPARKASSEN- UND GIROVERBAND (DSG)

The umbrella organisation of the SPARKASSEN comprising the regional organisations and based in BONN. The DEUTSCHER STÄDTE- UND GEMEINDEBUND, DEUTSCHER STÄDTETAG and DEUTSCHER LAND- KREISTAG all have representatives on the board of the organisa-tion because of the close links of the *Sparkassen* with local authorities. The DSGV has a public-relations function, lobbies for the interests of *Sparkassen* with the relevant authorities, and carries out training for the personnel employed in *Sparkassen*. See also: SPITZENVERBAND

DEUTSCHER SPORTBUND (DSB)
The umbrella organisation for all sports in Germany was founded in 1950 and is based in BERLIN.

DEUTSCHER STÄDTE- UND GEMEINDEBUND (DStGB)
The national association of smaller towns (i.e. within a KREIS) and GEMEINDEN. The association lobbies for the interests of small towns and Gemeinden in any new legislation and carries out public-relations exercises. See also: DEUTSCHER STÄDTETAG

DEUTSCHER STÄDTETAG
The national association of KREISFREIE STÄDTE, which lobbies for their interests in any new legislation and carries out public-relations exercises.

DEUTSCHER WETTERDIENST (DWD)
The German meteorological service providing weather forecasts and reports. The service is based in Offenbach (HESSEN) and is part of the BUNDESMINISTERIUM FÜR VERKEHR.

DEUTSCHES ARCHÄOLOGISCHES INSTITUT (DAI)
The German archaeological institute was founded in 1874. It is based in BERLIN and comes under the authority of the AUSWÄRTIGES AMT. The institute provides grants and carries out archaeological excavations in its own right.

DEUTSCHES ARZNEIBUCH (DAB)
The official pharmacopoeia containing the register of medicinal drugs with their uses, preparation, dosages, formulas, etc. The register gives details of the properties, testing and storage of pharmaceutical products.

DEUTSCHES ATOMFORUM e.V.
An association founded in 1959 with headquarters in BONN. The association promotes research and development into peaceful uses of nuclear energy.

DEUTSCHES ELEKTRONEN-SYNCHROTRON (DESY)

A research centre in HAMBURG established in 1964. The centre carries out research into elementary particle physics.

DEUTSCHES FERNSEHEN See: *ERSTES PROGRAMM*

DEUTSCHES FILMMUSEUM

Film museum in FRANKFURT AM MAIN with a permanent exhibition on the history of film, a reconstruction of the café frequented by the Lumière brothers and a cinema.

DEUTSCHES GESUNDHEITSMUSEUM

A museum of public health founded in 1949 in KÖLN. It is the federal centre for promoting awareness of health issues among the population.

DEUTSCHES HYGIENE-MUSEUM

The biggest museum of health and hygiene in the world was founded in 1930 in DRESDEN. The museum promotes public health and holds exhibitions on the history of medicine, the function of the human body and the prevention of disease.

DEUTSCHES INSTITUT FÜR FERNSTUDIEN-FORSCHUNG

This institute for distance-learning courses was founded in 1967 at TÜBINGEN (EBERHARD-KARLS-UNIVERSITÄT). It is responsible for processing correspondence courses in conjunction with the FERN-UNIVERSITÄT-GESAMTHOCHSCHULE HAGEN.

DEUTSCHES INSTITUT FÜR FILMKUNDE

German institute for film founded in 1947 in WIESBADEN holding an archive for film and image as well as a library and documentation centre.

DEUTSCHES INSTITUT FÜR NORMUNG e.V. (DIN)

The German standards institute is based in BERLIN and has published more than 25,000 DIN standards on all aspects of engineering and technology. The institute promotes the use of German standards at home and abroad, and advises the government on matters relating to standardisation.

DEUTSCHES INSTITUT FÜR WIRTSCHAFTS-FORSCHUNG e.V. (DIW)

Institute founded in 1925 and based in BERLIN. It is financed by public bodies and SPITZENVERBÄNDE. The institute carries out independent research into economic conditions and developments in Germany and abroad.

DEUTSCHES KABARETT-ARCHIV

An archive of German cabaret founded in 1976 and based in MAINZ.

DEUTSCHES MUSEUM

The Deutsches Museum von Meisterwerken der Natur-wissenschaft und Technik in MÜNCHEN was founded by engineer Oskar von Miller in 1903 and houses a massive collection showing the triumphs of science and technology through scientific demonstrations and exhibits such as cars, aeroplanes and a replica coalmine.

DEUTSCHES PATENTAMT (DPA)

The German patent office was founded in 1877 and is based in MÜNCHEN. It has 1.1 million volumes and some 35 million patent specifications.

DEUTSCHES ROTES KREUZ (DRK)

The German Red Cross was founded in 1921 and has its head-quarters in BONN. It is a federal organisation with LANDESVER-BÄNDE and a youth organisation, the Jugendrotkreuz. The DRK has its own hospitals, ambulances, training facilities and centres for blood donation. The DRK has an extensive social programme, running KINDERGÄRTEN, children's homes, old-people's homes, rehabilitation centres, homes for the disabled and out-patient services.

DEUTSCHES SPORTFERNSEHEN (DSF)

A commercial TV sports channel with a substantial holding by SPRINGER VERLAG. The channel broadcasts national and international sporting events.

DEUTSCHES SPRACHARCHIV

A sound archive of contemporary spoken German maintained by the INSTITUT FÜR DEUTSCHE SPRACHE.

DEUTSCHES STUDENTENWERK e.V. (DSW)

The umbrella organisation for 65 local STUDENTENWERKE. It campaigns on all social issues affecting students.

DEUTSCHES THEATER BERLIN

Theatre in east BERLIN founded in 1883 that gained a world reputation under Max Reinhardt for productions of the Greek classics, Shakespeare, classical German and modernist drama in the early part of the century. Today it produces a steady stream of new interpretations of classics and productions of contemporary plays.

DEUTSCHES WEINSIEGEL

A quality mark for German wines conferred by the DEUTSCHE LANDWIRTSCHAFTS-GESELLSCHAFT. The mark takes the form of a red seal for sweet wines, a green seal for medium-dry wines and yellow for dry.

DEUTSCHES WÖRTERBUCH

The monumental and invaluable 32-volume dictionary of the German language started by the Grimm brothers in the middle of the nineteenth century and only finished in 1961. Its coverage is erratic, however, with two volumes being devoted to the letters A to D, while S alone occupies more than six volumes. Even before the final volumes were completed, work started on a revised version of the letters A to F, which were compiled by the Grimm brothers themselves more than 150 years ago. This revision is due to be finished in 2005.

DEUTSCHLANDLIED

The official national anthem taken from the poem '*Deutschland, Deutschland über alles*' by Hoffmann von Fallersleben. The tune follows that of an old Austrian anthem in praise of the Austrian emperor, '*Gott erhalte Franz den Kaiser*' by Joseph Haydn. The *Deutschlandlied* was the national anthem from 1922 to 1945 and was then adopted by the BRD in 1952, though it is only the third verse that constitutes the anthem, avoiding the nationalistic associations of the first two verses.

DEUTSCHLANDRADIO (DLR)

A national radio station that went on air at the beginning of 1994. It was formed in a merger between Deutschlandfunk, the former American station RIAS Berlin (Hörfunk), and the former DDR radio station Deutschlandsender Kultur. It is one of two national radio stations and is based in KÖLN and BERLIN. It comes under the umbrella of ARD and ZDF. See also: BUNDESRUND-FUNKANSTALTEN

DEUTSCHLANDVERTRAG

The BONN Convention – a treaty signed on 26 May 1952 that came into force on 5 May 1955 regulating the relationship between the young BRD and the US, Great Britain and France. It was necessitated by the fact that no peace treaty had been signed between Germany and the Allied powers, and gave the government of the BRD jurisdiction over internal and foreign affairs. The ZWEI-PLUS-VIER-VERTRAG (12 September 1990) returned full sovereignty to the BRD and superseded the Deutschlandvertrag. See also: EINIGUNGSVERTRAG

DEZERNAT

An organisational unit in a local authority covering a number of ÄMTER. Also known as a REFERAT.

DEZERNENT

A KOMMUNALBEAMTER with decision-making responsibilities who is in charge of a DEZERNAT in local government. Known as a REFERENT in BAYERN.

DFB See: *DEUTSCHER FUSSBALLBUND*

DFG See: *DEUTSCHE FORSCHUNGSGEMEINSCHAFT e.V.*

DG BANK (DEUTSCHE GENOSSENSCHAFTSBANK)

The central bank for the KREDITGENOSSENSCHAFTEN with the right to open its own branches. DG Bank was founded in 1949 and company headquarters are at FRANKFURT AM MAIN. The bank is one of Germany's biggest banks and it has substantial holdings in industry.

DGB See: *DEUTSCHER GEWERKSCHAFTSBUND*

DGRV See: *DEUTSCHER GENOSSENSCHAFTS- UND RAIFFEISENVERBAND e.V.*

DGZ See: *DEUTSCHE GIROZENTRALE*

DHKT See: *DEUTSCHER HANDWERKSKAMMERTAG*

DIAKONISCHES WERK DER EVANGELISCHEN KIRCHE IN DEUTSCHLAND e.V.
Protestant charitable organisation established in 1957. The organisation runs the famine-relief initiative *Brot für die Welt*. It has some 260,000 employees and runs hospitals, KINDERGÄRTEN and centres carrying out various types of social work.

DIE AKTUELLE
Weekly women's magazine established in 1979 and published in NÜRNBERG with a circulation of 623,000. It is published by Gong-Verlag and is intended for middle-aged women.

DIE GRÜNEN
The environmental party formed at the beginning of the 1980s from regional groupings known as Grün-Alternative-Listen. The party marked a radical departure from traditional politics and promoted an environmentalist platform based on social democracy and non-violence. The new ABGEORDNETE were not afraid to heckle the traditional politicians and broke established precepts by attending in jeans and bringing their knitting along. They first crossed the five-percent threshold in 1983 and were successful in some LÄNDER, notably in HESSEN with the opposition to the new runway at FRANKFURT AM MAIN's airport (STARTBAHN-WEST). The party lost its way at the beginning of the 1990s when it failed to obtain the five percent necessary to enter the BUN-DESTAG in the 1990 elections (FÜNFPROZENTKLAUSEL), but was successful in 1994, when it joined forces with Bündnis 90, gaining 49 seats. See also: BÜNDNIS 90/DIE GRÜNEN; FUNDI; REALO

DIE RHEINPFALZ
A regional daily established in 1945 and published in LUD-
WIGSHAFEN with a circulation of 244,000.

DIE WELT
A right-wing daily newspaper (ÜBERREGIONALE ZEITUNg) established in 1946 and published by SPRINGER VERLAG in HAMBURG with
a circulation of 203,000. *Die Welt* has a major business section
and is widely read in business circles. It is distributed throughout
Germany, although it is particularly popular in Hamburg and
NORDRHEIN-WESTFALEN.

DIE ZEIT
A serious weekly newspaper published by Zeitverlag in HAMBURG
with a circulation of 470,000. This bulky newspaper aims
unashamedly at the intellectual élite, eschewing news as such
and providing a collection of thorough and erudite articles on
politics, culture and the arts in a style that is formidable in its
complexity. See also: DÖNHOFF, MARION GRÄFIN; SCHMIDT, HELMUT

DIEHL GmbH & CO
Metals and engineering company founded in 1902, producing
clocks, control systems and munitions. Company headquarters
are in NÜRNBERG. Diehl has some 12,000 employees.

DIENST MITTLERER TAGESZEITUNGEN GmbH
(DIMITAG/dmt)
A news agency founded in 1938 and based in BONN.

DIENSTERFINDUNG
A patentable invention made by an ARBEITNEHMER while working
for an ARBEITGEBER. The *Arbeitgeber* has the right to the invention but is obliged to pay an appropriate remuneration for it. See
also: FREIE ERFINDUNG

DIEPGEN, EBERHARD (1941–   )
Lawyer and CDU politician. He became a member of the ABGE-
ORDNETENHAUS in West BERLIN in 1971. He was appointed chairman of the CDU-FRAKTION in the Abgeordnetenhaus in 1980 and
chairman of the CDU in Berlin in 1983. From 1984–1989 he was

REGIERENDER BÜRGERMEISTER of West Berlin and since 1991 he has been Regierender Bürgermeister of united Berlin.

DIHT See: *DEUTSCHER INDUSTRIE- UND HANDELSTAG*

DIMITAG/dmt See: *DIENST MITTLERER TAGESZEITUNGEN GmbH*

DIN See: *DEUTSCHES INSTITUT FÜR NORMUNG e.V.*

DIPLOM
A *Diplom* is the degree issued to a student who has successfully completed the prescribed course of study and examinations at a HOCHSCHULE, generally in natural sciences, economics or social sciences. It also refers to the document conferring the degree. In BAYERN, BADEN-WÜRTTEMBERG and RHEINLAND-PFALZ the *Diplom* conferred at a FACHHOCHSCHULE is qualified by the initials 'FH'.

DIREKTMANDAT
A candidate elected by achieving a majority of direct votes through ERSTSTIMMEN in the system of mixed elections in Germany.
See also: BUNDESTAGSWAHL; LANDTAGSWAHL; ÜBERHANGMANDAT

DISTEL, DIE
Cabaret theatre in east BERLIN famous before reunification for its satire directed at the Communist regime.

DIW See: *DEUTSCHES INSTITUT FÜR WIRTSCHAFTSFORSCHUNG e.V.*

DJ See: *DEMOKRATIE JETZT*

DJV See: *DEUTSCHER JOURNALISTEN-VERBAND*

DKP See: *DEUTSCHE KOMMUNISTISCHE PARTEI*

DLG See: *DEUTSCHE LANDWIRTSCHAFTS-GESELLSCHAFT*

DLH See: *DEUTSCHE LUFTHANSA AG*

DLR See: *DEUTSCHE FORSCHUNGSANSTALT FÜR LUFT- UND RAUMFAHRT; DEUTSCHLANDRADIO*

DLV See: *DEUTSCHER LEHRERVERBAND*

DM See: *DEUTSCHE MARK*

DOCUMENTA

A trend-setting international exhibition of innovative, contemporary art held every four to five years in KASSEL. Avant-garde art had been banned as degenerate by the Nazis (*entartete Kunst*), and the first 'documenta' exhibition in 1955 signalled its re-emergence and acceptance in Germany. In 1992 the exhibition attracted a record 600,000 visitors during its 100 days. The budget for 1997 is DM 20 million.

DOKTORAND

Postgraduate studying for a doctorate at a HOCHSCHULE.

DOKTORGRAD

A doctorate awarded to a postgraduate student (e.g. *Dr. phil.* in a faculty of philosophy (arts)) after the completion and acceptance of a doctoral thesis (*Doktorarbeit*). The candidate has to pass an oral examination (*Rigorosum*) in two or three subjects and is awarded one of four grades: *rite* (satisfactory), *cum laude* (good), *magna cum laude* (very good), *summa cum laude* (excellent).

DOLDINGER, KLAUS (1936–   )

Jazz musician and composer who combines elements of dixieland, free jazz and pop. He formed his band Passport in 1971 and his recordings include *Oceanliner* (1979), *Talk Back* (1988) and *Blues Roots* (1991). His numerous compositions for films include the music for *Das Boot*, and TV compositions include the music for crime series TATORT.

DOMOTECHNICA (WELTMESSE DER HAUSGERÄTETECHNIK)

The world's leading trade fair for domestic appliances and utensils, built-in kitchens and accessories is held in KÖLN every two years with around 70,000 visitors.

DOMOTEX HANNOVER (WELTMESSE FÜR TEPPICHE UND BODENBELÄGE)

The 'World Trade Fair for Carpets and Floor Coverings' is held in HANNOVER annually with around 30,000 visitors.

DOMSCHATZKAMMER

AACHEN's cathedral treasury houses one of Europe's richest collections of ecclesiastical treasure, assembled over a millennium. Some of the most valuable items are kept in the basement for maximum security.

DÖNHOFF, MARION GRÄFIN (1909–)

Journalist and joint HERAUSGEBER of weekly newspaper DIE ZEIT with Helmut SCHMIDT. She was appointed editor of *Die Zeit* in 1946, editor-in-chief in 1968–1972 and *Herausgeberin* in 1973. She stands for political policies that promote international consensus and understanding and her books include *Weit ist der Weg nach Osten* (1985), *Eine Kindheit in Ostpreußen* (1988), *Namen, die keiner mehr nennt* (1989) and *Versöhnung: Polen und Deutsche* (1991, co-editor).

DOPPELBELASTUNG

This term designates the dual commitment of women who work and have prime responsibility for child care.

DOPPELSTUDIUM

Two STUDIENGÄNGE with different ABSCHLUSSPRÜFUNGEN that a student pursues concurrently (e.g. MAGISTER and STAATSEXAMEN).

DORMANN, JÜRGEN (1940–)

Industrialist with HOECHST AG since 1963 who was appointed VORSTANDSMITGLIED in 1984 and has been chairman of the VORSTAND since 1994.

DORN, DIETER (1935–)

Theatre producer whose productions are noted for their daringly contemporary presentation of classic dramas and his emphasis on the dramatic text, e.g. Goethe's *Iphigenie auf Tauris* (1981) and *Torquato Tasso* (1985). Dorn has been INTENDANT at the Münchner Kammerspiele since 1983 and regularly presents contemporary playwrights such as Botho STRAUSS, e.g. *Die Besucher* (1988).

DORST, TANKRED (1925–)
Playwright who first reached an international audience with his anti-war play *Große Schmährede an der Stadtmauer* (1962) and with *Toller* (1968), which focuses on the revolutionary dramatist Ernst Toller (1893–1939). Other plays include *Merlin oder Das wüste Land* (1981) and *Karlos* (1990). Dorst has also written films, radio plays, opera libretti, adaptations and translations. In 1990 he received the GEORG-BÜCHNER-PREIS.

DORTMUND
Dortmund is situated in NORDRHEIN-WESTFALEN on the Dortmund-Ems-Kanal in the east of the RUHRGEBIET (dialling code 02 31, postal area code 44...). Dortmund is the biggest town in Westfalen and was a member of the Hanseatic League during the Middle Ages. The development of iron and coalmining, and the completion of the Dortmund-Ems-Kanal in 1899 heralded the industrial growth that made Dortmund the biggest city in Westfalen. Now, however, restructuring has caused widespread redundancy in the steel industry and the last coalmine closed in 1987. Home to the Dortmunder Union brewery, the city was granted brewing rights in 1293 and now has the distinction of being Europe's number one city for beer production, even putting MÜNCHEN in the shade. Dortmund also houses the computer that allocates places to candidates at HOCHSCHULEN all over Germany.

The city has a population of some 605,000 with a total student population of around 33,000 (1 UNIVERSITÄT and 1 FACHHOCHSCHULE) and about 12% foreigners (40% Turkish). The SPD runs the city and has been in office since 1952. Dortmund's industry is based on iron and steel. Other industries include electrical engineering, printing, computer software and, of course, beer. See also: ZENTRAL-STELLE FÜR DIE VERGABE VON STUDIENPLÄTZEN

DORTMUND, UNIVERSITÄT
New university in NORDRHEIN-WESTFALEN with a modern, concrete campus, founded in 1966 and teaching some 25,000 students. The

Universität Dortmund has departments of mathematics, physics, chemistry, chemical engineering, urban and regional planning, mechanical engineering, computer science, statistics, electrical engineering, architecture, economics and social science, education, biology, special education and rehabilitation, sociology and philosophy and theology, languages and literature, journalism and history, music and arts, sport and geography.

DOUGLAS HOLDING AG
Wholesale and retail company founded in 1949, trading in perfumes, fashion, confectionery, health and household products. Company headquarters are in Hagen (NORDRHEIN-WESTFALEN). Douglas has some 14,000 employees.

DOZ. See: *DOZENT*

DOZENT
A lecturer at a HOCHSCHULE, VOLKSHOCHSCHULE or other institution of higher or further education. A *Hochschuldozent* is a lecturer who has not yet been appointed PROFESSOR and who has the status of BEAMTER, usually for a fixed period of time. The term *Dozenten* is also used generally to refer to the lecturers at a *Hochschule*. See also: PRIVATDOZENT

DP See: *DEUTSCHE POST*

DPA See: *DEUTSCHES PATENTAMT*

dpa DEUTSCHE PRESSE-AGENTUR GmbH (dpa)
The leading German press agency founded in 1949 and based in HAMBURG with offices in BONN and all the LAND capitals. dpa supplies newspapers, TV and radio stations and subscribing members with national and regional news and information. It also supplies other news agencies throughout the world with news in English, German, Spanish and Arabic.

DPG See: *DEUTSCHE POSTGEWERKSCHAFT*

DRB See: *DEUTSCHER RICHTERBUND*

DREIZEHNTES MONATSGEHALT
A thirteenth month's salary paid by many companies roughly

equal to one month's pay. It is normally paid at Christmas or during the summer holiday period.

DRESDEN

Dresden is the LANDESHAUPTSTADT of SACHSEN and is situated on the river Elbe (dialling code 03 51, postal area code 01...). Dresden was the capital of the Albertine line that ruled Saxony from 1485 to 1918. Under August der Starke Dresden became the centre for German baroque art and developed into one of Europe's most beautiful cities, known as 'Elbflorenz'. After the Allies obliterated the city centre on the night of 13–14 February 1945, Dresden – alongside Hiroshima – became a symbol of the futility of war. Although its architectural treasures were reduced to ruins, the people of Dresden have painstakingly reconstructed the buildings around the Residenzschloß and a new city has grown up outside the old centre. The buildings restored by the DDR include the renaissance Semperoper, and a multimillion-mark programme is now under way to restore the Schloß by the city's 800th anniversary in 2008. The cultural metropolis where Weber and Wagner conducted has continued its musical tradition with the Staatskapelle Dresden, the Dresdner Philharmonie, the Kreuzchor and three major festivals every summer: the Opernfestspiele in March/April, the Dresdner Musikfestspiele in May/June and the International Dixieland Festival in May.

The city has a population of some 470,000 with a total student population of around 22,000 (1 UNIVERSITÄT and 5 other HOCH-SCHULEN) and about 2% foreigners (15% Polish). The CDU has been running the city without an absolute majority since 1990. The industrial revolution was brought to Dresden by Germany's first 'Intercity' running between Dresden and LEIPZIG in 1839. The city's western industrial area is being torn down and rebuilt. BP reckons to have built Europe's biggest petrol station just outside Dresden and SIEMENS is building Europe's most modern microchip factory. Industries include microelectronics, pharmaceuticals, optical instruments and construction. Probably Dresden's best-loved product is the *Dresdner Christstollen*.

DRESDEN, TECHNISCHE UNIVERSITÄT

University in SACHSEN founded in 1828 (university status 1961) and teaching some 20,000 students. The Technische Universität Dresden has faculties of natural sciences and mathematics, computer science, electrical and mechanical engineering, economics, education, law, medicine, architecture, forestry and hydrology and geosciences, philosophy, linguistics and literature, transport and traffic engineering.

DRESDNER BANK AG

The second of the 'big three' German banks founded in 1872. It is a full-service UNIVERSALBANK. Dresdner Bank has some 38,000 employees and company headquarters are in FRANKFURT AM MAIN. Reunification meant that the Dresdner was able to return to its home town of DRESDEN.

DRITTES PROGRAMM

The third German public TV channel, operated by the public-service broadcasting corporations in the LÄNDER to form a regional channel. Programmes tend to have a regional interest and cover topics ranging from politics to culture. This channel carries TV for schools and fulfils an important educational function. It also shows foreign films with subtitles rather than the usual dubbing. See also: LANDESRUNDFUNK- UND FERNSEHANSTALTEN

DRITTES REICH

The term 'Drittes Reich' is used to describe the Nazi period between 1933 and 1945. Adolf Hitler came to power in Germany by constitutional means and became Chancellor on 30 January 1933. He quickly consolidated his power and effectively dissolved the WEIMARER REPUBLIK with the introduction of the *Ermächtigungsgesetz* (Enabling Act). Hitler enjoyed considerable popular support as he stood for a strong Germany and rejection of the Versailles Treaty, which had imposed harsh conditions and reparations and was seen by many Germans as unjust. He gave the population full employment and relative economic prosperity to the detriment of personal freedom and civil rights. He strengthened his hold on the reins of power by systematically removing political and trade-union opposition and dismantling the democratic apparatus of the state in a process of *Gleichschaltung*. When President Hindenburg died in 1934,

Hitler combined the offices of Chancellor and head of state to become *Führer*, and took personal command of the armed forces. He then continued to pursue a policy of secret rearmament and centralising power to form a totalitarian state, stamping out opposition in the process. His foreign policy was directed towards reversing the terms of the Versailles Treaty by diplomatic means and he successively regained the SAARLAND following a plebiscite (1935), re-occupied the demilitarized RHEINLAND (1936), seized Austria in the *Anschluß* (1938), annexed the SUDETENLAND (1938), made *Böhmen* and *Mähren* a protectorate (March 1939) and the *Slovakei* a satellite state (March 1939), occupied the MEMELLAND (March 1939) and occupied the free city of Danzig (1 September 1939).

On 1 September 1939, Germany invaded Poland. Britain and France declared war on 3 September signalling the start of the Second World War. After spectacular early German successes the tide started to turn when Germany invaded the Soviet Union during the summer of 1941 and the US entered the war in December 1941. Defeat at the Battle of Stalingrad (1943), and landings by the Allies in Africa (1942), Italy (1943) and France (1944) were the prelude to Hitler's suicide (30 April 1945) and Germany's unconditional surrender (8 May 1945).

The Second World War generated untold suffering, left tens of millions dead, Germany in ruins and a power vacuum at the centre of Europe. Nazi policies of racial purity led to the systematic mass murder of more than six million Jews in the '*Endlösung*', the virtual elimination of Europe's population of gypsies and the murder of thousands of political opponents and groups of people that the Nazis considered socially undesirable. Hitler had exploited and created the conditions under which organised genocide became a reality within a highly cultured European society.

Following defeat, Germany was divided into four zones (American, British, French, Soviet) with BERLIN being divided into four sectors. Initially there was considerable cooperation between the four powers but differences between the aims of the Soviet Union and the Western powers soon brought tensions and divergence of policy. Rapid introduction of the KPD in the Soviet zone, nationalisation of major industries and banking, and redistribution of land led to a political and economic transformation in the Soviet zone over the next few years. On the Western side, the Marshall Plan introduced in 1947, the WÄHRUNGSREFORM (June 1948) and the West's commitment to a democratic Germany exemplified by the Berlin airlift (1948–1949) led inexorably to the setting up of the BUNDESREPUBLIK DEUTSCHLAND in May 1949, which was followed five months later by the establishment of the DEUTSCHE DEMOKRATISCHE REPUBLIK in the Soviet zone in October 1949. See also: ODER-NEISSE-LINIE; POTSDAMER ABKOMMEN; REICH

DRK See: *DEUTSCHES ROTES KREUZ*

DRUPA (INTERNATIONALE MESSE DRUCK UND PAPIER)
'International Printing and Paper Fair' – a trade fair for paper and printing technology held in DÜSSELDORF every five years with nearly half a million visitors.

DSB See: *DEUTSCHER SPORTBUND*

DSF See: *DEUTSCHES SPORTFERNSEHEN*

DSGV See: *DEUTSCHER SPARKASSEN- UND GIROVERBAND*

DSL BANK See: *DEUTSCHE SIEDLUNGS- UND LANDESRENTENBANK*

DStGB See: *DEUTSCHER STÄDTE- UND GEMEINDEBUND*

DSU See: *DEUTSCHE SOZIALE UNION*

DSW See: *DEUTSCHES STUDENTENWERK e.V.*

DtA-BANK See: *DEUTSCHE AUSGLEICHSBANK*

DUALE RUNDFUNKORDNUNG
The legal framework for the provision of broadcasting services in Germany whereby public and private broadcasting exist alongside each other. However, in 1986 the BUNDESVERFASSUNGSGERICHT

produced a landmark ruling laying down that public-service broadcasting was the primary provider of broadcasting services and private broadcasting fulfilled a complementary role.

DUALES ABFALLSYSTEM See: *DUALES SYSTEM DEUTSCHLAND*

DUALES SYSTEM
The combination of compulsory part-time attendance at the BERUFSSCHULE primarily for the age group 15 to 18 combined with practical training on-the-job within the structured framework of the vocational training system. This combination of practical skills with theoretical knowledge has produced a highly skilled workforce which forms the backbone of German commerce and industry. See also: BERUFSAUSBILDUNG; MADE IN GERMANY

DUALES SYSTEM DEUTSCHLAND (DSD)
The private-sector system of waste disposal introduced on 1 January 1993. The system is run by Duales System Deutschland GmbH, a subsidiary of Der Grüne Punkt Duales System Deutschland Gesellschaft für Abfallvermeidung und Sekundärrohstoffgewinnung mbH, and operates alongside local refuse collection services. The aim of the system is to ensure that manufacturers and retailers are involved in the collection of packaging. Manufacturers pay a licence fee for the right to use the GRÜNER PUNKT that designates the packaging as recyclable. Consumers place packaging in sacks or bins that are regularly collected or emptied by an ENTSORGUNGSFIRMA.

The system has come in for a lot of criticism. It almost went into liquidation owing to the deficit of available capacity for recycling and owing to the fact that consumers included packaging from manufacturers who had not paid licence fees. A further criticism levelled at the system is that the consumer pays higher product prices, and the manufacturers have no incentive to cut down packaging. See also: RECYCLING; VERPACKUNGSVERORDNUNG; WERTSTOFFANNAHMESTELLE

DUDEN
A trade mark for reference works produced by the Bibliographisches Institut AG, MANNHEIM. The works include a

series of single volumes on aspects of the German language such as grammatical rules, loan words, etc., and an eight-volume dictionary of the German language.

Konrad Duden's *Vollständiges orthographisches Wörterbuch der deutschen Sprache* (1880) instigated a process of orthographical standardisation in German, for which *Duden* remains the acknowledged standard. See also: RECHTSCHREIBUNG; HOCHDEUTSCH

DUDENPREIS

A prize awarded every two years for services to the German language. The prize-winner is selected by the GEMEINDERAT in MANNHEIM on the recommendation of a jury.

DUISBURG

Duisburg is situated in NORDRHEIN-WESTFALEN at the point where the river Ruhr enters the Rhine (dialling code 02 03, postal area code 47...). The city was already a university town in the Middle Ages, and the medieval town changed little until the industrial revolution swept away the walls. The Deutsche Oper am Rhein is a theatre company shared by Duisburg and DÜSSELDORF with productions of international standing. The WILHELM-LEHMBRUCK-MUSEUM houses one of Germany's most important collections of 20th-century sculpture.

The city has a population of some 537,000 with a total student population of around 17,400 (1 UNIVERSITÄT and 2 other HOCHSCHULEN) and about 16% foreigners (61% Turkish). The SPD runs the city and has been in office since 1948. It has the biggest inland port system in the world and is connected to the sea ports in the north by the Rhein-Herne-Kanal. Industry got under way at the end of the nineteenth century when coal and steel production started up. Duisburg went on to become the biggest producer of steel in Germany although savage rationalisation is now introducing a post-industrial economy. Important industries include chemicals, paper, machinery and shipbuilding, and important companies include THYSSEN, HANIEL and KLÖCKNER.

DUISBURG, GERHARD-MERCATOR-UNIVERSITÄT-GESAMTHOCHSCHULE

University in NORDRHEIN-WESTFALEN founded in 1972 and teaching some 16,000 students. The Gerhard-Mercator-Universität-Gesamt-hochschule Duisburg has departments of philosophy and Protestant theology and Catholic theology and social sciences, educational science, psychology and physical education, linguistics, art and music, economics, biology and chemistry and geography, construction engineering, metallurgy and ceramics, electrical and control engineering, physics and technology, mathematics.

DÜRR, HEINZ (1933–   )

Chairman of electrical appliance manufacturer AEG in 1980–1990, he became chairman of the DEUTSCHE BUNDESBAHN in 1991–1993 and then chairman of the newly privatised DEUTSCHE BAHN AG in 1994.

DÜSSELDORF

Düsseldorf is the LANDESHAUPTSTADT of NORDRHEIN-WESTFALEN and is situated on the river Rhine at the mouth of the Düssel (dialling code 02 11, postal area code 40. . .). The city started life as a fishing village. It received a town charter in 1288, and the Palatinate Electors made Düsseldorf their seat of residence. The arrival of the railways and proximity to the river Ruhr acted as a magnet to industry; Belgian industrialists brought metal industries and machinery to Düsseldorf in the mid-1800s, and the Mannesmann brothers, who had revolutionised the steel-tubing industry, made Düsseldorf their headquarters. Düsseldorf later developed into the administrative centre, or 'Schreibtisch' of the RUHRGEBIET. The architecture in Düsseldorf is a monument to the industrial might of the Ruhrgebiet and the city's array of outdoor sculptures provides an esoteric contrast. The KÖNIGSALLEE (KÖ) is the city's shop window where Germany's most stylish women buy the latest in international design. Düsseldorf is a big centre for KARNEVAL in February, and the Großes Schützenfest in July is a festival on the banks of the Rhine lasting eight days accompanied by the RHEINLAND's biggest funfair (*Kirmes*). The KOM(M)ÖDCHEN is a famous venue for cabaret, and the Deutsche Oper am Rhein shared with DUISBURG has an international reputation.

The city has a population of some 572,000 with a total student population of around 30,000 (1 UNIVERSITÄT and 4 other HOCHSCHULEN) and about 15% foreigners (17% Turkish). A coalition between the SPD and DIE GRÜNEN, and latterly BÜNDNIS 90/DIE GRÜNEN, has been running the city since 1984. Düsseldorf is now a trading city, home to the DEUTSCHER GEWERKSCHAFTSBUND, and the *Japan-Center* is a monument to the scale of Japanese investment, which has made the city the home of the largest Japanese community in Europe. Düsseldorf's industries include iron and steel, glass, chemicals and brewing. The administrative headquarters of many large companies are located there, and it has the reputation of being Germany's fashion capital. Important companies include METRO, VEBA, MANNESMANN, THYSSEN HANDELSUNION and HENKEL. The city's trade-fair complex is a major centre for trade fairs in capital goods and holds fairs such as BOOT DÜSSELDORF (boat show), IGEDO (fashion), DRUPA (printing and paper), INTERKAMA (measurement and automation) and INTERPACK (packaging technology). See also: RHEINISCH-WESTFÄLISCHES INDUSTRIEGEBIET

DÜSSELDORF, HEINRICH-HEINE-UNIVERSITÄT
New university in NORDRHEIN-WESTFALEN founded in 1965 with a modern, concrete campus and teaching some 20,000 students. The Heinrich-Heine-Universität Düsseldorf has faculties of economics, mathematics and natural sciences, philosophy (arts), medicine.

DÜSSELDORFER WIRTSCHAFTSBEZIRK
The economic zone centred on the city of DÜSSELDORF.

DVU See: *DEUTSCHE VOLKSUNION*

DVW See: *DEUTSCHE VERKEHRSWACHT e.V.*

DW See: *DEUTSCHE WELLE RADIO & TV*

DWD See: *DEUTSCHER WETTERDIENST*

DYCKERHOFF & WIDMANN AG (DYWIDAG)
Construction company founded in 1865. Company headquarters are in MÜNCHEN. DYWIDAG has some 17,000 employees.

DYWIDAG See: *DYCKERHOFF & WIDMANN AG*

e.V. See: *EINGETRAGENER VEREIN*

E-PLUS
Cellular telephone network offering a business service (*Profi-Tarif*) and a service for private consumers (*Partner-Tarif*).

EDEKA ZENTRALE AG
Germany's biggest cooperative trading group, selling to 22 cooperatives of independent food retailers with over 11,000 retail outlets. The company also has nearly 400 retail outlets of its own. Group headquarters are in HAMBURG with some 800 employees.

EHRENAMT
An honorary post held in a public capacity without remuneration but in some cases with compensation for time and expenses.

EHRENAMTLICHER BÜRGERMEISTER See: *BÜRGERMEISTER, EHRENAMTLICHER*

EHRENAMTLICHER LANDRAT See: *LANDRAT, EHRENAMTLICHER*

EHRENAMTLICHER OBERBÜRGERMEISTER See: *OBERBÜRGERMEISTER, EHRENAMTLICHER*

EHRENAMTLICHER RICHTER
An honorary judge acts in a lay capacity and receives compensation for time and expenses. The honorary judge requires no legal training and sits in all types of court with equal rights alongside professional judges (*Berufsrichter*). Honorary judges in criminal cases are known as *Schöffen.*

EICHEL, HANS (1941–   )
Teacher and SPD politician. He was OBERBÜRGERMEISTER of KASSEL in 1975–1991 and was the first mayor in Germany to work with

DIE GRÜNEN in local government. He has been MINISTERPRÄSIDENT of HESSEN since 1991.

EICHINGER, BERND (1949–   )

Film producer and distributor who founded the production company Solaris in 1974 and took over production company Neue Constantin in 1979. He has enjoyed international box-office successes with productions such as *Das Boot* (1981) and *The Name of the Rose* (1986). *Das Geisterhaus* (1994) was also a smash-hit with more than four million tickets sold in the BRD. His other productions include *Falsche Bewegung* (1974) directed by W. WENDERS, and *Hitler. Ein Film aus Deutschland* (1976/1977) directed by H.-J. SYBERBERG.

EICHSTÄTT, KATHOLISCHE UNIVERSITÄT

University in BAYERN founded in 1972 and teaching some 4,000 students. The Katholische Universität Eichstätt has faculties of theology, philosophy and education, languages and literature, history and social sciences, mathematics and geography, economics, religious education, social studies.

EIGEN, MANFRED (1927–   )

Physicist who was awarded the Nobel Prize (with R.G.W. Norrish and G. Porter) in 1967 for research on high-speed chemical reactions. He was appointed professor at the Max-Planck-Institut für biophysikalische Chemie in Göttingen (NIEDERSACHSEN) in 1964. He presented a model for the origin of life in *Die Selbstorganisation der Materie und die Evolution biologischer Makromoleküle* (1970).

EIGENHEIM

A 'home of one's own' is the dream of many Germans, and they save long and hard to build their *Eigenheim*. Plots of land – priced by the square metre – are expensive, especially in the south, and houses are well built, which again drives up the price. Consequently, the level of home ownership is lower than in many European countries. Germans tend to regard buying or building a house as providing a house for life, which can make them reluctant to relocate to a new workplace. See also: BAU-SPARVERTRAG

EIGENTUMSWOHNUNG
An owner-occupied flat or apartment.

EINFUHRUMSATZSTEUER
A turnover tax charged on imports.

EINGEMEINDUNG
A process of concentration of local authorities when one GEMEINDE is absorbed by another. This process may occur voluntarily (*freiwillige Eingemeindung*) or is imposed on a Gemeinde (*Zwangseingemeindung*) in the public interest.

EINGETRAGENER VEREIN (e.V.)
A non-profit-making organisation that attains the status of a legal person by being registered in the VEREINSREGISTER at the AMTSGERICHT. The *Verein* must have a VORSTAND, it can be sued and take legal action itself, and any debtors only have a claim on the assets of the *Verein.*

EINIGUNGSVERTRAG
The treaty signed by the BRD and the DDR on 31 August 1990 by which the DDR was integrated within the BRD in accordance with *Artikel* 23 of the GRUNDGESETZ. The treaty made BRANDEN-BURG, MECKLENBURG-VORPOMMERN, SACHSEN, SACHSEN-ANHALT and THÜRINGEN new LÄNDER and made BERLIN the new capital of Germany while leaving the question of the seat of government open. A vote taken in the BUNDESTAG on 20 June 1991 subsequently paved the way for transferring both the Bundestag and the seat of government to the new capital. See also: NEUE BUN-DESLÄNDER

EINKOMMENSTEUER
Income tax paid in Germany by individuals and legal persons (e.g. companies) on the income earned. The tax is a personal tax and is collected directly from every individual and from legal entities such as companies. Items such as advertising costs, reference books and workwear are deductible expenses. *Einkommensteuer* includes LOHNSTEUER, VERANLAGTE EINKOMMENSTEUER, KAPITALERTRAGSTEUER and KÖRPERSCHAFTSTEUER. *Einkommensteuer* is shared by the BUND, the LAND and the GEMEINDE, the

precise proportions by which the tax is allocated being subject to continual revision.

EINS PLUS
Commercial TV channel run by the ARD and the Schweizerische Radio- und Fernsehgesellschaft.

EINSCHREIBUNG
Enrolment as a student at a HOCHSCHULE.

EINSCHULUNG
The first day at school for the new year's intake at the age of six. New school children are traditionally accompanied by a conical *Schultüte* containing pens, pencils and other equipment for use at school as well as a selection of sweets and other goodies.

EINWOHNERMELDEAMT
The office in large towns and cities where individuals have to register when they change address or move from another area.

EKD See: *EVANGELISCHE KIRCHE IN DEUTSCHLAND*

ELECTRONICA (INTERNATIONALE FACHMESSE FÜR BAUELEMENTE UND BAUGRUPPEN DER ELEKTRONIK)
The 'International Trade Fair for Components and Assemblies in Electronics' is a trade fair for the electrical-engineering and components industries held in MÜNCHEN every two years with around 80,000 visitors.

ELLE
Monthly fashion and lifestyle magazine for women established in 1988 and published in MÜNCHEN with a circulation of 218,000.

ELTERNAUSSCHUSS See: *ELTERNVERTRETUNG*

ELTERNBEIRAT See: *ELTERNVERTRETUNG*

ELTERNVERTRETUNG
The parents' association at a school has a role that is generally restricted to advising, although in HESSEN it has a say in how the school is run. *Elternvertretungen* in some LÄNDER also have

teacher representatives or representatives of the GEMEINDE and Church.

EMMA

Magazine with a feminist agenda. It was established in 1977 by Alice SCHWARZER and is published with a circulation of 50,000 in KÖLN every two months. *emma* tackles political and cultural issues and has a female and male readership.

ENERGIE-VERSORGUNG-SCHWABEN AG

Electricity generation and distribution company founded in 1939. Company headquarters are in STUTTGART. Energie-Versorgung-Schwaben has some 4,500 employees.

ENGHOLM, BJÖRN (1939–   )

Typesetter, lecturer and SPD politician. He was a MITGLIED DES BUNDESTAGES in 1969–1982 and STAATSSEKRETÄR in the BUNDESMINISTERIUM FÜR BILDUNG, WISSENSCHAFT, FORSCHUNG UND TECHNOLOGIE in 1981–1982. He became a member of the LANDTAG in SCHLESWIGHOLSTEIN and chairman of the SPD-FRAKTION in 1983 and went on to become MINISTERPRÄSIDENT in 1988. He was appointed chairman of the SPD in March 1993 but resigned all his posts in May 1993 due to revelations about false statements he had made to the Landtag in KIEL connected with the BARSCHEL-AFFÄRE.

ENTGELT

General term used officially to cover both LOHN and GEHALT. This is intended to remove the distinction between blue-collar and white-collar workers as more and more companies go over to paying wages and salaries monthly direct into employees' bank accounts.

ENTSORGUNGSFIRMEN

Waste disposal companies that collect and dispose of refuse. See also: DUALES SYSTEM DEUTSCHLAND

ENZENSBERGER, HANS MAGNUS (1929–   )

Poet and essayist who is highly critical of the society and civilisation of today. He started out as a member of GRUPPE 47 and went on to become one of the major German poets of the post-war era. From 1965 to 1975 Enzensberger was HERAUSGEBER of the influential literary journal *Kursbuch,* which proclaimed the 'death of literature' in 1968. His poetry is characterised by strict form and juxtapositions of different styles, with colloquialisms and neologisms. Collections include *verteidigung der wölfe* (1957), *Mausoleum. 37 Balladen aus der Geschichte des Fortschritts* (1975), *Der fliegende Robert* (1989) and *Kiosk* (1995). Enzensberger has also written in other genres, compiled anthologies (*Allerleirauh*, 1961) and continued his work as editor (*Die Andere Bibliothek*, since 1985).

EPD See: *EVANGELISCHER PRESSEDIENST*

EQUITANA (WELTMESSE DES PFERDESPORTS)
'Equestrian Sports World Fair' – a trade fair for horses, riding equipment and feedstocks held in ESSEN every two years with around a quarter of a million visitors.

ERFURT
Erfurt is the LANDESHAUPTSTADT of THÜRINGEN and is situated in the Thuringian Basin on the river Gera (dialling code 03 61, postal area code 99...). A bishopric was founded at Erfurt in 842 and a university in 1392 – later Martin Luther's Alma Mater. The university was closed by the Prussians in 1816 and reopened after the city celebrated its 1250th anniversary in 1992. A meeting in 1970 between Willy Brandt and Willi Stoph (DDR *Vorsitzender des Ministerrats*) ushered in Brandt's OSTPOLITIK – a policy of rapprochement with East Germany. Much of Erfurt came through the Second World War intact and the city provides a unique snapshot of pre-war Germany.

  The city has a population of some 213,000 with a total student population of around 3,000 (1 UNIVERSITÄT and 4 other HOCHSCHULEN) and only about 1% foreigners (25% Vietnamese). The CDU has been running the city as the strongest party since 1990, although lack of an absolute majority has necessitated the support of other parties. Erfurt's industry includes engineering, office machines, footwear and microelectronics, and the city hosts a massive international horticultural exhibition (iga) every year.

ERFURT, UNIVERSITÄT
New university due to start teaching in 1999 with faculties of phi-

losophy (arts), law and economics. It is envisaged that by the year 2010 there will be 6,000 funded places with something in the region of 10,000 students.

ERLANGEN-NÜRNBERG, FRIEDRICH-ALEXANDER-UNIVERSITÄT

University in BAYERN founded in 1743 and teaching some 26,000 students. The Friedrich-Alexander-Universität Erlangen-Nürnberg has faculties of theology, law, medicine, philosophy and history and social sciences, languages and literature, mathematics and physics, biology and chemistry, geosciences, economics and social sciences, technology, education.

ERSATZDIENST See: *ZIVILDIENST*

ERSATZKASSEN

Health-insurance funds (e.g. the DEUTSCHE ANGESTELLTEN-KRANKENKASSE, BARMER ERSATZKASSE) which provide health insurance for their members. Membership of an *Ersatzkasse* is voluntary and exempts members from paying contributions to a PFLICHTKRANKENKASSE. Membership of an *Ersatzkasse* is traditionally geared to a particular trade or professional group although *Ersatzkassen* may now also accept members outside their original membership group. See also: KRANKENKASSEN

ERSTES PROGRAMM

The main German public TV channel, operated by the ARD.

ERSTSTIMME

The first vote by which the electorate chooses between individual candidates on the voting paper and elects ABGEORDNETE directly (DIREKTMANDAT). See also: BUNDESTAGSWAHL; LANDTAGSWAHL; ÜBERHANGMANDAT

ERWACHSENENBILDUNG

Continuing education and training for adults including retraining, refresher courses, advanced vocational courses, etc. The VOLKSHOCHSCHULEN are one of the main vehicles for delivering *Erwachsenenbildung.*

ERZGEBIRGE

A range of hills across the south of SACHSEN that were an important area for mining iron and silver. The area is famous for its wooden toys and Christmas ornaments, and for lace-making. A popular area with tourists in both winter and summer, despite the fact that the forests are suffering from severe environmental problems due to air pollution from factory emissions.

ESSEN

Essen is situated between the rivers Emscher and Ruhr and is the biggest city in NORDRHEIN-WESTFALEN (dialling code 02 01, postal area code 45...). It started life as a convent for the daughters of Saxony's aristocrats in 852 and passed to PREUSSEN in 1802. The Krupp dynasty transformed a sleepy town into a steel metropolis during the nineteenth century and Essen's fortunes were founded on iron, coal and steel. Essen used to be the RUHRGEBIET's biggest coalmining centre, and although the last mine closed in 1986 the city is still the headquarters of RUHRKOHLE AG (Germany's biggest coalmining company) and many industrial associations have their headquarters here. The Münsterkirche in Essen is one of Germany's oldest churches, and the city also has northern Europe's largest synagogue, built in 1911–1913 and now housing a memorial exhibition.

The city has a population of some 619,000 with a student population of around 21,800 (1 UNIVERSITÄT) and about 9% foreigners (32% Turkish). The SPD has been running the city since 1956. The Krupp name lives on in a corporation based on heavy industry and armaments, and other industries include construction, energy, machinery and vehicles, food processing and service industries. Important companies include RWE, KARSTADT and ALDI. The city has a port on the Rhein-Herne-Kanal and hosts trade fairs such as DEUBAU (construction), EQUITANA (equestrian) and SECURITY.

ESSEN, UNIVERSITÄT-GESAMTHOCHSCHULE

University in NORDRHEIN-WESTFALEN founded in 1972 and teaching some 23,000 students. The Universität-Gesamthochschule Essen has departments of philosophy and religious studies and sociology, education, languages and literature, art and design, economics, mathematics, physics, chemistry, architecture and biosciences and geosciences, construction engineering, surveying, mechanical engineering and electrical engineering, medicine.

ESSEN & TRINKEN

Gourmet magazine established in 1972 with a circulation of 221,000. This is Germany's leading culinary magazine, published monthly by GRUNER + JAHR. It caters for a mainly female readership of working age with a good education and the money to take an aesthetic interest in wining, dining and haute cuisine.

ESSO AG

Oil company founded in 1890. It is a subsidiary of EXXON Corporation and has over 1,600 service stations. Company headquarters are in HAMBURG. Esso has some 2,300 employees.

EUROPAKANAL See: *RHEIN-MAIN-DONAU-GROSS-SCHIFFAHRTSWEG*

EUROSCHECK

Eurocheques are commonly used in Germany and are guaranteed by a banker's card up to DM 400.

EVANGELISCH

General term used for the Protestant Churches (usually Lutheran) when differentiating them from the Catholic Church and other denominations. See also: EVANGELISCHE KIRCHE IN DEUTSCHLAND; KATHOLISCH

EVANGELISCHE KIRCHE IN DEUTSCHLAND (EKD)

The federation of the 26 Lutheran, united and reformed Churches in Germany. The EKD has around 30 million members and is the country's biggest Protestant Church. Most adherents of the Christian faith in the former DDR were Protestant, and the Protestant Church in the DDR formed a focus of opposition to the Communist regime culminating in the peaceful marches in LEIPZIG in the autumn of 1989.

EVANGELISCHE ZENTRALSTELLE FÜR WELTANSCHAUUNGSFRAGEN (EZW)

An institution in STUTTGART set up by the EVANGELISCHE KIRCHE IN

DEUTSCHLAND in 1960 to look into contemporary philosophical and religious movements and to promote discussion within the Church.

EVANGELISCHER PRESSEDIENST (EPD)

A specialist news agency providing news and information about the Lutheran Church.

EVERDING, AUGUST (1928–   )

Theatre producer and director. He was appointed director of the Münchner Kammerspiele in 1963 and has also been director of the Staatsoper in HAMBURG. His international reputation was established with stunning performances of Wagner at New York's Metropolitan Opera in 1971 and 1976. Since 1982 Everding has been GENERALINTENDANT in MÜNCHEN of the four Bayerische Staatstheater (Bayerische Staatsoper, Residenztheater, Staatstheater am Gärtnerplatz, Prinzregententheater). As such he has exerted tremendous influence on the dramatic arts in Germany and his productions include *Lohengrin* (1976) in New York, *Die Entführung aus dem Serail* (1980) in München and *Der Ring des Nibelungen* (1988/89) in Warsaw.

EXPRESS

Daily newspaper established in 1963 and published in KÖLN with a circulation of 389,000.

EXTERNER

Pupil taking the final examination in a school that they have not attended.

EZW See: *EVANGELISCHE ZENTRALSTELLE FÜR WELTANSCHAUUNGSFRAGEN*

FACH See: *STUDIENFACH*

FACHARBEITER

A skilled worker in a registered trade or craft who will generally have completed three years of vocational training and obtained a FACHBRIEF. The *Facharbeiter* is able to operate independently and apply a range of skills.

FACHARZT

A doctor who, following basic training, has undergone several years of further specialist training. The doctor is then recognised by the ÄRZTEKAMMER as a specialist in a particular area of medicine. A high proportion of German doctors train and set up as *Fachärzte*. Patients may consult them direct without going through a general practitioner. See also: KRANKENKASSEN

FACHBEREICH (FB)

The administrative grouping of related subjects into a department at a HOCHSCHULE. Several *Fachbereiche* may form a FAKULTÄT, for example a *Philosophische Fakultät* might have the following *Fachbereiche: Sprach- und Literaturwissenschaft; Kunst- und Altertumswissenschaft; Geschichte, Philosophie und Sozialwissenschaften; Erziehungswissenschaften; Musik und Sport.* A *Fachbereich* is administered by a *Fachbereichsrat*. The responsibilities of the *Fachbereichsrat* include teaching, research, the STUDIENORDNUNG and the PRÜFUNGSORDNUNG.

FACHBRIEF

The certificate awarded to a FACHARBEITER at the end of three years of vocational training.

FACHGESCHÄFT

A retailer for a specialist range of goods where the staff will have been specially trained and are qualified to give specialist advice on the products they are selling.

FACHGYMNASIUM

A GYMNASIUM that builds on a REALSCHULABSCHLUSS or equivalent qualification, taking pupils to a general or vocational ABITUR. The LEHRPLAN includes specialist areas of study such as music, technology, social sciences, economics, etc. in addition to the usual general subjects. *Fachgymnasien* include the *technisches Gymnasium*, *naturwissenschaftliches Gymnasium* and *neusprachliches Gymnasium*. See also: HUMANISTISCHES GYMNASIUM; WIRTSCHAFTSGYMNASIUM

FACHHOCHSCHULE

A vocationally oriented tertiary institution where students study for a DIPLOM in subjects such as engineering, business studies, social work, fine arts and agriculture. The *Fachhochschule* offers a more practical education than a *wissenschaftliche Hochschule*, and courses are shorter. Applicants must complete at least 12 years of schooling, and the FACHHOCHSCHULREIFE is the entrance qualification. Courses last six SEMESTER, often with two additional practical *Semester* in a job placement. The student is awarded a diploma (accompanied by the abbreviation FH in BAYERN, BADEN-WÜRTTEMBERG and RHEINLAND-PFALZ) and is qualified to continue studying at a university with a specified number of *Semester*'s credit. *Fachhochschulen* do not have the right to confer doctorates (PROMOTION), and completion of a course of study at a *Fachhochschule* does not qualify the student to commence research for *Promotion*. However, there is a general trend for *Fachhochschulen* to become more research-oriented. See also: HOCHSCHULEN

FACHHOCHSCHULREIFE

Entrance qualification for a specified STUDIUM at a FACHHOCHSCHULE obtained at a FACHOBERSCHULE or FACHGYMNASIUM.

FACHIDIOT

A derogatory term for a person highly specialised in a narrow field of study who has no thoughts other than for their narrow specialism.

FACHOBERSCHULE
A secondary school for pupils in the classes 11 and 12 that provides theoretical study and practical training for particular subject areas such as business studies, engineering or design. The entrance requirement is the REALSCHULABSCHLUSS, and after two years of study students obtain the FACHHOCHSCHULREIFE.

FACHRICHTUNG
Specialist field of study within a student's chosen STUDIENFACH at a HOCHSCHULE.

FACHSCHAFT
The body of students studying a subject in a particular FACHBEREICH or FACHRICHTUNG at a HOCHSCHULE. The students elect representatives (*Fachschaftsrat* and *Fachschaftssprecher*) to represent their interests. See also: VERFASSTE STUDENTENSCHAFT

FACHSCHULE
Educational institution providing specialist training for people who have completed a registered BERUFSAUSBILDUNG and have several years of job experience. *Fachschulen* prepare candidates for a number of vocational examinations including the MEISTERPRÜFUNG.

FACHSCHULREIFE
Leaving certificate awarded to students at the BERUFSAUFBAUSCHULE and some BERUFSFACHSCHULEN. The certificate is a qualification for entrance to the FACHSCHULE and class 12 of the FACHOBERSCHULE.

FACHSEMESTER
A SEMESTER that has been completed for a STUDIENGANG in a particular STUDIENFACH. In order to register for the ABSCHLUSSPRÜFUNG a student must have completed a prescribed number of *Fachsemester*.

FACHSPITZENVERBAND
A national organisation that represents the interests of all the ARBEITGEBERVERBÄNDE in a particular sector of industry and commerce at the level of the BUND.

FACHVERBAND
Voluntary organisation of companies operating in the same sector that performs tasks in the common interests of all its members.

FACHWERK
A type of half-timbered construction with a house being built around a wooden framework. *Fachwerkhäuser* are characteristic of the ALTSTADT in many German towns and cities, such as those along the ROMANTISCHE STRASSE.

FACHWIRT
A vocational title that holders of a qualification from a FACHSCHULE are entitled to use. The title is specific to a particular area, for example banking or insurance.

FACHZEITSCHRIFT
A specialist magazine or periodical that is published at regular intervals and keeps readers up to date in a particular field.

FAG KUGELFISCHER GEORG SCHÄFER AG
Ball-bearings manufacturer founded in 1883. Company headquarters are in Schweinfurt (BAYERN). FAG has some 15,000 employees.

FAHRERLAUBNIS See: *FÜHRERSCHEIN*

FAHRSCHULE
In order to obtain a FÜHRERSCHEIN, a learner driver has to undertake a training course involving both theory and practice with an approved driving school. *Fahrschulen* are generally privately owned and the examination is held by an accredited testing centre. Driving instructors require a *Fahrschulerlaubnis* and learner drivers have to carry out all driving practice with a driving school.

FAKULTÄT
The traditional organizational unit at a HOCHSCHULE headed by a DEKAN. It is responsible for organising teaching and examinations and for appointing staff. The *Fakultät* has increasingly been replaced by FACHBEREICHE or *Abteilungen.* The term is also used to refer to the teaching body within the *Fakultät.*

FAMETA (INTERNATIONALE FACHMESSE FÜR METALLBEARBEITUNG)

The 'International Trade Fair for Metal-Working' is a trade fair for industrial and production engineering (machine tools, robotics, instrumentation and welding) held in NÜRNBERG every two years with around 27,000 visitors.

FASCHING

The run-up to Lent in the south of BAYERN, culminating in ROSENMONTAG and FASCHINGSDIENSTAG with wild fancy-dress parties and street processions.

FASCHINGSDIENSTAG

The Tuesday before Ash Wednesday and the 41st day before Easter. It is the final day of FASCHING, which finishes on *Faschingsdienstag* at 12.00 pm. Although not officially a public holiday, employees very often get a half-day holiday in areas that celebrate *Fasching*. See also: ROSENMONTAG

FASTNACHT

Originally *Fastnacht* referred to the 'night before fasting', i.e. Shrove Tuesday, but the carnival season has come to be extended to the entire period before Lent and is said to begin '*am elften elften elf Uhr elf*' (on 11.11. at 11.11 am), although it only really gets under way after HEILIGE DREI KÖNIGE. Variously termed KARNEVAL (in the RHEINLAND), *Fastnacht* (around MAINZ, *Määnzer Fassenacht*), *Fasnet* (SCHWABEN and south-west BAYERN), *Fosnat* (FRANKEN) and FASCHING (around MÜNCHEN), the carnival season is marked by wild fancy-dress parties and culminates in street processions, normally on ROSENMONTAG (the Monday preceding Shrove Tuesday). In some areas of Germany (the rural south, especially Schwaben and south-west Bayern) ancient customs continue, with wooden masks to drive out the evil spirits of winter and usher in the fertile spring, culminating in *Altweiberfastnacht* on the Thursday before Lent begins. Carnival celebrations tend to be concentrated in the Catholic areas of Germany.

FAZ See: *FRANKFURTER ALLGEMEINE ZEITUNG*

FB See: *FACHBEREICH*

FBW See: *FILMBEWERTUNGSSTELLE WIESBADEN*

FDP See: *FREIE DEMOKRATISCHE PARTEI*

FELTEN & GUILLEAUME ENERGIETECHNIK AG

Electrical engineering company founded in 1874. Company headquarters are in KÖLN. Felten & Guilleaume has some 4,200 employees.

FERNHEIZUNG

District heating is a popular means of supplying heat to buildings or small towns near a power station. Hot water or steam is piped to consumers from the industrial plant and provides heat in buildings some distance from the original source.

FERNSEHWOCHE

A TV guide established in 1969 and published weekly with a circulation of 1.7 million. In addition to programme information it also features leisure and humour.

FERNSTRASSE

Major road, often part of the AUTOBAHN network, linking up cities and industrial centres separated by long distances.

FERNSTUDIUM

A distance-learning course of study carried out at the FERNUNI-VERSITÄT and leading to a degree. The students attend study centres at regular intervals and are supported by correspondence courses, FUNKKOLLEGE, VOLKSHOCHSCHULEN and institutes of further and higher education.

FERNUNIVERSITÄT

Any type of 'open university' where study is carried out in the student's home through correspondence courses, and lectures are relayed primarily on television. In Germany, a *Fern-universität* was opened in HAGEN in 1975. See also: HAGEN, FERN-UNIVERSITÄT − GESAMTHOCHSCHULE

FERNUNTERRICHT

Correspondence courses, very often run by private institutions offering further vocational training based on STUDIENBRIEFE. These courses are monitored by the STAATLICHE ZENTRALSTELLE

FÜR FERNUNTERRICHT and the BUNDESINSTITUT FÜR BERUFSBILDUNG. Distance learning continues to expand access to education and training.

FERNVERKEHRSSTRASSE See: *FERNSTRASSE*

FERNWÄRME See: *FERNHEIZUNG*

FETSCHER, IRING (1922–   )

Political scientist whose criticism of society follows in the tradition of the FRANKFURTER SCHULE. His research is primarily concerned with the history of political theories and of Marxism in particular. Fetscher was appointed professor in FRANKFURT AM MAIN (JOHANN WOLFGANG GOETHE-UNIVERSITÄT) in 1963. He identifies three main problems that endanger the survival of the human species: the destruction of the environment, the population explosion and world hunger. His publications include *Modelle der Friedenssicherung* (1972), *Überlebensbedingungen der Menschheit – Zur Dialektik des Fortschritts* (1976) and *Utopien, Illusionen, Hoffnungen. Plädoyer für eine politische Kultur in Deutschland* (1990).

FEUILLETON

This forms the arts section of a newspaper and generally carries articles on cultural matters including book reviews and theatre reviews, and often a serialised novel.

FFA See: *FILMFÖRDERUNGSANSTALT*

FhG See: *FRAUNHOFER-GESELLSCHAFT ZUR FÖRDERUNG DER ANGEWANDTEN FORSCHUNG e.V.*

FILMBEWERTUNGSSTELLE WIESBADEN (FBW)

An authority founded in 1951 by the LÄNDER to classify full-length and short films submitted for production and distribution. The classification is awarded for artistic excellence and is important for obtaining subsidies and tax breaks under the FILM-FÖRDERUNGSGESETZ.

FILMFÖRDERUNGSANSTALT (FFA)

An organisation set up in 1951 to administer the subsidies created by the FILMFÖRDERUNGSGESETZ.

FILMFÖRDERUNGSGESETZ

A law for the promotion of the German film industry compelling all cinema-owners to contribute a proportion of their annual turnover to a central fund. The promotion of the film industry is coordinated by the FILMFÖRDERUNGSANSTALT in BERLIN.

FINANZAMT

The tax office at a local level (STADT or KREIS) responsible for assessing and collecting taxes due to the LAND and the BUND. The Finanzamt is responsible for the collection of EINKOMMENSTEUER and UMSATZSTEUER (*Mehrwertsteuer*) and many other taxes.

FINANZBERICHT

The financial report produced every year by the BUNDESREGIERUNG, which reports on the expenditure of all the BEHÖRDEN. It provides the background for the HAUSHALTSPLAN.

FINANZIERUNGSNACHWEIS

Evidence required from foreign students showing that they have sufficient funds available in order to pay for living expenses and the expenses incurred by a STUDIUM.

FINANZREFORMGESETZ

A reform of the financial and tax system in 1969 that amended the GRUNDGESETZ in an attempt to make the distribution of taxes more equitable. See also: GEWERBESTEUER

FISCHER, ERNST OTTO (1918–   )

Chemist who was awarded the Nobel Prize for chemistry in 1973 (with G. Wilkinson) for research showing that certain organometallic compounds have a sandwich molecular structure. He was appointed professor in MÜNCHEN (TECHNISCHE UNIVERSITÄT) in 1964.

FISCHER, JOSEPH (JOSCHKA) (1948–   )

Politician in BÜNDNIS 90/DIE GRÜNEN who was a MITGLIED DES BUNDESTAGES in 1983–1985 and the environment minister in HESSEN in 1985–1987 and 1991–1994. He was also deputy MINISTERPRÄSIDENT in 1991–1994. Fischer has been Mitglied des Bundestages and head of the FRAKTION of Bündnis 90/Die Grünen since 1994. He symbolises the pragmatic face of the Green movement favourably disposed to form coalitions. He supported military protection for the safe havens in the Bosnian conflict despite fierce opposition within the party.

FISCHER-DIESKAU, DIETRICH (1925–   )

Baritone singer who joined the Städtische Oper BERLIN in 1948 and has been a guest at most of the world's leading opera houses and music festivals. His interpretations of Schubert, Schumann and Hugo Wolf captured the imagination and brought renewed popularity for lieder recitals of solo voice and piano. He was appointed professor at the Hochschule der Künste in Berlin in 1982 and has made numerous recordings. His books include *Töne sprechen, Worte klingen. Zur Geschichte und Interpretation des Gesangs* (1985) and *Wenn Musik der Liebe Nahrung ist* (1990).

FKK See: *FREIKÖRPERKULTUR*

FLÄCHENSTAAT

A LAND other than the STADTSTAATEN of BERLIN, BREMEN and HAMBURG, which covers a large geographical area.

FLORA

Popular gardening magazine published monthly by GRUNER + JAHR with a circulation of 218,000. In the main, it addresses a young, well-to-do audience that is interested in topical issues concerned with gardening and the environment.

FOCUS

Current affairs and news magazine published weekly by BURDA in MÜNCHEN with a circulation of 677,000. *Focus* was established in 1993 as a centre-right competitor to DER SPIEGEL. It is aimed at business people and decision-makers in the 30–49 age bracket and provides a weekly overview of politics, business, science and technology. With its more attractive layout and shorter articles, *Focus* is proving a serious competitor for *Der Spiegel*.

FORD-WERKE AG

The German subsidiary for Ford was set up in 1925. Company headquarters are in KÖLN. Ford has some 44,000 employees.

FORTBILDUNG See: *WEITERBILDUNG*

FRAGERECHT

The right to put questions to witnesses, experts and other parties (including the defendant) in a criminal case in order to establish the material facts surrounding a case. The court or sometimes the presiding judge decides on the admissibility of questions.

FRAKTION

A political group of like-minded representatives within the BUNDESTAG, a LANDTAG or other elected assembly. In the Bundestag a *Fraktion* normally consists of all the MITGLIEDER DES BUNDESTAGES belonging to one party with at least 5%. The FÜNFPROZENT-KLAUSEL avoids a multitude of small *Fraktionen* in the Bundestag, although parties that fail to overcome that hurdle are still represented if they have at least three DIREKTMANDATE. They may then form a *Gruppe* but not a *Fraktion*. Only *Fraktionen* have full membership rights on parliamentary committees (BUNDESTAGSAUSSCHÜSSE). See also: FRAKTIONSZWANG

FRAKTIONSVORSITZENDER

The chairperson of a FRAKTION.

FRAKTIONSZWANG

The obligation of an ABGEORDNETER to vote in accordance with the policy of the FRAKTION. Although the exercise of *Fraktionszwang* contravenes the principle of the FREIES MANDAT as laid down in *Artikel* 38 of the GRUNDGESETZ, it is possible for an *Abgeordneter* to be excluded from the *Fraktion* or party if he or she does not vote according to policy. This cannot, however, lead to a withdrawal of the MANDAT.

FRANKEN

The northern part of BAYERN with the cities of NÜRNBERG and WÜRZBURG. The people of Franken have a long cultural history and their distinctive dialect (*Fränkisch*) and cultural identity set them apart from the rest of Bayern. Nürnberg differs from the other parts of Bayern by being predominantly Protestant and having an SPD mayor. The area around Würzburg is renowned for the dry *Frankenwein*.

FRANKFURT AM MAIN

Frankfurt am Main (as distinct from Frankfurt an der Oder in

BRANDENBURG) is the LANDESHAUPTSTADT of HESSEN. It is situated on the river Main just before it joins the Rhine (dialling code 0 69, postal area code 60–65...). Frankfurt's importance as a river-crossing dividing north and south Germany was recognised in Roman times, and Frankfurt's central position in Europe has made it a centre for trade and commerce since the Middle Ages. Most German emperors were crowned in Frankfurt and in 1848–1849 the city was the site of the first German national assembly (*Nationalversammlung*), but the city lost out to BONN as the site for a provisional capital of West Germany. The decision to start with a clean slate rather than restore extensively after the Second World War means that the architecture has an American feel to it, typified by the twin towers of the DEUTSCHE BANK and by the Messeturm, completed in 1991 and reputedly Europe's tallest building. The city has always had a reputation for liberal ideas: it has a left-wing university and is now home to Daniel COHN-BENDIT (one of the leaders of the Paris student revolts in 1968), a Frankfurt city councillor. Frankfurt is also a city of art, culture and publishing, and is the birthplace of Johann Wolfgang von Goethe (1749–1832).

The city has a population of some 654,000 with a total student population of around 48,000 (1 UNIVERSITÄT and 4 other HOCHSCHULEN) and about 28% foreigners (25% Yugoslav). A coalition between the SPD and BÜNDNIS 90/DIE GRÜNEN has been running the city since 1989. The first mention of the 'Frankfurt Fair' occurred as far back as 1240, and today's trade-fair complex is a monumental fairground of glass and concrete hosting the spring and autumn INTERNATIONALE FRANKFURTER MESSE (consumer goods), the world-famous FRANKFURTER BUCHMESSE (books), the INTERNATIONALE AUTOMOBILAUSSTELLUNG (motor show) and other specialist fairs such as INTERSTOFF (textiles). Banking has also been central to Frankfurt's development: today the city houses the DEUTSCHE BUNDESBANK and more than 400 banks have offices here. The BÖRSE in Frankfurt is Germany's largest stock exchange. Frankfurt considers the RHEIN-MAIN-FLUGHAFEN to be the biggest airport in Europe (if freight is included). Hoechst, a suburb of Frankfurt, is home to Germany's biggest chemical company – HOECHST. The FRANKFURTER ALLGEMEINE ZEITUNG

(Germany's premier broadsheet and business newspaper) and the centre-left FRANKFURTER RUNDSCHAU are published here.

FRANKFURT, JOHANN WOLFGANG GOETHE-UNIVERSITÄT

University in HESSEN founded in 1914 and teaching some 37,000 students. The Johann Wolfgang Goethe-Universität Frankfurt has departments of law, economics, social sciences, education, psychology, Protestant theology, Catholic theology, philosophy, history, classics, modern languages, East European and non-European languages and cultures, mathematics, physics, chemistry, biochemistry and pharmacology, biology, geosciences, geography, medicine, information science, sport.

FRANKFURT AN DER ODER See: *BRANDENBURG*

FRANKFURTER ALLGEMEINE ZEITUNG (FAZ)

Founded in 1949, the *FAZ* is one of Germany's most serious dailies, published in FRANKFURT AM MAIN but with nationwide coverage. It provides general news and maintains an objective, independent viewpoint in rather a dry style. It is slanted towards the business community with a substantial section on business every day. The *FAZ* has a circulation of 395,000 and is distributed in nearly 150 countries.

FRANKFURTER BUCHMESSE

The world-famous 'Frankfurt Book Fair' held in FRANKFURT AM MAIN annually. The fair hosts more than 6,000 exhibitors and receives over 250,000 visitors. See also: AUSSTELLUNGS- UND MESSE-GMBH DES BÖRSENVEREINS DES DEUTSCHEN BUCHHANDELS

FRANKFURTER RUNDSCHAU

This centre-left daily, founded in 1945, was the first newspaper to receive a licence in the Western zone (1 August 1945, American zone). It is published in FRANKFURT AM MAIN with a circulation of 188,000 and is also distributed in other big cities (ÜBERREGIONALE ZEITUNG). During the 1960s the paper was the only newspaper in which the majority of students had any faith. It remains one of Germany's more liberal dailies and gives the GEWERKSCHAFTEN and DIE GRÜNEN a fair hearing.

FRANKFURTER SCHULE
A group of neo-Marxist sociologists and philosophers centred on the Institut für Sozialforschung at FRANKFURT (JOHANN WOLFGANG GOETHE-UNIVERSITÄT) during the 1960s, which had a considerable influence on the student movement. Major exponents were Max Horkheimer, Theodor W. Adorno, Herbert Marcuse and Jürgen HABERMAS.

FRAUEN
The 1980s and 1990s have seen a number of initiatives intended to encourage the participation of women in the workforce. Systematic *Frauenförderung* and *Frauenquoten* have increased the numbers of women in some fields, though the higher echelons of business, industry and government are still dominated by men. In the universities, women are notoriously underrepresented at the top, where they barely make up six percent of C4 PROFESSOREN. In politics, the participation of women in lower-ranking jobs has increased, and parties are now also endeavouring to give them a higher profile in leading positions. Endeavours to increase equality of opportunity have led to widespread use of gender-neutral designations in job advertisements and elsewhere, e.g. *Beamter/ Beamtin*, *Mitarbeiter/in*, *Angestellte(r)* and *StudentInnen.*

FRAUNHOFER-GESELLSCHAFT ZUR FÖRDERUNG DER ANGEWANDTEN FORSCHUNG e.V. (FhG)
Society for the promotion of applied research which has 46 research institutes and a budget of some 1,000 million marks. The society has around 8,000 employees and is dedicated to providing solutions to scientific and engineering problems for the private and public sector. It is committed to transferring research results to industrial applications as fast as possible and is a non-profit-making organisation. The society's research programme offers industry a service right through to prototype as well as providing other services to industry such as advice on financing research, testing, feasibility studies and training.

FREIBAD
An outdoor swimming pool in a public place, or next to a river or lake. Many local authorities maintain open-air swimming

pools with changing facilities and smaller pools for young children. In summer it is normal for families to spend fine afternoons at the local *Freibad*. See also: HALLENBAD

FREIBERG, TECHNISCHE UNIVERSITÄT BERGAKADEMIE

University in SACHSEN founded in 1765 and teaching some 2,000 students. The Technische Universität Bergakademie Freiberg has faculties of mathematics and computer science, chemistry and physics, geophysics and geotechnology and mining engineering, mechanical engineering, materials science, economics and business studies.

FREIBETRAG

The allowance of an individual's income that is free of income tax and taken into account in the calculation of EINKOMMENSTEUER and other taxes.

FREIBURG, ALBERT-LUDWIGS-UNIVERSITÄT

One of Germany's oldest universities, founded in 1457. The university is in BADEN-WÜRTTEMBERG and teaches some 24,000 students. The Albert-Ludwigs-Universität Freiburg has faculties of theology, law, economics, medicine, philosophy (arts), mathematics, physics, chemistry and pharmacology, biology, geosciences, forestry.

FREIE BERUFE

Professions where the individual is generally self-employed rather than employed. These include doctors, RECHTSANWÄLTE, STEUERBERATER, architects, artists, writers, musicians, etc. These professions work for an HONORAR and have their own BERUFSVERBÄNDE.

FREIE DEMOKRATISCHE PARTEI (FDP)

The FDP was founded in 1948 from a mixture of liberal groupings. Theodor Heuss, first president of the BUNDESREPUBLIK, was first chairman of the FDP. In 1994 the FDP had just under 100,000 members in 16 LANDESVERBÄNDE. The FDP has formed coalition governments with both the SPD and the CDU/CSU and has effectively held the balance of power in post-war politics. The strength of the FDP's hand is shown by the fact that they have generally held the post of AUSSENMINISTER in coalition governments of which they formed a part. The FDP obtained 6.9% of the vote in the 1994 elections and has 47 MANDATE in the BUNDESTAG. Außenminister Klaus KINKEL was *Parteivorsitzender* of the FDP from 1993 to 1995, when he resigned following a series of poor results in LANDTAGSWAHLEN. Wolfgang GERHARDT was appointed as successor.

The FDP espouses liberal values with emphasis on the political and economic freedom of the individual in society. The party's official abbreviation is F.D.P. – emphatically with full stops.

FREIE ERFINDUNG
Any invention other than a DIENSTERFINDUNG. Non-exclusive rights on a *freie Erfindung* made by an ARBEITNEHMER that relates to the business of the ARBEITGEBER have to be offered to the *Arbeitgeber*.

FREIE HANSESTADT
BREMEN and HAMBURG are today independent LÄNDER and represent a form of independence and autonomy once enjoyed by around 100 free trading cities in the Hanseatic League. LÜBECK was an autonomous Freie Hansestadt (*Königin der Hanse*) until 1937 when it was incorporated into SCHLESWIG-HOLSTEIN. ROSTOCK remains proud of its history as a Hansestadt.

FREIE HANSESTADT BREMEN See: *BREMEN, FREIE HANSESTADT (LAND)*

FREIE UND HANSESTADT HAMBURG See: *HAMBURG, FREIE UND HANSESTADT (LAND)*

FREIES MANDAT
A free vote is guaranteed by *Artikel* 38 of the GRUNDGESETZ. BUNDESTAGSABGEORDNETE should vote according to their conscience rather than along party lines or following directions from the voters. See also: FRAKTIONSZWANG

FREIHERR
A title indicating membership of the lower ranks of the aristocracy and now part of the surname. A *Freiherr/Freifrau* is traditionally addressed as *Baron/Baronin*. See also: GRAF

FREIKÖRPERKULTUR (FKK)

A cult of nude bathing in public places started in summer colonies on the beaches of the north coast at the beginning of the century and has spread through the country to parks and lakesides. This form of open expression reached its peak in the early 1980s when passengers in MÜNCHEN trams were shocked by nudists who had ventured out of the Englischer Garten onto public transport. See also: SYLT

FREILICHTMUSEUM

Germany has a large number of open-air museums showing folk traditions. They attempt to give a representative picture of life and work in the past and include typical houses, farm buildings and craft workshops.

FREILICHTTHEATER

Open-air theatre has experienced a revival in Germany during the twentieth century as part of the proliferation of VOLKSFESTE in villages, towns and cities.

FREISTAAT BAYERN See: *BAYERN, FREISTAAT*

FREISTAAT SACHSEN See: *SACHSEN, FREISTAAT*

FREISTAAT THÜRINGEN See: *THÜRINGEN, FREISTAAT*

FREIWILLIGE SELBSTKONTROLLE DER FILMWIRTSCHAFT (FSK)

The film board within the SPITZENORGANISATION DER FILMWIRTSCHAFT E.V. was founded in 1949 and is responsible for classifying all films and videos for public showing in Germany. Committees are independent and are made up of representatives of the state, society (church, youth organisations, etc.) and the film industry. The GRUNDGESETZ prohibits censorship of the film industry by the state but the independent committees of the FSK have the power to place restrictions on the showing of films to youth audiences and on public holidays.

FREIZEIT

Modern Germans have a very acute appreciation of *Freizeit* or leisure, and the older generation bemoans the decline of the ARBEITSMORAL. The concept of *Freizeit* covers anything that is not work including all the usual leisure activities such as cinema, sport and holidays. The reduction of working hours to give workers more leisure time was a major theme in union negotiations with industry in the late 1980s, while distribution of the work available in order to reduce unemployment is the issue of the 1990s.

FREIZEIT REVUE
Magazine established in 1970 and published by BURDA every Thursday with a circulation of 1.2 million and a readership that is roughly one-third men and two-thirds women. It carries features of topical interest and general articles on subjects such as leisure, health, fashion and money.

FREIZÜGIGKEIT
The basic right guaranteed in the GRUNDGESETZ that grants all German citizens the right of WOHNSITZ or AUFENTHALT anywhere on German territory. It allows German citizens free right of passage with their goods, allows them to take up work in their new home and permits them to travel freely in and out of Germany.

FREUDENBERG & CO
Group of companies manufacturing seals, gaskets, fabrics and leatherware, founded in 1921. Company headquarters are in Weinheim (BADEN-WÜRTTEMBERG). Freudenberg has some 25,000 employees.

FRIED. KRUPP AG HOESCH-KRUPP See: *KRUPP AG HOESCH-KRUPP, FRIED.*

FRIEDENSPREIS DES BÖRSENVEREINS DES DEUTSCHEN BUCHHANDELS
A literature prize established in 1950 as the *Friedenspreis des Deutschen Buchhandels* with an award of DM 10,000 provided by 15 publishers. The prize – since 1979 DM 25,000 – is awarded annually to authors or organisations whose writing has contributed to peace, humanity and understanding. Its award to

Annemarie SCHIMMEL in 1995 for her work on Islam caused controversy and she was criticised especially by German writers (e.g. Günter GRASS) for not firmly enough rejecting Islamic fundamentalism and the fatwa against Salman Rushdie. See also: BÖRSEN-VEREIN DES DEUTSCHEN BUCHHANDELS E.V.

FRISTENLÖSUNG See: *SCHWANGERSCHAFTS-ABBRUCH*

FRONLEICHNAM
Corpus Christi is a religious festival on the second Thursday after Whitsun and is a public holiday in mainly Catholic LÄNDER (BADEN-WÜRTTEMBERG, BAYERN, HESSEN, NORDRHEIN-WESTFALEN, RHEINLAND-PFALZ, SAARLAND and Catholic areas in SACHSEN and THÜRINGEN).

FSK See: *FREIWILLIGE SELBSTKONTROLLE DER FILMWIRTSCHAFT*

FUGGEREI
Estate of seventeenth-century houses in AUGSBURG built by the wealthy Fugger family in 1514 for the deserving Catholic poor and arguably the world's oldest social housing project. It is inhabited today by some 300 residents at the same rent as in 1514, though with a supplement payable to the local authorities for modern amenities.

FÜHRERSCHEIN
Driving licences are divided into seven classes depending on the type of vehicle. A driving licence is issued to a driver over the minimum age (18 years for vehicles in class III – private cars) who has passed the theoretical and practical components of the driving test. The theoretical test consists of questions on the highway code, and an official list of all the questions for the current year is published every year. The practical test is taken at an accredited testing centre that also issues driving licences. The theoretical test can be taken a maximum of three times, and if a candidate fails the practical test three times he/she has to undergo a psychological examination. A driver is required by law to carry a driving licence when driving. See also: FAHRSCHULE

FÜHRUNGSZEUGNIS
Certificate of conduct based on the information held at the BUN-DESZENTRALREGISTER (criminal convictions, etc.). It is issued to the individual concerned by the GENERALBUNDESANWALT on receipt of an application.

FUN See: *D2–NETZ*

FUNDI
Member of the more radical, fundamentalist wing of BÜNDNIS 90/DIE GRÜNEN, opposed to compromises designed to ensure power at local level, in the LANDESPARLAMENT or in the BUNDESTAG if these involve watering down key policies. See also: REALO

FÜNFPROZENTKLAUSEL
The five-percent clause is intended to avoid the proliferation of political parties that had contributed to the downfall of the WEIMARER REPUBLIK. This clause specifies that only those parties which have obtained at least five percent of the votes cast in a BUNDESTAGSWAHL can take up seats in the BUNDESTAG unless a party obtains at least three DIREKTMANDATE through ERSTSTIMMEN in which case the *Fünfprozentklausel* does not apply and the party is allocated MANDATE in accordance with the number of ZWEITSTIMMEN cast. A similar rule applies in most LAND-TAGSWAHLEN. See also: ÜBERHANGMANDAT

FUNK UHR
Weekly radio and TV guide published by the SPRINGER VERLAG in HAMBURG. It was established in 1967 and has a circulation of 1.5 million. It offers a programme guide for TV and radio together with articles on health, travel and general trends.

FUNKKOLLEG
A series of radio lectures that are accompanied by study material and study groups, and are followed by an examination.

FWU See: *INSTITUT FÜR FILM UND BILD IN WISSENSCHAFT UND UNTERRICHT*

GADAMER, HANS-GEORG (1900–   )

Philosopher whose pioneering system of criticism and philosophical hermeneutics has been influential in twentieth-century philosophy, aesthetics and theology. He was a pupil of Martin Heidegger's and a professor at LEIPZIG (UNIVERSITÄT) in 1939–1947, professor at FRANKFURT AM MAIN (JOHANN WOLFGANG GOETHE-UNIVERSITÄT) in 1947–1949 and then professor at HEIDELBERG (RUPRECHT-KARLS-UNIVERSITÄT) in 1949–1968. Gadamer formulated his statement on hermeneutic theory, partly derived from concepts of Wilhelm Dilthey, in his major work *Wahrheit und Methode. Grundzüge einer philosophischen Hermeneutik* (1960), where he elucidates the possibility of finding truth by means that go beyond the traditional analytical tools. His other works include *Hegels Dialektik. Fünf hermeneutische Studien* (1971), *Vernunft im Zeitalter der Wissenschaft* (1976) and *Das Erbe Europas* (1989).

GASTARBEITER

Foreign worker from countries such as Italy, Turkey, the former Yugoslavia or Greece who has come to work in Germany on a temporary basis. *Gastarbeiter* may hold papers from another country or they may be stateless. They have no right to vote in Germany unless they apply for German citizenship; in some LÄNDER *Gastarbeiter* may vote in local elections. The immigrant workers have by and large not been well-integrated into German society. Financial incentives for *Gastarbeiter* to return to their country of origin have not resolved this problem, especially as many *Gastarbeiter* who came in the 1960s and early 1970s now have grown-up children who have been educated in Germany. See also: AUSLÄNDER

GASTEIG
Cultural, educational and conference complex in MÜNCHEN completed in 1985 with a lending library, concert hall, the Richard-Strauss-Konservatorium and a VOLKSHOCHSCHULE.

GASTHÖRER
Visiting student at a HOCHSCHULE who pays a fee for the privilege of sitting in on lectures or SEMINARE. The *Gasthörer* is not permitted to register for a STUDIENGANG or ABSCHLUSSPRÜFUNG.

GAUCK-BEHÖRDE
The Bundesbeauftragter für die Unterlagen des Staatssicherheitsdienstes der ehemaligen Deutschen Demokratischen Republik ('Gauck-Behörde') is Joachim Gauck, a leading clerical opponent of the Communist regime in the DDR. The authority has some 180 km. of files, 88 million documents on microfilm and some 5 million index cards. All citizens of the BRD have a right to file a request as to whether the STAATSSICHERHEITSDIENST held a file on them. The files may also be accessed in the public interest and for scholarly purposes. See also: STASI-AKTEN

GdED See: *GEWERKSCHAFT DER EISENBAHNER DEUTSCHLANDS*

GdP See: *GEWERKSCHAFT DER POLIZEI*

GEBIRGSDIVISION
The BUNDESWEHR has one mountain division consisting of troops trained in mountain warfare.

GEBÜHRENORDNUNG
Scale of charges laid down for lawyers, doctors, dentists and other professions.

GEHALT
The salary earned by an ANGESTELLTER that is paid monthly by the ARBEITGEBER. The terms *Gehalt* and LOHN have officially been subsumed under the umbrella term ENTGELT. See also: BESOLDUNG

GEHE AG
Pharmaceuticals group founded in 1903. Company headquarters are in STUTTGART. Gehe has some 11,800 employees.

GEISSENDÖRFER, HANS WILHELM (1941–)

Film director who created Germany's first and longest-running soap LINDENSTRASSE (from 1985). His other works include successful horror film *Joachim* (1969), crime series *Lobster* (1976), a controversial film of Thomas Mann's novel *Der Zauberberg* (1981), *Bumerang, Bumerang* (1989) and *Justiz* (1993).

GELERNTER ARBEITER See: *FACHARBEITER*

GELSENKIRCHEN

Gelsenkirchen is an industrial city situated on the Rhein-Herne-Kanal and the Emscher river in NORDRHEIN-WESTFALEN (dialling code 02 09, postal area code 45…). The city received a charter only in 1875. It is home to the Ruhr Zoo, and there is an inland port on the Rhein-Herne-Kanal.

The city has a population of some 295,000 with a total student population of around 2,000 (2 HOCHSCHULEN) and about 14% foreigners (60% Turkish). The SPD has been running the city since 1946. Coalmining turned a tiny nineteenth-century village into a flourishing industrial centre based on mining and heavy industry. Today's industries include coalmining, glass, petrochemicals, power engineering and water, and the development of small and medium-sized companies is being promoted. Important companies include VEBA, Flachglas and RUHRKOHLE.

GEMEINDE

The smallest unit of local government with the right to administer local affairs within the framework of the legislation laid down in the GEMEINDEVERFASSUNGSRECHT. See also: KOMMUNAL

GEMEINDEDIREKTOR

The most senior BEAMTER in a GEMEINDE in NORDRHEIN-WESTFALEN and NIEDERSACHSEN, responsible for administration and executive duties. The equivalent of the HAUPTVERWALTUNGSBEAMTER in other LÄNDER.

GEMEINDEGETRÄNKESTEUER See: *GETRÄNKE-STEUER*

GEMEINDEHOHEIT

The powers given to the GEMEINDE to perform all local functions

unless otherwise prescribed by law. See also: GEMEINDEVERFAS-
SUNGSRECHT

GEMEINDEORDNUNG
The local-government law enacted by each LAND prescribing the
organisation and powers of the GEMEINDE in that Land. This law
is also known as the *Amtsordnung, Kreisordnung* and *Landkreis-
ordnung*, depending on the Land.

GEMEINDERAT
The local council in the GEMEINDE elected in local elections.
The chairperson of the council is the BÜRGERMEISTER. The
Gemeinderat decides all important issues in the local community
and is responsible for drawing up a budget and for passing local
by-laws. The Gemeinderat is also referred to as STADTRAT in
towns. See also: GEMEINDERATSMITGLIED; STADTRAT

GEMEINDERATSMITGLIED
An elected member of the GEMEINDEVERTRETUNG, also known as a
Gemeindevertreter, GEMEINDERAT or Ratsherr depending on the
specific LAND.

GEMEINDESTEUERN
The taxes used to finance local government and from which the
GEMEINDEN derive their revenue. The most important *Gemeinde-
steuern* are GEWERBESTEUER, GRUNDSTEUER, VERGNÜGUNGSSTEUER,
GETRÄNKESTEUER and SCHANKERLAUBNISSTEUER.

GEMEINDEVERBAND
A term referring to local-government units that are composed of
a number of administrative units on a lower tier. See: AMT; KREIS;
SAMTGEMEINDE

GEMEINDEVERFASSUNGSRECHT
The legislation laying down the constitutional basis for the
GEMEINDEN. The body of law relating to the constitutional status
of local authorities is enshrined in the GRUNDGESETZ, the constitutions of the LÄNDER, and in the GEMEINDEORDNUNGEN and *Land-
kreisordnungen.* The Gemeindeverfassungsrecht prescribes that
all local communities should have a local authority or council
that is elected by secret ballot. This local authority is referred to

in general terms as the GEMEINDEVERTRETUNG. The *Gemeindevertretung* is also known as the GEMEINDERAT, the STADTRAT, the RAT DER STADT, and the STADTVERORDNETENVERSAMMLUNG. The *Gesetz über die Selbstverwaltung der Gemeinden und Landkreise* was passed in 1990, regulating the formation and government of the Gemeinde and KREIS in the NEUE BUNDESLÄNDER.

There are four forms of local constitution depending on the part of the country in which the local authority is located: MAGISTRATSVERFASSUNG, BÜRGERMEISTERVERFASSUNG, SÜDDEUTSCHE RATSVERFASSUNG, NORDDEUTSCHE RATSVERFASSUNG. The complex and varied nature of German local authorities is due to the fact that Germany was divided into four zones at the end of the Second World War, and each of the three Western Allied powers set up local authorities based on their own systems of local government.

GEMEINDEVERTRETER See: *GEMEINDERATSMITGLIED*

GEMEINDEVERTRETUNG
The body elected to serve local communities in accordance with the GEMEINDEVERFASSUNGSRECHT, known as the GEMEINDERAT, STADTRAT, RAT DER STADT or STADTVERORDNETENVERSAMMLUNG.

GEMEINDEVORSTAND
A term used for the HAUPTVERWALTUNGSBEAMTER or the MAGISTRAT.

GEMEINSCHAFTSTEUERN
The taxes that the GRUNDGESETZ allocates jointly to the BUND and LÄNDER. These taxes are EINKOMMENSTEUER, KÖRPERSCHAFTSTEUER, UMSATZSTEUER.

GENERALBUNDESANWALT
The federal public prosecutor who is head of the STAATSANWALTSCHAFT at the BUNDESGERICHTSHOF. In certain cases the Generalbundesanwalt may appear before an OBERLANDESGERICHT.

GENERALINSPEKTEUR DER BUNDESWEHR
The commander-in-chief of the BUNDESWEHR and the highest military position in the German armed forces. The General-

inspekteur is directly responsible to the BUNDESMINISTER DER VERTEIDIGUNG and advises the ministry and government on defence matters. See also: BAGGER, HARTMUT

GENERALINTENDANT
Director of a theatre or theatres usually presenting more than one genre (opera, ballet, drama).

GENERALSEKRETÄR
The top executive position in political parties and organisations. In the DDR power was effectively in the hands of the *Generalsekretär des Zentralkomitees* of the SED.

GENERALSTAB
The general staff of the military machine comprising specially trained officers who provide support for troop commanders in the field and plan strategy, tactics, logistics, etc.

GENSCHER, HANS-DIETRICH (1927–   )
Lawyer and FDP politician who moved to the BRD from the DDR in 1952. He has been a member of the BUNDESTAG since 1965, was deputy chairman of the FDP in 1968–1974 and party chairman in 1974–1985. Genscher was BUNDESMINISTER DES INNERN in 1969–1974 and AUSSENMINISTER and VIZEKANZLER from 1974 until his resignation on grounds of ill health in 1992. He played a central role in tilting the balance of power between the SPD and CDU/CSU in 1982 and ushering in the enduring coalition between the FDP and CDU/CSU. When Mikhail Gorbachev came to power in the Soviet Union, Genscher recognised that the tide of history had turned, opening up new opportunities for détente. His style as Außenminister was characterised by extensive travel throughout the world, and at home he played a crucial role in bringing about reunification in the ZWEI-PLUS-VIER-VERHANDLUN-GEN and cementing Germany's links within Europe.

GEO
Up-market monthly magazine on the world about us aimed at a young, educated readership with careers in management and the

professions. It is published by GRUNER + JAHR and has a circulation of 530,000.

GEORG-BÜCHNER-PREIS

A literature prize first awarded in 1923 by the *Volksstaat Hessen* in memory of author Georg Büchner (1813–1837) and reinstated in 1945 for authors who had originated from HESSEN. Since 1951 it has been awarded annually by the DEUTSCHE AKADEMIE FÜR SPRACHE UND DICHTUNG to authors writing in the German language who have made a significant contribution to contemporary German culture. This award is the most important literary award in Germany and is accompanied by a cash sum of DM 60,000. Authors awarded the prize include Hans Magnus ENZENSBERGER (1963), Günter GRASS (1965), Christa WOLF (1980), Botho STRAUSS (1989), Wolf BIERMANN (1991), Peter RÜHMKORF (1993) and Sarah KIRSCH (1996).

GEORGE, GÖTZ (1938–   )

Actor who won acclaim as Kommissar Schimanski in the TV series Tatort in 1981–1991. Films include *Der Bruch* (1988), *Blauäugig* (1989) and *Schtonk* (1991) and in 1995 he was awarded the prize for the best actor at the 52nd Venice Biennale for his role as 1920s mass murderer Fritz Haarmann in the film *Der Totmacher* (1995).

GEPRÜFTE SICHERHEIT See: *GS-ZEICHEN*

GERHARDT, WOLFGANG (1943–   )

FDP politician and member of the LANDTAG in HESSEN since 1978. Appointed *Bundesvorsitzender* of the FDP in 1995.

GERICHTSBERICHTERSTATTUNG

Media coverage by the press, radio and television of events inside the courtroom. Live coverage is not permitted inside the courts, and public information on trials is provided by journalists' reports.

GERICHTSBEZIRK

An area for which a particular court has jurisdiction.

GERICHTSFERIEN

The court recess during the summer between 15 July and 15

September. The EINIGUNGSVERTRAG excludes the NEUE BUNDESLÄN-DER from this recess.

GERMANISCHES NATIONALMUSEUM
Museum in NÜRNBERG founded in 1852 housing a collection of Germanic art and culture from prehistoric times to the present day, including prehistoric artefacts, religious and folk art, sculpture and carvings (in particular by Veit Stoß and Tilman Riemenschneider), German Renaissance painting, arms and musical instruments.

GERMANISTIK
The academic discipline of German language and literature.

GESAMTHOCHSCHULEN
Institutions of tertiary education established in some LÄNDER that integrate the functions of HOCHSCHULEN in the traditional mould such as UNIVERSITÄT, PÄDAGOGISCHE HOCHSCHULE and FACHHOCH-SCHULE to form a single administrative and teaching unit, although in some cases the institutions within the *Gesamthochschule* retain a degree of autonomy. This type of university resulted from the university reforms in the 1960s and allows the institutions to offer students a choice of modular courses within the same faculty.

GESAMTSCHULE
A comprehensive school at secondary level with mixed-ability teaching, which started to be introduced in the 1970s. The *integrierte Gesamtschule* replaces the traditional secondary schools of HAUPTSCHULE, REALSCHULE and GYMNASIUM while the *kooperative Gesamtschule* simply merges these schools to allow sharing of resources and premises. *Gesamtschulen* have meanwhile become well established in a number of LÄNDER and are intended to foster the child's individual abilities.

GESCHÄFTSFÜHRER
Managing director of a GMBH. Also used for the administrative head of a VEREIN. A Parlamentarischer Geschäftsführer is responsible for organisation and tactics within a FRAKTION.

GESCHÄFTSORDNUNG

The rules of procedure laid down to assist the decision-making process and internal structure in any official organisation, in BEHÖRDEN, the courts and in the BUNDESTAG, BUNDESREGIERUNG and BUNDESRAT. The *Geschäftsordnung* of the Bundestag lays down the procedures for holding elections, the formation of a FRAKTION and of committees, the obligations and duties of the ABGEORD-NETE, and the voting procedures.

GESELLE

Skilled worker in a registered vocation (AUSBILDUNGSBERUF) who has completed a vocational training in the German apprentice-ship system but not yet taken the MEISTERPRÜFUNG.

GESELLENZEIT

The time during which a skilled worker who has completed voca-tional training works as a GESELLE before taking the MEISTERPRÜ-FUNG and obtaining the MEISTERBRIEF.

GESELLSCHAFT

The collective term for society and also the term for a company (GMBH, AG) or partnership (PERSONENGESELLSCHAFT).

GESELLSCHAFT MIT BESCHRÄNKTER HAFTUNG (GmbH)

Private company with limited liability not listed on the open stock exchange. The GmbH is headed by one or more GESCHÄFTS-FÜHRER.

GESELLSCHAFTER

Partner in a PERSONENGESELLSCHAFT or a shareholder in a GMBH or AG.

GESELLSCHAFTSRECHT

The body of law regulating the organisation and activities of partnerships and companies. See also: PERSONENGESELLSCHAFT; KAPITALGESELLSCHAFT

GESETZ- UND VERORDNUNGSBLATT

The official gazette of individual LÄNDER containing the *Gesetze* and regulations specific to each Land.

GESETZLICHE KRANKENVERSICHERUNG See:
KRANKENVERSICHERUNG

GESUNDHEITSAMT
The health department in every KREIS and KREISFREIE STADT that is responsible for carrying out the medical functions of the *Gesundheitspolizei* and for providing advice on health and safety, health care in schools, and advice to mothers on child care.

GETRÄNKESTEUER
A consumer tax levied by the GEMEINDEN on drinks (apart from beer, milk, milk shakes and pure fruit juices) that are served and consumed on licensed premises.

GEW See: *GEWERKSCHAFT ERZIEHUNG UND WISSENSCHAFT*

GEWALTENTRENNUNG
Gewaltentrennung or *Gewaltenteilung* denotes the separation of the powers of the state into the executive (BUNDESREGIERUNG), the legislature (BUNDESTAG) and the judiciary (*Gerichte*). Essentially the same principle operates at the level of the LAND and to some extent at local level (KREIS, GEMEINDE).

GEWERBE
A trade or business as defined in the GEWERBEORDNUNG. It is any independent activity carried on for profit, but excludes the extraction and exploitation of raw materials and the creative and academic professions.

GEWERBEORDNUNG (GewO)
The legal code specifying the conditions for a GEWERBE and regulating its activity.

GEWERBESTEUER
The most important tax for the GEMEINDEN. It is a tax that is calculated by the FINANZAMT based on the capital and profits of a business. Since the FINANZREFORMGESETZ in 1969, part of this tax has to be paid to the LAND and the BUND, and the Gemeinden

receive a proportion of the revenue from EINKOMMENSTEUER in return.

GEWERKSCHAFT

Approximately 30% to 35% of the German workforce are organised in unions with a trend towards lower levels of membership. The main trade-union organisation is the DEUTSCHER GEWERKSCHAFTSBUND with 13 trade unions. Trade-union organisations not affiliated to the Deutscher Gewerkschaftsbund include the DEUTSCHE ANGESTELLTEN-GEWERKSCHAFT, DEUTSCHER BEAMTEN-BUND and CHRISTLICHER GEWERKSCHAFTSBUND DEUTSCHLANDS.

Individual unions are responsible for negotiating centralised collective agreements (TARIFVERTRÄGE) with the employers or ARBEIT-GEBERVERBÄNDE. These agreements are legally binding, and strikes are illegal while an agreement is in force or negotiations are under way. Any strike requires a 75% mandate from a secret ballot of the membership. BEAMTE (civil servants) are not allowed to strike.

The power of German unions derives in part from the absence of demarcation, and the trade-union movement was built up on the principle of one union for each industry, with the closed shop and politically motivated strikes being illegal. Workers' conditions in many industries were such that by the end of the 1980s there was little left to fight for; the big issue of the 1980s was a shorter working week. The big issues of the 1990s are parity of workers in east Germany with those in the west, unemployment, and a better distribution of the work available (more part-time work, job-sharing, reduction of overtime). Union membership has been falling steadily during the 1990s and union power has diminished with the decline of traditional industries and the trend towards a post-industrial economy.

GEWERKSCHAFT DER EISENBAHNER DEUTSCHLANDS (GdED)

Trade union with some 400,000 members representing workers in the railway industry.

GEWERKSCHAFT DER POLIZEI (GdP)

Trade union with some 200,000 members representing the police.

GEWERKSCHAFT ERZIEHUNG UND WISSENSCHAFT (GEW)

Trade union with some 300,000 members representing workers in education and science.

GEWERKSCHAFT HANDEL, BANKEN UND VERSICHERUNGEN (HBV)

Trade union with some 500,000 members representing workers in commerce, banking and insurance.

GEWERKSCHAFT HOLZ UND KUNSTSTOFF (GHK)

Trade union with some 160,000 members representing workers in the wood and plastics industries.

GEWERKSCHAFT LEDER See: *INDUSTRIEGEWERK-SCHAFT CHEMIE – BERGBAU – ENERGIE*

GEWERKSCHAFT NAHRUNG – GENUSS – GASTSTÄTTEN (NGG)

Trade union with some 300,000 members representing workers in the food, drink, tobacco and catering industries.

GEWERKSCHAFT ÖFFENTLICHE DIENSTE, TRANSPORT UND VERKEHR (ÖTV)

Trade union with some 1.8 million members representing workers in the public services and transport industry.

GEWERKSCHAFT TEXTIL – BEKLEIDUNG (GTB)

Trade union with some 200,000 members representing workers in the textile and clothing industries.

GewO See: *GEWERBEORDNUNG*

GG See: *GRUNDGESETZ*

GHK See: *GEWERKSCHAFT HOLZ UND KUNSTSTOFF*

GIESSEN, JUSTUS-LIEBIG-UNIVERSITÄT

University in HESSEN founded in 1607 and teaching some 22,000 students. The Justus-Liebig-Universität Gießen has departments of law, economics, social sciences, education, art and music and sport, psychology, religion, history, German, English, Mediterranean and East European studies, mathematics, physics, chemistry, biology, geology and geography, agriculture, veterinary medicine, nutrition, medicine.

GIROZENTRALEN See: *LANDESBANKEN*

GLOBO
Up-market magazine for regular travellers published monthly by Ringier Verlag in MÜNCHEN. It has a circulation of 99,000 and enjoys an affluent readership with the balance tilted towards a male audience.

GLÜCKS-REVUE
Weekly compendium of games, puzzles, entertainment and advice with a circulation of 433,000. It was established in 1986 and also carries features on young personalities, and hints on health, beauty and cooking.

GmbH See: *GESELLSCHAFT MIT BESCHRÄNKTER HAFTUNG*

GmbH & Co KG
A KOMMANDITGESELLSCHAFT in which the partner with unlimited personal liability is in fact a limited-liability company (GMBH). The shareholders of the GmbH are generally the limited-liability partners (*Kommanditisten*). In certain circumstances this confers tax advantages over a straight GmbH.

GOETHE-INSTITUT
A network of 16 institutes in Germany and over 150 institutes in 78 countries abroad, with the task of fostering the German language and culture. The organisation was founded in 1951 and is based in MÜNCHEN. The institutes have a library with German books, newspapers, etc., hold classes teaching the German language, organise seminars for teachers and promote German culture with film showings, exhibitions and a variety of other events.

GOETHE-NATIONALMUSEUM
The Goethehaus in Weimar (THÜRINGEN) where Johann Wolfgang von Goethe (born 1749) lived from 1782 until his death in 1832 has been preserved as Goethe knew it, complete with *Arbeitszimmer* and *Sterbezimmer*. The Goethe National-

museum is next to the *Wohnhaus* and houses a collection of manuscripts and memorabilia. The museum forms part of the STIFTUNG WEIMARER KLASSIK.

GONG

One of Germany's older TV and radio guides, published weekly since 1948 with a circulation of 803,000.

GORLEBEN

A GEMEINDE in NIEDERSACHSEN which hit the headlines when violent protests and action by BÜRGERINITIATIVEN halted plans for a nuclear reprocessing plant in 1979, although a nuclear storage site has been in operation since 1983. Gorleben came to prominence again in May 1996 when violent protests erupted as the first train of plutonium and nuclear waste to cross European borders, under French legislation requiring the return of waste to the country of origin, came into Germany from France on its way to storage at Gorleben. More than 100 trainloads of nuclear waste are destined for this storage facility over the coming ten years in the face of strong opposition from all walks of life in the local population.

GOSLAR

The ALTSTADT of this erstwhile imperial city in NIEDERSACHSEN and the historic Rammelsberg silver mines are a UNESCO world heritage site.

GÖTTINGEN, GEORG-AUGUST-UNIVERSITÄT

One of Germany's most prestigious old universities, founded in 1737. The university is in NIEDERSACHSEN and teaches some 30,000 students. The Georg-August-Universität Göttingen built up a strong reputation in mathematics and science and has faculties of theology, law, medicine, history and philology, mathematics, physics, chemistry, geology, biology, forestry, agriculture, economics, social sciences, education.

GOTTSCHALK, THOMAS (1950–   )

Moderator and TV entertainer who first made his mark with radio series *Pop nach acht* and went on to become a moderator with ZDF show *Na sowas* (1982–1987). He hosts the regular

Saturday-evening star show WETTEN, DASS. . .? and started the first German midnight show on RTL.

GRADUIERTENSTUDIUM
An AUFBAUSTUDIUM or further course of study taken after the first degree.

GRAF
The aristocratic title of count (female form *Gräfin*) which was abolished in 1919 but is still used as part of a person's name. See also: FREIHERR

GRAF, STEFANIE (STEFFI) (1969–   )
Germany's star female tennis player who triumphed at the Wimbledon ladies' championships in 1988–1989, 1991–1993 and 1995. She was seeded no. 1 in 1987–1991 and has been no. 1 since 1993. She won the Grand Slam and a gold medal at the Seoul Olympic Games in 1988. In the mid-1990s she was beset by difficulties between her father and the German tax authorities.

GRASS, GÜNTER (1927–   )
Political author and chronicler of post-war Germany who has written novels, poems and plays while also working as a sculptor and graphic artist. The work of the most prominent author of the second post-war generation was moulded by his childhood in petit bourgeois society in Danzig and his experiences of the totalitarian state under National Socialism. He was a member of GRUPPE 47 and has been an active advocate of social democracy and a peace campaigner. He studied sculpture and graphic arts before turning to writing and establishing an international reputation with *Die Blechtrommel* (1959), part I of the 'Danziger Trilogie', filmed in 1979 by Volker SCHLÖNDORFF. Other novels include *Katz und Maus* (1961) and *Hundejahre* (1963) – parts II and III of the 'Danziger Trilogie' –, *Der Butt* (1977) and *Die Rättin* (1986). During the 1980s he also turned to the graphic arts and produced two volumes of drawings and writings entitled *Zeichnen und schreiben* (1982–1984) and a travel diary with drawings, *Zunge zeigen* (1988). Grass' complex critique of reunification *Ein weites Feld* (1995) gained considerable publicity

when it was panned in a polemical SPIEGEL review by Marcel REICH-RANICKI.

GRAUE PANTHER See: *SENIOREN-SCHUTZ-BUND „GRAUE PANTHER" e.V.*

GRAUEN, DIE
A political party with just over 6,000 members, formed in 1989 to promote the interests of the older members of society. See also: SENIOREN-SCHUTZ-BUND „GRAUE PANTHER"

GREIFSWALD, ERNST-MORITZ-ARNDT-UNIVERSITÄT
University in MECKLENBURG-VORPOMMERN founded in 1456 and teaching some 5,000 students. The Ernst-Moritz-Arndt-Universität Greifswald has faculties of Protestant theology, law and economics, medicine, philosophy (arts), mathematics and natural sciences.

GRENZPOLIZEI, BAYERISCHE
The border police force in BAYERN, which is the only LAND with its own border police.

GRIMM See: *DEUTSCHES WÖRTERBUCH*

GROSSE KOALITION
Grand coalition between the two biggest political groupings in the BRD, the CDU/CSU and the SPD. A *große Koalition* was formed in 1966–1969 under Kurt Georg Kiesinger (CDU) to solve the economic problems at that time but the lack of effective parliamentary opposition led to the formation of the AUSSERPARLAMENTARISCHE OPPOSITION. A *große Koalition* between the CDU and SPD under Erwin TEUFEL ran BADEN-WÜRTTEMBERG from 1992–1996 and a CDU/SPD coalition under Eberhard DIEPGEN has run BERLIN since 1991.

GROSSGEMEINDE
A large GEMEINDE that covers a geographical area previously administered by a number of Gemeinden of smaller size.

GRUNDAUSBILDUNG
The three months of basic training for all new recruits to the BUNDESWEHR at the commencement of their WEHRDIENST. Soldiers

are taught self-defence and are generally prepared for their role in the military.

GRUNDBUCH

The register of land maintained by the GRUNDBUCHAMT. All transactions involving the transfer of ownership of land are entered in this register, which is open to public inspection by any individual with a justification. Legal ownership of title is only transferred once the transfer has been entered in the register. When the DDR ceased to exist, many claims for restitution of land and property were made by former owners (in 1995 there were over 1 million such claims outstanding). The *Grundbuch* for the local district was an important proof of ownership in these cases.

GRUNDBUCHAMT

A department within the AMTSGERICHT that is responsible for maintaining the GRUNDBUCH.

GRUNDERWERBSSTEUER

A tax that is levied on the transfer of ownership of land within Germany. The tax rate is 2% of the sale price.

GRUNDERWERBSSTEUERVERGÜNSTIGUNGEN

Tax exemptions from the GRUNDERWERBSSTEUER for the transfer of land between relatives or when the purchase is in the public interest.

GRUNDGESETZ (GG)

The written constitution of the BRD known as the Basic Law. The Grundgesetz was proclaimed on 23 May 1949; in the SAARLAND it became effective on 1 January 1957 after the population had voted to become part of the BRD. It was also the instrument by which the DDR was incorporated into the BRD on 3 October 1990.

The Grundgesetz lays down the legal framework for the state, the relationship between the BUND and the LÄNDER, and the rights of the citizens. The title of Grundgesetz was intended to highlight the provisional nature of the BRD and allowed for an eventual reunification of the divided Germany. This vision proved correct and certain parts of the Grundgesetz were amended when reunification rendered them superfluous. The Grundgesetz takes precedence over all other laws and can only be amended by passing a law which requires a majority of two-thirds of the MANDATE in the BUNDESTAG and two-thirds of the votes in the BUNDESRAT. The deployment of German troops abroad is prohibited except in cases expressly permitted by the Grundgesetz. This was an area of contention with the deployment of troops in Somalia and Bosnia, given the increasing pressure on Germany to play an active role in the new world order. In 1994, the BUNDESVERFASSUNGSGERICHT laid down that any deployments of troops or peace missions abroad have to be approved by the Bundestag. See also: VERFASSUNG

GRUNDIG AG
Hi-fi company founded in 1948. Company headquarters are in Fürth (BAYERN) and Grundig has some 13,000 employees.

GRUNDKURS
Compulsory course with about three hours teaching a week, taken by pupils at the GYMNASIUM. During the last two years of study, when preparing for their ABITUR, pupils have to take 22 *Grundkurse* in a range of core subjects (*Grundkursfächer*) including, for example, German, mathematics, a foreign language. See also: LEISTUNGSKURS

GRUNDRECHTE
The basic rights of German citizens guaranteed in the GRUNDGESETZ.

GRUNDSCHULE
Education in Germany normally starts after a child's sixth birthday (SCHULREIFE), with some 10% starting at seven. Pupils then attend the *Grundschule* for the next four years (six years in BERLIN).

GRUNDSTEUER
A tax on buildings and land that is collected annually and is an important source of revenue for the GEMEINDEN. See also: GEWERBESTEUER

GRUNDSTUDIUM
A university course consists of the *Grundstudium* (minimum of four SEMESTER) and the HAUPTSTUDIUM. The *Grundstudium*

concentrates on a range of compulsory subjects and is completed with the ZWISCHENPRÜFUNG or *Diplomvorprüfung* (VORDIPLOM).

GRÜNE See: *BÜNDNIS 90/DIE GRÜNEN; DIE GRÜNEN*

GRÜNE WOCHE BERLIN, INTERNATIONALE
'International Green Week Berlin' – a trade fair for food, drink, agriculture, forestry, fisheries, etc. held in BERLIN every three years with some half a million visitors.

GRUNER + JAHR AG
Printing and publishing company with a range of magazines and newspapers including Germany's biggest-selling general-interest magazine STERN. Media group BERTELSMANN has a majority share-holding and company headquarters are in HAMBURG. Gruner + Jahr has some 12,000 employees.

GRÜNER PUNKT
A green dot displayed on packaging indicating that it is recyclable within the DUALES SYSTEM DEUTSCHLAND. Manufacturers buy the right to designate packaging with the green dot by paying a licence fee to Duales System Deutschland GmbH. The manufacturers are then released from their legal obligation to collect the packaging. See also: VERPACKUNGSVERORDNUNG; WERT-STOFFANNAHMESTELLE

GRUPPE See: *FRAKTION*

GRUPPE 47
A loose-knit group of authors formed in 1947 by the left-wing authors Hans Werner Richter and Alfred Andersch in response to the banning of the journal *Der Ruf* by the American military authorities. Although most of the members were on the left, the group did not pursue a political agenda. They criticised both the material values of West Germany and the 'real socialism' pursued by the Communist DDR. Günter GRASS, Hans Magnus ENZENSBERGER and Heinrich Böll were all connected with the group as were other influential authors. The group believed that authors should play a prominent role in creating a new German democracy. The last major conference held by the group was in 1967.

GS-ZEICHEN
The GS seal of approval stands for *geprüfte Sicherheit* or 'safety tested'. The right to use the seal is granted to manufacturers of electrical equipment by a *Prüfstelle* of the VERBAND DEUTSCHER ELEKTROTECHNIKER E.V.

GTB See: *GEWERKSCHAFT TEXTIL – BEKLEIDUNG*

GUTENBERG-MUSEUM
Billed as the world museum of typography, the Gutenberg-Museum in MAINZ is a tribute to the inventions of Johannes Gutenberg that paved the way for the development of moveable typefaces and the mass-production of books. The museum holds a copy of the *42–zeilige Gutenberg-Bibel* (1452–1455), a recreation of Gutenberg's printing workshop and a collection of printing machines.

GYMNASIALE OBERSTUFE
The last three years at the GYMNASIUM that constitute the *Sekundarstufe II.*

GYMNASIUM
Secondary school that prepares students for the ABITUR. Pupils generally go to a *Gymnasium* after four years (six in BERLIN) at the GRUNDSCHULE (*Primarstufe*) and study at the *Gymnasium* for nine years until the age of 19 or 20. The *Gymnasium* covers the *Sekundarstufe I* and *Sekundarstufe II.* The GYMNASIALE OBERSTUFE (class 11 to 13) spans the last three years at school with the final two years (classes 12 and 13) forming the basis for the coursework assessment included in the *Abitur* result.

GYSI, GREGOR (1948–   )
Lawyer and PDS politician. He was chairman of the PDS in 1989–1993, has been a member of the BUNDESTAG since 1990 and is chairman of the PDS *Bundestagsgruppe.* He went on a week's hunger strike in December 1994 to persuade the courts to take tax debts from funds belonging to the old SED rather than those of the PDS.

HAB See: *HOMÖOPATHISCHES ARZNEIBUCH*

HABERMAS, JÜRGEN (1929–)
Philosopher and sociologist who with Theodor W. Adorno and Max Horkheimer was a leading proponent of '*kritische Theorie*' and a member of the FRANKFURTER SCHULE. He was a professor in FRANKFURT (JOHANN WOLFGANG GOETHE-UNIVERSITÄT) in 1964–1971 and from 1983, and was director at the Max-Planck-Institut für Sozialwissenschaft in MÜNCHEN in 1971–1980. His main work is *Theorie des kommunikativen Handelns* (1981) in which he formulates the theory that the normative principles of society are rooted in language. His other publications include *Theorie und Praxis* (1963), *Technik und Wissenschaft als Ideologie* (1968), *Die neue Unübersichtlichkeit* (1985), *Der philosophische Diskurs der Moderne* (1985) and *Wenn ich an Deutschland denke* (1990). Habermas has consistently criticised society in the BRD and spoke in favour of reforming the education system in the 1950s. He triggered the HISTORIKERSTREIT by an attack on revisionist rewriting of history in 1986, and more recently he criticised German policy in recognising Croatia during the war in the Balkans.

HABILITAND
A candidate for HABILITATION.

HABILITATION
The procedure for gaining the right to teach at a HOCHSCHULE. Following successful completion of a doctoral thesis (PROMOTION), candidates submit a HABILITATIONSSCHRIFT on a different subject and have to give a lecture, followed by a discussion. The successful candidate is then entitled to teach as a PRIVATDOZENT and gives an inaugural lecture in public.

HABILITATIONSSCHRIFT
The thesis submitted for HABILITATION.

HACKETHAL, JULIUS (1921–   )
Orthopaedic surgeon who was appointed professor at ERLANGEN-NÜRNBERG (FRIEDRICH-ALEXANDER-UNIVERSITÄT) in 1962. Hackethal has been a controversial critic of the medical establishment and has acted as an expert witness in trials involving medical negligence. He has drawn attention to high mortality rates following routine operations and inefficient cancer prevention, and has called for reform of the health-care system. His publications include *Auf Messers Schneide. Kunst und Fehler der Chirurgie* (1976), *Keine Angst vor Krebs* (1978), *Krankenhaus. Gegen ein patientenfeindliches Gesundheitswesen* (1978) and *Humanes Sterben. Mitleidstöten als Patientenrecht und Arztpflicht* (1988).

HACKS, PETER (1928–   )
Playwright in the tradition of Bertolt Brecht, whose plays frequently take up historical subjects or adapt works by earlier authors. He moved from the BRD to the DDR in 1955 for political reasons and there supported Communist policies such as the building of the BERLINER MAUER and the expulsion of Wolf BIERMANN, while criticising conditions in the DDR. His works include, *Die Schlacht bei Lobositz* (1958), *Amphitryon* (1968), *Das Jahrmarktfest zu Plundersweilern* (1973), *Pandora* (1981), *Fredegunde* (1989) and *Der Geldgott* (1993). Hacks has also written children's books, radio and TV plays, poetry and essays.

HAGEN
Hagen is situated in NORDRHEIN-WESTFALEN on the eastern edge of the RUHRGEBIET in the SAUERLAND (dialling code 0 23 31, postal area code 58...). Armourers imported from SOLINGEN in 1661 started the city's industrial development and Hagen received a civic charter in 1746. A prominent industrialist established an artists' colony as a centre for JUGENDSTIL and the city's architecture bears testimony to the influence of art nouveau.

The city has a population of some 216,000 with about 14% foreigners (35% Turkish). Germany's FERNUNIVERSITÄT was founded at Hagen in 1975 and now has some 55,000 students. The city also has two other HOCHSCHULEN with a total of around 1,300 students. The SPD has been running the city since 1994. The city's economy is based on iron and steel, and other industries include paper and food. Important companies include KRUPP-HOESCH, VARTA and DOUGLAS.

HAGEN, FERNUNIVERSITÄT-GESAMTHOCHSCHULE

Germany's open university was founded in HAGEN in 1975 and has 65 regional study centres and 55,000 students. Like other universities it is administered by the LAND (NORDRHEIN-WESTFALEN). The university offers courses leading to degrees in economics, social sciences, electrical engineering, law, mathematics and computer sciences.

HAGEN, NINA (1955–   )

Rock singer who has gained an international reputation. She was born in the DDR and left when Wolf BIERMANN was expelled in 1976. She now lives mainly in the US.

HALLE AN DER SAALE

Halle is situated on the river Saale in SACHSEN-ANHALT (dialling code 03 45, postal area code 06. . .). The salt trade around Halle started in the Bronze Age, and following Roman occupation a settlement was established in 806 to exploit the salt deposits in the area. The city received a charter in 1150 and salt was the basis of medieval wealth. Industrialisation set in during the latter half of the nineteenth century. Immediately after the Second World War, Halle was chosen as the capital of Sachsen-Anhalt by the Russian occupying forces. When Sachsen-Anhalt was re-established in 1990, however, the city lost out to MAGDEBURG. The university was founded in 1694 and became a centre of learning in the Age of Enlightenment. The city is the birthplace of Georg Friedrich Händel, and the annual Händelfestspiele in June celebrate his music. Other festivals are the Laternenfest at the end of August and the Drachenfest in October.

   The city has a population of some 290,000 with a total student population of around 14,000 (1 UNIVERSITÄT and 2 other HOCHSCHULEN) and about 2% foreigners (18% Vietnamese). The CDU has been running the city since 1990, although election results in 1994 left it as a minority administration dependent on the support of other parties; both the PDS and the SPD have a larger number of seats. Halle was a centre for the chemicals industry in the DDR and was heavily polluted. Industries now include machinery and rolling-stock construction, pharmaceuticals, food, drink and tobacco.

HALLE-WITTENBERG, MARTIN-LUTHER-UNIVERSITÄT

University in SACHSEN-ANHALT founded in 1817 as an amalgamation of the universities of Wittenberg (1502) and Halle (1694) and teaching some 12,000 students. The Martin-Luther-Universität Halle-Wittenberg has faculties of theology, law, economics, medicine, agriculture, philosophy (arts), mathematics and sciences and technology.

HALLENBAD

An indoor swimming pool maintained with changing and washing facilities and toilets. See also: FREIBAD

HALLSTEIN, INGEBORG (1937–)

Opera singer (soprano) famous for her roles in Mozart, Verdi and Richard Strauss and her interpretations of contemporary music. She became a member of the Bayerische Staatsoper in MÜNCHEN in 1961 and has appeared as a guest performer in many cities including Buenos Aires, London, Montreal and Paris. Hallstein was appointed professor at the Musikhochschule in WÜRZBURG in 1981.

HAMBURG, FREIE UND HANSESTADT (LAND)

The LAND Hamburg is a STADTSTAAT covering an area of 755 sq. km., with a population of some 1.7 million. The BÜRGERSCHAFT (LANDESPARLAMENT) enacts legislation and comprises 121 members elected every four years with the next election in autumn 1997. The SENAT (LANDESREGIERUNG) holds executive powers and the SENATOREN are elected by the Bürgerschaft. The Land Hamburg was created in 1946 in the British occupation zone and consists of the city of Hamburg. Two of the senators are elected BÜRGERMEISTER and one of the mayors is simultaneously Präsident des Senats (SENATSPRÄSIDENT). The Freie und Hansestadt

Hamburg is Germany's biggest port and the country's '*Tor der Welt*', with hundreds of trading companies dealing in exports and imports, and associated traditional industries of shipbuilding, fisheries and refineries in the harbour's industrial complex. The merchant élite have always been slow to encourage new industries but the decline in shipbuilding and competition from Rotterdam have encouraged the growth of new industries such as electronics, aerospace and engineering. The fuselage for the Airbus is constructed at the DAIMLER-BENZ-AEROSPACE plant at Finckenwerder and PHILIPS have invested heavily in a new microchip facility. Hamburg is also an important centre for banking, insurance and publishing. The city has a free-thinking, independent tradition that never really embraced the Nazi regime wholeheartedly and the city was ruled by the SPD continuously from 1946 to 1987 with a four-year interlude in the mid-1950s. They continued to rule in an SPD/FDP coalition formed in 1987, were voted back in with a majority in 1991, and following this election being declared null and void, the 1993 elections yielded a coalition in which the SPD is supported by the STATT-PARTEI-GRUPPE. See also: HAMBURG (STADT); LAND; VOSCHERAU, HENNING

HAMBURG (STADT)

Known as the 'Free Hanseatic City of Hamburg' (FREIE UND HANSESTADT HAMBURG), Hamburg is both a city and a STADTSTAAT and as such it is the LANDESHAUPTSTADT of LAND Hamburg. Hamburg is a city of bridges (2,195); it is situated on the river Elbe and straddles the Alster lake (dialling code 0 40, postal area code 20..., 21... and 22...).

Hamburg is Germany's second biggest city and developed early in the Middle Ages as a flourishing commercial centre with a charter dating from 1189. The city's merchants developed Hamburg into a leading member of the Hanseatic League. Following the First World War the city's development was curtailed with almost all the city's merchant fleet being taken as reparations. Extensive bombing during World War II destroyed residential areas and harbour installations on a massive scale, and the subsequent division of Germany cut the city off from its traditional hinterland.

Hamburg is now an industrial city with a modern harbour complex, and a thriving media city with stunning contemporary architecture. During the 1980s the city was the focus of radical protest when squatters (*Hausbesetzer*) occupied waterfront houses on the Hafenstraße in the heart of an area ripe for development and attracted considerable media attention. The SENAT approved the sale of the houses to the cooperative 'Alternative am Elbufer' at the end of 1995. The city's Kunsthalle has a vast range of paintings from the medieval period through to the present. Hamburg's district of St. Pauli is famous for the REEPER-BAHN, originally home to the ropemakers producing the huge ropes necessary for ocean-going vessels, and St. Pauli also launched the Beatles on their musical career. Live music in the city flourishes with three classical orchestras and a top opera house at the Hamburgische Staatsoper, and particular emphasis on jazz at the city's many venues. An open-air theatre festival comes to Hamburg in the summer and the Übersee Tag in May commemorates the founding of Hamburg's port in 1189.

The city has a population of some 1.7 million with a total student population of around 64,000 (3 UNIVERSITÄTEN and 6 other HOCHSCHULEN) and about 15% foreigners (27% Turkish). A coalition between the SPD and the STATT-PARTEI-GRUPPE has been running the city since 1993. Modern Germany's first BÖRSE was founded in Hamburg in 1558 and the city celebrated 800 years as a port in 1989. Today, Hamburg is the country's biggest port and trading centre with over 60 km. of docks. Port facilities have been modernised but high levels of unemployment have resulted from mechanization and rationalisation. The city has developed into Germany's second largest industrial centre and is the country's media capital as the headquarters of the SPRINGER VERLAG and GRUNER + JAHR, the DPA DEUTSCHE PRESSE-AGENTUR, the centre for the production of STERN, DER SPIEGEL and DIE ZEIT, and many radio and TV broadcasting companies. The shipbuilding industry has inevitably declined but is being replaced by modern electronics industries with heavy investment in education at the city's technical university. The city's *Messegelände* hosts specialist trade fairs such as INTERNORGA HAMBURG and HANSEBOOT. Hamburg's industries include shipbuilding, oil and chemicals, engineering and electronics, food processing, cigarettes and brewing. See also: HAMBURG (LAND)

HAMBURG, UNIVERSITÄT
University in HAMBURG founded in 1919 and teaching some 45,000 students. The Universität Hamburg has faculties of Protestant theology, law, economics, medicine, philosophy and social sciences, education, philology, languages and literature, history, oriental studies, mathematics, physics, chemistry, biology, geography, psychology, computer science, physical education.

HAMBURG, UNIVERSITÄT DER BUNDESWEHR
University in HAMBURG founded in 1972 for members of the BUNDESWEHR and teaching some 2,000 students. The Universität der Bundeswehr Hamburg has faculties of economics and management, education, electrical engineering, mechanical engineering.

HAMBURG-HARBURG, TECHNISCHE UNIVERSITÄT
University in Harburg, a suburb of HAMBURG. It was founded in 1978 and teaches some 3,000 students. The Technische Universität Hamburg-Harburg has departments of civil engineering, electrical engineering, mechanical engineering, process engineering.

HAMBURGER ABENDBLATT
The daily evening newspaper *Hamburger Abendblatt* was founded in 1948 and has a circulation of 311,000. It is published by the SPRINGER VERLAG and distributed in HAMBURG and northern Germany. It carries national and regional news and also reports on travel, the arts, sport, etc.

HAMBURGER ARBITRAGE
A form of amicable arbitration that may be specified in contracts relating to the grain trade and overseas trade. Arbitration is carried out by the INDUSTRIE- UND HANDELSKAMMER in HAMBURG, where both parties agree to seek arbitration. One party informs the other of their preferred arbitrator, and the other party is invited to select an arbitrator within a reasonable time period.

HAMBURGER KUNSTHALLE

HAMBURG's prestigious art gallery founded in 1869 has a magnificent collection of paintings from the medieval period to the present day. It also has a collection of sculpture from the nineteenth and twentieth centuries.

HAMBURGISCHES WELT-WIRTSCHAFTS-ARCHIV See: *HWWA – INSTITUT FÜR WIRTSCHAFTSFORSCHUNG*

HANDELSBLATT

This is Germany's most respected business daily, published in DÜSSELDORF with full and objective coverage of business affairs at home and abroad. It has a circulation of 129,000 and is widely read by executives.

HANDELSGESETZBUCH (HGB)

The commercial code, contained in five volumes.

HANDELSKAMMER See: *INDUSTRIE- UND HANDELSKAMMER*

HANDWERK

A craft trade is a GEWERBE that requires a long period of training and is characterised by the high level of skill of the individual worker. *Handwerk* is regulated by the HANDWERKSORDNUNG, and it is difficult to distinguish between *Handwerk* and industry. It is, however, generally accepted that businesses tend to be smaller, that a HANDWERKER can work independently, and that the products of *Handwerk* tend to be custom-made rather than mass-produced.

HANDWERKER

A general term for a skilled worker or craftsman who has received a training in a registered trade (AUSBILDUNGSBERUF). *Handwerker* are respected throughout society for their skills and charge premium rates for their work.

HANDWERKSINNUNG

A guild of self-employed craftsmen in a particular trade, subject to the supervision of the appropriate HANDWERKSKAMMER. Membership of the guild is voluntary, and the guild promotes the interests of the trade, and oversees BERUFSAUSBILDUNG in the trade.

HANDWERKSKAMMER

Regional chambers of craft trades generally based on the REGIERUNGSBEZIRK and organised by the LAND. Members include: independent craftsmen, proprietors of craft businesses, GESELLEN and AUSZUBILDENDE in craft trades. The *Handwerkskammern* represent the interests of craft trades, approve examination regulations for *Gesellen* and MEISTER, lay down ground-rules for training *Auszubildende* and craft examinations, mediate in disputes between HANDWERKER and ARBEITGEBER, and generally promote the interests of craft trades.

HANDWERKSORDNUNG (HandwO)

The legal code specifying the conditions for HANDWERK and regulating the activity. It lays down a code of practice, and contains regulations for training, the MEISTERPRÜFUNG and the use of the title of MEISTER.

HANDWERKSROLLE

A register of HANDWERKER drawn up by the HANDWERKSKAMMER and listing the trade for which an individual is registered. Passing the MEISTERPRÜFUNG successfully is the criterion for registration, and an entry in the *Handwerksrolle* is a prerequisite for running an independent business.

HandwO See: *HANDWERKSORDNUNG*

HANIEL & CIE. GmbH

Trading company founded in 1756, with headquarters in DUISBURG. Haniel has some 25,000 employees.

HANNOVER

Hannover is the LANDESHAUPTSTADT of NIEDERSACHSEN and is situated on the Leine river and Mittelland Kanal (dialling code 05 11, postal area code 30...). Hannover originated as a market town, received a charter in 1241 and joined the Hanseatic League in 1386. Modern Hannover is an important industrial city, and the development of Hannover as a *Messestadt* with a massive *Messegelände* in the south-east has had a big effect on the city. Hannover's Schützenfest is held at the end of June and includes processions and fireworks. The city's series of ornamental gardens feature many original baroque aspects and are some of the most impressive in Europe.

The city has a population of some 518,000 with a total student population of around 44,000 (1 UNIVERSITÄT and 5 other HOCHSCHULEN) and about 14% foreigners (33% Turkish). The SPD has been running the city since 1949, although lack of an absolute majority has made it dependent on the support of other parties. VOLKSWAGEN's headquarters are at Wolfsburg (NIEDERSACHSEN) just outside Hannover, and the city's industries include the manufacture of machinery, batteries, optical instruments, tyres and biscuits. The HANNOVER MESSE was first held in 1947 and has now become the world's biggest industrial trade fair – with up to half a million visitors it doubles the city's population every April. Other trade fairs include DOMOTEX (carpets and floor coverings), CEBIT (IT and telecommunications) and CONSTRUCTEC HANNOVER (building, construction and architecture). Hannover is due to host the World Fair Expo 2000 at 'Expo City' for five months from 1 June in the year 2000 with the theme 'Man – Nature – Technology'.

HANNOVER, MEDIZINISCHE HOCHSCHULE
Medical school in NIEDERSACHSEN founded in 1965 and teaching some 3,400 students.

HANNOVER, TIERÄRZTLICHE HOCHSCHULE
School of veterinary medicine in NIEDERSACHSEN founded in 1778 and teaching some 2,300 students.

HANNOVER, UNIVERSITÄT
University in NIEDERSACHSEN founded in 1831 and teaching some 32,000 students. The Universität Hannover has departments of mathematics, physics, chemistry, earth sciences, biology, architecture, civil engineering, mechanical engineering, electrical engineering, horticulture, planning, linguistics and literature, education, history and philosophy and social sciences, law, economics.

HANNOVER MESSE
The 'Hannover Fair' is the world's biggest industrial trade fair covering the vast area of industry and technology. Some of the

areas covered by the fair include plant construction, research and development, manufacturing equipment and machine tools, robotics materials, logistics and industrial automation. The fair features a core of areas every year with some areas alternating in even and odd numbered years. The Hannover Messe is held in HANNOVER every year with around 450,000 visitors.

HANNOVERSCHE ALLGEMEINE ZEITUNG (HAZ)
Regional newspaper published daily in HANNOVER and distributed in the surrounding areas. It was established in 1949 and has a circulation of 557,000.

HANSEBOOT (INTERNATIONALE BOOTSAUS-STELLUNG HAMBURG MIT HANSEBOOT-HAFEN)
The 'International Boat Show Hamburg' is a trade fair for boats and boating accessories held in HAMBURG every year with around 150,000 visitors.

HANSESTADT See: *FREIE HANSESTADT*

HAPAG-LLOYD AG
Shipping, airline and tourism company with a world-wide container service. Company headquarters are in HAMBURG. Hapag-Lloyd has some 8,300 employees.

HARZ
A range of mountains in NIEDERSACHSEN and SACHSEN-ANHALT, and formerly separated by the barbed wire of the DDR border. The DDR side was a magnet for holidaymakers and is now making the most of its relatively good tourist facilities including narrow-gauge steam railways that were closed down in the west.

HASCHISCH-URTEIL
The BUNDESVERFASSUNGSGERICHT ruled in the autumn of 1994 that the possession of small amounts of cannabis should no longer result in criminal proceedings. The Gesundheitsminister of 11 out of the 16 LÄNDER have agreed to carry out a five-year experiment in HAMBURG and SCHLESWIG-HOLSTEIN with cannabis products being sold in pharmacies from 1997. The plan has to be approved by the Bundesinstitut für Arzneimittel und Medizinprodukte in BERLIN and has received substantial criticism from pharmacists.

Trials are already under way for legalising the cultivation of cannabis plants with a maximum 0.3 percent content of the active ingredient tetrahydrocannabinol (THC) by farmers, for the production of hemp papers, cooking oil and other hemp products.

HAUPTAMTLICHER BÜRGERMEISTER See: *BÜRGERMEISTER, HAUPTAMTLICHER*

HAUPTAMTLICHER LANDRAT See: *LANDRAT, HAUPTAMTLICHER*

HAUPTAMTLICHER OBERBÜRGERMEISTER See: *OBERBÜRGERMEISTER, HAUPTAMTLICHER*

HAUPTSATZUNG
A SATZUNG that regulates the organisation of a GEMEINDE. It lays down the number of BEIGEORDNETE, prescribes expenses payable, defines the coat of arms and seal, etc.

HAUPTSCHULABSCHLUSS
The school-leaving qualification awarded to pupils leaving the HAUPTSCHULE at the age of 15/16. The *Hauptschulabschluß* is a qualification that allows pupils to start a BERUFSAUSBILDUNG and is the entrance requirement for the BERUFSFACHSCHULE.

HAUPTSCHULE
A secondary school that takes pupils from the GRUNDSCHULE or ORIENTIERUNGSSTUFE and lasts until the age of 15 (when pupils are permitted to leave school) or in many cases 16. The *Hauptschule* is intended to provide pupils with a general education and the HAUPTSCHULABSCHLUSS qualifies them to begin a BERUFSAUSBILDUNG or to carry on formal education at a BERUFSFACHSCHULE.

HAUPTSEMINAR
SEMINAR in the HAUPTSTUDIUM for which students must have passed the ZWISCHENPRÜFUNG.

HAUPTSTUDIUM
The *Hauptstudium* follows on from the GRUNDSTUDIUM and offers a wider range of subject choices and scope for specialisation and

independent study. It is completed with a degree such as the MAGISTER, DIPLOM or STAATSEXAMEN.

HAUPTVERWALTUNGSBEAMTER

The most senior BEAMTER in a GEMEINDE, carrying out executive duties.

HAUSHALTSGESETZ

The law passed by the BUNDESTAG to implement the HAUSHALTS-PLAN.

HAUSHALTSJAHR

The financial year in Germany commences on 1 January.

HAUSHALTSPLAN

The budget plan is prepared by the BUNDESFINANZMINISTER well before the beginning of the HAUSHALTSJAHR and is first presented to the BUNDESRAT, which has six weeks in which to debate and approve the plan. The BUNDESTAG then approves the *Haushaltsplan* and a HAUSHALTSGESETZ is passed.

HAZ See: *HANNOVERSCHE ALLGEMEINE ZEITUNG*

HBV See: *GEWERKSCHAFT HANDEL, BANKEN UND VERSICHERUNGEN*

HDTV

Analogue high-definition TV with a resolution of 1,250 lines. Such programmes were first broadcast in Germany in 1992.

HEER

The land forces of the BUNDESWEHR are divided into three corps and come under the command of the BUNDESMINISTER DER VERTEI-DIGUNG in peacetime and the BUNDESKANZLER if the country is under attack.

HEIDELBERG, RUPRECHT-KARLS-UNIVERSITÄT

Germany's oldest university was founded in 1386. It is in BADEN-WÜRTTEMBERG and teaches some 30,000 students. The Ruprecht-Karls-Universität Heidelberg has faculties of theology, law, medicine, philosophy and history, oriental and classical studies, languages and literature, economics, social sciences, mathematics, chemistry, pharmacology, physics and astronomy, biology, geosciences.

HEIDELBERGER ZEMENT AG

Company supplying building materials and services, founded in 1873. Company headquarters are in Heidelberg (BADEN-WÜRTTEMBERG). Heidelberger Zement has some 24,000 employees.

HEILIGE DREI KÖNIGE

Epiphany on 6 January is a public holiday in BADEN-WÜRTTEMBERG and BAYERN. In some rural areas of Bayern, children dress up as the three kings and do the rounds writing K + M + B (*Kaspar, Melchior, Balthasar*) on each front door in chalk.

HEIMAT

The concept of a person's roots being in a particular environment, be it a village, region or country. The notion of *Heimat* – a problematic concept since its appropriation by the Nazis – was epitomised in the two epic films by Edgar REITZ: *Heimat* (1984) and *Zweite Heimat* (1992).

HEIMATMUSEUM

A museum reflecting the local culture of a particular area. A FREILICHTMUSEUM will often have all the characteristics of a *Heimatmuseum.*

HEIMATPRESSE See: *LOKALPRESSE*

HEIN, CHRISTOPH (1944–)

Writer who gave a critical picture of the DDR within the socialist system, rejecting utopian views of society. He studied philosophy and logic in LEIPZIG and East BERLIN and after a spell at the *Volksbühne* in East Berlin and became an independent writer in 1979. His works include *Cromwell und andere Stücke* (1981), *Der fremde Freund* (1982, published under the title *Drachenblut* in the BRD), *Horns Ende* (1985), *Der Tangospieler* (1989), *Exekution eines Kalbes und andere Erzählungen* (1994) and *Randow. Eine Komödie* (1994).

HEINE-PREIS

An award worth DM 25,000 made by the city of DÜSSELDORF in memory of the poet Heinrich Heine (1797–1856) to personalities who by their intellectual achievements have contributed to improving human rights, promoted social and political advancement, or have contributed to understanding between peoples. The prize was originally awarded every three years but has been awarded biennially since 1981. Recipients of the award include Richard v. WEIZSÄCKER (1991) and Wolf BIERMANN (1993).

HEINRICH-BÖLL-PREIS (KÖLNER LITERATURPREIS)

A literature prize awarded by the city of KÖLN for outstanding achievement in the field of German literature. Originally a prize of DM 20,000 was awarded annually, but since 1995 a prize of DM 35,000 is awarded every two years. Prizewinners include Hans Magnus ENZENSBERGER (1985), Alexander KLUGE (1993) and Jürgen BECKER (1994).

HEISSENBÜTTEL, HELMUT (1921–)

Exponent of experimental literature and concrete poetry in the tradition of Dada. He was head of *Radio-Essay* at the SÜDDEUTSCHER RUNDFUNK from 1959 to 1981. Heißenbüttel creates combinations of words, parts of words and idioms as well as quotations from other authors, transcending the boundaries between poetry and prose. He was awarded the GEORG-BÜCHNER-PREIS in 1969 and the Österreichischer Staatspreis für Europäische Literatur in 1990. His work includes *Topographien* (1956), series of *Textbücher* (1960–1987) and *Projekte* (1970–1980, including the prose work *D'Alemberts Ende)* and *Fünf Kommentare und sechs Gedichte* (1987).

HENKEL KGaA

Chemicals group founded in 1876 producing washing and cleaning agents (inventors of *Persil*) and health and health-care products. Company headquarters are in DÜSSELDORF. Henkel has some 41,000 employees.

HENZE, HANS WERNER (1926–)

Composer and conductor with an international reputation who has lived in Italy since 1953. He founded the music workshop

Cantiere internazionale d'arte in Montepulciano to foster cooperation between professional and amateur musicians. His prolific output includes ballets, symphonies, piano and violin concertos, and many vocal works. He is, however, best known for operas such as *Der Prinz von Homburg* (1960), *La Cubana oder ein Leben für die Kunst* (1975) and *Das verratene Meer* (1989). His versatile musical language combines with the socialist message in his compositions to make him one of Germany's great contemporary composers.

HERAEUS HOLDING GmbH

Holding company with interests in metals, chemicals and technology, founded in 1985. Company headquarters are in Hanau (HESSEN). Heraeus has some 9,300 employees.

HERAUSGEBER

Editor of a publication where the content is written by different authors. In the case of newspapers and magazines the term *Herausgeber* normally refers to the editor-in-chief who is the controlling editor of the publication and responsible for its direction and content. However, the roles and terminology vary: a publication may have a *Herausgeber* and a CHEFREDAKTEUR (e.g. DER SPIEGEL) or one person acting as *Herausgeber* and *Chefredakteur* (e.g. DIE WELT) or one or more *Chefredakteure* with the *Verlag* acting as *Herausgeber* (e.g. SÜDDEUTSCHE ZEITUNG). Some newspapers have two or more *Herausgeber,* e.g. FRANKFURTER ALLGEMEINE ZEITUNG, where these are the nominal point of contact for letters from the public: *Briefe an die Herausgeber.* See also: REDAKTEUR; VERLEGER

HERBOLZHEIMER, PETER (1935–   )

Jazz musician, trombonist, composer and arranger who has his own band, Rhythm Combination & Brass, formed in 1969. The band has been one of Europe's top big bands since the 1970s and combines rock instruments with traditional jazz instruments. Herbolzheimer's recordings include *My kind of Sunshine* (1972), *Jazz Gala Concert* (1976), *20 Jahre Peter Herbolzheimer* (1990) and *Friends and Silhouettes* (1991).

HERTIE WAREN- UND KAUFHAUS GmbH

A chain of department stores founded in 1882. Company head-quarters are in FRANKFURT AM MAIN. Hertie has some 28,000 employees.

HERZOG, ROMAN (1934–   )

Judge, CDU politician and the first BUNDESPRÄSIDENT to be elected by the BUNDESVERSAMMLUNG representing reunited Germany. He was professor at BERLIN in 1964–1966 and then at the Hochschule für Verwaltungswissenschaften Speyer in 1969–1972. Herzog joined the CDU in 1970 and was Kultusminister in 1978–1980 and then Innenminister in BADEN-WÜRTTEMBERG in 1980–1983. He was appointed president of the BUNDESVERFASSUNGSGERICHT in 1987, where he defended the judicial system from political inter-ference and proposed faster integration of AUSLÄNDER. He was elected Bundespräsident in 1994 and his period of office contin-ues until 1999, when he may be elected for a second term.

HERZOG, WERNER (1942–   )

Film director (real name Werner Stipetic) with a taste for exotic locations and eccentric subjects. Herzog studied in the US and has travelled widely in search of subjects for his cinematic fan-tasies and during the 1970s was one of the foremost exponents of the *Neuer deutscher Film*. Herzog's characters are often bizarre and irrational. His most famous films include *Jeder für sich und Gott gegen alle* (1975), *Woyzeck* (1979), *Fitzcarraldo* (1982), *Cobra Verde* (1987), *Echos aus einem düsteren Reich* (1990) and *Schrei aus Stein* (1991). Despite Herzog's popularity abroad, his films repel many German cinema-goers, and audiences can be thin.

HERZOG-ANTON-ULRICH-MUSEUM

This museum in BRAUNSCHWEIG houses Duke Anton-Ulrich's col-lection of paintings and was opened to the public in 1754 as Germany's first museum.

HERZOG AUGUST BIBLIOTHEK WOLFENBÜTTEL

Library in Wolfenbüttel (NIEDERSACHSEN) founded in 1572. It spe-cialises in cultural history from the Middle Ages to the Enlightenment and was Europe's largest library during the 17th century. Its most famous librarians were the philosopher and polymath G.W. Leibniz and the dramatist G.E. Lessing. It has over 700,000 volumes and 12,000 manuscripts.

HESSEN

Hessen is a FLÄCHENSTAAT covering an area of 21,114 sq. km., with a population of just over 6 million. The LANDTAG (LAN-DESPARLAMENT) enacts legislation and comprises 110 members elected every four years with the next election in autumn 1999. The Landtag elects the MINISTERPRÄSIDENT, head of the Hessische Landesregierung, which holds executive powers. The Ministerpräsident appoints the ministers with responsibility for individual portfolios. Hessen is divided into three REGIERUNGS-BEZIRKE comprising five KREISFREIE STÄDTE and 21 KREISE. The LAN-DESHAUPTSTADT is WIESBADEN, and present-day Hessen was formed in 1945 from the former Hessian provinces of PREUSSEN included in the American occupation zone. Although German *Kaiser* were crowned in FRANKFURT AM MAIN for centuries, Hessen also has a republican tradition with the first national assembly being convened at Frankfurt in 1848. A bastion of the Lutheran Church during the Reformation, about two-thirds of the population of Hessen are Protestant and one-third Catholic.

Frankfurt is the engine for the region as Germany's banking centre and the city lies at the heart of one of Germany's most powerful economic regions – the RHEIN-MAIN-GEBIET with major industries in chemicals and engineering. Hessen is also central to Germany's transport system with a dense AUTOBAHN network, major rail junctions and waterways, and the RHEIN-MAIN-FLUGHAFEN, Germany's air-transport hub in Frankfurt. More than 400 banks are located in Frankfurt, which is also home to chemicals giant HOECHST and the world-famous INTERNATIONALE FRANK-FURTER MESSE. Other industrial centres are Darmstadt and Wiesbaden with chemicals, KASSEL with heavy engineering, and Offenbach as the centre of Germany's leather industry. Apart from the industrial areas Hessen has a rural landscape of mountains, rolling hills, lush valleys and forests, and the LAND is at the geographical centre of present-day Germany where the cultures from the north and south meet and intermingle. Around 40% of

Hessen is wooded, and some of Germany's best wines are grown in the Bergstraße and RHEINGAU.

The SPD was the strongest party in the Landtag until the early 1980s and formed the ruling coalition with the FDP until 1984. After four years of minority government by the SPD with the support of DIE GRÜNEN (from 1985 as a coalition), a CDU/FDP coalition ruled Hessen from 1987–1991. The SPD formed a ruling coalition with DIE GRÜNEN/BÜNDNIS 90 in 1991, which was reaffirmed in the 1995 elections. See also: EICHEL, HANS; LAND; LANDESREGIERUNG

HESSISCH

One of the *westmitteldeutsche Mundarten*, spoken around FRANKFURT AM MAIN. The pronunciation of the local summer tipple '*Apfelwein*' as '*Ebbelwoi*' gives an indication of the typical weakening of consonant 'p' to 'b', the dropping of 'f' in 'pf', the tendency to omit final 'n' and the difference of certain vowels by comparison with HOCHDEUTSCH.

HESSISCHER RUNDFUNK (hr)

A regional public-service radio and TV broadcasting corporation based in FRANKFURT AM MAIN and broadcasting principally to HESSEN. Hessischer Rundfunk is a member of the ARD. See also: LANDESRUNDFUNK- UND FERNSEHANSTALTEN

HEUTE

TV news on ZDF, the main *heute* being at 7 pm.

HEWLETT PACKARD GmbH

Subsidiary of American electronics company, founded in 1959. Company headquarters are in Böblingen (BADEN-WÜRTTEMBERG). Hewlett Packard GmbH has some 6,200 employees.

HEYM, STEFAN (1913–   )

Writer and MITGLIED DES BUNDESTAGES. After spending the years of the DRITTES REICH in exile (changing his name from Helmut Flieg), he joined the US army in 1943. Heym co-founded the American newspaper *Neue Zeitung* in MÜNCHEN in 1945 but was sent back to the US for pro-Communist views. He then went to the DDR in 1952 in protest at McCarthyism and lived there as an independent writer where he criticised society in both East and West Germany. The novel *5 Tage im Juni* (1974) addressed the uprising of 17 June 1953 in the DDR and could only be published in the BRD. Heym similarly published the novel *Collin* (1979) in the West, without prior consultation of the DDR authorities, a practice that other DDR authors were to follow. Together with his criticism of the decision to strip Wolf BIERMANN of DDR citizenship, this led to Heym's expulsion from the *Schriftstellerverband* in 1979. During the autumn of 1989 Heym spoke out for peaceful revolution but was against reunification and argued for a socialist alternative to the BRD. In the 1994 elections Heym was nominated by the PDS as a candidate for the Prenzlauer Berg WAHLKREIS in BERLIN and received a DIREKTMANDAT. He opened the 13th session of the BUNDESTAG as the *Alterspräsident.* His other works include *The Crusaders* (1948) and the German version *Der bittere Lorbeer* (1950), his autobiography *Nachruf* (1988), *Auf Sand gebaut* (1990) and *Radek* (1995).

HEYME, HANSGÜNTHER (1935–   )
Theatre producer whose innovative performances of the classics are an evergreen subject of controversy. He has worked at theatres in KÖLN, STUTTGART and ESSEN and has been GENERALINTENDANT in BREMEN since 1992. Heyme's theatre productions include Schiller's *Wilhelm Tell* (1965) – slated as '*Klassikermord*' –, Hebbel's *Maria Magdalena* (1972) and Aeschylus' *Orestie* (1988). Other productions include the TV film *Miele, ein deutsches Schicksal* (1987).

HGB See: *HANDELSGESETZBUCH*

HILDESHEIM
Hildesheim (NIEDERSACHSEN) suffered severe damage at the close of the Second World War and the cathedral and Michaeliskirche were both badly bombed. The city's decision to carry out an ambitious restoration programme was vindicated when these two churches were made UNESCO world heritage sites.

HILDESHEIM, UNIVERSITÄT

University in NIEDERSACHSEN founded in 1978 and teaching some 4,000 students. The Universität Hildesheim has faculties of theology and philosophy and education, linguistics and literature, music and art, translation, natural sciences and mathematics and computer science.

HISTORIKERSTREIT

A controversy between historians, philosophers and journalists in Germany about the role and analysis of National Socialism. It was triggered in 1986 by an article in DIE ZEIT in which philosopher Jürgen HABERMAS attacked what he perceived as revisionist writings that sought to play down the crimes committed during the DRITTES REICH. The controversy commanded considerable public attention and highlighted the enduring problems of Germany's relationship with its past. See also: AUSCHWITZ-LÜGE; MOMMSEN, HANS; NOLTE, ERNST

HIT!

Weekly magazine for teenagers with a circulation of 208,000. It reports on stars from the world of pop music, TV and cinema.

HIWI See: WISSENSCHAFTLICHE HILFSKRAFT

HOCHDEUTSCH

Spoken German held to be free of regional colouring. The 'purest' form of spoken German is considered to be that used around HANNOVER. See also: DEUTSCHE MUNDARTEN; RECHTSCHREIBUNG

HOCHHUTH, ROLF (1931–)

Writer and dramatist who has caused a number of scandals with his documentary dramas, notably *Der Stellvertreter* (1963) and most recently *Wessis in Weimar* (1993).

HOCHSCHULASSISTENT

Postgraduate assistant under a PROFESSOR at a HOCHSCHULE, who is appointed for a period of three years (occasionally renewable for a further three years) and has the status of a fixed-term BEAMTER. These assistants have normally completed their PROMOTION and are working on their HABILITATION. They carry out research and teaching assignments under the guidance of the *Professor.* Although specific conditions will vary with the LAND, these posts are normally C1 or C2 on the academic salary scale. See also: WISSENSCHAFTLICHER ASSISTENT

HOCHSCHULDOZENT

Lecturer at a HOCHSCHULE who has completed the HABILITATION and is generally employed on a fixed-term contract. See also: PROFESSOR

HOCHSCHULEN

Institutions of tertiary education carrying out teaching, training and research, and providing a course of study that leads to a higher degree. The term *wissenschaftliche Hochschule* is commonly used to include the traditional UNIVERSITÄTEN, TECHNISCHE UNIVERSITÄTEN, UNIVERSITÄTEN-GESAMTHOCHSCHULEN, PÄDAGOGISCHE HOCHSCHULEN, *Bundeswehr-Universitäten*, the FERNUNIVERSITÄT in HAGEN and certain specialist *Hochschulen.* Excluded from the category of *wissenschaftliche Hochschulen* are the FACH-HOCHSCHULEN, which confer a DIPLOM in applied and vocationally-oriented subjects but are not permitted to confer a doctorate (PROMOTION). Additionally there are also KUNSTHOCHSCHULEN, MUSIKHOCHSCHULEN and THEOLOGISCHE HOCHSCHULEN.

There are no tuition fees at German *Hochschulen* and except for subjects with NUMERUS CLAUSUS a pass at ABITUR (HOCHSCHUL-REIFE) constitutes the entry qualification. Students typically take longer than the basic eight SEMESTER to complete their studies, and there is a high drop-out rate. Numbers have increased rapidly in the post-war period with actual student numbers far exceeding funded places, and this has made studying at large institutions impersonal. The crisis engendered by overcrowding and under-funding has been a standard topic especially since the 1980s. The introduction of tuition fees is often suggested as a remedy, but this still seems unlikely.

HOCHSCHULRAHMENGESETZ (HRG)

This law was passed in 1976 and lays down uniform guidelines for the provision of higher education at HOCHSCHULEN. The law provides the basis for individual *Hochschulgesetze* in the LÄNDER and gives the BUND some control in developing uniform higher-education policies. See also: KULTURHOHEIT DER LÄNDER

HOCHSCHULREIFE
The entrance requirement for a place at a HOCHSCHULE. The ABITUR is the standard requirement and a student must have studied at least two foreign languages in the course of secondary education. Completion of a course of study at a FACHHOCHSCHULE or an aptitude test may act as substitutes.

HOCHSCHULREKTORENKONFERENZ (HRK)
A voluntary association of the 213 HOCHSCHULEN in Germany, founded in 1991 as the successor to the *Westdeutsche Rektorenkonferenz*. The idea behind the association is to coordinate policy on *Hochschulen*. The association carries out public-relations exercises and cooperates with government bodies.

HOCHSCHULZUGANGSBERECHTIGUNG (HZB)
Evidence of being qualified for admission to a STUDIUM at a HOCHSCHULE. The standard qualification is the ABITUR.

HOCHTIEF AG
Construction and civil-engineering company founded in 1875, with a majority shareholding now in the hands of RWE AG. Company headquarters are in ESSEN. Hochtief has some 35,000 employees.

HOCKENHEIMRING
Famous Formula One race track in the town of Hockenheim (BADEN-WÜRTTEMBERG). The ring was rebuilt in 1980 and is 7.58 km. long.

HOECHST AG
Germany's biggest chemicals and pharmaceuticals company with headquarters and its own suburb in FRANKFURT AM MAIN. Hoechst has some 166,000 employees.

HOFFMANN, REINHILD (1943–   )
Choreographer and director whose productions are inspired by classical ballet and contemporary dance. She was head of the Bremer Tanztheater from 1981 until 1986, when she moved with

the dance troupe to Tanztheater Bochum. Her work includes *Hochzeit* (1980), *Callas* (1983), *Machandel* (1987) and *Zeche I und II* (1992/1993).

HOFMAN, PETER (1944–)

Opera tenor who has sung Wagner at the Bayreuther Festspiele and all the major opera houses in the world. He embarked on a second career as a rock singer and TV star in the 1980s. His performances include the title role in Webber's *Phantom der Oper* (1990) and his recordings *Rock-Classics* (1982).

HOHENHEIM, UNIVERSITÄT

University in BADEN-WÜRTTEMBERG (in a suburb of STUTTGART) founded in 1818 and teaching some 5,000 students. The Universität Hohenheim has faculties of natural sciences, biology, agricultural sciences, economics.

HOLSTEN-BRAUEREI AG

Brewer and distiller founded in 1879. Company headquarters are in HAMBURG. Holsten has some 3,100 employees.

HOLZMANN AG, PHILIPP

Construction company founded in 1849. Company headquarters are in FRANKFURT AM MAIN. Holzmann has some 45,000 employees.

HOMÖOPATHISCHES ARZNEIBUCH (HAB)

The official register of homoeopathic remedies.

HOMOSEXUALITÄT

Campaigners for gay rights have gained some landmark victories in recent years, notably a decision by the BUNDESARBEITSGERICHT in 1994 that an individual may not be sacked on the grounds of sexual orientation.

HONORAR

A fee charged by members of FREIE BERUFE for services rendered.

HÖPPNER, REINHARD (1948–)

Scientist and SPD politician. He played an active role in the Evangelische Kirche in the DDR and became vice-president of the VOLKSKAMMER in 1989. Höppner became head of the

SPD-FRAKTION in SACHSEN-ANHALT in 1990 and MINISTERPRÄSIDENT in 1994 at the head of a minority government consisting of a coalition between the SPD and BÜNDNIS 90/DIE GRÜNEN.

HORT See: *KINDERHORT*

HORTEN AG
Company with nearly 60 department stores, the first store being founded in DUISBURG in 1936. Company headquarters are in DÜSSELDORF. Horten has some 11,000 employees.

HÖRZU
Weekly TV guide distributed nationally with six regional editions and published every Friday by SPRINGER VERLAG. It was founded in 1946 and has a circulation of 2.4 million. As well as giving details of programmes for TV and radio, *Hörzu* is a family magazine with articles of general interest.

hr See: *HESSISCHER RUNDFUNK*

HRG See: *HOCHSCHULRAHMENGESETZ*

HRK See: *HOCHSCHULREKTORENKONFERENZ*

HUBER, ROBERT (1937–)
Biochemist and director of the Max-Planck-Institut für Biochemie near MÜNCHEN, who was awarded the Nobel Prize for chemistry in 1988 (with J. DEISENHOFER and H. MICHEL) for determining the structure of a photosynthetic reaction centre using X-ray diffraction techniques.

HÜLS AG
Chemicals company owned by VEBA and founded in 1938. Company headquarters are in Marl (NORDRHEIN-WESTFALEN). Hüls has some 31,000 employees.

HUMANISTISCHES GYMNASIUM
The old-style GYMNASIUM where the LEHRPLAN includes Greek and Latin in addition to the usual general subjects. The numbers of this type of *Gymnasium* have been drastically reduced over the years.

HUMBOLDT-UNIVERSITÄT See: *BERLIN, HUMBOLDT-UNIVERSITÄT ZU*

HUNSRÜCK
A hilly, wooded area in RHEINLAND-PFALZ made famous in the film *Heimat* by Edgar REITZ.

HWWA – INSTITUT FÜR WIRTSCHAFTSFORSCHUNG (HWWA)
Independent research institute for economic research founded in 1908 and based in HAMBURG. Originally the *Hamburgisches Welt-Wirtschafts-Archiv*, it has an international library and archive and is one of Germany's leading institutes for economics. Research at the institute is focused on developing empirical tools for practical applications in economics and politics.

HYPO-BANK See: *BAYERISCHE HYPOTHEKEN- UND WECHSEL-BANK AG*

HYPOTHEK
A loan in the form of a mortgage against property or land. A *Hypothek* must be entered in the GRUNDBUCH.

HYPOTHEKENBANK
A private bank whose main business is based on issuing mortgages. These banks also issue local-government bonds to finance lending to local authorities and provide loans to companies.

HZB See: *HOCHSCHULZUGANGSBERECHTIGUNG*

IAA (INTERNATIONALE AUTOMOBILAUSSTELLUNG PERSONENKRAFTWAGEN)
The 'Frankfurt Motor Show' is held in FRANKFURT AM MAIN annually and has around three-quarters of a million visitors.

IBM DEUTSCHLAND GmbH
German subsidiary of electronics giant IBM founded in 1992. Company headquarters are in STUTTGART. IBM has some 24,000 employees.

IC See: *INTERCITY*

ICE-ZUG
A high-speed train reaching speeds up to 250 km./h. The service currently operates on a number of routes between major cities with the routes HANNOVER – WÜRZBURG and MANNHEIM – STUTTGART having special tracks for such trains.

IDS See: *INSTITUT FÜR DEUTSCHE SPRACHE*

IfA See: *INSTITUT FÜR AUSLANDSBEZIEHUNGEN*

IfD See: *INSTITUT FÜR DEMOSKOPIE ALLENSBACH*

IFO-INSTITUT FÜR WIRTSCHAFTSFORSCHUNG e.V.
Independent economics research institute founded in 1949 and based in MÜNCHEN. It is concerned with studying the business cycle using the IFO-KONJUNKTURTEST, providing macroeconomic analyses, structural studies and market analysis.

IFO-KONJUNKTURTEST
An empirical test originated by the IFO-INSTITUT FÜR WIRTSCHAFTS-FORSCHUNG involving monthly questionnaires on current trends to around 6,000 businesses in industry, wholesalers and retailers.

IfW See: *INSTITUT FÜR WELTWIRTSCHAFT*

IG See: *INDUSTRIEGEWERKSCHAFT*

IG BAU See: *INDUSTRIEGEWERKSCHAFT BAUEN – AGRAR – UMWELT*

IG CBE See: *INDUSTRIEGEWERKSCHAFT CHEMIE, BERGBAU UND ENERGIE*

IG CHEMIE See: *INDUSTRIEGEWERKSCHAFT CHEMIE, BERGBAU UND ENERGIE*

IG MEDIEN See: *INDUSTRIEGEWERKSCHAFT MEDIEN – DRUCK UND PAPIER, PUBLIZISTIK UND KUNST*

IG METALL See: *INDUSTRIEGEWERKSCHAFT METALL*

IGEDO (INTERNATIONALE MODEMESSE)
'International Fashion Trade Fair' for clothing and fashion held in DÜSSELDORF every two years with around 40,000 visitors.

IGM See: *INDUSTRIEGEWERKSCHAFT METALL*

IHK See: *INDUSTRIE- UND HANDELSKAMMER*

ILA-BERLIN-BRANDENBURG (INTERNATIONALE RAUMFAHRTAUSSTELLUNG)
'International Aerospace Exhibition' – a trade fair for aerospace and airport systems held in BERLIN every two years with around 150,000 visitors.

ILMENAU, TECHNISCHE UNIVERSITÄT
University in THÜRINGEN founded in 1953 (university status 1992) and teaching some 3,000 students. The Technische Universität Ilmenau has faculties of mathematics and natural sciences, electrical engineering and information technology, computer science, automation, mechanical engineering and economics.

IMMATRIKULATION See: *EINSCHREIBUNG*

IMMATRIKULATIONSFRIST
The period of time during which students at a HOCHSCHULE must enrol at the beginning of a SEMESTER.

IMPRESSUM
The details that newspapers and magazines publish in each copy

of an edition, as required by law. They include the place of publication, HERAUSGEBER, CHEFREDAKTEUR, REDAKTEURE and the names of those legally liable for the accuracy of information in particular sections.

IMPULSE (OST)

A complement to the main edition of IMPULSE specifically targeted at the east German market. It started up in 1990 and is published every month to address the special requirements of the new breed of entrepreneur and manager and the associated problems and challenges in east Germany. Circulation stands at around 33,000.

IMPULSE (WEST)

Monthly magazine established in 1980 for owners of small and medium-sized businesses giving news, ideas and advice of interest to entrepreneurs and managers. It is published by GRUNER + JAHR and has a circulation of 133,000.

INDUSTRIE

Industrie is distinguished from HANDWERK by a greater separation between management and production, much larger production facilities, the capability for mass production and the use of different types of production in a single enterprise.

INDUSTRIE- UND HANDELSKAMMER (IHK)

There are 83 regional chambers of industry and commerce in Germany. Membership of an *Industrie- und Handelskammer* is mandatory for all businesses in Germany (apart from HANDWERK) and they are financed by a compulsory levy on their members. The chambers are independent, and they are responsible for safeguarding the general interests of trade and industry and their members in particular. They advise the LAND authorities and government departments, and they also administer Germany's extensive programme of BERUFSAUSBILDUNG.

Before a local company is allowed to take on trainees, the local chamber establishes that the company has skilled personnel eligible to carry out training. The chamber ensures that the AUSZUBILDENDER has a proper contract with the employer. The chamber is also responsible for the examination process, with *Auszubil-*

dende being examined by a committee made up of representatives of the employers, employees and BERUFSSCHULEN. See also: DEUTSCHER INDUSTRIE- UND HANDELSTAG; HANDWERKSKAMMER

INDUSTRIEGEWERKSCHAFT (IG)

A trade union is based on the principle of one union to one company with members drawn from a particular sector of industry or public service. For example, workers in the chemical industry join IG CHEMIE whether they are computer programmers, secretaries or technicians. This concept was applied in Germany after the Second World War to create a strong union movement and to prevent politically motivated industrial unrest. See also: GEWERKSCHAFT

INDUSTRIEGEWERKSCHAFT BAUEN – AGRAR – UMWELT (IG BAU)

Trade union with some 740,000 members representing workers in the building and construction industry.

INDUSTRIEGEWERKSCHAFT BERGBAU UND ENERGIE See: *INDUSTRIEGEWERKSCHAFT CHEMIE – BERGBAU – ENERGIE*

INDUSTRIEGEWERKSCHAFT CHEMIE – BERGBAU – ENERGIE (IG CBE)

Union representing chemical workers, miners and the energy industry (merger of the unions *Industriegewerkschaft Chemie – Papier – Keramik*, the *Industriegewerkschaft Bergbau und Energie* and the *Gewerkschaft Leder* in October 1997). The combined union has some 1.1 million members. Traditionally known as IG CHEMIE.

INDUSTRIEGEWERKSCHAFT MEDIEN – DRUCK UND PAPIER, PUBLIZISTIK UND KUNST (IG MEDIEN)

Trade union with some 200,000 members representing workers in the media, the printing industry and the arts.

INDUSTRIEGEWERKSCHAFT METALL (IGM)

The world's biggest trade union, with some 2.8 million members, representing workers in the engineering industry. Usually known as IG METALL, this is by far the biggest of the German unions and wields considerable power in Germany's important engineering sector, although it has experienced a drain in membership during the 1990s. Because of the union's size and influence it acts as a trend-setter in the pay-bargaining round and plays a major role in developing union policy within the DEUTSCHER GEWERKSCHAFTS-BUND.

INDUSTRIEMEISTER
A qualification for a skilled worker who has followed a course of study leading to the INDUSTRIEMEISTERPRÜFUNG. An *Industriemeister* is not permitted to run his or her own business.

INDUSTRIEMEISTERPRÜFUNG
Examination set by the INDUSTRIE- UND HANDELSKAMMER providing the qualification of INDUSTRIEMEISTER.

INFO-CITY
Multimedia network in the RUHRGEBIET started up by energy-based conglomerate VEBA providing a range of multimedia services including tele-shopping.

INFOBRIEF
A new service launched by the DEUTSCHE POST on 1 April 1995 in a drive to become more efficient. *Infobrief* is intended to meet competition for bulk mailing introduced at the beginning of the year which allows the private sector to deliver direct advertising weighing over 250 g (coming down to 100 g from 1996). The service allows users to send mailings of at least 50 letters with the same content without sorting at a cost of DM 0.70 with overnight delivery.

INNUNGSKRANKENKASSE
PFLICHTKRANKENKASSE run by a HANDWERKSINNUNG for all those employed by members of the guild. The members of the guild must employ at least 450 employees on a regular basis.

INSTITUT
Institute devoted to research, education, etc. At HOCHSCHULEN it is generally the smallest autonomous administrative unit within a FAKULTÄT or FACHBEREICH specialising in a particular subject, e.g.

an *Institut für Soziologie* within the *Philosophische Fakultät.* Such a unit may also be called a SEMINAR.

INSTITUT FÜR AUSLANDSBEZIEHUNGEN (IfA)
An institute for international relations founded in 1951 and based in STUTTGART. It promotes international cultural exchange between peoples of different cultures, runs cultural awareness courses for business people and organises German language courses for foreigners.

INSTITUT FÜR DEMOSKOPIE ALLENSBACH (IfD)
Germany's most widely respected opinion poll institute, founded in 1947 and based in Allensbach (BADEN-WÜRTTEMBERG). The Allensbach surveys give a snapshot of public opinion on matters ranging from politics to consumer goods and the media. See also: NOELLE-NEUMANN, ELISABETH

INSTITUT FÜR DEN WISSENSCHAFTLICHEN FILM (IWF)
An institute founded in 1949 and based in Göttingen (NIEDER-SACHSEN). It produces educational films for tertiary education and research.

INSTITUT FÜR DEUTSCHE SPRACHE (IDS)
An institute for the study of the German language founded in 1964 and based in MANNHEIM. It carries out research into the written and spoken German language. The institute compiles a database of contemporary German and also has an extensive sound archive of spoken language, the DEUTSCHES SPRACHARCHIV.

INSTITUT FÜR FILM UND BILD IN WISSENSCHAFT UND UNTERRICHT (FWU)
An institute founded in 1950 and based in MÜNCHEN that lends audiovisual educational material to schools and authorised educational institutions.

INSTITUT FÜR WELTWIRTSCHAFT (IfW)
A leading institute for economic research in Germany, founded in 1914 at KIEL (UNIVERSITÄT). It aims to promote research in macroeconomic interrelationships on a global scale.

INSTITUT FÜR ZEITGESCHICHTE
A foundation based in MÜNCHEN for research into contemporary history.

INTENDANT
The director of a theatre or of a radio or television broadcasting organisation.

INTERCITY (IC)
The *Intercity* train service was introduced in 1971 and the *Intercity* network now includes all major towns and cities. See also: DEUTSCHE BAHN AG

INTERFAB (INTERNATIONALE FACHAUSSTELLUNG FÜR ARZT- UND ANSTALTSBEDARF)
The 'International Trade Exhibition for Medical and Hospital Equipment and Supplies' is a trade fair for manufacturers supplying the health-care sector held in NÜRNBERG every two years with around 40,000 visitors.

INTERGASTRA (INTERNATIONALE FACHAUS-STELLUNG FÜR DAS HOTEL-, GASTSTÄTTEN-GEWERBE UND KONDITORENHANDWERK)
The 'International Trade Fair for the Hotel, Catering and Confectionery Trades' is held in STUTTGART every two years with around 65,000 visitors.

INTERKAMA (INTERNATIONALE FACHMESSE FÜR MESS- UND AUTOMATISIERUNGSTECHNIK
'International Trade Fair for Measurement and Automation' – a trade fair for CIM (computer-integrated manufacture), instrumentation and control engineering held in DÜSSELDORF every three years with around 90,000 visitors.

INTERNAT
In Germany boarding schools are very much the exception to the rule. Although these schools are for the well-to-do, attendance there normally carries no special kudos. Germany has 18 *Landerziehungsheime*, the most famous being Schloß Salem (established by Kurt Hahn, founder of Gordonstoun in Scotland) and the Odenwaldschule. The *Fürstenschule* SCHULPFORTA is a

GYMNASIUM in the form of an *Internat*, with a long and distinguished history.

INTERNATIONALE AUSSTELLUNG FÜR WEINBAU UND KELLERWIRTSCHAFT, OBSTBAU UND VERARBEITUNG, ABFÜLL- UND VERPACKUNGS-TECHNIK See: *INTERVITIS/INTERFRUCTA*

INTERNATIONALE AUTOMOBILAUSSTELLUNG PERSONENKRAFTWAGEN See: *IAA*

INTERNATIONALE BOOTSAUSSTELLUNG HAMBURG MIT HANSEBOOT-HAFEN See: *HANSEBOOT*

INTERNATIONALE FACHAUSSTELLUNG FÜR ARZT- UND ANSTALTSBEDARF See: *INTERFAB*

INTERNATIONALE FACHAUSSTELLUNG FÜR DAS HOTEL-, GASTSTÄTTENGEWERBE UND KONDITORENHANDWERK See: *INTERGASTRA*

INTERNATIONALE FACHAUSSTELLUNG FÜR HOTELLERIE, GASTRONOMIE, GEMEINSCHAFTS-VERPFLEGUNG, BÄCKEREIEN UND KONDITO-REIEN See: *INTERNORGA HAMBURG*

INTERNATIONALE FACHMESSE FÜR BAUSTOFFE, BAUSYSTEME, BAUERNEUERUNG See: *BAU*

INTERNATIONALE FACHMESSE FÜR BIOCHEMISCHE UND INSTRUMENTELLE ANALYTIK, DIAGNOSTIK UND LABORTECHNIK See: *ANALYTICA*

INTERNATIONALE FACHMESSE FÜR BÜROEINRICH-TUNG UND IFCOM – ANWENDERMESSE FÜR INFOR-MATION UND COMMUNIKATION See: *ORGATEC KÖLN*

INTERNATIONALE FACHMESSE FÜR JAGD- UND SPORTWAFFEN UND ZUBEHÖR See: *IWA*

INTERNATIONALE FACHMESSE FÜR MESS- UND AUTOMATISIERUNGSTECHNIK See: *INTERKAMA*

INTERNATIONALE FACHMESSE FÜR METALLBEARBEITUNG See: *FAMETA*

INTERNATIONALE FACHMESSE FÜR TECHNISCHE GEBÄUDESYSTEME, BAUTECHNIK UND ARCHITEKTUR See: *CONSTRUCTEC HANNOVER*

INTERNATIONALE FRANKFURTER MESSE

The Internationale Frankfurter Messe in FRANKFURT AM MAIN has three trade fairs for consumer goods held annually: *Ambiente* (around 100,000 visitors) and Herbstmesse (around 100,000 visitors) in spring and autumn for tableware, interior design, lighting and giftware, and *Premiere* (around 50,000 visitors) for paper and office supplies, perfumes, cosmetics, hairdressing, accessories and giftware. The Frankfurter Messe has a long tradition, being first mentioned in 1240.

INTERNATIONALE FUNKAUSSTELLUNG

'International Audio and Video Fair Berlin' – a trade fair for consumer electronics, multimedia, broadcasting and telecommunications held in BERLIN every two years with nearly half a million visitors.

INTERNATIONALE GRÜNE WOCHE BERLIN See: *GRÜNE WOCHE BERLIN*

INTERNATIONALE MESSE DRUCK UND PAPIER See: *DRUPA*

INTERNATIONALE MESSE FÜR VERPACKUNGS-MASCHINEN, PACKMITTEL, SÜSSWAREN-MASCHINEN See: *INTERPACK*

INTERNATIONALE MODEMESSE See: *IGEDO*

INTERNATIONALE RAUMFAHRTAUSSTELLUNG See: *ILA-BERLIN-BRANDENBURG*

INTERNATIONALE SICHERHEITS-FACHMESSE See: *SECURITY*

INTERNATIONALE SPIELWARENMESSE MIT FACHMESSE MODELLBAU, HOBBY UND BASTELN

The 'International Toy Fair with a Special Show of Model

Construction Kits and Hobby Crafts' is the world's biggest trade fair for the toy industry, held in NÜRNBERG annually with around 60,000 visitors.

INTERNATIONALE TOURISMUS-BÖRSE See: *ITB BERLIN*

INTERNATIONALES ZEITUNGSMUSEUM DER STADT AACHEN
Museum of newspapers and journalism in AACHEN, founded in 1885 and housing a collection of more than 150,000 newspapers.

INTERNER NC
An internal NUMERUS CLAUSUS operated within an individual HOCHSCHULE. This type of *Numerus Clausus* does not apply throughout the BUND and is used to restrict numbers in oversubscribed subjects at a particular institution.

INTERNORGA HAMBURG (INTERNATIONALE FACHAUSSTELLUNG FÜR HOTELLERIE, GASTRONOMIE, GEMEINSCHAFTSVERPFLEGUNG, BÄCKEREIEN UND KONDITOREIEN)
The 'International Exhibition for the Hotel, Restaurant, Catering, Baking and Confectionery Trades' is a trade fair for gastronomy, fast-food, hospitality, hotel and catering equipment, and shop fittings held in HAMBURG annually with around 100,000 visitors.

INTERPACK (INTERNATIONALE MESSE FÜR VERPACKUNGSMASCHINEN, PACKMITTEL, SÜSSWARENMASCHINEN)
'International Fair for Packaging Machinery, Packing Materials and Confectionery Machinery' – a trade fair for food processing and packaging held in DÜSSELDORF every three years with around 200,000 visitors.

INTERREGIO-ZUG (IR)
A new generation train that is gradually replacing the SCHNELL-ZUG. These trains travel between stations that act as regional hubs and have carriages with a new design including a small café.

INTERSTOFF

The 'International Fabric & Accessories Show' is a trade fair for fabrics, accessories, CAD (computer-aided design), CAM (computer-aided manufacture) and CIM (computer-integrated manufacture) held in FRANKFURT AM MAIN twice a year with around 20,000 visitors.

INTERVITIS/INTERFRUCTA (INTERNATIONALE AUS-STELLUNG FÜR WEINBAU UND KELLERWIRT-SCHAFT, OBSTBAU UND VERARBEITUNG, ABFÜLL-UND VERPACKUNGSTECHNIK)

The 'International Trade Exhibition for Viticulture and Enology, Cultivation and Processing of Fruit, Bottling and Packaging' is a trade fair for the wine-making and fruit-processing industries held in STUTTGART every three years with around 60,000 visitors.

IR See: *INTERREGIO-ZUG*

ITB BERLIN (INTERNATIONALE TOURISMUS-BÖRSE)

'International Tourism Exchange' – a trade fair for tourism, travel and conference centres held in BERLIN annually with around 140,000 visitors.

IWA (INTERNATIONALE FACHMESSE FÜR JAGD- UND SPORTWAFFEN UND ZUBEHÖR)

The 'International Trade Fair for Hunting and Sporting Arms and Accessories' is a trade fair for manufacturers of firearms, hunting equipment and clothing held in NÜRNBERG annually with around 13,000 visitors.

JAHRESZEITEN VERLAG GmbH

Publisher founded in 1948 with a group of magazine titles including the up-market MERIAN series. Company headquarters are in HAMBURG. Jahreszeiten Verlag has some 550 employees.

JANOSCH (1931–)

Children's writer and illustrator (real name Horst Eckert) whose children's books include *Oh, wie schön ist Panama* (1978) and *Die Tigerente und der Frosch* (1988). He has also written short stories, comics and novels. He was awarded the *Deutscher Jugendbuchpreis* (DEUTSCHER JUGENDLITERATURPREIS) in 1979.

JENA, FRIEDRICH-SCHILLER-UNIVERSITÄT

University in THÜRINGEN founded in 1558 and teaching some 10,000 students. The Friedrich-Schiller-Universität Jena has faculties of theology, law, medicine, philosophy (arts), economics, mathematics and computer science, chemistry and geosciences, biology and pharmacology, physics and astronomy, psychology and education and sport.

JENS, WALTER (1923–)

Writer, critic and academic, professor of classics at TÜBINGEN (EBERHARD-KARLS-UNIVERSITÄT) from 1956 and professor of rhetoric from 1963 to 1988. He was an early member of the GRUPPE 47, writing novels including *Nein. Die Welt der Angeklagten* (1950) and *Der Mann, der nicht alt werden wollte* (1955), essays and radio plays. Jens was awarded the GEORG-BÜCHNER-PREIS in 1988. He has written TV reviews for DIE ZEIT since the 1960s under the pseudonym Momos and has also translated Greek classics and the Gospel according to St Matthew.

JOURNAL FÜR DIE FRAU

Fortnightly magazine for women published by SPRINGER VERLAG

in HAMBURG. It has a circulation of 483,000 and is popular with young and middle-aged women, covering topics such as fashion, cookery, career and travel.

JUGEND

A term for youth, the definition of which varies but generally includes young people between the ages of 12 and 25. Criminal law distinguishes between KINDER (up to the age of 14) and JUGENDLICHE (from 14 to 18). In civil law the age of majority at 18 is a deciding factor.

JUGENDAMT

The youth office in KREISE and KREISFREIE STÄDTE that delivers all the services prescribed by law under JUGENDHILFE. The office is responsible for children in care, guardianship and supervision of children's homes. They also provide a variety of other services including advice on upbringing and careers advice.

JUGENDDORF

An institution in the programme of JUGENDHILFE where young people requiring help live with youth workers. Children from the age of ten sometimes also receive this form of support. The emphasis is on education, training and integration in society.

JUGENDHILFE

The social services provided by the JUGENDAMT to young people.

JUGENDLICHER

Young person between the ages of 14 and 18 as defined in law.

JUGENDPRESSE

The youth press includes all the magazines read by JUGENDLICHE and children. They are generally focused on specific age groups.

JUGENDSTIL

Highly stylised art form expressed as architecture and interior design and known as *art nouveau* outside Germany. The name originated in conjunction with *Die Jugend*, a popular review published in MÜNCHEN from 1896. *Jugendstil* was a reaction to the historicism of the latter half of the nineteenth century, and most of the examples of *Jugendstil* date from the period between 1900 and 1915. A centre of *Jugendstil* was the artists' colony in Worpswede (NIEDERSACHSEN, near BREMEN).

JUGENDTOURISMUS

Tourism for the under-thirties from the age of about 14, that gives young people the chance to go on holiday and socialise among people of their own age away from dependence on adults. This type of holiday is run by JUGENDVERBÄNDE and also by commercial organisations, with discounts being given to schoolchildren, JUGENDLICHE who are working, and students.

JUGENDVERBÄNDE

Youth organisations, usually on a national scale, catering for the needs of JUGENDLICHE and in some cases having a political or religious purpose.

JUGENDWEIHE

Formerly a DDR ceremony at which JUGENDLICHE were ceremonially welcomed to adulthood at the age of 14. It has been continued informally following reunification as a secular celebration without the formal trappings of the state.

JÜNGER, ERNST (1895–)

Controversial author who celebrated his centenary in 1995 and whose work has reflected political developments in Germany over the twentieth century as well as being notable for its elegant style. Works such as *In Stahlgewittern* (1920) were used by the Nazis to support their dogma while *Auf den Marmorklippen* (1939) was a veiled critique of the Nazi regime. His essays since the Second World War have been concerned with war, power and the role of technology. Novels include *Heliopolis* (1949), *Eumeswil* (1977) and *Eine gefährliche Begegnung* (1985).

JUSTIZMINISTERIUM See: *BUNDESMINISTER[IUM] DER JUSTIZ*

KABARETT

Intimate theatre has a long history in Germany. The genre is characterised by songs and short cameos of a humorous or satirical nature, with politicians often being the butt of the joke. Following the heyday of cabaret in the 1920s and its brutal suppression in the 1930s, political cabaret gained some popularity again in the post-war era both in the BRD and the DDR. It was a particularly important medium for criticising the system in East Germany, where a certain amount of criticism was tolerated by the Communist authorities as long as it did not go too far and remained confined to small circles. Since the removal of Communist authoritarianism in the East, cabaret has lost impetus and no longer has the cutting edge of harsh satire. Today, cabaret in the BUNDESREPUBLIK tends more towards carefully manicured titillation for stylish, middle-class audiences.

KABEL 1

Commercial TV channel with a substantial holding owned by PRO 7, transmitting films and family programmes.

KABELFERNSEHEN

More than 50% of all households are linked up to cable television, and a total of 31 cable channels are currently planned.

KAGEL, MAURICIO (1931–   )

Composer and conductor born in Argentina who has lived in KÖLN since 1957. He has written experimental compositions, radio plays, film scripts and plays for theatre in which he creates avant-garde forms that combine elements of music and theatre. Kagel was appointed professor at the Musikhochschule in KÖLN in 1974. His works include *Match* (1964), *Der Schall* (1968), *Sankt-Bach-Passion* (1985) and *Worte über Musik* (1991).

KAISER-WILHELM-GEDÄCHTNIS-KIRCHE
Church built as a national memorial for Kaiser Wilhelm I in 1891–1895 and bombed in 1943, leaving a ruined tower as a symbol of BERLIN's past. The adjacent new church (built 1959–1961) contrasts by its modern octagonal design with blue glass.

KAISERSLAUTERN, UNIVERSITÄT
University in RHEINLAND-PFALZ founded in 1970 as the Universität Trier-Kaiserslautern (present status 1975) and teaching some 9,000 students. The Universität Kaiserslautern has faculties of mathematics, physics, chemistry, biology, mechanical engineering, electrical engineering, architecture and planning and civil engineering, computer science, social sciences and economics.

KANTHER, MANFRED (1939–   )
Lawyer and CDU politician who has been a member of the LANDTAG in HESSEN since 1974. He has been Finanzminister and chairman of the CDU in Hessen since 1991 and was appointed BUNDESMINISTER DES INNERN in 1993.

KANZLEI
The offices of a RECHTSANWALT, STEUERBERATER or NOTAR.

KANZLER
Short for BUNDESKANZLER. At an UNIVERSITÄT, the head of the administration, who is responsible to the LAND for the budget.

KANZLERKANDIDAT
The candidate adopted by a political party in Germany to run for the post of BUNDESKANZLER in the elections for the BUNDESTAG.

KAPITALERTRAGSTEUER
EINKOMMENSTEUER that is payable on dividends on shares, interest from fixed-interest shares, government bonds and other fixed-interest securities. This tax is also payable on interest earned from savings or current accounts if the annual total exceeds DM 6,100 (1995) per individual.

KAPITALGESELLSCHAFT
A company with limited liability that may either be a private company or a public company with shares quoted on the open

stock market. See also: GESELLSCHAFT MIT BESCHRÄNKTER HAFTUNG;
AKTIENGESELLSCHAFT

KARFREITAG
Good Friday is a public holiday throughout Germany and is a
time for being with the family and reflecting on life. The traditional food is fish.

KARL-MARX-STADT See: *CHEMNITZ*

KARL-MAY-MUSEUM
A tribute to one of the curiosities of German literature – popular
children's writer Karl May (1842–1912) has entertained generations with his stories of the American *Wilder Westen*, e.g.
Winnetou (1893–1910), with international sales of his works
totalling some 80 million. The museum in Radebeul (DRESDEN)
houses the most important collection of North American Indian
culture in Europe.

KARLSRUHE
Karlsruhe is situated on the eastern bank of the Rhine in BADEN-
WÜRTTEMBERG near the French border (dialling code 07 21, postal
area code 76. . .). The city was only established in 1715 and went
on to become an important centre for the arts and sciences in the
nineteenth century. Although it was bombed during the Second
World War, it remains one of the country's cultural centres, and
it is the seat of Germany's supreme courts – the BUNDESGERICHT-
SHOF and the BUNDESVERFASSUNGSGERICHT.

The city has a population of some 270,000 with a total student
population of around 29,700 (1 UNIVERSITÄT and 6 other
HOCHSCHULEN) and about 12% foreigners (20% Turkish). The
CDU has been running the city as the strongest party since 1975,
although lack of an absolute majority has necessitated the support of other parties. The construction of a harbour in 1901
enabled Karlsruhe to develop its industrial base, and today's
industries include telecommunications, electronics, precision
engineering, chemicals and oil refineries.

KARLSRUHE, UNIVERSITÄT FRIDERICIANA
University in BADEN-WÜRTTEMBERG founded in 1825 and teaching

some 20,000 students. The Universität Fridericiana Karlsruhe has faculties of mathematics, physics, chemistry, biological sciences and geosciences, arts and social sciences, architecture, economics, construction engineering, mechanical engineering, chemical engineering, electrical engineering, information science.

KARNEVAL
Karneval is the run-up to Lent in the RHEINLAND. The city of KÖLN is the heartland of *Karneval*, and the parties in the Rheinland seem to be wilder and more extravagant than elsewhere in Germany, culminating in the partying and street processions on ROSENMONTAG. Television on *Rosenmontag* is invariably dominated by the *Karneval am Rhein*. See also: FASTNACHT

KARSTADT AG
Germany's biggest department-store group, founded in 1920. Karstadt also owns mail-order company Neckermann Versand AG. Company headquarters are in ESSEN and Karstadt has some 108,000 employees.

KASSE See: *KRANKENKASSEN*

KASSEL
Kassel is situated on the river Fulda in HESSEN (dialling code 05 61, postal area code 34. . .). It was granted rights as a town in the twelfth century (1189) and progressed to become the capital of the kingdom of *Westfalen* between 1806 and 1813. A centre for aircraft and tank production, the city was virtually destroyed during the Second World War and while much of the centre is now utilitarian, some of its past glories were painstakingly restored and the green Wilhelmshöhe allows the city to breathe. Kassel was home to the Grimm brothers when they were writing their collection of fairy tales. Every four years, Kassel hosts DOCUMENTA, Germany's premier exhibition of modern art. Other festivals include the Zissel in early August with processions, jousting and music; the Lichtfest on the first Saturday of September with a fair and fireworks; and one of Europe's oldest music festivals, the Kasseler Musiktage at the beginning of November.

The city has a population of some 202,000 with a total student

population of around 18,000 (1 UNIVERSITÄT) and about 15% foreigners (35% Turkish). The CDU has been running the city since
1993, although lack of an absolute majority has necessitated the
support of other parties. Kassel is essentially a big industrial city
with industries including machinery and tram construction, electrical and precision engineering, steel, rubber and textiles.
Important companies include VOLKSWAGEN, DAIMLER-BENZ and AEG.

KASSEL, UNIVERSITÄT-GESAMTHOCHSCHULE
University in HESSEN founded in 1970 and teaching some 18,000
students. The Universität-Gesamthochschule Kassel has departments of humanities and education, ergonomics, psychology and
physical education and music, social sciences, languages and literature, economics, architecture, civil engineering, mechanical
engineering, electrical engineering, mathematics, physics, biology and chemistry, agriculture, planning, art, visual communication, product design.

KATHOLISCH
A term used to distinguish the Catholic Church from the
Protestant Churches. See also: EVANGELISCH

KATHOLISCHE AKADEMIEN
Educational conference centres set up after the Second World
War by the KATHOLISCHE KIRCHE to promote an exchange of opinions between different philosophies, cultures and political per-
suasions.

KATHOLISCHE KIRCHE
Germany has around 27 million Catholics (*Katholiken*) with centres of Catholicism in the RHEINLAND and in BAYERN and other
parts of southern Germany.

KATHOLISCHE NACHRICHTENAGENTUR (KNA)
A specialist news agency providing news and information about
the Catholic Church.

KATHOLISCHE PRESSE
Around nine million copies of newspapers and magazines promoting Catholic views are published every year.

KAUFHOF HOLDING AG

The holding company owning the Kaufhof department stores founded in 1879. Company headquarters are in KÖLN. Kaufhof has some 69,000 employees.

KAUFRING AG

Trading company supplying goods and services to department and specialist stores, founded in 1921. Company headquarters are in DÜSSELDORF. Kaufring has some 31,000 employees.

KBA See: *KRAFTFAHRT-BUNDESAMT*

KdöR. See: *KÖRPERSCHAFT DES ÖFFENTLICHEN RECHTS*

KFT AUTO-ZEITSCHRIFT

Monthly car magazine established in 1990 specifically for car owners in the NEUE BUNDESLÄNDER. It provides technical background information and reports on new developments in automotive engineering (*Kraftfahrzeugtechnik* or *KFT*). The magazine has a circulation of 119,000

KfW See: *KREDITANSTALT FÜR WIEDERAUFBAU*

KG See: *KOMMANDITGESELLSCHAFT*

KGaA See: *KOMMANDITGESELLSCHAFT AUF AKTIEN*

KICKER-SPORTMAGAZIN

Twice-weekly football magazine founded in 1920 and published in NÜRNBERG by Olympia-Verlag GmbH. It has a circulation of some 337,000 and appeals to young male readers.

KIEFER, ANSELM (1945–   )

Artist who studied under Joseph Beuys and produces large-scale works depicting scenes from mythology and political history. His pictures incorporate materials such as sand, dust, straw, petals and ash. Kiefer's first monumental sculpture *Zweistromland* was exhibited in 1989. It was composed of 200 books cast in lead and weighed 32 tonnes. His works include *Photobearbeitungen* and *Malen = Verbrennen* (1974). A retrospective was held in BERLIN in 1991. Kiefer lives in the ODENWALD and continually returns to contemporary German history as subject matter.

KIEL

Kiel is the LANDESHAUPTSTADT of SCHLESWIG-HOLSTEIN and is situated at the head of the Kieler Förde (dialling code 04 31, postal area code 24...). The city was founded in 1242 and joined the Hanseatic League in 1284. After the Prussian fleet was transferred to Kiel in 1865, the city developed rapidly, and the opening of the NORD-OSTSEE-KANAL linking the North Sea and the Baltic in 1895 increased Kiel's significance as a port. The Kiel mutiny in 1918 precipitated the abdication of Kaiser Wilhelm II and ushered in the WEIMARER REPUBLIK. Kiel's importance as a naval base and the presence of U-boat pens ensured massive bomb damage and the centre is now dominated by unimpressive 1950s architecture. The KIELER WOCHE is Germany's prestigious annual sailing regatta held every June with an accompanying cultural festival.

The city has a population of some 243,000 with a total student population of around 29,000 (1 UNIVERSITÄT and 2 other HOCHSCHULEN) and about 8% foreigners (43% Turkish). A coalition between the SPD and BÜNDNIS 90/DIE GRÜNEN has been running the city since 1994. Kiel remains an important naval base and port with the associated industries of shipbuilding, fishing and fish-processing. Other industries include machinery and vehicle construction, precision engineering, optics, paper and printing.

KIEL, CHRISTIAN-ALBRECHTS-UNIVERSITÄT ZU

University in SCHLESWIG-HOLSTEIN founded in 1665 and teaching some 23,000 students. The Christian-Albrechts-Universität zu Kiel has faculties of theology, law, economics and social sciences, medicine, philosophy (arts), mathematics and natural sciences, agriculture, engineering and education.

KIELER WOCHE

Annual June regatta held at KIEL since 1882. This is Germany's premier boating event and is accompanied by a cultural festival.

KIND

A child is generally classified as eligible to attend KINDERGARTEN between the ages of three and six, becoming *schulreif* at six and attending school as a *Schulkind* between the ages of six and 14, when it enters the phase of JUGEND. See also: SCHULREIFE

KINDERDORF

A children's village where children who have lost their parents or been abandoned are brought up in a family atmosphere. The best-known organisation is the world-wide SOS-Kinderdorf e.V.

KINDERFREIBETRAG

Tax-free allowance received by high-income parents or guardians of children instead of KINDERGELD.

KINDERGARTEN

Play school for children between the ages of three and six years old, usually in the morning only. *Kindergärten* are intended to complement family life by helping children to interact and play with other children. A *Kindergarten* may be run by the Church or the GEMEINDE, and there are a few privately run *Kindergärten.*

As part of the new legislation on abortion (SCHWANGER-SCHAFTSABBRUCH) a law was passed in 1992 that guarantees every child a place in a *Kindergarten* from three years until he or she starts school at the age of six (SCHULREIFE). This legislation came into effect at the beginning of 1996, although in 1995 the system was still lacking around half a million places and there was a deficit of trained staff. Current provision of *Kindergarten* places varies considerably from LAND to Land with rural districts coming off worse in comparison with inner cities. See also: KINDER-TAGESSTÄTTE

KINDERGELD

A benefit payable for every child to cover basic needs. Regulations coming into effect at the start of 1996 give parents a choice between *Kindergeld* and the KINDERFREIBETRAG. *Kindergeld* is paid monthly up to the age of 18 irrespective of the income of parents or child, and it may be payable up to the age of 27 or in certain cases even beyond if the child is still in full-time education or training. The *Familienkasse* at the ARBEITSAMT assesses each claim on application and pays the benefit in cases where this is not paid through ARBEITGEBER. Employers pay it to their employees as part of their pay and deduct it from tax payable (employers with fewer than 50 employees may apply to be exempted from this obligation). *Kindergeld* increases with the number of children from DM 200 each for the first and second child (DM 220 from 1997) to DM 300 for the third child and DM 350 for each child thereafter. Parents may apply for a *Kinderfreibetrag* (tax allowance) instead of *Kindergeld*, but this is only favourable if the parents have a joint annual taxable income of above DM 146,555. It is expected that approximately 10% of taxpayers will choose the *Kinderfreibetrag* instead of *Kindergeld.*

KINDERGOTTESDIENST
A children's service geared specifically to children's needs at the local church on a Sunday. The tradition of *Kindergottesdienst* goes back to the end of the eighteenth century.

KINDERHEIM
A home for children below school age and those attending school with special needs such as a mental or physical disability and for children without parents.

KINDERHORT
Afternoon day-care facility for children of school age providing a structured environment for children of working parents after school.

KINDERKRIPPE
A crèche providing day care for infants aged between six months and three years, for working mothers. In the former DDR there was an extensive system of state *Kinderkrippen* to allow mothers to go to work, but in west Germany these crèches are generally restricted to large cities. The sharp decline of public day-care provision in the NEUE BUNDESLÄNDER has been the cause of considerable resentment among the population there.

KINDERTAGESSTÄTTE
A KINDERGARTEN that looks after children all day.

KINKEL, KLAUS (1936–)
Lawyer and FDP politician who was president of the BUNDESNACHRICHTENDIENST from 1979 to 1982 and went on to become STAATSSEKRETÄR in the JUSTIZMINISTERIUM in 1982–1990. Kinkel was BUNDESMINISTER DER JUSTIZ for a short period in 1991–1992 and

was then appointed BUNDESMINISTER DES AUSWÄRTIGEN. He was chairman of the FDP from 1993 to 1995.

KIRCH, LEO (1926–   )
Media mogul, head of SAT 1 and the KirchGruppe, who built up a media empire based on the production and distribution of films and TV series.

KIRCHE
The two main established Churches in Germany are the KATHOLISCHE KIRCHE and the EVANGELISCHE KIRCHE IN DEUTSCHLAND, with the south being predominantly Catholic and the north and NEUE BUNDESLÄNDER predominantly Protestant. The Churches derive considerable incomes directly from a KIRCHENSTEUER that is levied on individual taxpayers. This gives them a high profile in German society: they run schools, ambulance services, hospitals, charities and other activities. The high numbers of registered church members belie a decline in attendance at regular church services. Increasing numbers are opting out of the Church and hence out of *Kirchensteuer* (800,000 Catholics in 1989–1995 and 1.5 million Protestants in 1989–1996), posing a threat to the Christian fabric of the nation.

KIRCHENSTEUER
Tax paid by individuals to one of the established Churches. The tax is levied by the FINANZAMT as an additional 8% to 10% (depending on the LAND) of a person's EINKOMMENSTEUER or LOHN-STEUER and is then forwarded to the respective Church. It is necessary to renounce Church membership officially if a taxpayer does not wish to pay *Kirchensteuer*. He or she is then not entitled to burial in consecrated ground or to other offices of the Church, although exceptions are commonly made.

KIRSCH, SARAH (1935–   )
Poet and writer expelled from the SED in 1977 when she protested about the expatriation of Wolf BIERMANN. She moved to West BERLIN in the same year and then into the country in SCHLESWIG-HOLSTEIN in 1985. Her poetry explores human relationships in simple language and richly evocative images. Kirsch's work includes *Zaubersprüche* (1973), *Die Pantherfrau* (1973),

Katzenkopfpflaster (1978), *Schneewärme* (1989), *Schwingrasen* (1991), *Erlkönigs Tochter* (1992) and *Das simple Leben* (1994). She was awarded the GEORG-BÜCHNER-PREIS in 1996.

KLAPHECK, KONRAD (1935–)

Artist who paints realistic representations of objects from industry and technology such as telephones, typewriters, taps and sewing machines to embody human characteristics. Taps are portrayed as erotic symbols and the typewriter represents the rational male psyche.

KLASSIK

A term applied to anything that represents first-class standards, especially where it harks back to the standards of ancient Greece and Rome. The *Weimarer Klassik* in the late eighteenth century established the works of Goethe and Schiller as canonical for German literature. In the DDR, Weimar Classicism together with nineteenth-century Realism formed the model writers were to emulate. See also: STIFTUNG WEIMARER KLASSIK

KLAUSUR

An examination (normally at university level) that has to be completed under supervision within a specified period of time.

KLEBE, GISELHER (1925–)

Composer of orchestral and chamber music, and opera whose *Weihnachtsoratorium* (1989) received great public acclaim. His music originated in the 1950s based on the twelve-tone technique and he experimented extensively with electronic music in KÖLN. Klebe's compositions include *Zwitschermaschine. Metamorphosen über das Bild von Paul Klee* (1950), *Figaro läßt sich scheiden* (1963), *Ein wahrer Held* (1975) and *Die Fastnachtsbeichte* (1983).

KLEIHUES, JOSEF PAUL (1933–)

Architect and planning director of the Internationale Bauausstellung (BERLIN) in 1987, whose buildings include innovative museums and galleries in Germany.

KLEIST-PREIS

A literature prize that was founded by the editor of the *Berliner*

Tageblatt in 1911 on the occasion of the 100th anniversary of the death of author Heinrich von Kleist (1777–1811). It was awarded to young German poets and was considered the peak of literary achievement in the interwar years. The prize was revived in 1985, and the BUNDESMINISTERIUM DES INNERN and several publishers provide a sum of DM 25,000 annually that is awarded for work in the areas in which Kleist himself was active. Award-winners – selected by a single judge – have included Alexander KLUGE (1985), Heiner Müller (1990) and Herta MÜLLER (1994).

KLITZING, KLAUS VON (1943–   )
Physicist, professor in STUTTGART (UNIVERSITÄT) and director of the Max-Planck-Institut für Festkörperforschung, who received the Nobel Prize for physics in 1985 for discovering that under certain conditions the resistance of an electrical conductor is quantised, thus allowing scientists to study the conducting properties of electronic components with very high precision.

KLÖCKNER & CO AG
International trading company in steel, chemicals, environmental technology, energy, etc., founded in 1906 and now a member of the VIAG group. Company headquarters are DUISBURG. Klöckner has some 10,000 employees.

KLÖCKNER-HUMBOLDT-DEUTZ AG
Engineering company producing diesel engines and machinery, founded in 1864. Company headquarters are in KÖLN. Klöckner-Humboldt-Deutz has some 9,400 employees.

KLÖCKNER-WERKE AG
Steel and engineering company founded in 1897 with interests in plastics, machinery, plant construction, process engineering and packaging. Company headquarters are in DUISBURG. Klöckner-Werke has some 20,000 employees.

KLUGE, ALEXANDER (1932–   )
Writer, film director and lawyer who combines fact and fiction in film, novels and short stories. His written work includes *Lebensläufe* (1962, 1974, 1986), *Geschichte und Eigensinn* (1981), *Maßverhältnisse des Politischen* (1992) and films include *Deutschland im Herbst* (1978, with R.W. Fassbinder, E. REITZ and

V. SCHLÖNDORFF), *Die Macht der Gefühle* (1983), *Vermischte Nachrichten (1986)* and *Die Zukunft der Aufklärung* (1988). Kluge was awarded the HEINRICH-BÖLL-PREIS in 1993.

KMK See: *STÄNDIGE KONFERENZ DER KULTUS-MINISTER DER LÄNDER IN DER BUNDESREPUBLIK DEUTSCHLAND*

KNA See: *KATHOLISCHE NACHRICHTENAGENTUR*

KNAPPSCHAFTSVERSICHERUNG
A PFLICHTKRANKENKASSE for employees and trainees in the mining industry. The *Knappschaftsversicherung* is divided into KRANKEN-VERSICHERUNG and RENTENVERSICHERUNG.

KÖ See: *KÖNIGSALLEE*

KOBLENZ-LANDAU, UNIVERSITÄT
Germany's first private university for business management founded in 1984 and financed by industry and student fees. The Universität Koblenz-Landau (RHEINLAND-PFALZ) teaches some 7,000 students.

KOHL, HELMUT (1930–   )
Politician and the first BUNDESKANZLER of reunited Germany. He studied history and political science and has been at the helm of the CDU for more than 20 years. Kohl comes from RHEINLAND-PFALZ, where he was a member of the LANDTAG in 1959–1976 and MINISTERPRÄSIDENT in 1969–1976. He was deputy head of the CDU in 1969–1973, became chairman of the party in 1973 and then chairman of the CDU/CSU FRAKTION in the BUNDESTAG. He formed a government and became Bundeskanzler in October 1982 when the FDP defected from the SPD/FDP coalition government and a KONSTRUKTIVES MISSTRAUENSVOTUM was passed in the Bundestag against Bundeskanzler Helmut SCHMIDT. Since then Kohl has gone from strength to strength and is now the elder statesman of Europe, having won national elections in 1983, 1987, 1990 and 1994. He has a reputation for keeping a tight hold on the reins of power with a phenomenal grasp on the CDU and the party machinery, and an eye for detail. He is widely credited with having taken the decision to push German reunification through quickly

and for having steered Germany successfully through this difficult period, although initial euphoria for the CDU in the east has been replaced with a degree of cynicism, and the left in west Germany have accused him of exploiting the situation for personal political gain.

KOLLEG
An institute in the ZWEITER BILDUNGSWEG that permits young adult learners to study for the ABITUR. Students require a REALSCHULAB-SCHLUSS, some form of vocational training/experience and have to pass an aptitude test. Unlike those at an ABENDGYMNASIUM, students at a *Kolleg* are not permitted to work while studying, and the course of study is full-time over a period of three to four years.

KÖLN
Köln is situated on the western bank of the Rhine in NORDRHEIN-WESTFALEN (dialling code 02 21, postal area code 50. . .). The city's position where the Rhine intersects important European trade routes on land has made it a major centre since Roman times. Charlemagne (Karl der Große) created an archbishopric in Köln in the eighth century, and it was recognised as a free imperial city in 1475. The city was a leading member of the Hanseatic League (second only to LÜBECK at the peak of its power) and flourished as a mercantile and banking centre with the university a major centre for European scholarship. The coming of the railways in the nineteenth century strengthened the importance of the city but made it a prime target for Allied bombs during the Second World War. Miraculously the city's mighty Gothic cathedral survived the onslaught and was restored after the war. Konrad Adenauer, father of the new BUNDESREPUBLIK DEUTSCH-LAND, was OBERBÜRGERMEISTER in Köln from 1917 until he was removed by the Nazis in 1933.

Today, Köln remains the spiritual and cultural capital of the RHEINLAND as well as being a major commercial, industrial and trade-fair centre. The cathedral has more visitors than any other monument in Germany and contains the magnificent gold shrine venerating the relics of the three magi that prompted the

construction of the cathedral in the first place. Köln had its own
school of medieval painters and the city remains a leading centre
for art dealers. The city's Roman history is reflected in one of the
country's most important archaeological collections, and the
many Roman monuments remaining include a Roman sewer.
Köln is Germany's broadcasting capital with the headquarters of
the WESTDEUTSCHER RUNDFUNK being located here. The radio studios of the WDR were used by composer Karlheinz STOCKHAUSEN
and played an important role in the development of electronic
music. The KARNEVAL season is the highpoint of the cultural year
in Köln and the *Rheinländer* throw themselves into the celebrations with characteristic vigour. *Karneval* is a riot of fancy dress,
gaiety and processions, and ends with a spectacular parade on
ROSENMONTAG which is a mixture of historical pageant, satirical
humour and madness when tons of sweets, popcorn and choco-
late are thrown to the crowds from the floats.

The city has a population of some one million with a total student population of around 78,000 (1 UNIVERSITÄT and 9 other
HOCHSCHULEN) and about 23% foreigners (43% Turkish). The SPD
has been running the city since 1956, although lack of an
absolute majority has necessitated the support of other parties.
Köln is now Germany's fourth biggest city and one of the country's biggest inland ports with the Rhine big enough to accommodate ocean-going vessels. It is also the country's busiest
railway junction and the city's *Autobahnring* joins up ten separate AUTOBAHNEN. The Kölnmesse is a major trade-fair centre
hosting many international trade fairs including DOMOTECHNICA,
ANUGA and ORGATEC. Important industries are insurance, engineering, chemicals and pharmaceuticals, and brewing. Two of
Köln's most famous products are *Eau de Cologne* (*Kölnisch
Wasser*, originally produced as an aphrodisiac) and *Kölsch* (the
city's distinctive beer). Köln is a major brewing centre with more
breweries than any other city in the world. See also: RHEINISCH-
WESTFÄLISCHES INDUSTRIEGEBIET

KÖLN, UNIVERSITÄT ZU

University in NORDRHEIN-WESTFALEN founded in 1388 and teaching
some 57,000 students. The Universität zu Köln has a strong repu-

tation in economics and has faculties of economics and social sciences, law, medicine, philosophy (arts), mathematics and natural sciences and education.

KÖLNISCHE RUNDSCHAU
Daily newspaper established in 1946 and distributed in the RHEINLAND with a circulation of 155,000.

KOMBINAT
Large state-owned industrial grouping in the former DDR comprising production facilities for a particular product or sector and the associated industries. In 1990 all the *Kombinate* were broken up, converted to GMBHS or AGS and sold off by the TREUHAND-ANSTALT.

KOMMANDITGESELLSCHAFT (KG)
Partnership with at least one personally liable partner (*Komplementär*) and at least one partner whose liability is limited to the amount of capital invested (*Kommanditist*).

KOMMANDITGESELLSCHAFT AUF AKTIEN
Business enterprise consisting of a hybrid between a KOMMANDIT-GESELLSCHAFT and an AKTIENGESELLSCHAFT to form a partnership limited by shares.

KOMMENTAR
An opinion column in which an editor comments on a topical subject.

KOM(M)ÖDCHEN
Cabaret theatre founded in DÜSSELDORF by Kay and Lore Lorentz in 1947. A political cabaret with an international reputation which has brought the German cabaret tradition to home audiences on TV and international audiences on tour.

KOMMUNAL
Refers to matters concerned with local government (GEMEINDE or KREIS). See also: KOMMUNALPOLITIK; KOMMUNALVERWALTUNG

KOMMUNALANLEIHEN
Local-government bonds, also known as *Kommunalobligationen*,

are issued by a HYPOTHEKENBANK and other banks to finance loans to a GEMEINDE or GEMEINDEVERBAND.

KOMMUNALBEAMTER
BEAMTER working in local government (GEMEINDE or KREIS).

KOMMUNALBETRIEBE
Businesses run by GEMEINDEN and KREISE to provide local services such as local transport and utilities (water, gas, electricity).

KOMMUNALE PFLICHTAUFGABEN
Duties that local authorities are obliged to carry out.

KOMMUNALE SELBSTVERWALTUNG
The principle of local self-government that applies in Germany. See also: GEMEINDEVERFASSUNGSRECHT

KOMMUNALE SPITZENVERBÄNDE
Associations (ÜBERREGIONAL) representing the interests of local authorities, i.e. KREISE, KREISFREIE STÄDTE and GEMEINDEN, at the level of the LAND and BUND.

KOMMUNALER BEDIENSTETER
Local-government employee working for a KREIS or GEMEINDE.

KOMMUNALER WAHLBEZIRK
District in which a representative is elected in KOMMUNALWAHLEN.

KOMMUNALPOLITIK
All aspects of administration affecting the local GEMEINDEN and GEMEINDEVERBÄNDE. These may relate to actions and policies of the LAND, BUND, the local authorities, political parties, or the associated organisations and economic entities, down to the individual citizens. *Kommunalpolitik* covers the whole myriad of affairs relating to local communities such as utilities, health, education, social affairs, culture, environmental services, etc.

KOMMUNALRECHT
All law relating to the GEMEINDEN and GEMEINDEVERBÄNDE.

KOMMUNALREFORM
Reforms of local government were carried out in the BRD between 1967 and 1978, enlarging the units of local government

in order to increase the efficiency of the GEMEINDE. Reform focused on the small Gemeinde with no full-time administrator. The numbers of KREISANGEHÖRIGE GEMEINDEN, KREISFREIE STÄDTE and KREISE were drastically reduced. The number of honorary members of the GEMEINDEVERTRETUNGEN was substantially reduced, and for many people the administration and government moved away from their local environment and became more centralised. In 1990 a law was passed to allow the formation of the NEUE BUNDESLÄNDER and provide the framework for local government in the former DDR. See also: GEMEINDEVERFASSUNGSRECHT

KOMMUNALVERFASSUNGSRECHT See: *GEMEINDEVERFASSUNGSRECHT*

KOMMUNALVERWALTUNG
Local government in Germany is centred on the GEMEINDE, although some local government duties are also carried out by the KREIS.

KOMMUNALWAHL
Local-government elections to elect the GEMEINDEVERTRETUNG.

KOMMUNE
A term used to refer to the GEMEINDE.

KOMMUNISMUS
The political theory based on the writings of Karl Marx and Friedrich Engels of a classless society in which the means of production and distribution are owned by the workers. The notion of the individual is subsumed under the power of an all-embracing state that provides for all the individual's needs.

The KOMMUNISTISCHE PARTEI DEUTSCHLANDS was founded in 1919, and although it held 100 seats in the REICHSTAG in 1932, the party was brutally suppressed in 1933. After the Second World War the KPD was permitted in all zones of occupation. In the Soviet zone the KPD was amalgamated with the SPD to form the SOZIALISTISCHE EINHEITSPARTEI DEUTSCHLANDS in 1946, which governed the DDR effectively as a single-party state until the collapse of the DDR. In the BRD the KPD was declared contrary to the

constitution in 1956 and again dissolved. In 1968 the DEUTSCHE
KOMMUNISTISCHE PARTEI was formed but it has consistently failed to
achieve any electoral success.

Following the breakdown of the BERLINER MAUER, the SED
rapidly changed its name to the PARTEI DES DEMOKRATISCHEN
SOZIALISMUS, and the subsequent collapse of the Soviet Union
generally discredited the Communist system. The vote for the
PDS declined in the early 1990s but revived in the 1994 elections.
The party failed to break through the five-percent barrier but
gained four DIREKTMANDATE and was therefore able to enter the
BUNDESTAG with 30 ABGEORDNETE. See also: FÜNFPROZENTKLAUSEL

KOMMUNISTISCHE PARTEI DEUTSCHLANDS (KPD)
The German Communist Party was formed in 1919 and dissolved
in 1933 under the Nazis. It was revived after the Second World
War in the BRD but abolished in 1956 after being declared unconstitutional. See also: KOMMUNISMUS; PARTEIVERBOT

KONFERENZ DER DEUTSCHEN AKADEMIEN DER
WISSENSCHAFTEN
Conference of the German Academies of Sciences and
Humanities founded in 1973, which represents the interests of
the member academies. The conference coordinates research
activities between the members and arranges conferences.

The member academies are: Bayerische Akademie der
Wissenschaften, Berlin-Brandenburgische Akademie der
Wissenschaften, Akademie der Wissenschaften in Göttingen,
Heidelberger Akademie der Wissenschaften, Akademie der
Wissenschaften und der Literatur Mainz, Nordrhein-
Westfälische Akademie der Wissenschaften, Sächsische
Akademie der Wissenschaften zu Leipzig.

KÖNIGSALLEE (KÖ)
DÜSSELDORF'S fashion-conscious main thoroughfare where the
chic of Germany's richest city buy the latest international
designs. It was named Königsallee by the city's elders allegedly
as an act of contrition after the unpopular Prussian monarch
Friedrich Wilhelm IV had been pelted with horse dung by rowdy
citizens. This broad boulevard was laid out in the early 1800s and

is lined with banks, offices, exclusive stores, restaurants and street cafés – one of the places to be seen in Germany.

KONJUNKTUR
The business cycle relating to the ups and downs of economic activity. The *Konjunktur* refers to the alternation between boom and bust that governments throughout the world have been trying to stabilise since the war. A tight control on inflation and monetary supply combined with cooperation between ARBEITGEBER and ARBEITNEHMER has ensured that German governments have been more successful than most in providing a stable economic environment.

KONKURSAUSFALLGELD
Compensation payable to all employees who lose earnings as a result of the ARBEITGEBER becoming insolvent.

KONRAD-DUDEN-PREIS See: *DUDENPREIS*

KONSTANZ, UNIVERSITÄT
Small university in BADEN-WÜRTTEMBERG founded in 1966 and teaching some 10,000 students. The Universität Konstanz has faculties of mathematics, physics, chemistry, biology, social sciences, economics and statistics, law, arts and administration.

KONSTRUKTIVES MISSTRAUENSVOTUM
A vote of no-confidence in the BUNDESKANZLER passed by a majority of the BUNDESTAG. A *konstruktives Mißtrauensvotum* is only permissible under the GRUNDGESETZ if the Bundestag simultaneously elects a new Bundeskanzler. The Bundestag then requests the BUNDESPRÄSIDENT to dismiss the incumbent Bundeskanzler, a request which he has to grant. The only time this has been used was in 1982, when Helmut SCHMIDT failed to win a vote of no-confidence as a result of withdrawal of support by the FDP. Helmut KOHL formed a new government with the support of the FDP and won a resounding victory in the polls in 1983.

KONVENT See: *KONZIL*

KONZIL
Representative body at many HOCHSCHULEN on which PROFESSOREN,

academic and non-academic staff and the STUDENTENSCHAFT are represented. Members of this body are elected and decide on certain matters of principle relating to the *Hochschule*, including the appointment of the REKTOR or PRÄSIDENT.

KOPPER, HILMAR (1935–   )

Vorstandssprecher of DEUTSCHE BANK AG since 1989 when head of Deutsche Bank Alfred Herrhausen was murdered by terrorists from the ROTE-ARMEE-FRAKTION.

KÖRPERSCHAFT DES ÖFFENTLICHEN RECHTS (KdöR)

A legal person set up for the purpose of dealing with public-sector industries and other activities in the public interest. Their members are appointed rather than elected and although under indirect government control, they are autonomous in the daily management of executive duties. The personnel working in a *Körperschaft des öffentlichen Rechts* are mostly ÖFFENTLICHE BE-DIENSTETE or BEAMTE. Examples of this type of organisation are GE-MEINDEN and KREISE, HOCHSCHULEN, KRANKENKASSEN, BERUFSGENOS-SENSCHAFTEN, RECHTSANWALTSKAMMERN and ÄRZTEKAMMERN.

KÖRPERSCHAFTSTEUER

EINKOMMENSTEUER that is payable by legal persons (e.g. public companies). This tax is shared by the BUND, the LAND and the GEMEINDE, and the precise proportions in which the tax is allocated are subject to continual revision.

KORPORATION See: *STUDENTISCHE VERBINDUNGEN*

KPD See: *KOMMUNISTISCHE PARTEI DEUTSCHLANDS*

KRAFTFAHRT-BUNDESAMT (KBA)

The federal office under the BUNDESMINISTERIUM FÜR VERKEHR, based in Flensburg (SCHLESWIG-HOLSTEIN) and responsible for registering FÜHRERSCHEINE, KRAFTFAHRZEUGBRIEFE and for maintaining the VERKEHRSZENTRALREGISTER.

KRAFTFAHRZEUGBRIEF

The registration document for a vehicle giving a description of the vehicle and details of ownership. The document accompanies a vehicle from manufacture to scrap heap and should not be kept with the vehicle. See also: KRAFTFAHRZEUGSCHEIN

KRAFTFAHRZEUGKENNZEICHEN

The registration number for a car is issued by a *Zulassungsstelle* in a KREIS or KREISFREIE STADT and has to be changed every time a car owner moves. The first group of up to three letters in the registration number indicates the area of registration, e.g. M for MÜNCHEN or HH for HANSESTADT HAMBURG, and is followed by an identification number for the car.

KRAFTFAHRZEUGSCHEIN

Operating licence for a motor vehicle issued by the *Zulassungsstelle* in a KREIS or KREISFREIE STADT when a vehicle is registered in a particular area. The *Kraftfahrzeugschein* gives details of exhaust-emission and TÜV roadworthy tests and must accompany the authorised driver at all times when driving. See also: KRAFTFAHRZEUGBRIEF

KRANKENGELD

Benefit paid by the KRANKENVERSICHERUNG to cover time off while sick. It is paid when an employee has been ill longer than six weeks, at which point LOHNFORTZAHLUNG ceases.

KRANKENKASSEN

Health-insurance funds which are KÖRPERSCHAFTEN DES ÖFFENT-LICHEN RECHTS. They form the basis of health-care provision in Germany, where funding goes with the patient and various options for combining state and private funding put the patient in a strong position. *Krankenkassen* operate with a system whereby the patient takes a health-insurance card (*Kranken-versichertenkarte*) to a general practitioner (*praktischer Arzt/ Arzt für Allgemeinmedizin*) or directly to a specialist (FACHARZT). The spiralling costs of health care have constituted a perennial topic for reform. See also: PFLICHTKRANKENKASSEN; ERSATZKASSEN

KRANKENVERSICHERUNG

The *gesetzliche Krankenversicherung* is the part of the SOZIALVER-SICHERUNG paid to cover the cost of health care, pregnancy and sickness benefits, and death, and it is paid in equal parts by ARBEITNEHMER and ARBEITGEBER. Health insurance is obligatory for every *Arbeitnehmer* earning up to a specified ceiling. A *private Krankenversicherung* is voluntary and can be taken out by *Arbeitnehmer* earning more than the statutory limit for *gesetzliche Krankenversicherung* and by the self-employed. Private insurance can also be taken out as a top-up by those paying *gesetzliche Krankenversicherung.*

KRAUSS-MAFFEI AG
Engineering company engaged in the production of tanks and founded in 1838. Company headquarters are in MÜNCHEN. Krauss-Maffei has some 5,000 employees.

KREDITANSTALT FÜR WIEDERAUFBAU (KfW)
This bank was set up by the BUND and the LÄNDER in 1948 to provide loans for post-war reconstruction. Since the early 1960s it has provided long-term finance for domestic investment and guarantees for loans to developing countries. More recently it has been involved in providing loans for owner-occupied homes. See also: ÖFFENTLICH-RECHTLICHE KREDITINSTITUTE

KREDITGENOSSENSCHAFTEN
There are around 3,000 cooperative banks traditionally serving agriculture (RAIFFEISENBANKEN) and the MITTELSTAND (VOLKSBANKEN). The cooperative banks rival the SPARKASSEN for retail trade, and their central bank is the DEUTSCHE GENOSSENSCHAFTSBANK based in FRANKFURT AM MAIN.

KREFELD
Krefeld is situated on the left bank of the Rhine in NORDRHEIN-WESTFALEN (dialling code 0 21 51, postal area code 47. . .). The city received a charter in 1373 and became a centre for linen and silk production in the seventeenth and eighteenth centuries. At the beginning of the century Krefeld absorbed several neighbouring towns including Uerdingen, with the giant BAYER chemical works and a harbour on the Rhine, and Linn, where most of the city's museums are now located. Krefeld is renowned for its luxury silks and velvets and the city is Germany's number one textile centre. Not surprisingly it also has Germany's most comprehen-

sive textile museum, with textiles and costumes from all over the world.

The city has a population of some 247,000 with a student population of around 4,000 (1 HOCHSCHULE) and about 15% foreigners (39% Turkish). The CDU has been running the city on a slim majority since 1994. Krefeld's pre-eminence in textiles and clothing is complemented by other industries including machinery, stainless steel, chemicals and food. Important companies include Bayer and THYSSEN. See also: RHEINISCH-WESTFÄLISCHES INDUSTRIEGEBIET

KREIS
The Kreis or Landkreis is an administrative authority based on a geographical area, intermediate between GEMEINDEN and LAND. This exists in all the Länder apart from the city states of BERLIN, BREMEN and HAMBURG. The senior BEAMTER in a Kreis is the LANDRAT. In most Länder the Kreis carries out functions associated with the Gemeinde and the Land. See also: KREISFREIE STADT; KREISSTADT

KREISANGEHÖRIGE GEMEINDE
A GEMEINDE that forms part of a KREIS.

KREISANGEHÖRIGE STADT
A small town that is part of a KREIS.

KREISAUSSCHUSS
A second decision-making body in KREISE (the KREISTAG being the first), with the LANDRAT as chairman.

KREISDIREKTOR
The deputy to the OBERKREISDIREKTOR in a large KREIS in NORDRHEIN-WESTFALEN and NIEDERSACHSEN.

KREISFREIE STADT
A large town generally with more than 100,000 inhabitants that is not part of a KREIS. The local authority carries out the functions associated with the GEMEINDE and the Kreis.

KREISGERICHT
The lowest court in the NEUE BUNDESLÄNDER, corresponding to the AMTSGERICHT.

KREISHAUS See: *LANDRATSAMT*

KREISORDNUNG See: *GEMEINDEORDNUNG*

KREISPRÄSIDENT
Chairman of the KREISTAG in SCHLESWIG-HOLSTEIN, elected by the members of the Kreistag.

KREISRAT See: *KREISAUSSCHUSS*; *KREISTAGS-ABGEORDNETER*

KREISSTADT
A town that is the administrative centre of a KREIS. See also: KREISFREIE STADT

KREISTAG
The decision-making body elected by the electorate in a KREIS by secret ballot. The members of the Kreistag are honorary, and the chairperson of the Kreistag is the LANDRAT or a KREISPRÄSIDENT.

KREISTAGSABGEORDNETER
A member of the KREISTAG, also known as *Kreisrat*, *Kreisverordneter* or *Kreistagsmitglied.*

KREISTAGSMITGLIED See: *KREISTAGSABGEORDNETER*

KREISVERORDNETER See: *KREISTAGSABGEORDNETER*

KREISVERWALTUNG
The local authority governing a KREIS.

KRIEGSDIENST See: *WEHRDIENST*

KRIEGSDIENSTVERWEIGERER
A conscientious objector to WEHRDIENST. *Artikel* 4 of the GRUNDGESETZ provides that nobody should have to serve in the armed forces if they object on grounds of conscience. If a case is accepted, the individual has to serve for 13 months in ZIVILDIENST.

KRIMINALPOLIZEI (KRIPO)
The police responsible for preventing and investigating crimes. The *Kriminalpolizei* is concerned with detection in organised

crime, and other serious crimes such as rape, murder, blackmail, drugs, etc. They have special units available that can be deployed to combat terrorism and rescue hostages.

KRIPO See: *KRIMINALPOLIZEI*

KROETZ, FRANZ XAVER (1946–   )
Playwright, producer and actor who uses BAIRISCH to great effect and carries on the tradition of the *Volksstück*, depicting the struggle of the ordinary person against an impersonal, uniform society. His plays have caused a number of scandals, notably the première at the Münchner Kammerspiele of *Bauern sterben* (1985) with its realistic worm-ridden corpses, blood and *Scheiße* galore. Other plays include *Wildwechsel* (1973, film by R.W. Fassbinder 1972), *Heimarbeit* (1971), *Oblomow* (1989), *Der Drang* (1994) and *Ich bin das Volk* (1994). TV appearances have brought him popularity as an actor.

KRUPP AG HOESCH-KRUPP, FRIED.
Engineering group mainly involved in capital goods. The company was originally founded in 1811 and developed from a coalmining and steel company into an armaments manufacturer. Company headquarters are in ESSEN. Krupp has some 66,000 employees.

KRUZIFIX-URTEIL
A decision by the BUNDESVERFASSUNGSGERICHT in 1995 that declared a regulation in BAYERN requiring GRUNDSCHULEN and HAUPT-SCHULEN to have a cross in each classroom as contrary to the constitution. The decision attracted fierce criticism from the CSU and generated wide-ranging public debate.

KU'DAMM See: *KURFÜRSTENDAMM*

KUHN, ROLF (1929–   )
Leading jazz clarinetist who spent the 1950s and 1960s playing in the US (for some time with Benny Goodman) and then returned to Germany to form a big band at NDR.

KULTUR
The concept of *Kultur* denotes the realms of education, learning

and the arts (e.g. in KULTUSMINISTERIEN) and has high status. It is also used more broadly for 'civilisation'.

KULTURHOHEIT DER LÄNDER
The cultural autonomy of the LÄNDER is enshrined in the GRUNDGESETZ. The Länder are responsible for education, cultural affairs and broadcasting. However, in certain areas (e.g. HOCHSCHULEN) the BUND has the right to enact framework legislation (*Rahmengesetze*) laying down general principles within which the Länder are empowered to enact their own detailed legislation. See also: BUNDESMINISTERIUM FÜR BILDUNG, WISSENSCHAFT, FORSCHUNG UND TECHNOLOGIE; BUNDESRECHT; KULTUSMINISTERIUM

KULTURPOLITIK
Responsibility for cultural affairs in Germany is divided between the BUND, the LÄNDER, the Church and the individual. Education and internal cultural affairs fall mainly within the remit of the Länder, while cultural affairs abroad are the province of the AUSWÄRTIGES AMT. See also: KULTURHOHEIT DER LÄNDER; GOETHE-INSTITUT

KULTURPREIS DES DEUTSCHEN GEWERKSCHAFTSBUNDES
A prize of DM 20,000 for cultural achievements promoting social progress, sponsored by the DEUTSCHER GEWERKSCHAFTSBUND. The prize was started in 1963 and is awarded annually.

KULTUSMINISTERIUM
The ministry responsible for cultural affairs in each LAND. The BUNDESMINISTERIUM FÜR BILDUNG, WISSENSCHAFT, FORSCHUNG UND TECHNOLOGIE only regulates a carefully circumscribed and restricted range of matters relating to cultural affairs, e.g. general guidelines for tertiary education, grants, research funding and general legislation on press. For most aspects of KULTUR, i.e. education, the arts, sciences and cultural affairs, the *Kultusministerien* of the Länder are in effect the highest authorities in Germany. See also: KULTURHOHEIT DER LÄNDER

KULTUSMINISTERKONFERENZ See: *STÄNDIGE KONFERENZ DER KULTUSMINISTER DER LÄNDER IN DER BUNDESREPUBLIK DEUTSCHLAND*

KÜNDIGUNGSFRIST

The minimum period of notice that is laid down in a contract of employment.

KUNERT, GÜNTER (1929–)

Writer of poems, short stories, essays and plays for radio and television. He studied applied arts before turning to writing. Kunert was expelled from the SED in 1977 and moved to the BRD in 1979. His early poems were in the style of socialist realism but his work adopted an increasingly critical tone, which led to his expulsion from the SED. His works include *Offener Ausgang* (1972), *Berlin beizeiten* (1987), *Fremd daheim* (1990) and *Die letzten Indianer Europas* (1991).

KÜNG, HANS (1928–)

Catholic theologian and professor of theology at TÜBINGEN (EBER-HARD-KARLS-UNIVERSITÄT). A critic of the infallibility (*Unfehlbarkeit*) of the Pope, he was deprived of the right to teach at Catholic institutions, but a chair in ecumenical theology was created at Tübingen. He has written widely on the reunification of Churches and the relationship between the Church and the world. His works include *Struktur der Kirche* (1962), *Unfehlbar? Eine Anfrage* (1970), *Ewiges Leben?* (1982), *Theologie im Aufbruch* (1987), *Das Judentum* (1991) and *Große christliche Denker* (1994).

KUNSTHALLE BREMEN

Founded in 1823, the Kunsthalle Bremen is one of Germany's oldest municipal art galleries, housing a collection of European painting from the fifteenth to the twentieth centuries. It is particularly strong in the nineteenth and early twentieth centuries.

KUNSTHOCHSCHULEN

Germany has 22 HOCHSCHULEN for fine and applied arts.

KUNSTSAMMLUNG NORDRHEIN-WESTFALEN

Gallery in DÜSSELDORF with a remarkable collection of paintings by Paul Klee and an extensive array of twentieth-century art.

KUNZE, REINER (1933–)

Poet and writer who studied philosophy and journalism. He was a member of the SED in 1949–1968 but fell foul of the authorities and emigrated to the BRD in 1977, where he was awarded the GEORG-BÜCHNER-PREIS in the same year. Kunze's work includes *Sensible Wege* (1969), *Zimmerlautstärke* (1972), *Die wunderbaren Jahre* (1976, BRD, 1979), *Wohin der Schlaf sich schlafen legt* (1991) and *Wo Freiheit ist. Gespräche 1977–1993* (1994). The volume *Deckname »Lyrik«* (1990) documents his surveillance by the STAATSSICHERHEITSDIENST. Kunze has also written numerous children's books and translated from Czech.

KUR

A health cure normally lasting around a month. A massive industry has grown up around the propensity of many Germans to 'take the waters', breathe pure air, wallow in mud and engage in healthy exercise courtesy of the KRANKENKASSEN or privately. Sebastian Kneipp (1821–1897) was a pioneer of the German *Kur* industry and developed the popular *Kneipp-Kur*. Big spa ressorts include Bad Mergentheim (BADEN-WÜRTTEMBERG) on the ROMANTISCHE STRASSE and Bad Wörishofen (BAYERN). An essential adjunct for many is the *Kurschatten* of the opposite sex at the tea dance and the evening rumba.

KURFÜRSTENDAMM (KU'DAMM)

Famous shopping boulevard $3\frac{1}{2}$ km. long and over 50 m. wide in west BERLIN. Originally it was laid out in the sixteenth century as a causeway leading to the Elector's hunting lodge in the Grunewald.

KURS

General term for 'course'. Also more specifically a teaching module running for half the school year in the senior classes of the GYMNASIUM and the GESAMTSCHULE; pupils are able to draw up their own study programme from the *Kurse* offered in compulsory and optional subjects. See also: GRUNDKURS; LEISTUNGSKURS

KURZARBEIT

Short-time working introduced when there is a drop in work for the workforce of a business. If this includes a reduction in pay, management have to seek the agreement of the BETRIEBSRAT or the workforce. See also: KURZARBEITERGELD

KURZARBEITERGELD

An allowance paid under the ARBEITSLOSENVERSICHERUNG to short-time workers who are required to work and be paid less than their contracted number of hours each week due to a lack of work. It is paid when a company has officially registered KURZARBEIT with the ARBEITSAMT and at least a third of the workforce has been affected by a drop in work of 10% for a minimum of four weeks. The allowance is 63% (68% for employees with children) of the usual net pay and is generally paid for a maximum of six months.

LADENSCHLUSSZEITEN

Germany traditionally has some of the most restrictive opening hours for shops in Europe. Closing times have been governed by the *Ladenschlußgesetz* dating from 1956, with shops allowed to open Monday to Friday from 7.00 am but having to close by 6.30 pm (2.00 pm on Saturdays) with late-night shopping until 8.30 pm on Thursdays. There are certain exceptions for pharmacies, newspaper kiosks, hairdressers and service stations, and special rules apply to shops in railway stations and airports. Following considerable controversy, it was agreed in November 1995 to extend opening times to 8.00 pm on weekdays and to permit Saturday opening until between 2.00 and 6.00 pm depending on the LAND.

LAFONTAINE, OSKAR (1943–   )

Physicist and SPD politician. He was a member of the LANDTAG in SAARLAND in 1970–1975 and OBERBÜRGERMEISTER of SAARBRÜCKEN in 1976–1985. Lafontaine has been MINISTERPRÄSIDENT of the Saarland since 1985 and was selected as the KANZLERKANDIDAT in the 1990 BUNDESTAGSWAHL. Just before the election in 1990 he was stabbed in a maverick attack at an election rally. This election was fought on the issue of reunification and Lafontaine made much of the negative social consequences of the reunification of Germany but the CDU/CSU with Helmut KOHL gained a landslide victory. In 1995 Lafontaine was elected *Bundesvorsitzender* of the SPD in a dawn coup against Rudolf SCHARPING. He is known to be in favour of a red/green alliance for the 1998 elections that does not exclude the possibility of cooperation with the PDS.

LAG See: *LANDESARBEITSGERICHT*

LAGERFELD, KARL (1938–   )

Fashion designer and head of design at Chanel. He has lived in Paris since 1952 and is famous both for creative designs and off-the-peg collections. Lagerfeld has had his own firm in Germany, Karl Lagerfeld-Impression, since 1974 and has been designing collections for German fashion house Klaus Steilmann since 1987.

LAND

Germany consists of 16 Länder with three STADTSTAATEN (BERLIN, BREMEN, HAMBURG) and 13 FLÄCHENSTAATEN (BADEN-WÜRTTEMBERG, BAYERN, BRANDENBURG, HESSEN, MECKLENBURG-VORPOMMERN, NIEDER-SACHSEN, NORDRHEIN-WESTFALEN, SAARLAND, SACHSEN, SACHSEN-ANHALT, SCHLESWIG-HOLSTEIN, THÜRINGEN). The Land is the second tier of state government in Germany's federal system. Each Land collects all the taxes due to the BUND, from which it receives a share, as well as collecting its own taxes. The LAND is responsible for education, culture, broadcasting, police, environment, local government and planning. Members of the LANDTAG are elected every four or five years, and the individual Länder enjoy considerable autonomy even to the extent of having large holdings in companies (e.g. Niedersachsen holds shares in VOLKS-WAGEN). Each Land sends three to six members to the BUNDESRAT, depending on its population. See also: ABGEORDNETENHAUS, BÜR-GERSCHAFT

LANDESAMT FÜR DENKMALPFLEGE

The central office of a LAND that is responsible for the preservation and upkeep of the cultural heritage. The *Landeskonservator* is the head of this office and is directly responsible to the KULTUS-MINISTERIUM.

LANDESARBEITSGERICHT (LAG)

The court of second instance for settling labour disputes where the amount in dispute is greater than DM 800. Disputes may be between ARBEITNEHMER and ARBEITGEBER, between *Arbeitnehmer*, or between unions and management. The Landesarbeitsgericht also deals with cases related to the BETRIEBSVERFASSUNGSGESETZ and TARIFVERTRÄGE. The court is made up of a BERUFSRICHTER as chairperson and two EHRENAMTLICHE RICHTER (one *Arbeitnehmer*, one *Arbeitgeber*). The court settling this type of dispute in the NEUE BUNDESLÄNDER is known as the *Bezirksgericht*. See also: ARBEITSGERICHT; BUNDESARBEITSGERICHT

LANDESÄRZTEKAMMER
The professional body in each LAND to which all doctors have to belong.

LANDESBANKEN (GIROZENTRALEN)
Regional banks for the SPARKASSEN, owned partly by the LAND and partly by the *Sparkassen*. They provide finance for and promote the economy of the Land. They also act as clearing houses (*Girozentralen*) for the *Sparkassen* and manage the liquid reserves of the member *Sparkassen*. They approve loans which are beyond the authority of individual *Sparkassen* and manage payment transactions within the giro system. See also: DEUTSCHE GIROZENTRALE; DEUTSCHER SPARKASSEN- UND GIROVERBAND

LANDESDIREKTOR
The HAUPTVERWALTUNGSBEAMTER of a LANDSCHAFTSVERBAND.

LANDESHAUPTSTADT
The capital city of a LAND. The *Landeshauptstädte* are: BERLIN, BREMEN, DRESDEN, DÜSSELDORF, ERFURT, HAMBURG, HANNOVER, KIEL, MAGDEBURG, MAINZ, MÜNCHEN, POTSDAM, SAARBRÜCKEN, SCHWERIN, STUTTGART, WIESBADEN.

LANDESKRIMINALAMT (LKA)
The office responsible for the KRIMINALPOLIZEI in each LAND. The *Landeskriminalämter* are independent, although the BUNDESKRIMINALAMT helps to coordinate activities when crime goes beyond Land borders.

LANDESLISTE
The list of candidates selected by a party in a particular LAND, for which the electorate votes in a BUNDESTAGSWAHL.

LANDESPARLAMENT
The elected representative body or parliament in a LAND. It is

called the LANDTAG in BADEN-WÜRTTEMBERG, BAYERN, BRANDEN-
BURG, HESSEN, MECKLENBURG-VORPOMMERN, NIEDERSACHSEN, NORD-
RHEIN-WESTFALEN, SAARLAND, SACHSEN, SACHSEN-ANHALT, SCHLESWIG-
HOLSTEIN, THÜRINGEN. In BREMEN and HAMBURG the *Landesparlament*
is known as the BÜRGERSCHAFT and in BERLIN as the ABGEORD-
NETENHAUS.

LANDESRAT
A BEIGEORDNETER of a LANDSCHAFTSVERBAND.

LANDESRECHT See: *BUNDESRECHT*

LANDESREGIERUNG
The government of a LAND comprising the MINISTERPRÄSIDENT and
the MINISTER (*Staatsminister* in BAYERN, HESSEN and SACHSEN). In
the STADTSTAATEN (BERLIN, BREMEN and HAMBURG) the
Landesregierung is known as the SENAT and the ministers as SENA-
TOREN.

LANDESRUNDFUNK- UND FERNSEHANSTALTEN
There are 11 regional broadcasting stations in the BRD: BAY-
ERISCHER RUNDFUNK, HESSISCHER RUNDFUNK, MITTELDEUTSCHER RUND-
FUNK, NORDDEUTSCHER RUNDFUNK, OSTDEUTSCHER RUNDFUNK BRAN-
DENBURG, RADIO BREMEN, SAARLÄNDISCHER RUNDFUNK, SENDER FREIES
BERLIN, SÜDDEUTSCHER RUNDFUNK, SÜDWESTFUNK, WESTDEUTSCHER
RUNDFUNK. Together with the two BUNDESRUNDFUNKANSTALTEN
these form the ARD and produce programmes for the ERSTES PRO-
GRAMM. They also produce their own programmes for the DRITTES
PROGRAMM.

LANDESVERBAND
An association dedicated to a particular purpose at LAND level.
See also: BUNDESVERBAND

LANDESZENTRALBANKEN (LZB)
The main administrative centres for the DEUTSCHE BUNDESBANK in
each LAND. They carry out financial transactions between the
government, the authorities and the banks in each Land, and
coordinate payments within the Land.

LANDGEMEINDE
Term used to refer to a rural GEMEINDE. The term carries no legal status.

LANDGERICHT
The court in the German legal system above the AMTSGERICHT. The Landgericht is a regional court and is empowered to hear all civil claims that do not come under the jurisdiction of the Amtsgericht, as well as more serious criminal cases which carry a minimum sentence of one year or more. The court is divided into Zivilkammer, Strafkammer and Jugendkammer. The Landgericht hears the majority of appeals from the Amtsgericht. Appeals against the Landgericht are heard by the OBERLANDES-GERICHT.

LANDKREIS See: *KREIS*

LANDKREISORDNUNG See: *GEMEINDEORDNUNG*

LANDRAT, EHRENAMTLICHER
Honorary chairperson of the KREISTAG in NORDRHEIN-WESTFALEN and NIEDERSACHSEN. See also: OBERKREISDIREKTOR

LANDRAT, HAUPTAMTLICHER
The senior BEAMTER in a KREIS and chairperson of the KREISTAG. The Landrat is elected by the electorate or the Kreistag, or is appointed by the LAND with the agreement of the Kreistag. In some Länder the position of senior *Beamter* of the Kreis is separate from that of Kreistag chairperson, e.g. Kreise in NORDRHEIN-WESTFALEN and NIEDERSACHSEN have a full-time OBERKREISDIREKTOR and an honorary chairman of the Kreistag (LANDRAT, EHREN-AMTLICHER).

LANDRATSAMT
Building that accommodates the administrative offices of the LANDRAT.

LANDSCHAFTSVERBAND
Two regional authorities in NORDRHEIN-WESTFALEN (Rheinland and Westfalen-Lippe) that comprise the KREISFREIE STÄDTE and KREISE in the two areas. They are elected indirectly and are

responsible for certain statutory duties that are administered more effectively on a regional basis, e.g. welfare and roads.

LANDSHUTER FÜRSTENHOCHZEIT
Festival and procession held every three years, re-enacting the wedding of Bavarian Duke Georg der Reiche to the Polish princess Hedwig in 1475.

LANDTAG
The elected parliament at LAND level (LANDESPARLAMENT). This is known as the ABGEORDNETENHAUS in BERLIN and as the BÜRGER-SCHAFT in BREMEN and HAMBURG. The Landtag is elected every four or five years and enacts legislation. Executive power is in the hands of the LANDESREGIERUNG.

LANDTAGSABGEORDNETER See: *ABGEORDNETER*

LANDTAGSFRAKTION See: *FRAKTION*

LANDTAGSWAHL
The elections to the LANDTAG in each LAND are held every four or five years. Like BUNDESTAGSWAHLEN, the elections for the Landtag are a mixture of proportional representation and candidates elected directly. The ZWEITSTIMMEN hold the key to final percentages and therefore to the number of MANDATE for each party in the Landtag. The first *Landtagswahlen* were held in all four occupation zones in 1946.

LANDWIRT
Term used to describe an independent farmer or tenant farmer.

LANDWIRTSCHAFTLICHE KRANKENKASSEN
PFLICHTKRANKENKASSEN for LANDWIRTE and working members of their families.

LANDWIRTSCHAFTLICHE RENTENBANK
A national bank providing loans to agriculture. The bank was founded in 1949 and is based in FRANKFURT AM MAIN. See also: ÖFFENTLICH-RECHTLICHE KREDITINSTITUTE

LANDWIRTSCHAFTSKAMMER
Organisations representing the interests of agriculture and
forestry in part of a LAND or throughout a particular Land.

LANG, ALEXANDER (1941–   )
Actor and producer with the BERLINER ENSEMBLE in 1967–1969
and the Deutsches Theater in East BERLIN in 1969–1986 known
for his stylised productions. Lang was producer at the Thalia-
Theater HAMBURG in 1987–1989 and artistic director at the
Staatliche Schaubühne Berlin in 1990–1993. His productions
include Heiner Müller's *Philoktet* (1977), Lessing's *Miß Sara
Sampson* (1978), Schiller's *Don Carlos* (1985) and Bernhard's
Über allen Gipfeln ist Ruh' (1993).

LÄRMSCHUTZ
Protection against noise pollution is provided by comprehensive
regulations against excessive noise on building sites, in factories,
in the home and in the environment (e.g. motor vehicles, aircraft). Regulations are such that domestic use of power tools and
lawnmowers is prohibited on Sundays, and some SPIELPLÄTZE can
only be used between certain times to protect nearby residents
from noise.

LAST, JAMES (1929–   )
Bandleader, composer and arranger (real name Hans Last)
whose big band has remained popular since the 1960s. His popular arrangements of international hits, German folk songs, classical music, etc. have brought him many record awards.

LASTENAUSGLEICH
The system of compensation for injustices caused by the Nazi
regime and for the welfare of war veterans and dependants. The
system also provided compensation for losses and damage sustained as a result of the destruction during the Second World
War and compensation for the effects of the displacement of
German populations from the eastern territories during and
after the war. Over a period of 40 years this system of compensation helped more than eight million Germans who suffered damage to property, and 12 million refugees from the territories
overrun by the Soviet Union. The system will continue to pro-

vide pensions well into the next century. See also: DEUTSCHE AUS-
GLEICHSBANK; VERTRIEBENE

LASTENAUSGLEICHSBANK See: *DEUTSCHE AUSGLEICHSBANK*

LAUSITZ
A historical region divided into Oberlausitz and Niederlausitz,
most of the Oberlausitz now being in SACHSEN and Niederlausitz
being in BRANDENBURG. Those parts east of the river Neiße now
belong to Poland. Lausitz is the traditional home of the SORBEN.

LEBENSHALTUNGSKOSTEN
The costs used to calculate the official cost-of-living index based
on the WARENKORB of basic goods and services. It is used to mea-
sure changes in retail prices.

LEBENSLAUF
The curriculum vitae prepared by any applicant for a job. This
may be in tabular form or a discursive document. The requirement for a handwritten *Lebenslauf* is dying out, and the tabular
form generally takes precedence.

LEBENSMITTEL-KENNZEICHNUNGSVERORDNUNG
Regulations requiring manufacturers and importers of foodstuffs
to give certain information on the packaging, including the name
and place of manufacture, the contents, a description of the
ingredients, the best-by date and the alcohol content.

LEBENSRAUM
The concept of 'living space' which was used to justify territorial
expansion in the propaganda of the Nazis.

LEGISLATURPERIODE See: *WAHLPERIODE*

LEGITIMATION NICHTEHELICHER KINDER
The process by which children conceived out of wedlock can
acquire the legal status of a legitimate child.

LEHRAMT
The official title for the position of a teacher in a state school
(GRUNDSCHULE, HAUPTSCHULE, REALSCHULE, GYMNASIUM, GESAMT-
SCHULE, BERUFSSCHULE).

LEHRBRIEF See: *STUDIENBRIEF*

LEHRE
The old term for BERUFSAUSBILDUNG but still used extensively in spoken language to refer to an apprenticeship and the vocational training system in Germany.

LEHRERKONFERENZ
The official meeting of all the teachers in a school, which takes decisions on matters relating to the internal administration of a school.

LEHRHERR See: *AUSBILDENDER*

LEHRLING
The old term for AUSZUBILDENDER but still used extensively in industry and commerce to refer to apprentices or trainees.

LEHRPLAN
The curriculum for the different types of school in each LAND, based on principles agreed by the KULTUSMINISTERKONFERENZ.

LEHRSTUHL
Official chair in a particular subject at a HOCHSCHULE, to which a PROFESSOR is appointed.

LEHRVERGÜTUNG
The wage earned by an AUSZUBILDENDER during the two- or three-year training period. The wage rises annually.

LEHRVERTRAG
The contract governing the relationship between the AUSBILDEN-DER and the AUSZUBILDENDER.

LEHRZEIT
The period of time during which an AUSZUBILDENDER is undergoing training, generally between two and three years in accordance with the vocational skills taught on the training programme.

LEIPZIG
Leipzig is situated at the confluence of the rivers Weiße Elster and Pleiße in SACHSEN (dialling code 03 41, postal area code 04. . .).

It was granted a charter in 1165 and the city developed as an important commercial centre when the status of its two annual markets was raised to that of fairs. Until 1945 Leipzig was the centre of the German book trade with the world's biggest book fair, and it still houses the largest German-language library in the world – the DEUTSCHE BÜCHEREI. In 1989 Leipzig led the way in bringing about the downfall of the Communist regime when its people took to the streets in peaceful protest and the police looked on powerless. Leipzig has a proud musical heritage – Wagner was born there and Bach and Mendelssohn spent the last years of their lives in Leipzig. The city's festivals include a Bachfest at Easter; a festival of concerts in the Leipziger Kulturwoche in October; and the Lachmesse celebrating the city's satirical tradition at Leipzig's famous cabarets (Academixer, Funzel and Pfeffermühle).

The city has a population of some 488,000 with a total student population of around 23,000 (1 UNIVERSITÄT and 5 other HOCHSCHULEN) and about 3% foreigners (23% Polish). A coalition between the SPD, BÜNDNIS 90/DIE GRÜNEN and the CDU has been running the city since 1990. The Leipziger Messe has an unbroken tradition from the Middle Ages, and since reunification the traditional spring fair has been repositioned as a grouping of specialist fairs including the BAU-FACHMESSE LEIPZIG, LEIPZIGER BUCHMESSE and LEIPZIGER MESSE AUTO MOBIL INTERNATIONAL. Leipzig's main industries include chemical-plant and machinery construction, printing machinery, chemicals and pharmaceuticals, and exploitation of the area's lignite deposits. The city is home to Blüthner pianos and important companies include QUELLE and MITTELDEUTSCHER RUNDFUNK.

LEIPZIG, UNIVERSITÄT

University in SACHSEN founded in 1409 and teaching some 18,000 students. The Universität Leipzig has faculties of theology, law, economics, history and art and oriental studies, languages and literature, education, mathematics and computer science, life sciences and pharmacology and psychology, physics and earth sciences, chemistry and mineralogy, social sciences and philosophy, sports science, medicine, veterinary medicine.

LEIPZIGER BUCHMESSE
The 'Leipzig Book Fair' – Germany's biggest book fair before the Second World War – is held in LEIPZIG every two years with around 40,000 visitors.

LEIPZIGER MESSE AUTO MOBIL INTERNATIONAL
The 'Leipzig Fair Auto Mobil International' for cars, commercial vehicles and accessories is a trade fair for the automobile industry held in LEIPZIG annually with around 170,000 visitors.

LEIPZIGER VOLKSZEITUNG
Daily newspaper published in LEIPZIG with a circulation of 368,000.

LEISTUNGSGESELLSCHAFT
Term referring to present-day Western society with its consumerism, materialism and achievement, whereby an individual's social standing is based on achievements rather than class or a hereditary position in society. Many young people in Germany have traditionally sought ways of escaping from the pressures to achieve in society, and the ARBEITSMORAL so prevalent among the older generations in the 1950s and 1960s has given way to a mood that follows the pleasure principle.

LEISTUNGSKURS
Course lasting one *Halbjahr* in a special subject (*Leistungsfach*) taken by pupils during the last two years at the GYMNASIUM. *Leistungskurse* cover an area of study in greater depth than is the case with GRUNDKURSE. It is compulsory to take eight *Leistungskurse* in two *Leistungsfächer* for ABITUR (three *Leistungsfächer* in RHEINLAND-PFALZ and SAARLAND). *Leistungskurse* generally have five to six hours allocated in the school timetable each week. One of the *Leistungsfächer* must build on previous study, e.g. a foreign language, mathematics, science.

LEISTUNGSNACHWEIS
Certificate issued at a HOCHSCHULE confirming attendance and completion of a course of study (ÜBUNG, SEMINAR or PRAKTIKUM) during a STUDIUM. It generally has a grade and is necessary for

continuation to the next part of the *Studium* or for registration for examinations.

LEITARTIKEL

The leader article in a newspaper or magazine, in which a senior editor expresses an opinion on a major news item in the day's paper.

LEKTOR

A member of the teaching staff at a UNIVERSITÄT generally from another country and employed on a fixed-term contract to teach language classes and cultural studies. See also: DEUTSCHER AKADEMISCHER AUSTAUSCHDIENST

LEMPER, UTE (1963–   )

Actress, singer and dancer who rocketed to fame in the 1980s in roles such as Katze Bombalurina in *Cats* (1983), the leading role in *Peter Pan* (1984) and Sally Bowles in the musical *Cabaret* (1986) and with her interpretations of Kurt Weill's music. She made her ballet début in *La mort subite* (1991) and played the main role in the revue *Der blaue Engel* in 1992.

LEONHARD, WOLFGANG (1921–   )

Author, historian and journalist who emigrated from Germany in 1933, spending the years 1935–1945 in the Soviet Union and returning to the Soviet occupation zone with Walter Ulbricht in 1945. He taught at the SED *Parteihochschule Karl-Marx* in 1947–1949 before quitting the DDR for Yugoslavia and the BRD. Leonhard was professor of history at Yale in 1966–1987 and has worked on the problems of socialism, particularly as it was applied in the Soviet Union. His publications include *Die Revolution entläßt ihre Kinder* (1955), *Kreml ohne Stalin* (1959), *Dämmerung im Kreml* (1984), *Der Schock des Hitler-Stalin-Paktes* (1986), *Das kurze Leben der DDR* (1990) and *Die Reform entläßt ihre Väter. Der steinige Weg zum modernen Rußland* (1994).

LERNMITTELFREIHEIT

School books are supplied free of charge in most LÄNDER. Their content tends to be carefully controlled by the KULTUSMINISTERIUM of the respective Land.

LIDL & SCHWARZ STIFTUNG

Discount food chain founded in 1930 with over 1,000 discount food stores. Company headquarters are in Neckarsulm (BADEN-WÜRTTEMBERG). Lidl has some 30,000 employees.

LIMBACH, JUTTA (1934–   )

Judge, professor of law and PRÄSIDENTIN of the BUNDESVERFAS-SUNGSGERICHT. She was Justizsenatorin (SPD) in BERLIN in 1989–1994 and was head of a body investigating former DDR judges and STAATSANWÄLTE, restructuring the legal system in the NEUE BUNDESLÄNDER and looking into criminal actions by the government of the former DDR. She was the first woman to be appointed president of the Bundesverfassungsgericht in 1994 when Roman HERZOG was elected BUNDESPRÄSIDENT.

LINDE AG

Engineering company founded in 1879 and specialising in process engineering, materials-handling equipment, refrigeration and industrial gases. Company headquarters are in WIESBADEN. Linde has some 30,000 employees.

LINDENBERG, UDO (1946–   )

Rock musician and singer who hit the German pop scene in the 1970s with the LP *Udo Lindenberg & Das Panik-Orchester* (1972) and propagated rock with a social conscience. At the end of the 1980s he became a symbol uniting rock fans from east and west. His recordings include *Ball pompös* (1974), *Wotan Wahnwitz* (1975), *Sündenknall* (1985), *Casa Nova* (1989) and *Panik-Panther* (1992).

LINDENSTRASSE

The longest-running German TV soap (from 1985) with more than 500 weekly episodes and over 7 million regular Sunday-evening viewers. The series is based on famous British soap *Coronation Street* and aims to portray everyday life in the BRD.

LKA See: *LANDESKRIMINALAMT*

LOHN

Traditionally the wage earned by a blue-collar worker and paid weekly. In a term such as LOHNSTEUER, the GEHALT earned by an ANGESTELLTER is also considered as *Lohn*. The terms *Lohn* and *Gehalt* have officially been subsumed under the umbrella term ENTGELT.

LOHNFORTZAHLUNG

The pay that an ARBEITGEBER has to pay an ARBEITNEHMER for a period of six weeks after the first day of illness, at which point the KRANKENKASSE pays KRANKENGELD during continued sickness. The employee is obliged to notify the employer how long the illness is likely to last and if the illness lasts longer than three days he or she must provide a doctor's certificate (*ärztliche Bescheinigung*) by the following working day.

LOHNSTEUER

A personal tax on income (i.e. a type of EINKOMMENSTEUER) that is deducted at source from all persons who are not self-employed. The tax is collected from an individual's ENTGELT by the ARBEITGEBER who forwards it to the FINANZAMT. Any adjustments necessary are made by means of the LOHNSTEUERJAHRES-AUSGLEICH. The amount of tax deducted is governed by the LOHNSTEUERTABELLE and the tax class entered on a person's LOHN-STEUERKARTE.

There are six tax classes. *Klasse I* is for single, divorced, separated or widowed individuals. *Klasse II* is for the same group if they have one or more children. *Klasse III* covers married couples where one spouse is earning (not self-employed) and the other is either unwaged or taxed under *Klasse V; Klasse III* also covers widowed individuals whose spouse died in the current fiscal year or the previous year. *Klasse IV* is for married couples where both partners are earning and not self-employed. *Klasse V* is an elective tax class for married couples where both partners are earning (not self-employed); married couples may elect the combination *Klasse III/V* or *Klasse IV/IV*: where earnings are unequal the couple would choose *Klasse III/V* (because

Klasse III is a more favourable tax class for the higher earner) while two spouses with relatively equal earnings would choose *Klasse IV/IV. Klasse VI* is for individuals who have earnings from a second (and third, etc.) employment.

LOHNSTEUERBESCHEINIGUNG

The certificate given to the ARBEITNEHMER by the ARBEITGEBER at the end of each financial year giving details of length of service, pay, KIRCHENSTEUER and LOHNSTEUER paid, and any other deductions.

LOHNSTEUERJAHRESAUSGLEICH

The procedure by which an ARBEITNEHMER's income is assessed for each fiscal year. This may be carried out by the ARBEITGEBER, or in certain cases an individual applies to the FINANZAMT. The purpose of the *Lohnsteuerjahresausgleich* is to ensure that the *Arbeitnehmer* pays no more tax than is due. Any refund is deducted from the next year's LOHNSTEUER or refunded directly.

LOHNSTEUERKARTE

A tax deduction card that is issued to an employee by the GEMEINDE or STADT indicating an individual's tax class and other details relevant to tax. See also: LOHNSTEUER

LOHNSTEUERTABELLE

Table issued by the FINANZAMT showing employers how much LOHNSTEUER to deduct from an employee's wage or salary.

LOKALPRESSE

The local or regional press that is centred on a particular town or city and its immediate surroundings. Germany's press is characterised by a large number of regional broadsheets.

LORIOT (1923–   )

Graphic artist, cartoonist and author (real name Vicco von Bülow), who has achieved cult status among aficionados. He rose to fame with his *Knollennasenmännchen* series of cartoons in which he satirises petty bourgeois behaviour in a humorous manner. This theme persists throughout his work and he has also written satirical TV series such as *Cartoon* (1967–1972). The films *Ödipussi* (1988) and *Papa ante Portas* (1991) take a humorously ironic look at everyday situations.

LORSCH
This Benedictine abbey in HESSEN founded in 764 has been made a UNESCO world heritage site.

LOVE-PARADE
Bizarre procession of 200,000 young people along the KURFÜRSTENDAMM held every summer in BERLIN since 1989 celebrating the TECHNO cult in a public display of hedonism.

LÜBECK
Lübeck is situated on the river Trave a few miles from the Ostsee in SCHLESWIG-HOLSTEIN (dialling code 04 51, postal area code 23...). The city was founded in 1143, became a *Reichsstadt* (free imperial city) in 1226 and in 1243 formed a trading alliance with HAMBURG which later developed into the Hanseatic League. Lübeck's influence receded with the decline of the Hanse and changes in trading patterns, and the free city was integrated into Schleswig-Holstein in 1937. Lübeck was home to Heinrich and Thomas Mann, and the city's Marienkirche houses the world's largest mechanical instrument (an organ). The city's architectural wealth of Gothic churches and merchants' houses was recognised in 1987 when the whole of the ALTSTADT was made a world heritage site by UNESCO. Festivals include the Markt anno dazumal in May and the biennial Altstadtfest in September.

The city has a population of some 216,000 with a total student population of around 5,000 (1 UNIVERSITÄT and 2 other HOCHSCHULEN) and about 8% foreigners (38% Turkish). The SPD has been running the city as the strongest party since 1990, although lack of an absolute majority has necessitated the support of other parties. The city's medieval wealth was built on trade and the port still trades in coal, timber, ores and manufactured goods. Industries include shipbuilding, engineering, medical equipment, food processing and the manufacture of the famous *Lübecker Marzipan*.

LÜBECK, MEDIZINISCHE UNIVERSITÄT ZU

Medical school in SCHLESWIG-HOLSTEIN founded in 1963 and teaching some 2,000 students.

LUDWIG, PETER (1925–   )

Owner of the Ludwig Schokoladen AG, art collector and patron of the arts. He donated his collection of American pop art comprising 340 pictures to the city of KÖLN to be housed in the Museum Ludwig in the WALLRAF-RICHARTZ-MUSEUM.

LUDWIGSHAFEN (AM RHEIN)

Ludwigshafen is situated on the left bank of the Rhine opposite MANNHEIM in RHEINLAND-PFALZ (dialling code 06 21, postal area code 67...). The city received its charter in 1859 and has developed into a modern industrial centre.

Ludwigshafen has a population of some 171,000 with a student population of around 3,000 (2 HOCHSCHULEN) and about 18% foreigners (31% Turkish). A coalition between the SPD and BÜNDNIS 90/DIE GRÜNEN has been running the city since 1994. The chemicals giant BASF (founded in 1865) dominates the city with Europe's biggest chemicals complex. Other industries include pharmaceuticals, steel, electrical engineering and glass.

LUFTHANSA See *DEUTSCHE LUFTHANSA AG*

LUFTWAFFE

The airborne forces of the BUNDESWEHR are divided into four divisions and come under the command of the BUNDESMINISTER DER VERTEIDIGUNG in peacetime and the BUNDESKANZLER if the country is under attack.

LÜNEBURG, UNIVERSITÄT

University in NIEDERSACHSEN founded in 1946 and teaching some 6,000 students. The Universität Lüneburg has faculties of education, economics and social sciences, cultural studies.

LÜNEBURGER HEIDE

Germany's largest area of heathland located in NIEDERSACHSEN and populated mainly by sheep. It is a popular recreational area for the city-dwellers in BREMEN, HAMBURG and HANNOVER.

LÜPERTZ, MARKUS (1941–   )

Artist whose 'dithyrambic' painting in the 1960s and 1970s presented stylised objects in abstract form. He turned to sculpture in 1981 and was appointed professor at the Kunstakademie DÜSSELDORF in 1986. His works include *Mexikanische Dithyrambe* (1964), *Deutsches Motiv* (1972) and *Pierrot Lunaire* (1984, sculpture).

LZB See: *LANDESZENTRALBANKEN*

MADAME

International monthly magazine published by Magazinpresse Verlag GmbH in MÜNCHEN. It was established in 1952 and has a readership among young and middle-aged women. *Madame* has a circulation of 108,000 and is aimed at the affluent with disposable income to match the magazine's exclusive taste in fashion, short stories, culture and travel.

'MADE IN GERMANY'

The slogan still holds cachet as representing quality and reliability in German products. It epitomises the skill of Germany's highly-trained workforce and is used to advertise German goods. The need to mark the origin of goods was introduced by the British government at the end of the nineteenth century to combat competition as the emerging industrial nation on the continent started to challenge the nineteenth century's industrial juggernaut. Ironically the slogan has become a powerful image for promoting the products of corporate Germany, which despite problems in the early 1990s looks set to hold sway beyond the year 2000. See also: DEUTSCHE WERTARBEIT

MAGDEBURG

Magdeburg is the LANDESHAUPTSTADT of SACHSEN-ANHALT and is situated on the river Elbe and the Mittellandkanal (dialling code 03 91, postal area code 39...). A Benedictine monastery was founded in 937 and the city was granted a charter in 1188. During the Middle Ages Magdeburg became a flourishing trading centre as a member of the Hanseatic League. Industrialisation started in the nineteenth century with the development of shipbuilding and engineering works. In 1990, Magdeburg triumphed over HALLE in the tussle to become the capital of Sachsen-Anhalt. This new status has prompted the city to shake off the drab image of the Communist era and generate a new dynamism.

The city has a population of some 266,000 with a total student population of around 7,400 (1 UNIVERSITÄT and 1 FACHHOCH-SCHULE) and about 2% foreigners (13% Vietnamese). A coalition between the SPD and BÜNDNIS 90/DIE GRÜNEN has been running the city since 1990, although lack of an absolute majority has necessitated the support of other parties. The city's industries include engineering, construction, food processing and sugar refining.

MAGDEBURG, OTTO-VON-GUERICKE-UNIVERSITÄT

University in SACHSEN-ANHALT founded in 1953 (university status 1993) and teaching some 6,000 students. The Otto-von-Guericke-Universität Magdeburg has faculties of humanities, social sciences, economics and management, mathematics, natural sciences, medicine, computer science, mechanical engineering, electrical engineering.

MAGDEBURGER DOM

The cathedral in MAGDEBURG was built between 1209 and 1520 and is particularly remarkable for its collection of sculptures ranging from the thirteenth-century sculpture of St George to Ernst Barlach's monument to the dead of the First World War. Documentation of Magdeburg's sculptural heritage is continued in the Kulturhistorisches Museum with the famous *Magdeburger Reiter* and other works, and in a collection of modern sculptures housed in the cultural complex in the former Kloster Unser Lieben Frauen.

MAGISTER

A qualification re-introduced in 1960 for arts subjects (*Magister/Magistra Artium*) and awarded after a minimum of eight SEMESTER of study at a UNIVERSITÄT. Students have to take examinations in one main subject and two subsidiary subjects as well as submitting a written dissertation (*Magisterarbeit*).

MAGISTRAT

The Magistrat is the executive administration in towns and cities in HESSEN and SCHLESWIG-HOLSTEIN that consists of the BÜRGERMEISTER as chairperson, and honorary and full-time STADTRÄTE (BEIGEORD-NETE).

MAGISTRATSVERFASSUNG

A type of local-authority constitution applicable in HESSEN and the towns of SCHLESWIG-HOLSTEIN. The MAGISTRAT (known as the GEMEINDEVORSTAND in GEMEINDEN in Hessen) is a collegiate body (elected by the GEMEINDEVERTRETUNG) carrying out executive duties; it consists of the BÜRGERMEISTER or OBERBÜRGERMEISTER as chairperson and the BEIGEORDNETE or STADTRÄTE. See also: GEMEINDEVERFASSUNGSRECHT

MAINZ

Mainz is the LANDESHAUPTSTADT of RHEINLAND-PFALZ and is situated on the Rhine opposite WIESBADEN and the mouth of the Main (dialling code 0 61 31, postal area code 55...). Mainz became a free city in 1244 and in 1477 a university was established. Johannes Gutenberg, a pioneer of printing with movable type, set up his printing press in Mainz in 1450. The power of the city's archbishops made the city a major ecclesiastical and political centre, and today Mainz is seat of the Catholic hierarchy in Germany. KARNEVAL is celebrated enthusiastically in FASTNACHT parties. The Johannisnacht celebrations in June have jousting and fireworks while wine is at the centre of the Weinmarkt at the end of August and beginning of September.

The city has a population of some 189,000 with a total student population of around 38,000 (1 UNIVERSITÄT, 3 HOCHSCHULEN) and about 17% foreigners (20% Turkish). The SPD has been running the city since 1948, although lack of an absolute majority has necessitated the support of other parties. Mainz is the centre for the RHEINLAND wine trade and is an important administrative, commercial and industrial centre. Industries include machinery, glass-making, chemicals, paper, cement and printing. The two major broadcasting stations ZDF and SWF are located in Mainz.

MAINZ, JOHANNES GUTENBERG-UNIVERSITÄT

University in RHEINLAND-PFALZ founded in 1477 (closed in 1816 and re-opened in 1946) and teaching some 29,000 students. The Johannes Gutenberg-Universität Mainz has faculties of Catholic theology, Protestant theology, law and economics, medicine, philosophy and education, psychology, social sciences, languages and literature, history, mathematics, physics, chemistry and pharmacology, biology, geosciences, fine arts, music, physical education.

MAINZELMÄNNCHEN
Gremlins based on the traditional helpful *Heinzelmännchen* dwarfs from German folklore. They introduce advertising on ZDF, *Mainzelmännchen* being a pun on MAINZ – the ZDF headquarters.

MAN AG
Holding company founded in 1986. Members of the group are involved in the production of commercial vehicles and machinery. Group headquarters are in MÜNCHEN. MAN has some 58,000 employees.

MANAGER MAGAZIN
One of Germany's leading monthly magazines for the business world. Owned by SPIEGEL VERLAG, it has a reputation for taking a controversial stance. It was founded in 1972 and is published monthly in HAMBURG with a circulation of 112,000. *Manager Magazin* focuses on profiles of leading personalities and organisations from the world of industry and finance, and reports on management methods and trends. It also gives critical appraisals of successes and failures.

MANDAT
The term of office for which a member of the BUNDESTAG or LANDTAG is elected, and represented by a seat in the Bundestag or Landtag. See also: BUNDESTAGSWAHL; LANDTAGSWAHL

MANGELSDORFF, ALBERT (1928–   )
Jazz trombonist who was an exponent of Cool Jazz in the 1950s and whose virtuoso technique adapts to all forms of modern jazz. He founded a jazz quintet at HESSISCHER RUNDFUNK in 1957 and appeared solo at the Newport Jazz Festival in 1969. His appearances since the 1980s have increasingly been as a solo or in a duet and he has released many recordings.

MANNESMANN AG

A steelmaker that produces seamless steel tubing and has diversified into communications and electronics. The company was founded in 1890 in BERLIN but company headquarters were moved to DÜSSELDORF in 1893. Originally a steelmaker, the company now generates a third of its earnings from service industries, including the mobile-telephone network D2-NETZ. Mannesmann now has some 125,000 employees.

MANNHEIM

Mannheim is situated opposite LUDWIGSHAFEN on a strip of land at the point where the Neckar enters the Rhine in BADEN-WÜRTTEMBERG (dialling code 06 21, postal area code 68...). Mannheim received its charter in 1607, and the centre of the city was laid out in a chessboard pattern during the seventeenth and eighteenth centuries with blocks of houses being labelled with letters of the alphabet and numbers. Between 1720 and 1778 the residence of the Palatine Electors was in Mannheim, and in 1778 Germany's first national theatre opened there. A large inland port was constructed in 1834 and 1876 and paved the way for industrialisation.

The city has a population of some 324,000 with a total student population of around 18,200 (1 UNIVERSITÄT and 6 other HOCHSCHULEN) and about 20% foreigners (33% Turkish). The SPD has been running the city since 1966, although lack of an absolute majority has necessitated the support of other parties. Mannheim's port is Germany's second biggest inland harbour after DUISBURG and handles trade in coal, construction materials, oil, ores and timber. Industries include electronics, machinery and vehicle construction, pharmaceuticals, chemicals, cellulose and textiles.

MANNHEIM, UNIVERSITÄT

University in BADEN-WÜRTTEMBERG founded in 1907 (university status in 1967) and teaching some 12,000 students. The Universität Mannheim has faculties of law, economics, political economics and statistics, social sciences, philosophy and psychology, education, languages and literature, history and geography, mathematics and information science.

MARBURG, PHILIPPS-UNIVERSITÄT
One of Germany's older universities, founded in 1527. The university is in HESSEN and teaches some 18,000 students. The Philipps-Universität Marburg has faculties of law, economics, social sciences, psychology, theology, history, classics and archaeology, languages and literature, mathematics, physics, chemistry, pharmacology, biology, geology, geography, medicine, education.

MARIÄ HIMMELFAHRT
The Assumption of the Blessed Virgin is a Catholic religious festival on 15 August and is a public holiday in SAARLAND and parts of BAYERN.

MARIE CLAIRE
Monthly women's magazine with a circulation of 171,000. It was started up in 1990 as a joint venture with *Marie Claire* in France and addresses young, well-educated women with their own careers who appreciate quality.

MARINE
The naval forces of the BUNDESWEHR have about 180 ships and come under the command of the BUNDESMINISTER DER VERTEIDIGUNG in peacetime and the BUNDESKANZLER if the country is under attack.

MARKWORT, HELMUT (1936–   )
HERAUSGEBER of FOCUS and GESCHÄFTSFÜHRER of BURDA. He has been editor-in-chief of BILD + FUNK and GONG, and established Germany's most successful private radio station Antenne Bayern in 1988.

MASKE, HENRY (1964–   )
Boxer who was light heavyweight champion in the DDR in 1983 and went on to become European champion three times. He gained a gold medal at the 1988 Olympic Games and was amateur world champion in 1989. Maske went professional in 1990 and became light heavyweight world champion and Germany's *Sportler des Jahres* in 1993. He successfully defended his title in 1995.

MASSA AG
Supermarket and furnishing stores chain with company headquarters at Alzey (RHEINLAND-PFALZ) and with some 7,500
employees.

MASUR, KURT (1927–   )
Chief conductor with Germany's oldest symphony orchestra
(Gewandhausorchester) in LEIPZIG and since 1991 with the New
York Philharmonic. International guest performances and a
steady stream of recordings have ensured an international reputation since the 1970s. Masur opened the Gewandhaus for political discussion in the autumn of 1989 and played a considerable
role in ensuring that the Monday demonstrations in Leipzig leading to the downfall of the DDR passed off peacefully.

MATRIKEL
The register of students studying at a HOCHSCHULE, or a church
register listing christenings, confirmations, marriages and deaths.

MATTES, EVA (1954–   )
Actress who was part of the management of the BERLINER EN-
SEMBLE in 1994–1995. Her film performances include *Mathias
Kneissl* (1971), *Wildwechsel* (1972) and *Woyzeck* (1979) and she
starred in the controversial TV comedy series *Motzki* in 1993 that
took a satirical look at the relationship between OSSIS and WESSIS.

MAUER See: *BERLINER MAUER*

MAULBRONN
This Cistercian monastery in BADEN-WÜRTTEMBERG dating from
1147 has been made a UNESCO world heritage site.

MAX
Monthly fashion magazine appealing to a young, basically male
audience that is well educated. It is published by Max Verlag in
HAMBURG and has a circulation of 220,000.

MAX-PLANCK-GESELLSCHAFT ZUR FÖRDERUNG
DER WISSENSCHAFTEN e.V.
A society for the advancement of science which is the successor
to the *Kaiser-Wilhelm-Gesellschaft zur Förderung der Wissen-*

schaften founded in 1911. It has 69 institutes and research centres and 27 short-term working groups in the NEUE BUNDESLÄNDER. The society is dedicated to scientific research with some 14,000 employees and a budget totalling 1,700 million marks.

MAXI
Monthly established in 1986. It is aimed at younger women and takes a look at life from a personal point of view. It is published by BAUER VERLAG and has a circulation of 404,000.

MAY, GISELA (1924–   )
Actress and member of the BERLINER ENSEMBLE in east Berlin since 1962. She is famous for her interpretations of East German writer Bertolt Brecht and became known in the West for her interpretations of political songs and ballads. Her theatre performances include Hauptmann's *Der Biberpelz* (1962) and Brecht's *Mutter Courage* (1978), recordings include *Gisela May singt Jacques Brel* (1984), and films include *Just a Movie* (1984).

MdB See: *MITGLIED DES BUNDESTAGES*

MDR See: *MITTELDEUTSCHER RUNDFUNK*

MECKLENBURG-VORPOMMERN
Mecklenburg-Vorpommern is a FLÄCHENSTAAT covering an area of 23,169 sq. km., with a population of some 1.8 million. The LANDTAG (LANDESPARLAMENT) enacts legislation and comprises 71 members elected every four years with the next election in autumn 1998. The Landtag elects the MINISTERPRÄSIDENT, head of the Landesregierung von Mecklenburg-Vorpommern, which holds executive powers. The Ministerpräsident appoints the ministers with responsibility for individual portfolios. Mecklenburg-Vorpommern is divided into six KREISFREIE STÄDTE and 31 KREISE. The LANDESHAUPTSTADT is SCHWERIN. Mecklenburg-Vorpommern in the former DDR was formed in 1990 and has a long tradition as the historic regions of *Mecklenburg* and *Vorpommern*, together with the vestigial part remaining in modern Germany of the former province of POMMERN, now mainly part of Poland. It is bordered by the Baltic coast and the Elbe and Oder rivers, and is covered by a myriad of lakes, ancient forests and agricultural prairies.

The population of Mecklenburg-Vorpommern is overwhelmingly Protestant and the LAND has Germany's lowest population density. Agriculture, forestry, fisheries and food processing are the main industries in Mecklenburg-Vorpommern and it is the least industrialised of all the Länder. Shipbuilding was developed along the coast during the 1950s with big shipyards and a container port in ROSTOCK and other yards in Stralsund, Wismar and Wolgast, but there have been massive cutbacks since reunification with heavy unemployment. Metalworking and engineering are the main industries in Schwerin, Greifswald and Neubrandenburg. During the days of the DDR, holiday crowds flocked to the coast and lakes during the summer, and the tourist trade is now rapidly developing and looks set to become an important economic pillar. Mecklenburg-Vorpommern has been ruled by the CDU since reunification in 1990. See also: LAND; LANDESREGIERUNG; SEITE, BERNDT

MEHRWERTSTEUER See: *UMSATZSTEUER*

MEIN SCHÖNER GARTEN
Monthly gardening magazine established in 1972 with a circulation of 483,000. Gives high-income readers information on gardening and lavishly illustrates the beauties of garden, balcony and window-box.

MEINE FAMILIE UND ICH
Monthly family magazine with the emphasis on menus, shopping and cooking. It was established in 1966 and has a circulation of 469,000. Appealing to a mainly female audience, the magazine is distributed through self-service stores.

MEISSNER PORZELLAN
The famous hand-painted figures and crockery from Europe's oldest manufacturer of porcelain in Meißen. Production was originally started up in DRESDEN in 1710 and later moved to Meißen. This was one of the few East German enterprises to come out of reunification with an exclusive range of products and well-established markets. See also: SACHSEN, FREISTAAT

MEISTER

A master craftsman who has completed the GESELLENZEIT and passed the MEISTERPRÜFUNG. The candidate either has to present evidence of having worked as a *Geselle* for a number of years or has to present a certificate from the INDUSTRIE- UND HANDELSKAMMER with details of the examination following the BERUFSAUSBILDUNG and demonstrate several years' work as a HANDWERKER. The *Meister* is allowed to run an independent business and is qualified to train AUSZUBILDENDE.

MEISTERBRIEF

The certificate issued after successful completion of the GESELLENZEIT or a recognized equivalent and the MEISTERPRÜFUNG. It qualifies the holder to set up an independent business and carry out training.

MEISTERPRÜFUNG

The examination taken to obtain the title of MEISTER comprising a practical examination, an examination in the specialist subject area, an examination in business management and an examination in training and educational theory.

MEISTERSCHULE

A specialist school for preparing a GESELLE for the MEISTERPRÜFUNG.

MEMELLAND

A region north of the river Memel that belonged to OSTPREUSSEN before the First World War. It was returned to the Soviet republic of Lithuania in 1948 after having been annexed by Germany in 1939. Apart from the mainly German Lutheran population of the port city of Memel, much of the rural population was Lithuanian. Most of the German population fled the Memelland before the advancing Soviet armies arrived at the end of the war. Today, the area is part of Lithuania.

MENSA

Student refectory run by the STUDENTENWERKE and providing subsidised food. Although students complain, there is a wide choice of reasonable quality food at cheap prices.

MENSCHENWÜRDE

Human dignity is held by the GRUNDGESETZ to be inviolable, and Germany's constitution imposes an obligation on the state not to infringe *Menschenwürde*. The responsibility of individuals in this respect is also upheld, and officers of the state (such as soldiers) cannot be punished for disobeying orders if they would result in injury to human dignity.

MERCEDES-BENZ AG

Luxury automobile manufacturer owned by DAIMLER-BENZ. Company headquarters are in STUTTGART. Mercedes-Benz has some 197,000 employees.

MERCK, E.

Chemicals and pharmaceuticals company founded in 1827. Company headquarters are in Darmstadt (HESSEN). Merck has some 26,000 employees.

MERIAN

A lavishly illustrated look at beautiful cities and places in the world. The series was established in 1947 and is published monthly by JAHRESZEITEN VERLAG in HAMBURG with a circulation of 179,000. It provides detailed analyses by top journalists and targets a wealthy élite with expensive tastes.

MERKEL, ANGELA (1954–)

Physicist and CDU politician who worked briefly for the *Akademie der Wissenschaften zu Berlin* in autumn 1989 and was one of the founders of the new party DEMOKRATISCHER AUFBRUCH. She was a spokeswoman for the short-lived DDR government after the March elections in 1990 and has been a member of the BUNDESTAG since December 1990 and deputy chairwoman of the CDU since 1991. She was *Bundesministerin für Frauen und Jugend* in 1991–1994 and was appointed BUNDESMINISTERIN FÜR UMWELT, NATURSCHUTZ UND REAKTORSICHERHEIT in 1994.

MESSEN

Germany is a world centre for trade fairs: out of a total of 150 leading international specialist trade fairs, 116 are held in Germany. In addition, about 130 regional trade fairs are held in

Germany every year. The most important trade-fair centres, or *Messestädte*, are BERLIN, DÜSSELDORF, ESSEN, FRANKFURT AM MAIN, HAMBURG, HANNOVER, KÖLN, LEIPZIG, MÜNCHEN, NÜRNBERG and STUTTGART. Other trade fair centres are DORTMUND, Friedrichshafen (BADEN-WÜRTTEMBERG), Idar-Oberstein (RHEINLAND-PFALZ), KARLSRUHE, Offenbach (HESSEN), Pirmasens (RHEINLAND-PFALZ) and SAARBRÜCKEN. The trade-fair complex in a city is known as the *Messegelände*.

METALLGESELLSCHAFT AG
Company founded in 1929 with activities in mining and processing ores, metals and minerals, environmental plant construction, chemicals, transport and trading. Company headquarters are in FRANKFURT AM MAIN. Metallgesellschaft has some 26,000 employees.

METRO-VERMÖGENSVERWALTUNGS KG
Trading group with nearly 60 independent hypermarkets. The group holds more than 50% of the shares in KAUFHOF and ASKO. Company headquarters are in DÜSSELDORF. Metro has some 13,000 employees. See also: CENTRE0

MEZ See: *MITTELEUROPÄISCHE ZEIT*

MICHEL, HARTMUT (1948–   )
Biochemist and director of the Max-Planck-Institut für Biophysik in FRANKFURT AM MAIN, who was awarded the Nobel Prize for chemistry in 1988 (with J. DEISENHOFER and R. HUBER) for determining the structure of a photosynthetic reaction centre using X-ray diffraction techniques.

MILITÄRDIENST See: *WEHRDIENST*

MINDESTSEMESTERZAHL
The minimum number of SEMESTER necessary to complete a STUDIUM.

MINETTI, BERNHARD (1905–   )
Actor and director who has played the main classical roles in a long career that started before the Second World War at the Berliner Staatstheater and continued in HAMBURG, DÜSSELDORF

and STUTTGART. Minetti turned increasingly to roles in plays by contemporary authors after the Second World War, and Austrian playwright Thomas Bernhard dedicated a number of plays to him including *Minetti* (1976) and *Der Weltverbesserer* (1980). His performances include Bernhard's *Die Jagdgesellschaft* (1974), Goethe's *Faust* (1982), Shakespeare's *König Lear* (1985) and STRAUSS' *Besucher* (1988). In 1995 he joined the BERLINER ENSEMBLE.

MINISTER

Member of a government at the level of the BUND or the LAND and head of a *Ministerium*. Ministers in the BUNDESREGIERUNG are officially known as BUNDESMINISTER and are head of a BUNDESMINI-STERIUM while ministers in the LANDESREGIERUNGEN are known as *Minister* (*Staatsminister* in BAYERN, HESSEN and SACHSEN) or, in the STADTSTAATEN, as SENATOREN.

MINISTERPRÄSIDENT

The head of a LANDESREGIERUNG who officially represents the LAND. The Ministerpräsident is known as the REGIERENDER BÜR-GERMEISTER in BERLIN, the ERSTER BÜRGERMEISTER in HAMBURG and the BÜRGERMEISTER UND SENATSPRÄSIDENT in BREMEN.

MITBESTIMMUNG

The concept of worker participation in German industry known as co-determination and based on the BETRIEBSVERFASSUNGSGESETZ of 1952. Employees are legally entitled to take part in the deci-sion-making process of the company they work in. This partici-pation is effected by worker representation on the AUFSICHTSRAT. Since 1951 companies in the coal and steel industry have had PARITÄT between shareholders and employees on the *Aufsichtsrat* with an additional neutral member agreed by both sides. The *Mitbestimmungsgesetz* of 1976 provides for 50% worker partici-pation on the *Aufsichtsrat* in companies with more than 2,000 employees, with the chairperson (elected by the shareholders) having a casting vote. AKTIENGESELLSCHAFTEN with up to 2,000 employees and other companies with 500 to 2,000 employees have 33% worker representation on the *Aufsichtsrat*.

MITGLIED DES BUNDESTAGES (MdB)

Members of the BUNDESTAG (*Bundestagsabgeordnete*) have to be over the age of 18 on the day of their election and have held a German passport for at least a year. They are elected every four years by a mixed system of first past the post and proportional representation. See also: ABGEORDNETER; BUNDESTAGSWAHL

MITTELDEUTSCHER RUNDFUNK (MDR)

A regional public-service radio and TV broadcasting corporation based in LEIPZIG. MDR was established in the NEUE BUNDESLÄNDER of SACHSEN, SACHSEN-ANHALT and THÜRINGEN following reunification in 1990. Mitteldeutscher Rundfunk is a member of the ARD. See also: LANDESRUNDFUNK- UND FERNSEHANSTALTEN

MITTELDEUTSCHLAND

A geographical area of Germany encompassing the central mountain ranges (including the HARZ, THÜRINGER WALD and ERZGEBIRGE). There is no real political consensus on the term as it derives from the imperial German REICH when German territories extended much further east to the river Memel.

MITTELEUROPA

The rather nebulous concept of Central Europe that is generally accepted to include Germany, Switzerland, Austria, Poland, the Czech and Slovak Republics, Hungary and Romania.

MITTELEUROPÄISCHE ZEIT (MEZ)

Central European Time is determined at the PHYSIKALISCH-TECHNISCHE BUNDESANSTALT, which transmits the exact time throughout Germany by a radio signal. It lies one hour behind Greenwich Mean Time.

MITTELGROSSES UNTERNEHMEN See: *MITTELSTAND*

MITTELSCHULE See: *REALSCHULE*

MITTELSTAND

Small and medium-sized companies in Germany which employ between 50 and 500 people. The 4th EC directive (1978) defines a *mittelgroßes Unternehmen* as having a balance sheet total between DM 3.9 and 15.5 million, a turnover between DM 8 and

32 million, and between 51 and 250 employees. In practice the lines are not quite so clearly drawn, and companies with three or four hundred employees may view themselves as still being part of the *Mittelstand*. This hard-working and enduring section of German industry formed the backbone of the WIRTSCHAFTSWUN-DER and sustains Germany's continued economic success.

MITTELSTÄNDISCHES UNTERNEHMEN See: *MITTELSTAND*

MITTLERE REIFE See: *REALSCHULABSCHLUSS*

MOBIL OIL AG
German subsidiary of Mobil Oil founded in 1898. Company headquarters are in HAMBURG. Mobil has some 1,800 employees.

MODE-WOCHE-MÜNCHEN
The 'INTERCOLLECTION – International Fashion Fair' for women's and children's clothing, menswear and accessories is a trade fair for the fashion industry held in MÜNCHEN in spring and autumn annually with around 10,000 visitors.

MOKSEL AG, A.
Meat-trading company founded in 1948. Company headquarters are in Buchloe (BAYERN). Moksel has some 3,000 employees.

MOMMSEN, HANS (1930–   )
Historian, professor in BOCHUM (RUHR-UNIVERSITÄT) and member of the SPD, whose main area of research is the labour movement and the Nazi period. He was involved in the HISTORIKERSTREIT and criticised those historians who propagated a revisionist perspective on the DRITTES REICH. His works include *Beamtentum im Dritten Reich* (1966) and *Die verspielte Freiheit* (1989). See also: HABERMAS, JÜRGEN; NOLTE, ERNST

MÖNCHENGLADBACH
Mönchengladbach is situated about 30 km. west of DÜSSELDORF in NORDRHEIN-WESTFALEN (dialling code 0 21 61/66, postal area code 41...). The city grew up around a Benedictine monastery founded in 974 and dissolved in 1802. The city developed as the centre of the RHEINLAND cotton and textile industry but after the Second

World War became headquarters for the British Rhine Army and NATO's operations base for northern and central Europe. The MUSEUM ABTEIBERG is one of Germany's most daring museums of modern art. Masterminded by Viennese architect and artist Hans Hollein, the museum favours iconoclasts and the avant-garde including Joseph Beuys, Cy Twombly and Sigmar POLKE. Like most Rheinland cities, Mönchengladbach celebrates KARNEVAL in a big way, but is unusual in that the main procession takes place on *Veilchendienstag* (Shrove Tuesday) rather than ROSENMONTAG.

The city has a population of some 269,000 with a student population of around 6,000 (1 HOCHSCHULE) and about 10% foreigners (35% Turkish). A coalition between the CDU and SPD has been running the city since 1989. Apart from textiles (silks, synthetics and woollens), industries include textile machinery, engineering, printing and brewing. See also: RHEINISCH-WESTFÄLISCHES INDUSTRIEGEBIET

MORRIS GmbH, PHILIP
Subsidiary of American tobacco giant founded in 1970. Company headquarters are in MÜNCHEN. Philip Morris has some 3,600 employees.

MÖSSBAUER, RUDOLF (1929–)
German-born physicist and professor at MÜNCHEN (TECHNISCHE UNIVERSITÄT), who was awarded the Nobel Prize for physics (with R. Hofstadter) in 1961 following his discovery of the Mössbauer effect, which allows the resonance absorption of gamma rays.

MÜLLER, HERTA (1953–)
Romanian-German writer, translator and teacher who moved from Romania to Germany in 1987 and whose stories in *Niederungen* (1982) and *Barfüßiger Februar* (1987) evoke life in the German-speaking villages of Romania. She has also published the novels *Der Fuchs war damals schon der Jäger* (1992), *Herztier* (1994) and the essays *Hunger und Seide* (1995). She was awarded the KLEIST-PREIS in 1994.

MÜNCHEN
München is the LANDESHAUPTSTADT of BAYERN and is situated on the river Isar within sight of the Alps (dialling code 0 89, postal

area code 80... and 81...). München was founded by Heinrich der Löwe in 1158 and granted a charter in 1214. It was ruled by the WITTELSBACH dynasty from 1255 until the abdication of the Bavarian König Ludwig III in 1918, and the city's traditionally minded citizens still accord high esteem to the Wittelsbach descendants. München developed relatively late and remained small until the nineteenth century, when König Ludwig I undertook an extensive programme of building to develop it into a city worthy of royal status, providing the impetus for its flowering as a centre for the arts, culture and scholarship. Hitler saw it as the capital of the Nazi movement and there are a number of monumental architectural reminders of the city's past (e.g. Haus der Kunst).

München is home to many clichés about Germany – *Dirndl, Lederhosen*, beer and the Hofbräuhaus – and although it has a cosmopolitan air to it as the most sought-after city in Germany, local people still retain a provincial disdain for the *Zugereiste* who have flocked to the '*Weltstadt mit Herz*' from all over Germany. Schwabing epitomises the city's attraction for artists, though in recent years it has been dominated by the local SCHICK-ERIA. The twin-towered Frauenkirche characterises München's skyline, complemented by the rococo splendour of the *Residenz*, the Italianate elegance of the Wittelsbach summer residence at Schloß Nymphenburg, and the tall *Olympiaturm*. The mighty DEUTSCHES MUSEUM is Europe's most impressive monument to science and technology and the Alte Pinakothek houses a comprehensive collection of the German School. The BAYERISCHE STAATSBIBLIOTHEK holds one of Europe's most valuable library collections and München's LUDWIG-MAXIMILIANS-UNIVERSITÄT is Germany's biggest university. The Bayerische Staatsoper is a glittering venue for top opera and the Münchener Opernfestspiele in mid-summer are only overshadowed by the world's premier beer festival – the OKTOBERFEST. Other festivals include FASCHING in the carneval season, Sommerfestspiele at the Olympiapark and the Christkindlmarkt (WEIHNACHTSMARKT) at Christmas.

The city has a population of some 1.3 million with a total student population of around 88,600 (3 UNIVERSITÄTEN and 5 other

HOCHSCHULEN) and just over 21% foreigners (30% Yugoslavian). Traditionally an SPD city, a coalition between the SPD and BÜNDNIS 90/DIE GRÜNEN has been running the city on a slim majority since 1994 together with the support of two individual representatives of other ecological parties; in fact, the CSU is now the strongest party. München is Germany's third largest city and a leading industrial centre. It is the capital of Germany's electronics industry, a leading European insurance centre and famous for beer production. The 1972 Olympic Games spurred the city's economic development with investment in the Olympic stadium complex and a new suburban railway and underground system. Since then, the S-BAHN and U-BAHN networks have been further expanded to form an integral part of an extensive integrated transport system. The latest addition to the city's transport system is the Franz-Joseph-Strauß-Flughafen commemorating Bavaria's jovial, right-wing patriarch. The European Patent Office and the BUNDESFINANZHOF are based in München. The city's trade fair complex hosts a wide range of international trade fairs including BAU, MODE-WOCHE, ANALYTICA, SYSTEMS and ELECTRONICA. Industries in the city include automobile manufacture, construction, aerospace, engineering, electronics, chemicals, fashion, publishing, broadcasting and film, banking and insurance, food processing and, of course, brewing. Important companies in the city include ALLIANZ, BMW, DAIMLER-BENZ AEROSPACE and SIEMENS.

MÜNCHEN, LUDWIG-MAXIMILIANS-UNIVERSITÄT

University in BAYERN founded in 1472 and teaching some 60,000 students. The Ludwig-Maximilians-Universität München has departments of Catholic theology, Protestant theology, law, business studies, economics, medicine, veterinary medicine, history and art, philosophy, mathematics, physics, chemistry and pharmacology, biology, geosciences, forestry, psychology and education, ancient history, languages and literature, social sciences.

MÜNCHEN, TECHNISCHE UNIVERSITÄT

University in BAYERN founded in 1868 and teaching some 20,000 students. The Technische Universität München has faculties of mathematics, physics, chemistry and biology and earth sciences, economics and social sciences, civil engineering and surveying, architecture, mechanical engineering, electrical engineering and information technology, computer science, agriculture, brewing and dairy science, medicine.

MÜNCHEN, UNIVERSITÄT DER BUNDESWEHR

University in BAYERN founded in 1973 for members of the BUNDESWEHR and teaching some 2,000 students. The Universität der Bundeswehr München has faculties of civil engineering and surveying and geodesy, electrical engineering, computer and information sciences, aerospace engineering, education, social sciences, economics and management, mechanical engineering, electrical engineering, business studies.

MÜNCHENER RÜCKVERSICHERUNGS-GESELLSCHAFT

The world's largest reinsurer, founded in 1880. Company headquarters are in MÜNCHEN. Münchener Rück has some 1,900 employees.

MÜNCHNER LACH- UND SCHIESSGESELLSCHAFT

Cabaret theatre in MÜNCHEN founded in 1956. Televised performances of this cabaret brought the political satire of founder Dieter Hildebrandt to German households.

MÜNCHNER MERKUR

Major regional daily newspaper in BAYERN. It was established in 1948 and is published in MÜNCHEN by the Münchener Zeitungsverlag, with a circulation of 198,000.

MUNICH See: *MÜNCHEN*

MÜNSTER

Münster is situated on the Dortmund-Ems-Kanal in NORDRHEIN-WESTFALEN (dialling code 02 51, postal area code 48. . .). The bishopric of Münster was founded in 805 and the city received a charter in 1170. The city was made the capital of the Prussian province of *Westfalen* and in 1945 became part of Nordrhein-Westfalen. It is Westfalen's cultural centre and as the seat of a Catholic bishop, the city is steeped in the Catholic tradition. During the Nazi dictatorship, the bishop of Münster defied government orders in 1936 by refusing to remove crucifixes from schools, one of the few points at which Nazism took heed of domestic opposition. Festivals include the 'Send' held three times a year at the *Schloß*, the Stadtfest, the Barockfest, and the Lambertusfest in September for children.

The city has a population of some 264,000 with a total student population of around 53,000 (1 UNIVERSITÄT and 6 other HOCHSCHULEN) and about 7% foreigners (11% Turkish). The CDU has been running the city as the strongest party since 1984, although lack of an absolute majority has necessitated the support of other parties. The city is a centre for trade and administration, and has a port on the Dortmund-Ems-Kanal. Industries include engineering, pharmaceuticals, chemicals, timber and plastics.

MÜNSTER, WESTFÄLISCHE WILHELMS-UNIVERSITÄT
One of Germany's older universities, founded in 1780 (university status 1780–1818 and from 1902). The university is in RHEINLAND-PFALZ and teaches some 45,000 students. The Westfälische Wilhelms-Universität Münster has departments of Protestant theology, Catholic theology, law, economics, medicine, philosophy (arts), social sciences, psychology, education, history, languages and literature, mathematics, physics, chemistry, biology, earth sciences.

MÜNSTERLAND
A flat plain surrounding the city of MÜNSTER that is predominantly agricultural and has over 50 moated castles known as *Wasserburgen*.

MURMANN, KLAUS (1932–   )
Lawyer who was chairman of the regional employers' association in SCHLESWIG-HOLSTEIN in 1975–1987 and went on to become president of the BUNDESVEREINIGUNG DER DEUTSCHEN ARBEITGEBERVERBÄNDE in 1986.

MUSEEN DAHLEM
A vast complex of culture in BERLIN that includes a gallery of painting from medieval times to the eighteenth century, a sculpture gallery of German masters, and sections devoted to anthropology and ethnography, German folk history, Indian, Islamic and East Asian art.

MUSEUM ABTEIBERG
Museum in MÖNCHENGLADBACH opened in 1982 with avant-garde art from the Expressionists to the present day, including work by Joseph Beuys, Sigmar POLKE, Cy Twombly and Andy Warhol.

MUSEUM FOLKWANG
The Museum Folkwang in ESSEN was founded in 1902 and houses an excellent collection of modern art, in particular French Impressionists and German Expressionists.

MUSEUM FÜR KUNSTHANDWERK
Museum of applied art in FRANKFURT AM MAIN founded in 1877, with an outstanding collection of some 30,000 exhibits including furniture, glass, ceramics and books.

MUSEUMSINSEL
An island in the river Spree in BERLIN that was designated by royal decree in 1841 to hold collections of art and archaeological finds. The island is home to the PERGAMONMUSEUM, the Bodemuseum, the Altes Museum, the Neues Museum and the Alte Nationalgalerie. These museums hold large collections spanning Egyptian, Asian and Amerindian cultures – the results of expeditions by German archaeologists. The Neues Museum was in ruins until recently and is now being renovated prior to housing the Egyptian section from the Bodemuseum.

MUSIKHOCHSCHULEN
Germany has 21 HOCHSCHULEN where students specialise in music.

MUTTER, ANNE-SOPHIE (1963–   )
Violinist who caused a sensation with her performance at the national competition *Jugend musiziert* as a child prodigy of six. Since her début at Salzburg in 1977 she has carried out international concert tours and was appointed to a post at the Royal Academy of Music in London in 1986.

MUTTERSCHAFTSGELD
Benefit for pregnant women paid by the KRANKENVERSICHERUNG for six weeks before the birth and eight weeks after the birth.

MwSt., Mw.-St. (MEHRWERTSTEUER) See:
UMSATZSTEUER

NACHLASSGERICHT

The court of probate – in most LÄNDER part of the AMTSGERICHT – is responsible for opening and making public the contents of a person's will in the presence of all interested parties. In certain cases the Nachlaßgericht is responsible for maintaining the integrity of the estate until it is accepted by the executor. It identifies rightful heirs, settles inheritance disputes and fulfils other duties relating to inheritance.

NACHRICHTENAGENTUR

A news agency that collects news and distributes it to newspapers, radio stations, TV channels and other institutions.

NATIONAL-ZEITUNG

Right-wing weekly newspaper published in MÜNCHEN. It promotes extreme right-wing views and nationalistic policies, and reveres military heroes of the past.

NATIONALDEMOKRATISCHE PARTEI DEUTSCHLANDS (NPD)

An extreme right-wing party formed in 1964 and gaining some representation in LANDTAG elections in the late 1960s. However, the party has declined to insignificance since it failed to enter the BUNDESTAG in 1969. Today it has around 4,500 members with a following totalling perhaps as much as 50,000. Although the NPD has no elected representatives it continues to present radical right-wing views, organise neo-Nazi marches, abuse Jews and AUSLÄNDER and deny the holocaust (*'Der Holo ist beendet'*).

NATUR

Nature magazine promoting environmental awareness, established in 1981 and published monthly with a circulation of 128,000 by Ringier Verlag.

NDR See: *NORDDEUTSCHER RUNDFUNK*

NEHER, ERWIN (1944–)
Physicist at the Max-Planck-Institut für biophysikalische Chemie in Göttingen (NIEDERSACHSEN), who received the Nobel Prize for medicine in 1991 (with Bert SAKMANN) for research on cellular ion channels and developing a method of measuring very small electrical currents in these channels.

NEOFASCHISMUS See: *RECHTSEXTREMISMUS*

NESTLÉ DEUTSCHLAND AG
Subsidiary of Swiss confectionery company, founded in 1922. Company headquarters are in FRANKFURT AM MAIN. Nestlé Deutschland has some 15,000 employees.

NEUE BUNDESLÄNDER
The new LÄNDER in the east of Germany that were created after the reunification of Germany based on the territory that was previously the DDR. They are BRANDENBURG, MECKLENBURG-VORPOMMERN, SACHSEN, SACHSEN-ANHALT and THÜRINGEN.

NEUE POST
Magazine for older women established in 1984 and published weekly by BAUER VERLAG in HAMBURG. It has a circulation of 1.5 million and covers leisure, fashion and advice on health etc.

NEUE REVUE
Family magazine for young men and women. It was established in 1966 and is published weekly by BAUER VERLAG in HAMBURG. *Neue Revue* has a circulation of 555,000 and covers a broad range of subjects including current affairs, consumer affairs, leisure and household.

NEUES DEUTSCHLAND
Previously the official mouthpiece of the SED with a circulation of around a million, this paper was established in 1946 and had to adapt to being run as a business after reunification. It is now the PDS newspaper and is published daily as a left-wing paper. Circulation, however, has slumped to 76,000 and the readership mainly belongs to the older generation in east Germany.

NEUES FORUM (NF)

A citizen's action group formed in the DDR on 9 September 1989 with the aim of campaigning about issues such as freedom to travel, political pluralism, reform of the constitution and disbanding of the STAATSSICHERHEITSDIENST. The movement developed into a powerful instrument of mass demonstration during the autumn of 1989 and played a central role in bringing about the peaceful revolution. However, the leaders of the movement lacked political experience and had only sketchy ideas about a political agenda. Neues Forum merged with other members of the movement advocating more democracy to form BÜNDNIS 90 in the spring of 1990. Some members of Neues Forum formed the *Deutsche Forumspartei*, which was absorbed into the FDP later that year. See also: BÜNDNIS 90/DIE GRÜNEN

NEUES WOHNEN

Lifestyle monthly focusing on house and home for educated young people with good jobs who are just starting up home. It is published by GRUNER + JAHR in HAMBURG and has a circulation of 182,000.

NEUJAHR

1 January, and a public holiday all over Germany. It is preceded by SILVESTER and is a time for relaxing with the family, celebrating and winter sports – for those who can afford it.

NF See: *NEUES FORUM*

NGG See: *GEWERKSCHAFT NAHRUNG – GENUSS – GASTSTÄTTEN*

NIEDERLAUSITZ See: *LAUSITZ*

NIEDERSACHSEN

Niedersachsen is a FLÄCHENSTAAT covering an area of 47,605 sq. km., with a population of some 7.7 million. The LANDTAG (LANDESPARLAMENT) enacts legislation and comprises 161 members elected every four years with the next election in spring 1998. The Landtag elects the MINISTERPRÄSIDENT, head of the Niedersächsische Landesregierung, which holds executive powers. The Ministerpräsident appoints the ministers with responsibility for individual portfolios. Niedersachsen is divided into four REGIERUNGSBEZIRKE comprising nine KREISFREIE STÄDTE and 38 KREISE. The LANDESHAUPTSTADT is HANNOVER. Niedersachsen was formed by the British military government in 1946 from the former duchies of *Braunschweig, Oldenburg*, the tiny state of *Schaumburg-Lippe* and the former Prussian province of *Hannover*. PLATTDEUTSCH is a unifying cultural tradition although the German spoken around Hannover is deemed to be the purest form of HOCHDEUTSCH. Around 65% of the population is Protestant with just under 20% being Catholic.

Agriculture is still an important component in the economy of Niedersachsen, reflecting the fertile valleys and lowlands contrasting with the barren heath and woodlands of the LÜNEBURGER HEIDE and the HARZ mountains. Mineral extraction has a long tradition in Niedersachsen with the prosperity of the medieval city of Lüneburg resting on the saltworks. Today, the potash industry is of importance, and the town of Salzgitter has vast iron-ore deposits mined by PREUSSAG. Virtually all of Germany's natural-gas production is in Niedersachsen and most of Germany's naturally occurring oil is pumped up here. Hannover is the site of the world's biggest industrial trade fair, the HANNOVER MESSE, and Wolfsburg rose from a tiny village in the 1930s to become the ultimate company city as the home of VOLKSWAGEN. Other important industrial centres include BRAUNSCHWEIG, Osnabrück, Hildesheim and Wilhelmshaven. Fisheries, shipbuilding and chemicals are important coastal industries, with tourism forming the dominant component of the local economy in some areas. Other industries include food and confectionery, electronics, rubber, machinery and textiles, with the world-famous Bockbier being brewed in the little town of Einbeck. The Lüneburger Heide is a vast nature reserve, the coastland area of OSTFRIESLAND has a thriving tourist industry (despite dreary weather) and the gentle curves of the Harz mountains have the reputation of being pensioners' walking country.

The political pendulum has swung to and fro in Niedersachsen with the SPD being the strongest party from the end of the Second World War and holding office in the early 1950s and throughout the 1960s to the mid-1970s with a brief interlude of the right-wing *Deutsche Partei* holding power in 1955–1959. The electorate turned in the CDU as the strongest party in 1976 and CDU or CDU/FDP governments ruled from 1976–1990. In 1990 the SPD were again returned to power in a coalition with BÜNDNIS 90/DIE GRÜNEN and in 1994 the party gained an absolute majority. See also: LAND; LANDESREGIERUNG; PREUSSEN; SCHRÖDER, GERHARD

N.N.

Abbreviation for Latin *nomen nescio* or *nomen nominandum*, 'name not (yet) known'. It is commonly used in VORLESUNGSVER-ZEICHNISSE to refer to lectures and classes that are part of the official timetable, but where details of who will be teaching are to be supplied at a later point.

NOELLE-NEUMANN, ELISABETH (1916–)

Opinion pollster and head of the INSTITUT FÜR DEMOSKOPIE ALLENS-BACH, which she founded in 1947. The institute carries out opinion polls, market research and election analyses. Noelle-Neumann was a journalist during the Second World War and a professor of journalism at MAINZ (JOHANNES GUTENBERG-UNIVER-SITÄT) in 1965–1983, and she has been professor in Chicago since 1978. Her publications include *Die Schweigespirale. Die öffentliche Meinung – unsere soziale Haut* (1980) and *Demoskopische Geschichtsstunde* (1991).

NOLTE, CLAUDIA (1966–)

CDU politician and the youngest member of the KOHL government. She has been BUNDESMINISTERIN FÜR FAMILIE, SENIOREN, FRAUEN UND JUGEND since 1994.

NOLTE, ERNST (1923–)

Historian and professor of history in BERLIN (FREIE UNIVERSITÄT) and author of *Der Faschismus in seiner Epoche*. Nolte was at the centre of the HISTORIKERSTREIT, in which it was claimed that he was attempting to excuse Nazi war crimes by comparison with the purges in the Soviet Union. His other publications include *Deutschland und der kalte Krieg* (1974), *Der europäische Bürgerkrieg 1917–1945. Nationalsozialismus und Bolschewismus* (1987), *Das Vergehen der Vergangenheit. Antwort an meine*

Kritiker im sogenannten Historikerstreit (1987) and *Geschichts-denken im 20. Jahrhundert* (1991). See also: DRITTES REICH; HABER-MAS, JÜRGEN; MOMMSEN, HANS

NORD-OSTSEE-KANAL

The canal linking the North Sea (Nordsee) and the Baltic (Ostsee), constructed in 1895. Formerly known as the *Kaiser-Wilhelm-Kanal*, the canal is 98.7 km. long. It is one of the world's most important and busiest man-made shipping lanes for commercial traffic.

NORD-SÜD-GEFÄLLE

The north-south divide became marked in the 1980s as the traditional industries of shipbuilding, coal and steel in the north suffered cutbacks and BAYERN and BADEN-WÜRTTEMBERG canvassed to bring new, high-tech industries to the attractive landscapes of the south. The north has followed suit by pouring resources into restructuring, regeneration and new industries. Since the WENDE the *Nord-Süd-Gefälle* has been overshadowed by the divide between east and west.

NORDDEUTSCHE RATSVERFASSUNG

A type of local-authority constitution applicable in NIEDERSACH-SEN and NORDRHEIN-WESTFALEN. The RAT is the elected body responsible for governing the GEMEINDE, and the BÜRGERMEISTER is the chairperson of the *Rat*. The GEMEINDEDIREKTOR is responsible for the executive duties of administration. In this form of local-authority constitution the elected GEMEINDEVERTRETUNG is clearly distinguished from the administration. See also: GEMEINDEVERFAS-SUNGSRECHT

NORDDEUTSCHER RUNDFUNK (NDR)

A regional public-service radio and TV broadcasting corporation based in HAMBURG, broadcasting to SCHLESWIG-HOLSTEIN, Hamburg and NIEDERSACHSEN. Norddeutscher Rundfunk is a member of the ARD. See also: LANDESRUNDFUNK- UND FERNSEHANSTALTEN

NORDRHEIN-WESTFALEN (NRW)

Nordrhein-Westfalen is a FLÄCHENSTAAT covering an area of 34,071 sq. km. It is Germany's most populous LAND with some

17.8 million inhabitants. The LANDTAG (LANDESPARLAMENT) enacts legislation and comprises 221 members elected every five years, with the next election in spring 2000. The Landtag elects the MINISTERPRÄSIDENT, head of the Landesregierung Nordrhein-Westfalen, which holds executive powers. The Ministerpräsident appoints the ministers with responsibility for individual portfolios. Nordrhein-Westfalen is divided into five REGIERUNGSBEZIRKE comprising 23 KREISFREIE STÄDTE and 31 KREISE. The LANDESHAUPT-STADT is DÜSSELDORF. Nordrhein-Westfalen was formed by the British military government in 1946 from the Prussian possessions of *Westfalen* and the *Rheinprovinz*, with the state of *Lippe* being added in 1947.

Despite containing Europe's most heavily industrialised area, Nordrhein-Westfalen is surprisingly rural with areas like SAUER-LAND, BERGISCHES LAND, SIEBENGEBIRGE, TEUTOBURGER WALD for the city-dwellers to relax in and enjoy their leisure time away from the city. Nordrhein-Westfalen is administered by Germany's wealthiest city – Düsseldorf. Post-war governments in the provisional capital of BONN steered West Germany through 40 years of democratic rule. AACHEN, BIELEFELD, BOCHUM, DORTMUND, DUIS-BURG, DÜSSELDORF, ESSEN, GELSENKIRCHEN, HAGEN, KÖLN, KREFELD, MÖNCHENGLADBACH, MÜNSTER, OBERHAUSEN, SOLINGEN, WUPPERTAL – Nordrhein-Westfalen is a roll-call of many of Germany's big industrial cities connected up by a dense network of AUTOBAHNEN and a complex network of public transport.

The Ruhr valley and the area around Aachen were rich in coal, and the mountain regions were abundant in iron ore and other minerals. Industry flourished around these raw materials in the nineteenth and twentieth centuries as the RUHRGEBIET went on to become Europe's most heavily industrialised area. An extensive system of dams in the mountains of the Bergisches Land, Sauerland and Eiffel provided the vast supplies of water necessary for industrial production. Industrial activity in the region is diversified, covering all areas of production, while certain areas are associated with particular activities – cars in Bochum, beer in Dortmund, the world's biggest inland port in Duisburg, steel in Essen, textiles in Krefeld, chemicals in Leverkusen with the sprawling BAYER works, cutlery in Solingen.

As mining and heavy industry were scaled down and drastically cut back in the 1970s and 1980s, Nordrhein-Westfalen has been devoting enormous efforts to attracting new industries, creating hundreds of thousands of new jobs. However, although many deep mines have been closed, open-cast mining still flourishes with many villages cleared and 8,000 people due to be relocated from the projected site of a second Garzweiler open-cast mine south of Mönchengladbach to permit the extraction of millions of tonnes of lignite. Mining remains important and more than 30 major power stations make Nordrhein-Westfalen Germany's most important energy-production area.

Köln is home to KARNEVAL, MÜNSTERLAND is a land of castles, and Aachen was the royal seat of Charlemagne. Düsseldorf is the country's fashion capital, and the Deutsche Oper am Rhein shared by Düsseldorf and Duisburg ranks among Germany's top opera companies. The steady immigration of Italians, Poles, Turks and other nationalities has given the cities a cosmopolitan air that has enriched the local culture. The diversity of the small states and principalities which made up the region meant that the religion of different areas may be predominantly Catholic or Protestant. Overall, just under 50% of the population are Catholic with roughly a third Protestant.

Nordrhein-Westfalen was governed by coalitions led alternately by the CDU and SPD until 1980, when the SPD was able to form a majority government. In 1995 the SPD lost their absolute majority and formed a coalition with BÜNDNIS 90/DIE GRÜNEN. See also: AACHENER REVIER; LAND; LANDESREGIERUNG; PREUSSEN; RAU, JOHANNES

NOTAR

A notary public is appointed by the legal authorities in a particular LAND to carry out conveyancing, authenticate documents and draw up wills. The *Notar* is obliged to keep all matters confidential and to maintain an independent stance. *Notare* charge according to a fixed list of fees for their services. See also: BEFÄHIGUNG ZUM RICHTERAMT; KANZLEI

NOTENDURCHSCHNITT

The average overall mark obtained by a candidate in the ABITUR on a scale of 1 (*sehr gut*) to 6 (*ungenügend*). The pass mark is 4.0, and a pass at *Abitur* allows a student to continue to a course of study at a HOCHSCHULE. Subjects which have a NUMERUS CLAUSUS may demand much higher grades which can vary from year to year.

NOTSTANDSGESETZE

Legislation giving the state emergency powers during a crisis. The highly controversial introduction of the *Notstandsgesetze* in 1968 followed two years of student and union unrest. See also: AUSSERPARLAMENTARISCHE OPPOSITION

NOTSTANDSVERFASSUNG

The emergency constitution giving the state powers to combat a threat both from within the state and from outside. The *Notstandsverfassung* was incorporated within the GRUNDGESETZ following violent protests from students and trade unionists in 1968. See also: AUSSERPARLAMENTARISCHE OPPOSITION; NOTSTANDS-GESETZE

NPD See: *NATIONALDEMOKRATISCHE PARTEI DEUTSCHLANDS*

NRW See: *NORDRHEIN-WESTFALEN*

NUMERUS CLAUSUS (NC)

A system of restricting student numbers at German universities, notably in medicine and other oversubscribed subjects, introduced in 1972. Whereas a pass at ABITUR (grade 4.0) is in principle an adequate entrance qualification, in subjects with *Numerus clausus* entry is restricted to a higher average mark (NOTENDURCHSCHNITT) obtained by a candidate in the *Abitur*. Additional factors may be taken into account for admission to a candidate's chosen field of study including *Wartezeit*, aptitude test and possibly interview. See also: INTERNER NC; ZENTRALSTELLE FÜR DIE VERGABE VON STUDIENPLÄTZEN

NÜRBURGRING

A famous racing track round the ruins of the Nürburg, a twelfth-century fortress. The track was built between 1925 and 1927 but is no longer used for Formula One because it is too dangerous.

NUREMBERG See: *NÜRNBERG*

NÜRNBERG

Nürnberg is situated on the river Pegnitz and the RHEIN-MAIN-DONAU-GROSSCHIFFAHRTSWEG in BAYERN (dialling code 09 11, postal area code 90...). The city was granted a charter in 1219, later attained the status of *Reichsstadt* (Free Imperial City), and became the most important trading centre in FRANKEN. The first German railway line linked Nürnberg with Fürth in 1835 and opened the way for industrialisation. Nürnberg was the scene of Hitler's showpiece Nuremberg rallies and, following the Allied victory, the Nuremberg Trials for war criminals. The medieval ALTSTADT was lovingly rebuilt after being reduced to rubble in the Second World War. Nürnberg hosts a number of cultural festivals in the summer including the Musica Franconia (period instruments), Kulturzirkus (theatre), Internationale Orgelwoche (organ music), Bardentreffen (open-air concerts), Ost-West Jazzfest and the Altstadtfest. The *Christkindlmarkt* (WEIHNACHTS-MARKT) during the four weeks of Advent has been held for more than 400 years.

The city has a population of some 496,000 with a total student population of around 16,600 (1 UNIVERSITÄT and 3 other HOCH-SCHULEN) and about 15% foreigners (30% Turkish). A coalition between the SPD and BÜNDNIS 90/DIE GRÜNEN has been running the city since 1982. Nürnberg is a flourishing trade-fair centre with fairs including the INTERNATIONALE SPIELWARENMESSE (toys), IWA (hunting and field sports), FAMETA (metal-working) and INTERFAB (medical and hospital supplies). Nürnberg is a world centre for the toy industry, and VEDES, a cooperative of Germany's specialist toy retailers, is based here. Nürnberg is also the headquarters of one of Europe's biggest mail-order companies, QUELLE. The city has Germany's newest inland port, and industries include electrical engineering, vehicles, office machinery, toys, food processing, paper and brewing. See also: ERLANGEN-NÜRNBERG, FRIEDRICH-ALEXANDER-UNIVERSITÄT

NÜRNBERGER NACHRICHTEN

Daily newspaper established in 1945 and published by Verlag Nürnberger Presse with a circulation of 342,000.

NÜSSLEIN-VOLHARD, CHRISTIANE (1942–   )

Biologist and director of the Max-Planck-Institut für Entwicklungsbiologie in Tübingen (BADEN-WÜRTTEMBERG), who won the Nobel Prize for medicine in 1995 (with E. F. Wieschaus and E. Lewis) for discovering a group of genes in the drosophila fruit fly that control embryonic development of the fertilized egg cell.

OBERBAYERN

The area of BAYERN surrounding MÜNCHEN including the Alps and many famous resorts such as Oberammergau and Garmisch-Partenkirchen. It forms a REGIERUNGSBEZIRK for administrative purposes.

OBERBÜRGERMEISTER, EHRENAMTLICHER

The official title of the honorary mayor with no executive functions in large towns in NORDRHEIN-WESTFALEN and NIEDERSACHSEN.

OBERBÜRGERMEISTER, HAUPTAMTLICHER

The official title of the mayor in a large town or city.

OBERHAUSEN

Oberhausen (the cradle of the RUHRGEBIET) is situated on the Rhein-Herne-Kanal in NORDRHEIN-WESTFALEN (dialling code 02 08, postal area code 46...). The development of this industrial city was based on coalmining, and the Ruhrgebiet's first iron-works were built here. The city was granted a charter in 1874 and heavy industry still forms the backbone of the city's economy. Since 1955, Oberhausen has hosted the Westdeutsche Kurzfilmtage, an international festival of short films, and in 1962 a group of 26 young directors drew up the OBERHAUSENER MANI-FEST denouncing the old film industry.

The city has a population of some 226,000 with about 11% foreigners. The SPD has been running the city since 1952. Industries include coalmining, iron and steel, metal-working and chemicals. Important companies include MAN, DEUTSCHE BABCOCK and THYSSEN. See also: CENTRE0

OBERHAUSENER MANIFEST

A manifesto drawn up by 26 young film-makers at the Westdeutsche Kurzfilmtage in OBERHAUSEN in 1962. The signatories included Edgar REITZ and Alexander KLUGE, who went on to achieve later fame. With the slogan '*Der alte Film ist tot. Wir glauben an den neuen!*', the manifesto denounced the old film industry as moribund and condemned society for not providing the economic basis for a new, healthy film industry. It demanded a new German film free from commercial constraints and limitations on creativity, and proved successful in prompting the government to provide subsidies for film-making. The *Oberhausener Manifest* marks the beginning of the *Neuer deutscher Film*. See also: FILMFÖRDERUNGSANSTALT; FILMFÖRDERUNGSGESETZ

OBERKREISDIREKTOR

The senior BEAMTER in a KREIS and head of the KREISVERWALTUNG in NORDRHEIN-WESTFALEN and NIEDERSACHSEN. See also: LANDRAT, EHRENAMTLICHER

OBERLANDESGERICHT (OLG)

The Oberlandesgericht is the highest court at LAND level. This court hears appeals on points of fact and law (*Berufungen*) from the LANDGERICHT and from the AMTSGERICHT (only in cases of custody and guardianship, and family law). The court also hears appeals on points of law only (*Revisionen*) in criminal cases from the Landgericht. Cases involving crimes against the state are heard by the Oberlandesgericht as a court of first instance. Appeals on points of law concerning judgements made by the Oberlandesgericht are heard by the BUNDESGERICHTSHOF in KARLSRUHE.

OBERLAUSITZ See: *LAUSITZ*

OBERPFALZ

A region in BAYERN based on historical links with the RHEINLAND and today a REGIERUNGSBEZIRK.

OBERSEMINAR

Seminar for advanced students, very often those preparing for examinations and DOKTORANDEN. Participation in these SEMINARE tends to be by invitation only.

OBERSTADTDIREKTOR

The official title of the HAUPTVERWALTUNGSBEAMTER in a KREISFREIE

STADT in NORDRHEIN-WESTFALEN and NIEDERSACHSEN. See also: STADTDIREKTOR

ODENWALD

An area of forest covering much of southern HESSEN and extending into BAYERN and BADEN-WÜRTTEMBERG. A large part of the Odenwald has been designated the nature reserve Bergstraße-Odenwald and traditional crafts still flourish in the half-timbered towns. Odenwald is designated a KREIS.

ODER-NEISSE-LINIE

The Oder-Neiße Line is the national border between Germany and Poland. This line running along the western bank of the rivers Oder and Neiße was laid down at the POTSDAM Conference between the Allied powers in 1945 and effectively meant the loss of Germany's eastern territories. The border was confirmed by Helmut KOHL with the signing of the DEUTSCH-POLNISCHER GRENZ-VERTRAG in November 1990. See also: POTSDAMER ABKOMMEN

OFFENE HANDELSGESELLSCHAFT (OHG)

A partnership in commerce that carries on business under the name of the partnership. The partners have unlimited liability for the debts of the firm.

ÖFFENTLICH-RECHTLICHE KREDITINSTITUTE

Public-sector banks that carry out many functions in the public interest. These banks include the SPARKASSEN, LANDESBANKEN, *Girozentralen, öffentliche* BAUSPARKASSEN, certain public mortgage banks (e.g. DEUTSCHE PFANDBRIEFANSTALT) and other public banks for specific purposes such as the DEUTSCHE AUSGLEICHSBANK and the LANDWIRTSCHAFTLICHE RENTENBANK.

ÖFFENTLICH-RECHTLICHE RUNDFUNKANSTALT

A public-service broadcasting corporation (radio, TV) financed by public money (e.g. NORDDEUTSCHER RUNDFUNK, ZWEITES DEUTSCHES FERNSEHEN). The BUND is responsible for laying down the legal framework for the technical transmission of broadcasts whereas the individual LÄNDER provide legislation for setting up broadcasting stations. See also: BUNDESRUNDFUNKANSTALTEN; LANDESRUNDFUNK- UND FERNSEHANSTALTEN

ÖFFENTLICHE HAND

A term referring to the public authorities that are responsible for administering public funds and for the industries within the public sector.

ÖFFENTLICHER BEDIENSTETER

Public-service employee working for the BUND, LAND, KREIS OR GEMEINDE.

ÖFFENTLICHER DIENST

Public service, referring to activities carried out by organisations under ÖFFENTLICHES RECHT in the service of the BUND, LAND, KREIS and GEMEINDE. Public servants are classified either as BEAMTE, who have special privileges and are not permitted to strike, or as ANGESTELLTE and ARBEITER, who have a normal contract of employment under PRIVATRECHT, although they may also have certain special privileges. Special conditions apply to government employees in the NEUE BUNDESLÄNDER. The *öffentlicher Dienst* effectively covers all public-sector activities including education, utilities, the courts, etc.

ÖFFENTLICHES RECHT

Public law covering the areas of law not included in PRIVATRECHT and governing the relationship between the individual and the state. *Öffentliches Recht* includes constitutional law, administrative law, the judiciary, civil and criminal proceedings, international law and European law. See also: BÜRGERLICHES RECHT; PRIVATRECHT

OHG See: *OFFENE HANDELSGESELLSCHAFT*

ÖKOBANK

Cooperative bank founded in 1982 to provide credit for alternative businesses and to promote projects related to the environment.

ÖKOCHONDER
Alleged hypochondriac whose fears focus on environmental dangers to personal health.

OKTOBERFEST
Reputedly the world's biggest beer festival, which is held in MÜNCHEN ironically in the latter part of September every year (ending on the first Sunday of October). The festival has its origins in the future König Ludwig I's royal wedding to Prinzessin Therese von Sachsen-Hildburghausen on 17 October 1810. It started out as an annual fair in honour of the king's bride. Now it is a mammoth beer festival launched by the OBERBÜRGERMEISTER with the announcement in BAIRISCH '*Ozapft is*' as he broaches the first beer barrel. Each of the six breweries in München has a massive beer tent, there is a huge funfair with sideshows, and gargantuan amounts of food and beer ('*Das Brot des Lebens*') are consumed by over 6 million visitors in the space of two weeks: in 1995 5.3 million litres of beer, 663,135 chickens, over 400,000 sausages, 17,550 kilos of fish, and 79 oxen roasted on spits. The price of beer at the festival is always a sore point and in 1995 the price of a *Maß* of beer (theoretically 1 litre but in fact nearer two-thirds) burst through the barrier of DM 10.

OLDENBURG, CARL VON OSSIETZKY UNIVERSITÄT
University in NIEDERSACHSEN founded in 1974 and teaching some 13,000 students. The Carl von Ossietzky Universität Oldenburg has faculties of education, communication and aesthetics, social sciences, economics and law, philosophy and psychology and sport, mathematics and computer science, biology, physics, chemistry, information science, languages and literature.

OLG See: *OBERLANDESGERICHT*

OPEL AG
Automobile manufacturer founded by engineer Adam Opel in 1862 as a workshop for manufacturing sewing machines. Bicycle production started up 15 years later and Opel then went over to car production in 1898. The company has been a subsidiary of American volume car manufacturer General Motors since 1829.

Company headquarters are in Rüsselsheim (HESSEN). Opel has some 47,000 employees.

ORB See: *OSTDEUTSCHER RUNDFUNK BRANDENBURG*

ORDINARIUS See: *PROFESSOR*

ORGANISATIONSEINHEIT
An organisational unit in a local authority providing a particular service.

ORGATEC KÖLN (INTERNATIONALE FACHMESSE FÜR BÜROEINRICHTUNG UND IFCOM – ANWENDER-MESSE FÜR INFORMATION UND COMMUNIKATION)
The 'International Office Trade Fair' for office furnishing and equipment, communications and IT is held in KÖLN every two years with around 130,000 visitors.

ORIENTIERUNGSSTUFE
A period of two years (classes 5 and 6) which may follow the GRUNDSCHULE to give pupils and teachers the opportunity to determine which type of secondary school is best suited to each pupil's individual abilities (HAUPTSCHULE, REALSCHULE or GYMNASIUM).

ORTHOGRAPHIEREFORM See: *RECHTSCHREIB-REFORM*

OSNABRÜCK, UNIVERSITÄT
University in NIEDERSACHSEN founded in 1973 and teaching some 13,000 students. The Universität Osnabrück has departments of law, economics, education, geosciences, languages and literature, psychology, mathematics and computer science, physics, biology and chemistry, Catholic theology, health sciences.

OSSI
Ossis is used colloquially for east Germans as opposed to west Germans (WESSIS) and is particularly applied by west Germans to people from east Germany. The TV comedy series *Motzki* (1993) proved unpopular when it took a satirical look at the relationship between *Ossis* and *Wessis* and was judged to widen the

gulf between east and west Germany, instead of bridging it as intended.

OSTDEUTSCHER RUNDFUNK BRANDENBURG (ORB)

A regional public-service radio and TV broadcasting corporation based in POTSDAM. ORB was established for BRANDENBURG after reunification in 1990. Ostdeutscher Rundfunk is a member of the ARD. See also: LANDESRUNDFUNK- UND FERNSEHANSTALTEN

OSTERMONTAG

Easter Monday is a public holiday throughout Germany.

OSTERSONNTAG

Easter Sunday is the time for the *Osterhase* to visit children with Easter eggs and sweeties. Popular traditions include dyeing hard-boiled eggs, blowing eggs out and painting them with intricate patterns, and arranging them on a bunch of spring branches just bursting into bud.

OSTFRIESLAND

A flat, rural area on the *Nordseeküste* in NIEDERSACHSEN between the city of BREMEN and the Netherlands, which is protected by a huge sea barrier stretching from Emden to Wilhelmshaven. The people of Ostfriesland – the butt of jokes known as *Ostfriesenwitze* elsewhere in Germany – have kept their own cultural identity and language (a variety of PLATTDEUTSCH). Despite a windy, rainy climate, the coastal towns, WATT and East Friesian islands attract large numbers of visitors who come to enjoy the bracing sea air.

OSTGEBIETE See: *DEUTSCHE OSTGEBIETE*

OSTPOLITIK

A policy of reconciliation and *détente* with the eastern Communist block initiated by BUNDESKANZLER Willy Brandt of the SPD in 1969 and continued by Helmut SCHMIDT. The policy was initially severely criticised by the right, but closer links with East Germany continued to be fostered under the right-wing government during the 1980s culminating in a visit by GENERALSEKRETÄR Erich Honecker to West Germany in 1987. See also: BUNDESRE-PUBLIK DEUTSCHLAND

OSTPREUSSEN
A former province of PREUSSEN that forms part of modern-day Poland and Russia. See also: ODER-NEISSE-LINIE; ZWEI-PLUS-VIER-VERTRAG

OTTO, FRANK (1957–   )
Owner of Radio OK in HAMBURG with shares in a string of other local radio stations including Radio Kiss FM (BERLIN), Delta-Radio (KIEL), Newstalk-Radio (Berlin) and Radio Europa FM. He also has interests in local TV stations including Hamburg 1 and music TV stations Viva and Viva 2.

OTTO, FREI (1925–   )
Engineer and architect who carried out pioneering work in the construction of suspended roofs and was the inspiration for the spectacular tent-like roofs of the sports complex built for the 1972 Olympics in MÜNCHEN. See also: BEHNISCH, GÜNTER

OTTO-VERSAND GmbH & CO
Founded in 1949, Otto-Versand rose to become one of the world's biggest mail-order companies, attracting middle-class customers to mail order. Company headquarters are in HAMBURG. Otto-Versand has some 48,000 employees.

ÖTV See: *GEWERKSCHAFT ÖFFENTLICHE DIENSTE, TRANSPORT UND VERKEHR*

PÄDAGOGISCHE HOCHSCHULEN (PH)
Institutions of tertiary education that specialise in teacher training and educational science for the GRUNDSCHULE and HAUPT-
SCHULE and in some cases the REALSCHULE. They combine theoretical study with practical training for the teaching profession.

PADERBORN, UNIVERSITÄT-GESAMTHOCHSCHULE
University in NORDRHEIN-WESTFALEN founded in 1972 and teaching
some 17,000 students. The Universität-Gesamthochschule Paderborn has departments of philosophy and history and geography
and social sciences, education and psychology and physical education, languages and literature, fine arts and music, economics
and business studies, physics, architecture, construction engineering, mechanical engineering, electrical engineering,
chemistry, agriculture, telecommunications, mathematics and
computer science, environmental technology.

PAL-SYSTEM
System of broadcasting colour TV programmes introduced by
Germany in 1967 and used by many other European countries.
An improved system called PALplus was introduced in 1994 for
wide-screen TVs.

PALAIS SCHAUMBURG
Official residence of the BUNDESKANZLER in BONN until the govern-
ment moves to BERLIN between 1998 and 2000. See also: SCHLOSS
BELLEVUE

PALAST DER REPUBLIK
The ruins of the royal *Schloß* in BERLIN were dynamited by the
Communist authorities in the early 1960s in an effort to erase all
memories of the imperial past. The Palast der Republik was
erected on the south-eastern side of the Schloßplatz in a thou-

sand days to house the DDR'S VOLKSKAMMER, while the car park for the parliament was built on the site of the former *Schloß*. The Palast der Republik was closed in 1990 and the large amount of asbestos present makes it likely that this example of Socialist Realism will in turn be demolished. Archaeologists have excavated the remains of the Kaiser's cellars which are destined to become a car park again until the city decides on plans for the vacuum at the centre of Berlin.

PALITZSCH, PETER (1918–   )

Producer and exponent of political theatre who was with the BERLINER ENSEMBLE in 1948–1961, working with Brecht until Brecht's death in 1956. He then moved to the BRD and worked at the Stuttgarter Schauspiel (1966–1971) and Frankfurter Schauspiel (1972–1979). His productions include WALSER'S *Überlebensgroß Herr Krott* (1963) and *Der schwarze Schwan* (1964), DORST'S *Toller* (1968), Brecht's (uncompleted) *Das wirkliche Leben des Jakob Geherda* (1983), Turrini's *Tod und Teufel* (1989) and DORST'S *Karlos* (1991).

PANZERDIVISION

The BUNDESWEHR has four tank divisions.

PANZERGRENADIERDIVISION

The BUNDESWEHR has three armoured divisions.

PARAGRAPH

Section of a law designated by the sign § and a serial number (e.g. §218 of the STRAFGESETZBUCH covering SCHWANGERSCHAFTSABBRUCH). *Paragraphen* may also be used to structure contracts, academic works, etc.

PARITÄT

The socio-political objective of obtaining equality for different groups within society in an attempt to achieve greater social justice. This may relate to equal pay for different groups of workers or equal representation of different interests within an organisation. The objective of obtaining *Parität* in the process of MITBESTIMMUNG has been a central union objective for many years. See also: ARBEITSDIREKTOR; BETRIEBSVERFASSUNGSGESETZ

PARKSCHEIBE
Cardboard parking clock that can be purchased from newsagents. Motorists set it at the time they arrive in a zone with restricted parking time, and display it in the windscreen.

PARTEI DES DEMOKRATISCHEN SOZIALISMUS (PDS)
After the fall of the BERLINER MAUER, the SED quickly renamed itself Partei des Demokratischen Sozialismus (PDS) on 4 February 1990 after an initial phase as SED-PDS. In the BUNDESTAGS-WAHLEN of 1990 and 1994 the party failed to poll sufficient votes to overcome the FÜNFPROZENTKLAUSEL and form a FRAKTION, but gained enough DIREKTMANDATE to enter the BUNDESTAG with 17 and 30 MANDATE respectively. The party has around 124,000 members with the vast majority of members living in the former DDR. The party has been unable to make any real progress because of its political and financial links with the SED past. At its party conference at the beginning of 1995 the PDS resolved to distance itself from Stalinist views.

Over 90% of PDS members were members of the old SED and the party's power base is almost exclusively in the NEUE BUN-DESLÄNDER with support virtually non-existent in the former BRD. In 1995 the Bundesamt für Verfassungsschutz classified the PDS as being extreme left-wing. See also: BISKY, LOTHAR; GYSI, GEORG

PARTEIVERBOT
The party ban permitted in the GRUNDGESETZ for political parties that are ruled to be unconstitutional because they present a threat to democracy or to the existence of the BRD. The case for a ban has to be put before the BUNDESVERFASSUNGSGERICHT by the BUNDESTAG, BUNDESRAT or BUNDESREGIERUNG. So far, only two parties have been banned, the *Sozialistische Reichspartei* (a neo-fascist party banned in 1952) and the KOMMUNISTISCHE PARTEI DEUTSCHLANDS, banned in 1956 and reconstituted in 1968 as the DEUTSCHE KOMMUNISTISCHE PARTEI, which has no stated commitment to overthrowing the state.

PARTNER-TARIF See: *E-PLUS*

PASSAU, UNIVERSITÄT

University in BAYERN founded in 1972 and teaching some 9,000 students. The Universität Passau has faculties of Catholic theology, law, business studies, philosophy (arts), mathematics and computer science.

PAUL, WOLFGANG See: *DEHMELT, HANS-GEORG*

PAULUSSCHLÖSSEL

The Paulusschlössel in Markneukirchen (SACHSEN) houses a musical-instrument museum with around 2,300 examples of ancient and modern musical instruments from all over the world.

PDS See: *PARTEI DES DEMOKRATISCHEN SOZIALISMUS*

PENCK, A. R. (1939–   )

Artist and sculptor (real name Ralf Winkler) who was self-taught during the late 1950s and denied admission to formal art training in DRESDEN and East BERLIN. He worked as a night-watchman and postman before a breakthrough when some of his work was exhibited at the Akademie der Künste in East Berlin (1961). He returned to the East from visiting Georg BASELITZ in West Berlin the evening before the BERLINER MAUER was built, drawn by his commitment to Socialism, and was not to return to the West until 1980. He took the name of geologist Albert R. Penck, who had written the book *Die Alpen im Eiszeitalter* in 1901–1909, partly to reflect the 'ice age' prevailing in the DDR. His first exhibition in the West was in 1969, he was represented at DOCUMENTA in 1972, and the Stadthalle in KÖLN held a retrospective in 1981. Penck left the DDR in 1980, moving first to Köln and then to London, where he started producing sculpture in bronze and marble. He was appointed professor at the Kunstakademie DÜSSELDORF in 1989. His work includes *Weltbilder* (1963–1965), the *Standart Bilder* (1968–1973), sculpture, music and poetry.

PERGAMONMUSEUM

The last museum to be built on the MUSEUMSINSEL in BERLIN and completed in 1930. The museum was built to house the collections from Asia Minor and Egypt excavated by German archaeologists including Heinrich Schliemann, excavator of Troy. Part of the treasure from Troy was exhibited at the Pushkin Museum in Moscow in 1996 where it had been kept, and officially denied, since the Second World War. The museum's centrepiece is the Pergamon Altar showing a battle between the Greek gods and the giants. The Pergamon forms part of the monumental museum complex on the Museumsinsel that was neglected during the DDR era and is due to be restored to its former glory.

PERSONENGESELLSCHAFT

A partnership with unlimited liability for the individual partners, as opposed to a KAPITALGESELLSCHAFT, which is a share company owned by the shareholders. See also: KOMMANDITGESELLSCHAFT; OFFENE HANDELSGESELLSCHAFT

PETRA

Monthly magazine for young women established in 1969 and published by JAHRESZEITEN VERLAG in HAMBURG with a circulation of 351,000. It focuses on fashion and beauty and aims at an intelligent, successful audience.

PEYMANN, CLAUS (1937–   )

Theatre producer and director of the Burgtheater in Wien since 1986. Peymann was co-founder of the Schaubühne am Halleschen Ufer in BERLIN in 1970, Schauspieldirektor at the Staatstheater STUTTGART in 1974–1979 and INTENDANT at the Schauspielhaus BOCHUM in 1979–1986. His innovative interpretations of plays by Thomas Bernhard, Peter Handke and Botho STRAUSS made his reputation. Theatre productions include Handke's *Publikumsbeschimpfung* (1966) and *Kaspar* (1970), Strauss' *Die Hypochonder* (1973), Bernhard's *Vor dem Ruhestand* (1979) and *Heldenplatz* (1988), Handke's *Das Spiel vom Fragen* (1990) and Turrini's *Alpenglühen* (1993).

PFÄLZER WALD

A hilly wooded region in RHEINLAND-PFALZ, much of which has been declared a nature reserve.

PFINGSTMONTAG
Whit Monday is a public holiday in most LÄNDER. In BADEN-WÜRTTEMBERG it was abolished in 1994 in order to finance the new PFLEGEVERSICHERUNG.

PFINGSTSONNTAG
Whit Sunday is the seventh Sunday after Easter and forms a long weekend with Whit Monday in most LÄNDER.

PFLEGEVERSICHERUNG
Invalidity insurance scheme introduced in 1995 as a fourth SOZIALVERSICHERUNG. It is intended to provide for the increasing numbers of elderly requiring care in the home when they become ill or incapacitated and unable to look after themselves. Contributions for the *Pflegeversicherung* are shared equally by ARBEITGEBER and ARBEITNEHMER as with SOZIALVERSICHERUNGEN, but the *Arbeitgeber* is compensated by the abolition of a public holiday (BUSS- UND BETTAG/PFINGSTMONTAG) in all LÄNDER except SACHSEN, where the *Arbeitnehmer* pays the full cost after the CDU rejected abolition of a public holiday. This is the first time that the burden of paying for a *Sozialversicherung* has effectively been placed on the *Arbeitnehmer*.

Nearly one million people applied for benefits during the first year of the scheme. Critics of the new scheme claim that it will be unable to provide the resources necessary in the long term for an ageing population.

PFLICHTKRANKENKASSEN
Compulsory health-insurance funds for providing mandatory health insurance to their members. The members are registered by the ARBEITGEBER, who deducts contributions from their pay. *Pflichtkrankenkassen* include ALLGEMEINE ORTSKRANKENKASSEN, BETRIEBSKRANKENKASSEN, INNUNGSKRANKENKASSEN, KNAPPSCHAFTS-VERSICHERUNG, *Seekasse* and LANDWIRTSCHAFTLICHE KRANKEN-KASSEN. See also: SEESOZIALVERSICHERUNG

PFLICHTLEHRVERANSTALTUNG
Compulsory class, seminar etc. for all students taking a particular subject (STUDIENFACH).

PFLICHTVERBAND

A ZWECKVERBAND that is set up compulsorily to deliver services.

PH See: *PÄDAGOGISCHE HOCHSCHULEN*

PHILIPS GmbH

German subsidiary of Dutch electronics giant, founded in 1926. Company headquarters are in HAMBURG. Philips GmbH has some 21,000 employees.

PHYSIKALISCH-TECHNISCHE BUNDESANSTALT (PTB)

The national authority for weights and measures in BRAUN-SCHWEIG is concerned with research and development in metrology and the mandatory tests and approvals for instrumentation. The authority also relays MITTELEUROPÄISCHE ZEIT by radio signal.

PIËCH, FERDINAND (1937–)

Engineer Ferdinand Piëch was chairman of VOLKSWAGEN subsidiary AUDI from 1988 to 1992, when he became chairman of Volkswagen AG.

PIERER, HEINRICH VON (1941–)

Lawyer and industrialist who joined SIEMENS in 1969 and was appointed chairman in 1993.

PISCHETSRIEDER, BERND (1948–)

Joined luxury automobile manufacturer BMW in 1973 and became chairman in 1993. He masterminded the purchase of the UK Rover Group in 1994.

PLANUNGSAMT

Local-authority office responsible for town planning at local level.

PLATTDEUTSCH

Low German dialects (*niederdeutsche Mundarten*) spoken in the north of Germany. *Plattdeutsch* or *Platt* has much in common with Dutch and English.

PLENZDORF, ULRICH (1934–)

Playwright, scriptwriter and author who studied philosophy in LEIPZIG before working in the DEFA film studios in the DDR. His most spectacular success was the play, film and novel *Die neuen Leiden des jungen W.*, first staged in 1972. The work provoked widespread discussion in the DDR on the state of mind of young people in East Germany. Other works include the film script *Die Legende von Paul und Paula* (1973), its sequel, the novel *Legende vom Glück ohne Ende* (1979), and the TV drama *Vater, Mutter, Mörderkind* (1993).

PLUS WARENHANDELSGESELLSCHAFT & CO OHG
Chain of cut-price supermarkets founded in 1972. Company headquarters are in Mülheim (NORDRHEIN-WESTFALEN). Plus has some 21,000 employees.

PM MAGAZIN
Popular science monthly established in 1987 and published by GRUNER + JAHR with a circulation of 418,000. It appeals to a young, educated, predominantly male readership.

POLENDEUTSCHE
A German minority of about 1 million ethnic Germans living mostly in the former Prussian province of SCHLESIEN, now part of Poland. They were largely ignored by the Communist authorities, but the DEUTSCH-POLNISCHER NACHBARSCHAFTSVERTRAG in 1991 has provided guarantees for their linguistic, cultural and religious integrity.

POLIZEI
Under the German constitution, internal security is the responsibility of each LAND while external security is the responsibility of the BUND. The only police directly under the control of the Bund are the BUNDESGRENZSCHUTZ and the BUNDESKRIMINALAMT, which coordinates the activities of the LANDESKRIMINALÄMTER. The SCHUTZPOLIZEI is under the control of the Ministerium des Innern in each Land.

POLIZEILICHES FÜHRUNGSZEUGNIS See: *FÜHRUNGSZEUGNIS*

POLKE, SIGMAR (1941–   )
Painter who moved to the BRD from the DDR in 1953 and whose work includes *Der Wurstesser* (1963), his large-format

Rasterbilder and *Stoffbilder*, and *Wachtturm III* (1985). Polke was represented at DOCUMENTA 5 (1972), 6 (1979) and 7 (1982) in KASSEL and at the Venice Biennale in 1986. He was appointed professor at the Kunsthochschule HAMBURG in 1977.

POLT, GERHARD (1942–   )
Cabaret artist and actor who draws on his native BAIRISCH to present a satirical view of society. After working as a translator and interpreter he commenced his artistic career in 1975 and has worked with the satirical music group *Biermösl Blos'n* since 1981. His successful TV series *Fast wia im richtigen Leben* ran from 1979–1983, his cabaret programme is entitled *Diridari* and he has made a number of satirical films including *Kehraus* (1986) and *Man spricht deutsh* (1987).

POMMERN
Region in present-day Germany and Poland that was historically divided into two regions, *Vorpommern* and *Hinterpommern*. The area formed the Prussian provinces of *Pommern* and WESTPREUSSEN after Napoleon's defeat in 1815. *Hinterpommern* became part of modern Poland after the Second World War with the German population being expelled, and *Vorpommern* west of the ODER-NEISSE-LINIE became part of the DDR and is today part of MECKLEN-BURG-VORPOMMERN. See also: DEUTSCH-POLNISCHER GRENZVERTRAG

PORSCHE AG, Dr. Ing. h.c. F.
Manufacturer of luxury sports cars founded in 1931 by engineer Ferdinand Porsche. Company headquarters are in STUTTGART and Porsche went public in 1971. Porsche has some 6,600 employees.

PORZNER, KONRAD (1935–   )
SPD politician who had two spells as Parlamentarischer Geschäfts-führer with the SPD-FRAKTION in the BUNDESTAG. He had a brief period as Finanzsenator in BERLIN and was then STAATSSEKRETÄR at the BUNDESMINISTERIUM FÜR WIRTSCHAFTLICHE ZUSAMMENARBEIT in 1981–1982. He was appointed president of the BUNDESNACHRICH-TENDIENST in 1990.

POSSEHL & CO mbH
Trading company founded in 1847. Company headquarters are in LÜBECK. Possehl has some 4,500 employees.

POSTAMT
A post office where services provided by the DEUTSCHE POST are delivered. However, with privatisation some local *Postämter* are being closed down and *Agenturen* delivering postal services are being opened up in shops.

POSTDIENST See: *DEUTSCHE POST AG*

POSTFACH
A lockable post box that can be rented from the DEUTSCHE POST for the receipt of mail. All mail has to be collected within seven days of receipt.

POSTGIRODIENST
The cashless money-transfer service provided by the DEUTSCHE POSTBANK AG, which allows holders of Postbank giro accounts to receive money from and transfer money to other accounts in the giro system. Cash can be withdrawn at all POSTÄMTER.

POSTLEITZAHL
Post code (zip code) comprising five digits. A new system of post codes was introduced in Germany on 1 July 1993. The system comprises 83 postal regions indicated by the first two digits, and the last three digits give the place, street, POSTFACH or individual recipient in the case of large companies or organisations. Small towns and villages have a single post code, and the 209 large towns and cities are divided into smaller delivery areas each with an individual post code. All the post codes are printed in the POSTLEITZAHLENBUCH which can be obtained from the POSTAMT.

POSTLEITZAHLENBUCH
A directory listing all the POSTLEITZAHLEN for Germany.

POSTRECHT
The body of law relating to post and telecommunications. This has been changed considerably in recent years with the reforms

in 1989 and 1994 and the projected reform in the late 1990s. The reforms are privatising postal and telecommunications services and opening up the telecommunications market to competition. See also: POSTREFORM

POSTREFORM

The first postal reform was carried out in 1989 splitting the DEUTSCHE BUNDESPOST into three operational units (postal services, banking service, telecommunications). Postreform II created three public companies on 1 January 1995: DEUTSCHE POST AG, DEUTSCHE POSTBANK AG and DEUTSCHE TELEKOM AG. The shares in these companies are held by the state in the form of the BUNDESANSTALT FÜR POST UND TELEKOMMUNIKATION. Postreform III is intended to finish the task of breaking up the old monopolies when the BUNDESMINISTERIUM FÜR POST UND TELEKOMMUNIKATION is disbanded at the end of 1997 and the telephone network is opened up to competition on 1 January 1998.

POSTSPARKASSE

Savings bank run by the DEUTSCHE POSTBANK. Holders of a savings account can withdraw up to DM 2,000 per month from post offices abroad.

POTSDAM

Potsdam is the LANDESHAUPTSTADT of BRANDENBURG and is situated to the south-west of BERLIN where the river Nuthe flows into the Havel (dialling code 03 31, postal area code 14...). Potsdam received its charter in 1317, and the Hohenzollerns turned it into a royal residence and Prussia's most important garrison town. In 1945, Churchill/Attlee, Truman and Stalin met at the Potsdam Conference in Schloß Cecilienhof to decide on the future of post-war Germany. After the fall of the BERLINER MAUER the remains of Friedrich der Große – removed to the West at the end of the war – were reinterred at Potsdam in 1991 and the last Russian troops moved out in 1994. As a royal residence for Prussia's rulers until 1918, Potsdam is home to SCHLOSS SANSSOUCI built by Friedrich der Große. More recently, the DDR's central state archives were located in Potsdam, and the DEFA film studios in Babelsberg were the centre for the East German film industry.

The city has a population of some 140,000 with a total student population of around 9,000 (1 UNIVERSITÄT and 2 other HOCHSCHULEN) and about 3% foreigners (19% Polish). Industry includes machinery, construction, transport, brewing and organ building. The SPD runs the city and has been in office since 1990.

POTSDAM, UNIVERSITÄT
University in BRANDENBURG founded in 1991 and teaching some 8,000 students. The Universität Potsdam has faculties of law, philosophy (arts), economics and social sciences, mathematics and natural sciences.

POTSDAMER ABKOMMEN
The Potsdam Declaration was agreed at the Potsdam Conference between the US, the Soviet Union and Great Britain on 2 August 1945. It regulated the military occupation of Germany in the four zones agreed at the Yalta Conference (effectively confirming the subsequent post-war frontiers of Europe). It set the western frontier of Poland along the ODER-NEISSE-LINIE and agreed the forcible repatriation of Germans living in the DEUTSCHE OSTGEBIETE east of this line and living in the SUDETENLAND. It also set up a Control Council composed of representatives of the four Allies (the US, the Soviet Union, Great Britain and France) to deal with issues affecting Germany and Austria as a whole based on the principles of demilitarisation, denazification, democratisation, decentralisation and deindustrialisation agreed at the Yalta Conference. The declaration foresaw Germany's being treated as a single economic unit but was rendered meaningless by the subsequent cold war, in which Germany became a divided state. See also: DEUTSCH-POLNISCHER GRENZVERTRAG; ZWEI-PLUS-VIER-VERTRAG

POTSDAMER PLATZ
The bustling centre of pre-war BERLIN was reduced to rubble by RAF bombers during the Second World War and became a barren wasteland when the city was divided. Reunification has given this square a new lease of life. Sony, DAIMLER-BENZ, ASEA BROWN BOVERI and HERTIE now own most of the area and a new commercial centre is planned here.

ppa See: *PROGRESS PRESSE AGENTUR*

PRAKTIKUM

A course of practical training during a theoretical course of study. This practical element is an integral part of medical training and is also found in other courses of study at HOCHSCHULEN leading to qualifications as teachers or social scientists (generally on work placements). Older school children may also carry out a vocational *Praktikum* or a *Sozialpraktikum* in the community (e.g. working in an old-people's home).

PRÄSENZBIBLIOTHEK

A reference library where books may not be borrowed. Most libraries at INSTITUTE are *Präsenzbibliotheken* although many permit readers to borrow books over a weekend. Some major research libraries are *Präsenzbibliotheken*, e.g. the SCHILLER-NATIONALMUSEUM UND DEUTSCHES LITERATURARCHIV and the HERZOG AUGUST BIBLIOTHEK WOLFENBÜTTEL.

PRÄSIDENT

President or head of an organisation. In HOCHSCHULEN it is the title for the full-time executive head, which has in many cases replaced the traditional title of REKTOR. See also: BUNDESPRÄSIDENT

PRAUNHEIM, ROSA VON (1942–   )

Actor and producer (real name Holger Mischwitzky) whose controversial films on lesbians and gays advocate a society that is free of prejudice about sexual orientation. His films include *Die Bettwurst* (1970), *Nicht der Homosexuelle ist pervers, sondern die Situation, in der er lebt* (1971), the AIDS trilogy: *Schweigen = Tod* (1989), *Positiv* (1990) and *Feuer unterm Arsch* (1990), *Affengeil* (1991) and *Ich bin meine eigene Frau* (1992).

PRESSE- UND INFORMATIONSAMT DER BUNDESREGIERUNG (BPA)

The government press office with the twin functions of keeping the government informed about news and opinions reported in the German and foreign press, and to provide information about government policy to the media. The BPA monitors the world's major press agencies as well as over 100 radio broadcasters and 25 TV channels in German and 22 other languages. The head of the BPA is a spokesperson for the government. In contrast to other countries, press conferences are always held by the press, and the government spokesperson goes to meet the press rather than the press coming to the government.

PRESSEFREIHEIT
Freedom of the press is zealously guarded in Germany and is guaranteed in *Artikel* 5 of the GRUNDGESETZ.

PREUSSAG AG
Holding company for a group of companies engaged in steel production, transport, energy and construction. The company was founded in 1923 as a coal and steel company. Company headquarters are in HANNOVER. The group has some 70,000 employees.

PREUSSEN
Originally a dukedom ruled by the Hohenzollerns, Prussia rose to prominence as a European power under Friedrich der Große and went on to become the largest and most powerful German state with nearly 42 million inhabitants in 1939. It forged a united Germany in 1871 as the German REICH under Bismarck, but after the Second World War *Preussen*, already reduced in size by the ODER-NEISSE-LINIE, was formally dissolved on 25 February 1947. The state was then broken up and use of the name banned as being associated with hegemony and militaristic traditions. The possessions of the state passed to the successor German states and the cultural heritage of *Preussen* has been gathered under the STIFTUNG PREUSSISCHER KULTURBESITZ.

PREUSSEN ELEKTRA AG
Electricity, gas and water generation and distribution company founded in 1927. The company is a wholly-owned subsidiary of VEBA. Company headquarters are in HANNOVER. Preussen Elektra has some 27,000 employees.

PREUSSLER, OTFRIED (1923–   )
Originally a teacher, who turned to writing children's books. *Die kleine Hexe* (1957) and *Der Räuber Hotzenplotz* (1962) with

their sequels remain popular, both as books and as cassettes. More recent works are *Der Engel mit der Pudelmütze* (1985) and *Mein Rübezahlbuch* (1993). He was awarded the *Deutscher Jugendbuchpreis* (DEUTSCHER JUGENDLITERATURPREIS) in 1963 and 1972.

PREY, HERMANN (1929–   )
Baritone singer who made his reputation as an opera singer with his performance of Rossini's Figaro in Wien in 1955 and with the Bayerische Staatsoper MÜNCHEN from 1960. He is also a well-known singer of lieder and oratorios. Prey was appointed professor at the Musikhochschule in HAMBURG in 1983, and made his début as an opera producer in 1988.

PRIMA
Monthly magazine established in 1987 and published in MÜNCHEN by GRUNER + JAHR with a circulation of 459,000. The emphasis of *Prima* is on information and advice for a young, creative female readership.

PRINZ
Monthly listings magazine with editions in ten major cities established in 1988 and published by JAHRESZEITEN VERLAG in HAMBURG with a circulation of 194,000. It provides a balance of news, local interest and listings and is aimed at a young, consumer-oriented audience living in big cities.

PRIVATDOZENT
A lecturer at a HOCHSCHULE without the status of BEAMTER who has obtained a licence to teach (*Lehrbefugnis*) following completion of a HABILITATION.

PRIVATE KRANKENVERSICHERUNG See: *KRANKENVERSICHERUNG*

PRIVATRECHT
The area of law regulating relationships between private individuals including BÜRGERLICHES RECHT, and also commercial and company law, copyright and competition law, and the law governing cheques and bills of exchange. Privatrecht contrasts with

ÖFFENTLICHES RECHT, which governs interactions between individuals and the state. See also: BÜRGERLICHES RECHT

PRO 7 TELEVISION GmbH
Germany's third biggest commercial TV channel, founded in 1989 and with a major holding by Thomas Kirch (son of media mogul Leo KIRCH). Company headquarters are at Unterföhring, a suburb of MÜNCHEN, and Pro 7 has some 700 employees. The channel mainly shows feature films together with news, documentaries and family programmes and beams its output to households 24 hours a day.

PROFESSOR
A *Professor* is appointed (*Berufung*) to a HOCHSCHULE by the KULTUSMINISTERIUM in the relevant LAND. *Professoren* are responsible for carrying out and organising research and teaching (*Forschung und Lehre*) in their specialist field. To qualify, the appointee must have completed a doctorate (PROMOTION) and normally a HABILITATION, and be under 55 years of age. A *Professor* is normally made a lifelong BEAMTER. Remuneration is on three salary scales, C2, C3, C4, of which C4 is the highest. At *wissenschaftliche Hochschulen* slightly over half the *Professoren* are C4 *Professoren*, with a LEHRSTUHL. These are equivalent to the old-style *Ordinarius* and have a secretary, assistant, etc.; C3 *Professoren* have fewer facilities provided as well as a lower salary. *Professoren* at FACHHOCHSCHULEN are paid according to the scales C2 and C3; they are not required to have a *Habilitation* but must have five years' vocational experience in their field.

PROFI-TARIF See: *E-PLUS*

PROGRESS PRESSE AGENTUR (ppa)
News agency founded in 1971 and based in DÜSSELDORF.

PROMOTION
The conferment of a doctor's degree attained by submitting a dissertation (*Doktorarbeit*) and undergoing an oral examination in two or three subjects (*Rigorosum*). The dissertation must be published with a print-run that will permit all German academic

libraries to receive a copy. See also: DOKTORAND; DOKTORGRAD; HABILITATION

PROSEMINAR
Foundation SEMINAR held during the GRUNDSTUDIUM.

ProTel See: *D1–NETZ*

PROTOKOLL
The minutes taken as a record of an official meeting.

PRÜFUNGSAMT
Organisation run by FAKULTÄTEN/FACHBEREICHE for purposes of organising examinations. They provide candidates with information on examinations, and candidates must obtain registration forms and register for examinations there.

PRÜFUNGSORDNUNG
The examination regulations for a particular FACHBEREICH.

PTB See: *PHYSIKALISCH-TECHNISCHE BUNDESANSTALT*

PWA PAPIERWERKE WALDHOF-ASCHAFFENBURG AG
Packaging, paper and printing company with headquarters in Raubling (BAYERN). PWA has some 12,000 employees.

QUADFLIEG, WILL (1914–)

Actor and producer who has played all the classic roles including Shakespeare's great tragic heroes and the protagonists in Lessing's *Nathan der Weise* and Goethe's *Faust* and *Tasso*. In 1958 Quadflieg played Faust alongside Gustaf Gründgens' Mephisto (film 1960) and he played Mephisto in Goethe's *Faust* at the *Salzburger Festspiele* in 1962–1964. He has appeared in numerous films including *Der große Bellheim* (1993).

QUEDLINBURG

The ALTSTADT in this remarkable east German town in SACHSEN-ANHALT with its wealth of half-timbered houses (including the birthplace of poet F. G. Klopstock) and the Stiftskirche high up on the Schloßberg have been made a UNESCO world heritage site.

QUELLE-SCHICKEDANZ AG & CO

One of Europe's biggest mail-order companies was founded in 1927. Company headquarters are in Fürth (BAYERN). Quelle has some 37,000 employees.

RAAB KARCHER AG
Trading and service company founded in 1848, now wholly owned by VEBA. Company headquarters are in ESSEN. Raab Karcher has some 27,000 employees and is Germany's biggest private security company, patrolling U-BAHN and S-BAHN stations.

RADIO BREMEN (RB)
A regional public-service radio and TV broadcasting corporation based in BREMEN and broadcasting principally to LAND BREMEN. Radio Bremen is a member of the ARD. See also: LANDESRUND-FUNK- UND FERNSEHANSTALTEN

RAF See: *ROTE-ARMEE-FRAKTION*

RAIFFEISENBANKEN
Cooperative banks traditionally serving agriculture with a full range of banking services. In 1972 they joined forces with the VOLKSBANKEN in the BUNDESVERBAND DER DEUTSCHEN VOLKSBANKEN UND RAIFFEISENBANKEN E.V. See also: KREDITGENOSSENSCHAFTEN; UNIVERSALBANKEN

RALLYE RACING
A racing and sports monthly published in HAMBURG with a circulation of 94,000 and a young, professional, predominantly male audience with an interest in Formula One.

RAT
General term for a legislative or administrative body (e.g. BUNDESRAT). In NORDRHEIN-WESTFALEN and NIEDERSACHSEN the *Rat* is the elected body responsible for governing a GEMEINDE. *Rat* is also a title for a senior BEAMTER in the civil service. See also: GEMEINDERAT; STADTRAT

RAT DER STADT
The official title for the STADTRAT in NORDRHEIN-WESTFALEN and NIEDERSACHSEN.

RATHAUS
The building accommodating the *Gemeindeverwaltung* or the main administrative offices in a large town.

RATSHERR See: *GEMEINDERATSMITGLIED; STADTRATSMITGLIED*

RATSVERSAMMLUNG
The official title of the STADTRAT in some towns in SCHLESWIG-HOLSTEIN.

RATSVORSITZENDER
The chairman of a GEMEINDERAT or STADTRAT.

RAU, JOHANNES (1931–   )
SPD politician and publisher. He has been a member of the LANDTAG in NORDRHEIN-WESTFALEN since 1958 and was minister for science and research in 1970–1978. He has been chairman of the SPD in Nordrhein-Westfalen since 1977 and MINISTERPRÄSIDENT since 1978. He was elected KANZLERKANDIDAT for the SPD in 1986, losing to Helmut KOHL in the 1987 elections, and he lost to Roman HERZOG in the elections for BUNDESPRÄSIDENT in 1994. The SPD lost its absolute majority in the 1995 elections in Nordrhein-Westfalen and he is now head of a coalition between the SPD and BÜNDNIS 90/DIE GRÜNEN. Since 1982 he has been deputy chairman of the SPD.

RB See: *RADIO BREMEN*

REALO
Member of the less radical, more pragmatic wing of BÜNDNIS 90/DIE GRÜNEN that advocates 'realistic' compromise, e.g. coalition with the SPD. See also: FUNDI

REALSCHULABSCHLUSS
The vocational school-leaving qualification awarded to pupils leaving the REALSCHULE and to pupils leaving a GYMNASIUM having completed the first stage of secondary school at the age of 16/17.

The *Realschulabschluß* is a qualification that allows pupils to start a BERUFSAUSBILDUNG and is the entrance requirement for the FACHOBERSCHULE. See also: FACHGYMNASIUM

REALSCHULE

A secondary school generally for pupils between the ages of 10 and 16 (12 and 16 in BERLIN). The *Realschule* follows on from the GRUNDSCHULE, and pupils can choose between compulsory subjects that prepare them for a wide range of vocations. When pupils have completed their course of study they can either start a training scheme combined with employment (BERUFSAUSBILDUNG) or continue their secondary education at the FACHOBERSCHULE.

RECHTSANWALT

A lawyer licensed to practise law at a particular court. The *Rechtsanwalt* can appear before any AMTSGERICHT and can appear before a higher court if registered there. The rules for appearance in court in the NEUE BUNDESLÄNDER are a modified version of those in the ALTE BUNDESLÄNDER, and fees may be liable to a 20% reduction subject to certain conditions. See also: BEFÄHIGUNG ZUM RICHTERAMT; KANZLEI

RECHTSANWALTSKAMMER

The professional association of RECHTSANWÄLTE registered with the BUNDESGERICHTSHOF and the OBERLANDESGERICHT. The association is a KÖRPERSCHAFT DES ÖFFENTLICHEN RECHTS. It administers the affairs of the profession and regulates the ethical conduct of its members.

RECHTSCHREIBREFORM

A reform of the written German language was agreed by the KULTUSMINISTERKONFERENZ in December 1995. The new rules for spelling and punctuation are due to come into effect on 1 August 1998 although the old rules will remain acceptable until the year 2005. By comparison with the long-standing big debates about eliminating capitalisation for nouns, the changes introduced are relatively minor, affecting use of ß (e.g. *Fass* instead of *Faß*), use of capitals in adverbial phrases (*im Allgemeinen* instead of *im allgemeinen*) and the splitting of words. There will be greater flexibility in the use of commas. The trend is towards fewer compound words, more capitalisation, and fewer orthographic rules (112 instead of 212). See also: RECHTSCHREIBUNG

RECHTSCHREIBUNG

Despite several early attempts to arrive at a standardised orthography for German, the first uniform set of orthographical rules was accepted at the end of the nineteenth century, when Konrad Duden produced a compendium of German orthography based on the rules used in Prussian schools. This orthography was also adopted in Switzerland. Since its introduction in Germany there have been numerous moves to carry out reforms, the principal target being the capitalisation of German nouns. The main consideration in any move towards reform has been the desire to maintain a uniform standard for all German-speaking countries and the necessity to carry out any reform in all German-speaking countries at the same time. The RECHTSCHREIBREFORM of 1995 constituted a moderate attempt to iron out some of the inconsistencies in spelling while resisting the temptation to abolish initial capitalisation for nouns and Germanicise foreign words (e.g. '*Kauboi*' for *Cowboy*). See also: DUDEN

RECHTSEXTREMISMUS

Neo-fascist parties and organisations opposed to the constitution are banned in the BRD, and one of the two parties to be banned under the constitution was the neo-fascist *Sozialistische Reichspartei*. Extreme right-wing organisations active today are the NATIONALDEMOKRATISCHE PARTEI DEUTSCHLANDS and the DEUTSCHE VOLKSUNION. The far-right REPUBLIKANER, though not overtly neo-fascist, has elements with extreme right-wing views and is the most right-wing party to have gained any electoral successes in recent years. Neo-fascist groups include the Aktionsfront Nationaler Sozialisten, and groups of skinheads and other right-wing extremists have been active in particular in a number of vicious attacks on foreigners. Fears of a nationalist revival following severe unemployment in the former DDR have been largely unfounded and neo-Nazis remain a marginal element in society. See also: AUSLÄNDERFEINDLICHKEIT; PARTEIVERBOT

RECHTSRADIKALISMUS See: *RECHTSEXTREMISMUS*

RECHTSSCHUTZVERSICHERUNG
Many Germans take out an insurance to cover legal expenses relating to third-party liability and other domestic matters. Germans are quite willing to go to law over the most minor matters and disputes.

RECHTSSTAAT
A state where the rule of law prevails, ensured in Germany by the GRUNDGESETZ.

RECHTSVERORDNUNG (RVO)
A regulation with the force of law issued by the BUNDESREGIERUNG, a BUNDESMINISTER or a LANDESREGIERUNG.

RECYCLING
Germany has pursued a formidable policy of recycling raw materials wherever possible, and it is nothing to see a line of six different waste bins alongside each other at a public resort, for paper, glass, plastic packaging, compostable material, metal and residual waste. Each local community has a WERTSTOFFANNAHMESTELLE where recyclable materials are sorted and categorised. The extensive recycling policy has been criticised for exporting waste to poorer countries and for sorting waste which is then simply put together again, but the recycling drive has been very successful at raising awareness of waste throughout the population. See also: DUALES SYSTEM DEUTSCHLAND

REDAKTEUR
Editor or sub-editor with a newspaper, responsible for editing reports sent in by correspondents and reporters and for preparing them for printing. See also: CHEFREDAKTEUR; HERAUSGEBER; REDAKTION

REDAKTION
The editorial staff of a newspaper or magazine. *Redaktion* may refer to all the editors and sub-editors that work for a publication or to its offices. See also: CHEFREDAKTEUR; HERAUSGEBER; VERLEGER

REDAKTIONSGEMEINSCHAFT
A method of cutting costs by small independent papers in which a joint editorial board is formed for a number of small papers. Each paper takes a core component of its news from the joint editorial board and then produces perhaps the local section of the newspaper itself. This way of pooling resources allows smaller papers to maintain their independence in a world of increasing concentration.

REEMTSMA CIGARETTENFABRIKEN GmbH
Cigarette manufacturer founded in 1910 producing some of Germany's best-known brands (e.g. *Peter Stuyvesant, Ernte, Reval, Roth-Händle*). Company headquarters are in HAMBURG. Reemtsma has some 8,000 employees.

REEPERBAHN
Entertainment quarter in HAMBURG with discos, night clubs and theatres. It is famed for its sex shows, blue movies and brothels.

REFERAT
The basic organisational unit for each *Abteilung* in a BUNDES-MINISTERIUM. Each *Referat* is headed by a REFERENT. See also: DEZERNAT

REFERATSLEITER See: *REFERENT*

REFERENDAR See: *REFERENDARZEIT*

REFERENDARZEIT
The period of time following the *Erstes* STAATSEXAMEN spent doing practical training in law and as a final stage of teacher training. It also relates to practical training for the higher echelons of government service.

REFERENT
A BEAMTER who is head of a REFERAT in a BUNDESMINISTERIUM. The term *Referent* can also refer in general to a spokesperson on a particular subject. See also: DEZERNENT

REFORMATIONSTAG
31 October, marking the day in 1517 when Luther precipitated the Protestant Reformation by nailing 95 Theses attacking

ecclesiastical abuses to a church door in Wittenberg (SACHSEN-ANHALT). It is a public holiday in the NEUE BUNDESLÄNDER (BRANDENBURG, MECKLENBURG-VORPOMMERN, SACHSEN, Sachsen-Anhalt, THÜRINGEN).

REGELSTUDIENZEIT

The officially prescribed period of time in which a particular STUDIUM can be completed, for most courses nine or ten SEMESTER. In 1994 only 10% of all students completed their *Studium* within that time, most needing a further two or three *Semester* due to overcrowding, irregular provision of courses and financial constraints requiring most students to work while studying.

REGENBOGEN-KOALITION

Coalition between several parties, often in a STADTRAT where, for example, the SPD (red) and BÜNDNIS 90/DIE GRÜNEN (green) form a coalition together with individual representatives of minor local parties such as David contra Goliath (ecology), Rosa Liste (gay rights). See also: AMPEL-KOALITION

REGENSBURG, UNIVERSITÄT

University in BAYERN founded in 1962 and teaching some 17,000 students. The Universität Regensburg has departments of Catholic theology, law, economics, medicine, philosophy and sport and art, education and psychology, history and social sciences and geography, languages and literature, mathematics, physics, biology, chemistry and pharmacology.

REGIERENDER BÜRGERMEISTER See:
BÜRGERMEISTER, REGIERENDER

REGIERUNGSBEZIRK

An administrative authority of the LAND comprising a number of KREISE and KREISFREIE STÄDTE.

REGIONALBANKEN

Commercial banks with a regional base as opposed to the big three (DEUTSCHE BANK, DRESDNER BANK, COMMERZBANK). The biggest regional banks are the BAYERISCHE HYPOTHEKEN- UND

WECHSELBANK and the BAYERISCHE VEREINSBANK, although these two banks have expanded well beyond their regional borders.

REICH

The first German *Reich* was the Holy Roman Empire (*Heiliges römisches Reich*), followed by the empire created by Bismarck (*Bismarckreich*). The term DRITTES REICH became a political slogan under the Nazis. It symbolised a new German order based on racial superiority, following on from the previous two empires.

REICH-RANICKI, MARCEL (1920–   )

Literature critic who moved from Poland to BERLIN in 1929, was deported to the Warsaw Ghetto and escaped in 1943, returning to the BRD in 1958 where he became involved in the GRUPPE 47. He was literary critic at DIE ZEIT in 1960–1973 and the FRANKFURTER ALLGEMEINE ZEITUNG in 1973–1988 and as such has been a powerful influence in the literary world of post-war Germany. Since 1988 he has been an independent critic with his own ZDF programme *Das literarische Quartett*. Reich-Ranicki has been a controversial figure and in 1995 slammed Günter GRASS's latest novel *Ein weites Feld* as being '*unlesbar*' and '*wertlos*'. He has published many anthologies (including the series *Frankfurter Anthologie* from 1976) and a number of other books including *Lauter Verrisse* (1970), *Thomas Mann und die Seinen* (1987) and *Ohne Rabatt. Über Literatur aus der DDR* (1991).

REICHSTAG

The name for the monumental building in BERLIN built in 1884–1894 to house the elected assembly (Reichstag) and to become a symbol of German unity inscribed with the words '*Dem deutschen Volke*' ('for the German people'). The original building was burnt down in 1933 leading to emergency powers being introduced that strengthened Hitler's control over Germany. In the summer of 1995, the Reichstag was completely shrouded in plastic to form an art installation by CHRISTO. Helmut KOHL wants to rename the building BUNDESTAG to signal a new beginning when the Bundestag moves to Berlin at the end of the century.

REICHSVERSICHERUNGSORDNUNG (RVO)

General legal basis for SOZIALVERSICHERUNG passed in 1911. Following a number of reforms which have transferred e.g. KRANKENVERSICHERUNG and RENTENVERSICHERUNG to the SOZIALGE-SETZBUCH, the Reichsversicherungsordnung now covers mainly insurance benefits for accident (UNFALLVERSICHERUNG) and maternity.

REIFEZEUGNIS   See: *ABITURZEUGNIS*

REIMANN, ARIBERT (1936–   )

Pianist and composer who accompanied Dietrich FISCHER-DIESKAU and has developed as an important contemporary composer of opera and other music, drawing his inspiration from Webern, Berg and Indian music. Operas include *Ein Traumspiel* (1965), *Melusine* (1971), *Lear* (1978), *Die Gespenstersonate* (1984) and *Troades* (1986). Reimann has also composed ballets (*Die Vogelscheuchen*, 1990, with libretto by Günter GRASS), piano and organ music, vocal works and chamber music.

REITZ, EDGAR (1932–   )

Film director who created the epic film HEIMAT (1984, $15\frac{1}{2}$ hours long), which portrays the rise of Nazism and the post-war WIRTSCHAFTSWUNDER through the eyes of a village in the HUNSRÜCK. The sequel *Zweite Heimat* (1992, 26 hours long) explores life among German artists and intellectuals in the 1960s and 1970s by following the musical career of Hermann Simon, the youngest son of Maria, central character in *Heimat*.

REKTOR

Head of a GRUNDSCHULE, HAUPTSCHULE, REALSCHULE or SONDER-SCHULE. Traditionally head of a HOCHSCHULE, where the term *Rektor* is equivalent to the vice-chancellor or principal, although many *Hochschulen* now have a PRÄSIDENT instead. See also: HOCHSCHULREKTORENKONFERENZ

RENTENBERECHNUNG

The pension calculation used to determine a person's entitlement to a pension from the state based on the state RENTENVER-SICHERUNG. The pension is calculated according to a formula that takes into account a person's level of earnings compared with average earnings, the type of pension and the purchasing power of the pension. An individual normally needs to have contributed to the state *Rentenversicherung* for 35 years in order to qualify for a full retirement pension. Pensions in the NEUE BUNDESLÄNDER are considerably lower than in the ALTE BUNDESLÄNDER.

RENTENVERSICHERUNG

The part of the SOZIALVERSICHERUNG paid to provide a pension on retirement from paid work at the end of the 65th or 63rd year for men and the 63rd or 60th year for women, depending on the number of years of insurance contributions paid and a variety of other factors.

REPORTAGE

A report in the press, or on radio or TV, especially one in which eye-witness accounts from the people involved are included. This presents a view that includes the emotions and experiences of protagonists and bystanders, and may include the reactions of the reporter. *Reportage* also refers to articles such as *Die Seite Drei* in the SÜDDEUTSCHE ZEITUNG, where an entire article is written in the form of a report.

REPUBLIKANER, DIE

An extreme right-wing party founded in 1983. The party has a membership of around 20,000 and campaigns vigorously for traditional values and against foreigners. It gained initial successes particularly in BAYERN, west BERLIN and BADEN-WÜRTTEMBERG between 1986 and 1992, but failed to cross the five-percent barrier in the LANDTAG and BUNDESTAG elections in 1994. It was classified as *verfassungsfeindlich* by the Bundesamt für Verfassungsschutz in 1995. The party was unable to capitalise on discontent in the former DDR in the 1990 elections, and fears of a right-wing revival have died down with the party's slump into relative obscurity. See also: RECHTSEXTREMISMUS

RESSORT

Area of responsibility or organisational unit (e.g. *Abteilung*) responsible for a particular sphere or group of functions, e.g. in government or publishing. In a REDAKTION journalists specialising in a particular area edit news as a team and constitute a *Ressort*.

The main *Ressorts* correspond to the main sections of a news-paper and are as follows: home and international news (*Nachrichten*, *Politik*), business (*Wirtschaft*), local (*Lokalteil*), arts (FEUILLETON), sport (*Sport*).

REWE-GRUPPE
Retail chain of supermarkets founded as a cooperative in the 1920s in the west of Germany and now also covering north and south Germany. The headquarters of the purchasing organisa-tion Rewe-Zentral-AG are in KÖLN. The Rewe-Gruppe has some 161,000 employees.

REXRODT, GÜNTER (1941–   )
Businessman and FDP politician who was Finanzsenator in West Berlin in 1985–1989 and a member of the board of the TREUHAND-ANSTALT in 1991–1992. He was appointed BUNDESMINISTER FÜR WIRTSCHAFT in 1993 and became MITGLIED DES BUNDESTAGES in 1994.

RHEIN-MAIN-DONAU-GROSSCHIFFAHRTSWEG (EUROPAKANAL)
This trans-European waterway stretches 3,500 km. from the Nordsee to the Black Sea and was opened in 1992.

RHEIN-MAIN-FLUGHAFEN
The airport serving the RHEIN-MAIN-GEBIET, claimed to be Europe's biggest if freight is included. It is a town in its own right, with over 50,000 employees, offering the facilities of a bustling metropolis including hotels, more than 100 shops, a medical centre and even somewhere to house your pet.

RHEIN-MAIN-GEBIET
The Rhein-Main-Gebiet is situated in HESSEN centred on FRANK-FURT AM MAIN and encompassing the area between Hanau (HESSEN) and WIESBADEN/MAINZ. After the RUHRGEBIET the Rhein-Main-Gebiet ranks with BERLIN as Germany's most powerful eco-nomic area.

RHEIN-ZEITUNG
Daily newspaper established in 1948 and published in Koblenz (RHEINLAND-PFALZ) with a circulation of 244,000.

RHEINGAU
Wine-growing region in HESSEN running along the river Rhine.

RHEINHESSEN
Major wine-growing area in RHEINLAND-PFALZ.

RHEINISCH-WESTFÄLISCHES ELEKTRIZITÄTSWERK AG See: *RWE AG*

RHEINISCH-WESTFÄLISCHES INDUSTRIEGEBIET
The heavily industrialised central area of NORDRHEIN-WESTFALEN with the lower Rhine and the Ruhr rivers passing through. It includes the RUHRGEBIET, SIEGERLAND, BERGISCHES LAND, and the areas around AACHEN, DÜSSELDORF, KÖLN, KREFELD and MÖNCHEN-GLADBACH.

RHEINISCH-WESTFÄLISCHES INSTITUT FÜR WIRTSCHAFTSFORSCHUNG (RWI)
One of the leading independent institutes for economic research, founded in 1926 and based in ESSEN. The institute is primarily concerned with analysing the business cycle in the BRD, with particular emphasis on the RUHRGEBIET.

RHEINISCHE POST
Daily newspaper established in 1946 and published in DÜSSEL-DORF with a circulation of 399,000. It is a regional paper centred on Düsseldorf and is distributed throughout NORDRHEIN-WESTFALEN.

RHEINISCHES BRAUNKOHLENREVIER
Europe's largest area of lignite deposits, around the city of Neuss (NORDRHEIN-WESTFALEN). The extensive open-cast mines produce lignite for the electricity industry, chemical processing and for domestic consumption.

RHEINISCHES LANDESMUSEUM BONN
Regional museum of the RHEINLAND in BONN, founded in 1820 and

housing a collection of prehistoric and Roman antiquities, Frankish artefacts from the Rheinland, and the skull of Neanderthal Man discovered near DÜSSELDORF.

RHEINLAND
A term with no precise historical definition, today used to refer to the area along the Mittelrhein and Niederrhein and including the REGIERUNGSBEZIRKE around the cities of AACHEN, DÜSSELDORF, Koblenz (RHEINLAND-PFALZ), KÖLN, TRIER and WIESBADEN.

RHEINLAND-PFALZ
Rheinland-Pfalz is a FLÄCHENSTAAT covering an area of 19,845 sq. km., with a population of nearly 4 million. The LANDTAG (LANDESPARLAMENT) enacts legislation and comprises 101 members elected every four years with the next election in 2000. The Landtag elects the MINISTERPRÄSIDENT, head of the Landes-regierung Rheinland-Pfalz, which holds executive powers. The Ministerpräsident appoints the ministers with responsibility for individual portfolios. Rheinland-Pfalz was formed by the French military government in 1946 from areas formerly part of BAYERN (*Pfalz*), PREUSSEN and the region *Rheinhessen*. Rheinland-Pfalz is divided into three REGIERUNGSBEZIRKE comprising 12 KREISFREIE STÄDTE and 24 KREISE. Koblenz was the LANDESHAUPTSTADT until 1950 when the seat of government was transferred to MAINZ. This is the true heartland of the Rhine where the *Lorelei* and *Nibelungen* legends of the river blend in with the enchanting reality of the towns perched on the banks. The vineyards along the Rhine and in the Mosel valley form Germany's most important wine-growing area, with Koblenz an important centre for the wine trade, and they yield to mountain and forest in the areas of the Eiffel, HUNSRÜCK, PFÄLZER WALD, TAUNUS and Westerwald.

Industry is not the main focus in Rheinland-Pfalz but there are important areas of industrial activity, notably the chemicals industry in Mainz and LUDWIGSHAFEN, which has Europe's biggest chemicals complex at BASF. Engineering is also important at Bad Kreuznach, Frankenthal and Kaiserslautern, while Pirmasens is Germany's biggest centre for manufacturing footwear. The abundance of precious stones in the Hunsrück has turned the town of Idar-Oberstein into Germany's centre for trade in precious stones (with Intergem an international trade fair for gems and jewellery) and oil is extracted at Landau. Other industries are media, forestry and tourism with more than 7 million visitors every year. The Pfälzer Wald is Germany's biggest area of continuous forest and is mostly a nature reserve attracting large numbers of tourists. The three historic towns of Mainz, Speyer and Worms have Germany's most impressive medieval cathedrals and have each made their contribution to history: Mainz as the ecclesiastical centre of the Catholic Church in Germany, Speyer as an imperial residence, and Worms for the rejection of Luther's theses. TRIER is Germany's oldest city and was capital of the Western Roman Empire. More recently it was the birthplace of Karl Marx, whose writings shaped the political map of twentieth-century Europe. The RHEINLAND has traditionally been a Catholic area and just over half the population of Rheinland-Pfalz is Catholic. Worms with Germany's earliest synagogue was a centre for Jewish culture for over 900 years until the rise of Nazism.

The CDU was the strongest party in the Landtag in 1947–1991, ruling with a majority government in 1971–1987 (Helmut KOHL was Ministerpräsident in 1969–1976). An SPD/FDP coalition was elected in 1991 and confirmed in the 1996 elections. See also: BECK, KURT; DEUTSCHE WEINSTRASSE; LAND; LANDESREGIERUNG

RHEINMETALL BERLIN AG
Armaments and engineering company founded in 1950. Company headquarters are in DÜSSELDORF. Rheinmetall has some 14,000 employees.

RICHARD-WAGNER-MUSEUM
The home of composer Richard Wagner, Haus Wahnfried (literally 'peace from delusion') in Bayreuth (BAYERN). It was founded as a museum in 1976 and includes an archive documenting the life and works of the composer.

RICHTER See: *BERUFSRICHTER; EHRENAMTLICHER RICHTER*

RICHTER, HORST-EBERHARD (1923–   )
Psychoanalyst and social psychologist whose theories and treatments aim to get away from the notion that the causes of mental illness are to be found in the individual, and advocate an approach that focuses on the family and social interaction. He was director of the Zentrum für Psychosomatische Medizin at Gießen (HESSEN) from 1962 until 1992. His publications include *Patient Familie* (1970), *Die Gruppe* (1972), *Zur Psychologie des Friedens* (1982) and *Die hohe Kunst der Korruption* (1989).

RICHTGESCHWINDIGKEIT
The recommended maximum speed of 130 km./h. introduced on many stretches of AUTOBAHN in Germany. The car lobby in Germany has strenuously resisted the imposition of an overall speed limit on the *Autobahn* network, and the *Richtgeschwindigkeit* is intended to keep speeds down for safety.

RIGOROSUM See: *PROMOTION*

RIHM, WOLFGANG (1952–   )
Composer of orchestral works, chamber music and opera whose music is representative of a *Neue Einfachheit* which seeks to move away from the highly structured music of the avant-garde that dominated the post-war years. Rihm draws his inspiration from the early Arnold Schönberg and was a pupil of Karlheinz STOCKHAUSEN. He has taught at the Musikhochschule in KARLSRUHE since 1973 and his prolific output includes *Jakob Lenz* (1979), *Die Hamletmaschine* (1987) and *Séraphin* (1994).

RINGVORLESUNG
A lecture circus comprising a series of lectures on a common theme given by representatives from different *Fächer*.

ROBERT BOSCH GmbH See: *BOSCH GmbH, ROBERT*

ROMANTISCHE STRASSE
The 'Romantic Way' passing mainly through BAYERN is Germany's oldest tourist route. It is more than 350 km. long, starting at WÜRZBURG and finishing in Füssen. It includes a string

of historic Bavarian towns such as Rothenburg ob der Tauber, Dinkelsbühl, Nördlingen and AUGSBURG.

RÖMISCH-GERMANISCHES MUSEUM

Museum in KÖLN with an important collection of Roman and Frankish archaeological remains including the *Dionysos-Mosaik* from the second century AD, which formed part of a villa in Roman *Colonia* and was excavated in 1941.

ROSENMONTAG

Rosenmontag is the Monday before Ash Wednesday and the 42nd day before Easter. Especially in the RHEINLAND it is the culmination of the KARNEVAL season, celebrated by street processions with elaborate decorated floats and by wild parties. Although not officially a holiday, employees very often get the day off in areas that celebrate *Karneval*.

ROSTOCK

Rostock is situated on the Baltic in MECKLENBURG-VORPOMMERN (dialling code 03 81, postal area code 18...). The city was granted a charter in 1218 and was a powerful member of the Hanseatic League during the fourteenth and fifteenth centuries. The city has been a cultural centre for the Baltic since northern Germany's first university was opened there in 1419. Rostock is now Germany's biggest Baltic port, but it is suffering from high unemployment as a result of reunification. The Hanseatische Hafentage are an annual event in August.

The city has a population of some 231,000 with a total student population of around 8,700 (1 UNIVERSITÄT and 1 HOCHSCHULE) and about 2% foreigners (20% Romanian). Although the PDS is the strongest party, a coalition between the SPD and CDU has been running the city on a slim majority since 1994. Industries include shipbuilding, construction, fish processing and communications.

ROSTOCK, UNIVERSITÄT

University in MECKLENBURG-VORPOMMERN founded in 1419 and teaching some 8,000 students. The Universität Rostock has faculties of medicine, mathematics and natural sciences, agriculture, economics and social sciences, philosophy (arts), theology, technology and law.

ROTE-ARMEE-FRAKTION (RAF)

Terrorist organisation that sustained a prolonged campaign of murder and robbery against capitalism and the German state throughout the 1970s and 1980s. The organisation murdered a number of prominent figures in the 1970s including Jürgen Ponto (head of the DRESDNER BANK), Siegfried Buback (prosecutor in the BAADER-MEINHOF trials) and Hanns-Martin Schleyer (head of the BUNDESVEREINIGUNG DER DEUTSCHEN ARBEITGEBERVERBÄNDE) and hijacked a Lufthansa airline to Mogadishu with the passengers on board as hostages – spectacularly thwarted by a German anti-terrorist squad.

German society was for the most part shocked and revolted by the campaign of violence, and although right-wing politicians called for a crackdown that would have severely curtailed democratic rights in the BRD, the government of Helmut SCHMIDT upheld democracy and resisted the calls for emergency measures. Most of the leaders were arrested by the early 1980s after the failure of the Mogadishu hijack but the group still proved powerful enough to murder Alfred Herrhausen, head of DEUTSCHE BANK, in 1989. After reunification it emerged that the remaining leaders of the RAF had gone to the DDR where some had continued to direct a terrorist campaign with the help of the STAATSSICHERHEITSDIENST and the tacit compliance of the Communist government. The Rote-Armee-Fraktion was one of the most potent destabilising threats to German democracy in the post-war years. See also: AUSSERPARLAMENTARISCHE OPPOSITION

RTL

Germany's most popular commercial TV channel, owned mainly by Luxemburg-based CLT and BERTELSMANN. The channel is based in KÖLN and competes head-on with SAT 1. It broadcasts a full programme schedule of film, entertainment, sport, news and politics to roughly two-thirds of German households. Its viewing figures are marginally higher than those of ARD and ZDF.

RTL 2
Commercial TV channel owned by BAUER VERLAG, Telemünchen, CLT and BERTELSMANN and transmitting films, soaps and family programmes.

RÜCKMELDUNG
The regular requirement for students to register (EINSCHREIBUNG) at the beginning of each SEMESTER.

RÜCKRIEM, ULRICH (1938–   )
Sculptor who started out as a stonemason's apprentice and worked on restoration of the cathedral in KÖLN before embarking on a career as a sculptor in 1961. Since 1974 he has held professorships first at DÜSSELDORF, and since 1988 at FRANKFURT AM MAIN and HAMBURG. He works in materials including steel and wood, but is best known for his monumental abstract sculptures in stone, including the *Heinrich-Heine-Denkmal* (1983) in BONN.

RÜGEN
The biggest island in Germany is off the *Ostseeküste* in MECKLEN-BURG-VORPOMMERN and connected to the town of Stralsund by a narrow neck of land. Its sandy beaches and towering cliffs have made it a popular tourist resort since the nineteenth century, and it is now being rediscovered by west Germans.

RÜHE, VOLKER (1942–   )
Teacher and CDU politician who was a member of the BÜRGER-SCHAFT in HAMBURG. He has been a member of the BUNDESTAG since 1976 and was GENERALSEKRETÄR of the CDU in 1989–1992. He was appointed BUNDESMINISTER DER VERTEIDIGUNG in 1992.

RÜHMKORF, PETER (1929–   )
Writer of poetry, essays and fairy-tales who was a member of GRUPPE 47, and won the GEORG-BÜCHNER-PREIS in 1993. He often works with parody, writing in response to German folk songs, Romantic poetry and the classical verse of F. G. Klopstock, addressing contemporary themes in traditional forms. His work includes *Kunststücke* (1962), *Haltbar bis Ende 1999* (1979), *Der Hüter des Misthaufens* (1983) and *Laß leuchten! Memos, Märchen, TaBu, Gedichte, Selbstporträt mit und ohne Hut* (1993).

Rühmkorf has often accompanied his poetry readings with jazz improvisations.

RUHR See: *RUHRGEBIET*

RUHR-NACHRICHTEN
Regional daily established in 1949 and published in DORTMUND with a circulation of 217,000.

RUHRGAS AG
Gas supply company with interests in oil and nuclear fuels, founded in 1926. Company headquarters are in ESSEN. Ruhrgas has some 11,000 employees.

RUHRGEBIET (RUHR)
The Ruhrgebiet is situated in NORDRHEIN-WESTFALEN and is traditionally Germany's industrial powerhouse and the most industrialized area in Europe. The area is named after the river Ruhr which runs through the region. The presence of coal and iron ore combined with the arrival of the railways to attract industry in the nineteenth century, especially the iron and steel industry. It is the country's most populated area, and although the 1980s saw a mushrooming of high-tech industries in BADEN-WÜRTTEMBERG and BAYERN, the Ruhrgebiet has also been successful in attracting new industries as heavy industry and coal and steel decline in importance. Important cities include BOCHUM, DORTMUND, ESSEN, DUISBURG, GELSENKIRCHEN, Herne, Mühlheim, OBERHAUSEN and Recklinghausen. The area is like a vast industrial park and sometimes it is difficult to know where one city ends and another begins. See also: NORD-SÜD-GEFÄLLE; RHEINISCH-WESTFÄLISCHES INDUSTRIEGEBIET

RUHRKOHLE AG
Holding company set up in 1968 to restructure the coal industry in the RUHRGEBIET. Company headquarters are in ESSEN. Ruhrkohle has some 107,000 employees.

RUHRREVIER
The coalmining area in the RUHRGEBIET.

RUSKA, ERNST See: *BINNIG, GERD*

RUSSLANDDEUTSCHE
There are nearly one million ethnic Germans in Russia with an estimated three million more living in Kazakhstan and other republics of the former Soviet Union. Catherine the Great recruited Germans to colonise the lower Volga as a bulwark against the Tartars and immigration continued throughout the nineteenth century. During the Second World War the German settlers were rounded up and deported to the eastern republics, and although they were partially rehabilitated in the mid-1960s they were not allowed to return to their Volga homeland. A wave of Russian Germans emigrated to Germany following the collapse of the Soviet Union, spurred by uncertainty about their future and the desire to retain their cultural identity. The open-door policy bred of the cold war obliged Germany to accept them, but a subsequent treaty with Russia in 1991 envisages a degree of autonomy and German financial aid to encourage ethnic Germans to stay in Russia. See also: AUSSIEDLER

RÜTTGERS, JÜRGEN (1951–   )
Lawyer and CDU politician who has been BUNDESMINISTER FÜR BILDUNG, WISSENSCHAFT, FORSCHUNG UND TECHNOLOGIE since 1994.

RVO See: *RECHTSVERORDNUNG; REICHSVERSICHERUNGSORDNUNG*

RWE AG (RHEINISCH-WESTFÄLISCHES ELEKTRIZITÄTSWERK AG)
One of Europe's biggest energy-supply companies, founded in 1898 and with interests in lignite mining, electricity production and nuclear power. Company headquarters are in ESSEN. RWE has some 118,000 employees.

RWI See: *RHEINISCH-WESTFÄLISCHES INSTITUT FÜR WIRTSCHAFTSFORSCHUNG*

S-BAHN

The rapid-transit suburban railway system in many big cities including BERLIN, MÜNCHEN and DÜSSELDORF.

SAARBERGWERKE AG

Coalmining and electricity company founded in 1957, owned by the BUND and SAARLAND. Company headquarters are in SAARBRÜCKEN. Saarbergwerke has some 20,000 employees.

SAARBRÜCKEN

Saarbrücken is LANDESHAUPTSTADT of the SAARLAND and is situated on the river Saar in the Saar valley at the mouth of the Sulz (dialling code 06 81, postal area code 61...). The city was granted a charter in 1321 and was the capital of the counts of Nassau-Saarbrücken from 1381 to 1801. Rich deposits of coal and iron ore made the city an important economic centre in the nineteenth and twentieth centuries, and Saarbrücken now forms the focal point for the economy and culture of the Saarland. Saarbrücken combines French and German lifestyles. Festivals include the Perspectives du Théâtre (new French theatre) held in May and the Max Ophüls-Preis film festival in January.

The city has a population of some 190,000 with a total student population of around 24,000 (1 UNIVERSITÄT and 6 other HOCHSCHULEN) and about 11% foreigners (23% Italian). A coalition between the SPD and FDP has been running the city since 1994. Saarbrücken's position on the French border makes it an important centre for Franco-German trade, and the SAARMESSE is held annually. Industries include coalmining, iron and steel, manufacture of machinery and vehicles, chemicals, textiles, food processing, brewing, and printing and publishing.

SAARBRÜCKEN, UNIVERSITÄT DES SAARLANDES
University in SAARLAND founded in 1948 and teaching some 20,000 students. The Universität des Saarlandes has faculties of law and economics, medicine, philosophy (arts), natural sciences, technology.

SAARBRÜCKER ZEITUNG
Regional daily newspaper established in 1761. It is published in SAARBRÜCKEN and distributed in SAARLAND with a circulation of 195,000.

SAARLAND
Saarland, named after the Saar river, is Germany's smallest FLÄCHENSTAAT, covering an area of 2,570 sq. km. and with a population of nearly 1.1 million. The LANDTAG (LANDESPARLAMENT) enacts legislation and comprises 51 members elected every five years, with the next election in spring 1999. The Landtag elects the MINISTERPRÄSIDENT, head of the Saarländische Landesregierung, which holds executive powers. The Ministerpräsident appoints the ministers with responsibility for individual portfolios in agreement with the Landtag. The LANDESHAUPTSTADT is SAARBRÜCKEN and Saarland comprises the Stadtverband Saarbrücken and six KREISE. The history of Saarland has been one of continual transfer between France and Germany and its predecessor states. At the end of the First World War it effectively passed under French control but was reunited with Germany following a referendum in 1935. At the end of the Second World War it was again under French control but the Saarland was integrated into West Germany as the BRD's tenth fully-fledged LAND in 1957 following a referendum that rejected further integration with France. The extensive Saar coalfields ensured rapid development of coalmining and iron and steel production in the nineteenth century. However, although highly industrialised, the Land today is west Germany's poorest.

The link with France continues to be strong, with French still being spoken and France as Saarland's biggest trading partner. The majority of the population are Catholic with just over 20% Protestant. Saarland is heavily forested, with the coalfields located beneath the Saar valley. The main industrial centre is

Saarbrücken and the surrounding area, with small mining or agricultural towns being prevalent in the rest of the Land. The traditional industries of coalmining, iron and steel have been subject to drastic cutbacks and rationalisation. Other industries include automotive and electrical engineering, food-processing, glass and ceramics, plastics and rubber. The CDU were the strongest party in the Landtag until 1980 when the SPD gained this advantage, and the SPD has ruled with an absolute majority since 1985. See also: LAFONTAINE, OSKAR; LAND; LANDESREGIERUNG

SAARLÄNDISCHER RUNDFUNK (SR)
A regional public-service radio and TV broadcasting corporation based in SAARBRÜCKEN and broadcasting to the SAARLAND. Saarländischer Rundfunk is a member of the ARD. See also: LANDESRUNDFUNK- UND FERNSEHANSTALTEN

SAARMESSE
The 'International Saar Fair' for capital and consumer goods is a trade fair for building materials and equipment, interior design, tools and machinery for wood, DIY, energy, household appliances, textiles and clothing held in SAARBRÜCKEN annually with around 120,000 visitors.

SACHENRECHT
The part of BÜRGERLICHES RECHT relating to property and the individual.

SACHSEN, FREISTAAT
The 'Free State of Saxony' is a FLÄCHENSTAAT covering an area of 18,408 sq. km., with a population of some 4.6 million. The LANDTAG (LANDESPARLAMENT) enacts legislation and comprises 120 members elected every five years, with the next election in autumn 1999. The Landtag elects the MINISTERPRÄSIDENT, head of the Staatsregierung Freistaat Sachsen, which holds executive powers. The Ministerpräsident appoints the ministers with responsibility for individual portfolios. Sachsen comprises six KREISFREIE STÄDTE and 48 KREISE and the LANDESHAUPTSTADT is DRESDEN. Sachsen in the former DDR is on the territory of the kingdom of Saxony and was re-formed as a LAND in 1990. At the beginning of the century Sachsen and THÜRINGEN formed

Germany's biggest industrial area. Sachsen remains the industrial heartland of MITTELDEUTSCHLAND and has the best economic prospects of all the former DDR Länder. Conversely it also has some of the worst environmental problems with diseased forests in the ERZGEBIRGE, a heavily polluted Elbe, a legacy of radiation pollution around the uranium mines in the Erzgebirge, and massive environmental damage and air pollution around the open-cast mines and lignite power station at Espenhain south of LEIPZIG.

The Saxon people have a reputation for being inventive and hard-working, if a little conventional. The mechanical loom was invented in Sachsen and more recently the world's first CFC-free refrigerator. CHEMNITZ, Dresden, and Leipzig are the major industrial locations in Sachsen for the traditional industries of textiles, machinery and vehicle manufacture, and electrical engineering. Dresden has a vision of developing as a high-tech centre for electronics and optics with SIEMENS investing in Europe's biggest microchip production facility. Leipzig has the reputation of being a boom town (the city's marketing slogan is *Leipzig kommt*), as the trade-fair complex is updated in a multimillion-mark building programme and mail-order company QUELLE has invested in Germany's most up-to-date logistics centre. Finnish papermaker Enso-Gutzeit Oy has built the world's biggest paper factory just outside Leipzig. Chemnitz is a centre for textile production and machinery. During the days of the DDR the TRABI was manufactured in Zwickau, which is now home to the *VW Golf* following investment in new production facilities by VOLKSWAGEN (although over-capacity in the world market means that new buildings stand empty). The town of Meißen produces world-famous hand-painted porcelain and the traditional industries of toy-making and wooden ornaments flourish in the Erzgebirge, while Markneukirchen and other VOGTLAND towns have a long tradition of handmade musical instruments. Other important industries are electrical engineering, printing, food processing and agriculture. As in the rest of east Germany the building industry is booming as AUTOBAHNEN are being constructed and modernised, housing stock is renewed and new companies spring up.

Sachsen has a distinguished cultural heritage with Johann Sebastian Bach spending the latter part of his life in Leipzig, and Dresden a baroque architectural masterpiece now being lovingly restored to some of its former glory. Historic towns like Wernigerode and Wittenberg are popular with tourists as are the Erzgebirge, Elbsandsteingebirge (which includes the SÄCHSISCHE SCHWEIZ) and the VOGTLAND. The town of Bautzen is the cultural capital of the minority Slav community – the SORBEN – with their own language and colourful traditional dress. Although a centre for the nascent labour movement in the mid-nineteenth century, and Leipzig a driving force behind the bloodless revolution in 1989, Sachsen is now the most right-wing of all German Länder. The CDU formed a majority government after elections in 1990 and was confirmed in office in the 1994 elections. See also: BIEDENKOPF, KURT; LAND; LANDESREGIERUNG

SACHSEN-ANHALT

Sachsen-Anhalt is a thinly-populated FLÄCHENSTAAT covering an area of 20,445 sq. km., with a population of some 2.7 million. The LANDTAG (LANDESPARLAMENT) enacts legislation and comprises 98 members elected every four years, with the next election in summer 1998. The Landtag elects the MINISTERPRÄSIDENT, head of the Regierung von Sachsen-Anhalt, which holds executive powers. The Ministerpräsident appoints the ministers with responsibility for individual portfolios. Sachsen-Anhalt is divided into three REGIERUNGSBEZIRKE comprising three KREISFREIE STÄDTE and 37 KREISE. The LANDESHAUPTSTADT is MAGDEBURG. Sachsen-Anhalt in the former DDR was formed in 1990 and lies on the territory of the Prussian province of *Sachsen* and former duchy of *Anhalt*. The Soviet authorities forged the two entities into a single administrative unit in 1945, which was then broken up into smaller BEZIRKE by the East German authorities. There was considerable popular support for the two areas to form one of Germany's new LÄNDER following reunification, with Magdeburg winning the struggle against HALLE to become the new *Landeshauptstadt*.

The DDR chemicals industry based on lignite was concentrated in Sachsen-Anhalt with big plants at towns in the chemical belt including Bitterfeld, Halle, Leuna, Schkopau and Wolfen. The open-cast mine at Mücheln is destined to become one of Germany's biggest lakes, and more than 200 new companies now occupy the site of the Bitterfeld chemicals complex with an Expo 2000 exhibition planned to demonstrate ecological and economic restructuring in Germany. Although industry has undergone massive restructuring with old industrial buildings being torn down and the east's most radical environmental clean-up, a core chemical industry is being retained with the American company Dow Chemical investing heavily in the area and Elf Aquitaine constructing Europe's most up-to-date refinery in Leuna. Dessau, Halle and Magdeburg are centres for heavy industry and machinery, and Stendal is a centre for food processing, machinery and natural-gas production. Other important industries are agriculture, electrical engineering and footwear.

The ALTMARK and Börde regions are mainly agricultural and the heavily forested HARZ forms Germany's northernmost mountain range. European history was profoundly affected by events in the little town of Wittenberg when Martin Luther composed his 95 theses in 1517 and thereby started the Reformation. The town of QUEDLINBURG with its beautifully preserved half-timbered architecture has been recognised as a world heritage site. Following elections in October 1990 a CDU/FDP coalition governed the Land only to be replaced by a coalition of the SPD and BÜNDNIS 90/DIE GRÜNEN in 1994. See also: HÖPPNER, REINHARD; LAND; LANDESREGIERUNG; PREUSSEN

SÄCHSISCH

Sächsisch, or more properly *Obersächsisch*, is one of the *ostmitteldeutsche Mundarten* and is spoken in the area south of BERLIN and around LEIPZIG and DRESDEN. A characteristic of this dialect by comparison with HOCHDEUTSCH is the weakening of the consonants 'p', 't' and 'k' to resemble 'b', 'd', and 'g' respectively, while 'g' becomes 'ch'. It has been said about the Saxons that '*die sin nich dodzegriechen*' ('*die sind nicht totzukriegen*') – showing both their toughness and the weakening of 't' and 'k'.

SÄCHSISCHE SCHWEIZ

A hilly area in SACHSEN following the river Elbe, that is actually something of a misnomer being heavily forested rather than mountainous. It is popular walking country with some stunning scenery.

SÄCHSISCHE ZEITUNG

Regional daily newspaper published in DRESDEN and distributed in SACHSEN with a circulation of 420,000.

SACHVERSICHERUNG

Non-life insurance that insures against risks relating to property.

SAGER, KRISTA (1953–)

Politician who joined the Grün-Alternative-Liste HAMBURG in 1982. She became a member of the BÜRGERSCHAFT in 1989 and was appointed spokeswoman of BÜNDNIS 90/DIE GRÜNEN in 1994.

SAKMANN, BERT (1942–)

Doctor and research scientist at the Max-Planck-Institut für Medizinische Forschung in Heidelberg (BADEN-WÜRTTEMBERG), who received the Nobel Prize for medicine in 1991 (with Erwin NEHER) for research on cellular ion channels and developing a method of measuring very small electrical currents in these channels.

SAMTGEMEINDE

An intermediate tier of local government in NIEDERSACHSEN formed by a number of GEMEINDEN joining together voluntarily. See also: AMT

SANDER, JIL (1943–)

Fashion designer for professional women who are into power dressing. She opened a boutique in HAMBURG in 1967 and formed the Jil Sander AG in 1989.

SAT 1 SATELLITEN FERNSEHEN GmbH

SAT 1 is a commercial TV channel with major holdings by the KIRCH media group and SPRINGER VERLAG. The channel is based in MAINZ and was the first private channel in Germany. It broadcasts a VOLLPROGRAMM of film, entertainment, sport, news and politics to nearly two-thirds of German households. Company headquarters are in Mainz and SAT 1 has some 760 employees.

3SAT
Satellite channel that is a joint venture between ARD, ZDF, Austrian TV and Swiss TV.

SATZUNG
Constitution or statutes. This is also the term used for a by-law enacted by a GEMEINDERAT covering a local area of jurisdiction.

SAUERLAND
A rugged upland area in NORDRHEIN-WESTFALEN with a well-developed tourist industry for the city-dwellers in the industrial towns of the RUHRGEBIET. Four national parks, a wealth of trails, rivers and lakes make this area a haven for outdoor pursuits despite being subject to a harsh climate that ensures tourism continues into winter sports. The area is also prized for beer with famous brews like *Warsteiner*.

SAURER REGEN
Acid rain became prominent in Germany during the 1980s, when the phenomenon of WALDSTERBEN came to public attention especially through the campaigns of the environmental groups in the Grün-Alternative-Liste. Acidic compounds – principally sulphur dioxide and oxides of nitrogen – from the burning of fossil fuels in cars and power stations are believed to be causing disease and death in Germany's extensive forests and elsewhere.

SAWALLISCH, WOLFGANG (1923–   )
Conductor who was appointed principal conductor of the Philadelphia Orchestra in 1992 as successor to Riccardo Muti. He was principal conductor of the Wiener Philharmoniker in 1960–1970 and musical director of the Philharmonie in HAMBURG in 1961–1973. Sawallisch was appointed musical director of the Bayerische Staatsoper in 1971 and INTENDANT in 1982. He is particularly famous for his performances of Wagner and Richard Strauss.

SCALL
Radio-paging service introduced by DEUTSCHE TELEKOM subsidiary DETEMOBIL in 1994. Scall subscribers can be reached within a range of 50 km. and can receive calls from any telephone within

that area. Messages are sent in code form, for example a telephone number or a pre-arranged numerical code containing up
to 15 digits.

SCHANKERLAUBNISSTEUER

A once-only tax levied by GEMEINDEN in a few LÄNDER on issuing a
licence for licensed premises, a small retailer or kiosk selling
spirits, or a bar selling non-alcoholic drinks. The tax is calculated
as a percentage of annual turnover and varies according to the
legislation in the Land.

SCHANKVERZEHRSTEUER See: *GETRÄNKESTEUER*

SCHARPING, RUDOLF (1947–   )

Political scientist and SPD politician. He entered the LANDTAG in
RHEINLAND-PFALZ in 1975 and was head of the SPD-FRAKTION in the
Landtag in 1985–1991 before being elected MINISTERPRÄSIDENT in
1991–1994. Scharping was *Bundesvorsitzender* of the SPD in
1993– 1995 when he was ousted in a surprise challenge by Oskar
LAFONTAINE. He was KANZLERKANDIDAT in the 1994 elections and
has been head of the BUNDESTAGSFRAKTION of the SPD since 1994.

SCHATZANWEISUNGEN

Financial instruments in the form of bonds that are used by the
BUND and the LÄNDER to finance spending requirements.

SCHÄUBLE, WOLFGANG (1942–   )

Lawyer and CDU politician who has been a member of the BUN-
DESTAG since 1972. He has held various ministerial positions
including BUNDESMINISTER im BUNDESKANZLERAMT in 1984–1989 and
BUNDESMINISTER DES INNERN in 1989–1991. He was head of the
team that negotiated the reunification of Germany and has been
chairman of the CDU/CSU-BUNDESTAGSFRAKTION since 1991.
Schäuble was confined to a wheelchair following a maverick
assassination attempt in 1990.

SCHEIN See: *LEISTUNGSNACHWEIS*

SCHERF, HENNING (1938–   )

Lawyer and SPD politician. He became chairman of the SPD in
BREMEN in 1972 and held the positions of SENATOR for social and

youth affairs in 1979–1990 and Senator for education, science, justice and constitutional affairs in 1991–1995. In 1995 he was elected BÜRGERMEISTER UND SENATSPRÄSIDENT in Bremen.

SCHERING AG
Pharmaceuticals company founded in 1871. Company headquarters are in BERLIN. Schering has some 18,000 employees.

SCHICKERIA
Brashly affluent set which likes to be seen swaggering in the right places wearing the latest fashions and pursuing leisure activities that are currently all the rage.

SCHIEDSGERICHT
The court of arbitration for the settlement of civil disputes arising from PRIVATRECHT following agreement to arbitrate in a SCHIEDSVERTRAG. It is generally made up of one or three arbitrators that may be selected by the two sides or appointed by a third party.

SCHIEDSVERTRAG
An agreement that in the event of a dispute in PRIVATRECHT two parties give a commitment to arbitration by a SCHIEDSGERICHT.

SCHIFFAHRTSMUSEUM
Museum in ROSTOCK recording the seafaring tradition with a fascinating collection of model boats from the days of sail to iron battleships.

SCHILLER-NATIONALMUSEUM UND DEUTSCHES LITERATURARCHIV
The national Schiller museum and German literature archive was founded in 1895. The library is in Marbach (BADEN-WÜRTTEM-BERG) and houses a collection of 400,000 volumes covering German literature since 1750. It is Germany's foremost research library for modern German literature.

SCHIMMEL, ANNEMARIE (1921–   )
Orientalist who was awarded the FRIEDENSPREIS DES BÖRSENVEREINS DES DEUTSCHEN BUCHHANDELS in 1995 for her work on Islam. The award was criticised by German intellectuals who were of the

view that she had not taken a clear stand against Islamic fundamentalism.

SCHLECHTWETTERGELD

An allowance paid to workers in the construction industry who
cannot work due to bad weather during the winter.

SCHLESIEN

The historic region of Silesia (most of which is now in Poland)
was Germany's second most important industrial region before
the First World War with extensive coalmines and steelworks.
The POTSDAMER ABKOMMEN provided for the return of most of
Schlesien to Poland, and the ethnic Germans living there were
expelled with about 1 million POLENDEUTSCHE remaining. The
DEUTSCH-POLNISCHER GRENZVERTRAG acknowledges that this region
is irretrievably lost to Germany and guarantees the integrity of
the ODER-NEISSE-LINIE. The only parts of *Schlesien* in Germany
today are the areas around Cottbus and DRESDEN in modern-day
SACHSEN.

SCHLESWIG-HOLSTEIN

Schleswig-Holstein is a FLÄCHENSTAAT covering an area of 15,738
sq. km. It is Germany's northernmost state and has a population
of some 2.7 million. The LANDTAG (LANDESPARLAMENT) enacts legislation and comprises 89 members elected every four years, with
the next election in 2000. The Landtag elects the MINISTERPRÄSI-
DENT, head of the Landesregierung Schleswig-Holstein, which
holds executive powers. The Ministerpräsident appoints the ministers with responsibility for individual portfolios. Schleswig-
Holstein comprises four KREISFREIE STÄDTE and 11 KREISE; the
LANDESHAUPSTADT is KIEL. Schleswig-Holstein, historically part of
Denmark and the subject of a long-running dispute between
Denmark and PREUSSEN in the nineteenth century, was formed as
a LAND from the Prussian province by the British military government in 1946. Schleswig has a Danish minority for which special
provision is made in the constitution to accommodate the SÜD-
SCHLESWIGSCHER WÄHLERVERBAND. The predominant Christian
faith is Protestant.

Schleswig-Holstein is a region of lakes, fjords and cliffs with a fertile eastern region. Its strategic position with two coastlines (Nordsee and Ostsee) has meant that the ports of Flensburg, Kiel and the *Hansestadt* LÜBECK have been important centres for trade, and the NORD-OSTSEE-KANAL is a very busy shipping lane. Shipbuilding is also important in these cities but is inevitably subject to gradual decline and Schleswig-Holstein remains a Land with a low level of industrialisation. Agriculture and fisheries are the traditional industries in Schleswig-Holstein, and new industrial development is being promoted in the small town of Brunsbüttel based on the nuclear power station and petrochemicals industry; other industries include machinery, electrical engineering, food processing, paper, printing and textiles.

Although there is little forest here, millions of trees are produced in Schleswig-Holstein for replanting in Germany's forests. Nordfriesland, the offshore island of SYLT and the Holsteinische Schweiz form some of Germany's most popular summer tourist areas though now facing new competition from MECKLENBURG-VORPOMMERN. The CDU ruled Schleswig-Holstein from 1947 until 1987 with a brief period of SPD rule in 1947–1950 (from 1971 with a majority government). After the BARSCHEL-AFFÄRE the SPD gained an absolute majority in the 1988 elections and were returned to power in 1992 with Heide SIMONIS becoming Germany's first female Ministerpräsident in 1993. See also: FREIE HANSESTADT; LAND; LANDESREGIERUNG

SCHLÖNDORFF, VOLKER (1939–   )

Film director of the *Neuer deutscher Film* who takes the view that cinema should appeal to a mass audience. His reputation is based on his widely acclaimed films of major works of German literature, for example H. von Kleist's *Michael Kohlhaas* (1968/1969), B. Brecht's *Baal* (1969), H. Böll's *Die verlorene Ehre der Katharina Blum* (1975), G. GRASS's *Die Blechtrommel* and M. Frisch's *Homo faber* (1991). He founded the Studio Babelsberg GmbH production company in 1992.

SCHLOSS BELLEVUE

Official residence of the BUNDESPRÄSIDENT in BERLIN. See also: PALAIS SCHAUMBURG

SCHLOSS SANSSOUCI

Begun in 1744, Schloß Sanssouci ('without cares') is the magnificent rococo masterpiece built by architect Georg von Knobelsdorff as a residence for Friedrich der Große in POTSDAM and recently made a UNESCO world heritage site. The splendid park of Sanssouci holds the Neptungrotte, Bildergalerie (17th century paintings), Große Fontäne, Chinesisches Teehaus, Orangerie (now an archive), Drachenhaus, Belvedere, Neues Palais (including a theatre), the Rehgarten and Schloß Charlottenhof.

SCHMALZ-JACOBSEN, CORNELIA (1934–)

FDP politician who was SENATOR with responsibility for youth and family affairs in BERLIN in 1985–1988 and general secretary of the FDP in 1988–1991. In 1991 she joined the BUNDESREGIERUNG with responsibility for foreign immigrants (*Ausländerbeauftragte der Bundesregierung*).

SCHMERZENSGELD

Compensation for pain and suffering arising as a result of an injury, impairment of health or unlawful deprivation of liberty. Most Germans have a RECHTSSCHUTZVERSICHERUNG, which makes them willing to go to law if they have sustained injury, with a view to obtaining *Schmerzensgeld*.

SCHMIDT, HELMUT (1918–)

Politician and BUNDESKANZLER in 1974–1982 with a reputation as a pragmatist. He joined the SPD in 1946 and was a member of the BUNDESTAG in 1953–1962 and 1965–1987. As Innensenator in HAMBURG from 1961 to 1965 he was responsible for organising relief work during the devastating floods in 1962. Schmidt was VERTEIDIGUNGSMINISTER in 1969–1972 and BUNDESFINANZMINISTER in 1972–1974 before becoming Bundeskanzler in 1974 following the resignation of Willy Brandt. He went on to win two elections in 1976 and 1980 as head of an SPD/FDP coalition before losing a KONSTRUKTIVES MISSTRAUENSVOTUM in 1982. He continued Brandt's policy of *détente* with the Soviet block and building bridges with the DDR while supporting the deployment of Pershing missiles to achieve a strategic balance. Schmidt pursued policies designed to maintain economic stability and full employment. Since leaving office he has written widely, including *Eine Strategie für den Westen* (1986) and *Handeln für Deutschland* (1993). He is joint HERAUS-GEBER of the weekly DIE ZEIT. See also: DÖNHOFF, MARION GRÄFIN

SCHMIDT-JORTZIG, EDZARD (1941–   )

Lawyer and FDP politician. Professor of law at KIEL (CHRISTIAN-ALBRECHTS-UNIVERSITÄT) and MITGLIED DES BUNDESTAGES since 1994. He was appointed BUNDESMINISTER DER JUSTIZ in January 1996 after the resignation of Sabine Leutheusser-Schnarrenberger because she disagreed with party policy on bugging private homes to combat rising crime.

SCHNEIDER, MANFRED (1938–   )

Lawyer and industrialist who has worked for BAYER since 1966. He was appointed VORSTANDSMITGLIED in 1987 and became chairman of the VORSTAND in 1994.

SCHNELLVERFAHREN See: *BESCHLEUNIGTES VERFAHREN*

SCHNELLZUG (D-ZUG)

A fast train operating on the rail network with few stops. These trains are gradually being replaced by the INTERREGIO trains.

SCHOLL, HERMANN (1935–   )

Joined BOSCH, Germany's biggest automotive components manu-facturer, in 1962 and became chairman in 1993.

SCHÖNER ESSEN

Monthly cookery magazine published by GRUNER + JAHR with a circulation of 143,000 and aimed at young working women with an interest in culinary matters.

SCHÖNER WOHNEN

House and home magazine published by GRUNER + JAHR with a circulation of 375,000. It appeals to a young, predominantly female readership, giving ideas and setting trends.

SCHORFHEIDE

Schorfheide north-east of BERLIN in BRANDENBURG is Germany's biggest conservation area covering a total of nearly 1,300 sq. km.

with a rich landscape of forest, moor and around 250 lakes. The area has been designated a world biosphere reserve by UNESCO.

SCHREIER, PETER (1935–   )

Tenor singer and conductor who started out as a chorister in the Dresdner Kreuzchor, joining the Dresdner Staatsoper in 1961, the Berliner Staatsoper in 1963 and the Metropolitan Opera New York in 1968. He has sung at the world's major opera houses and is famous for his interpretations of Mozart and his role as the Evangelist in Bach's Passions.

SCHREINEMAKER, MARGARETHE (1959–   )

Sociologist and TV moderator who started her television career in 1980 at WDR. She has a regular Thursday talkshow *Schreinemaker live* on SAT 1 with 5 million viewers but is due to transfer to RTL by 1997.

SCHREMPP, JÜRGEN (1944–   )

Engineer who after heading subsidiary Deutsche Aerospace became chairman of industrial conglomerate DAIMLER-BENZ in 1995.

SCHRÖDER, GERHARD (1944–   )

Lawyer and SPD politician. A MITGLIED DES BUNDESTAGES in 1980–1986, he became chairman of the SPD-FRAKTION in the LANDTAG in NIEDERSACHSEN and was MINISTERPRÄSIDENT of a coalition between the SPD and DIE GRÜNEN in 1990–1994. Since 1994 he has been Ministerpräsident of an SPD government in Niedersachsen.

SCHROETER, WERNER (1945–   )

Film director whose films include *Neapolitanische Geschwister* (1978), *Palermo oder Wolfsburg* (1980), *Der Rosenkönig* (1986) and *Malina* (1991, script by E. Jelinek based on the novel by I. Bachmann).

SCHULAMT

The local education office in a KREIS or KREISFREIE STADT. This office is responsible for school buildings and their upkeep and may carry out the function of the LAND for implementing education policy within schools.

SCHÜLERLOTSE
School crossing patrol with a white sign, to help school children across the road. This system of school patrols was introduced in the BRD in 1953. See also: DEUTSCHE VERKEHRSWACHT E.V.

SCHÜLERMITVERWALTUNG (SMV)
A system of school councils in which pupils play an active role in shaping school life. These councils were introduced in the BRD after the Second World War and are intended to develop pupils' initiative and a sense of social and political responsibility. They organise elections for class respresentatives, publish SCHÜLERZEIT-SCHRIFTEN, organise self-study groups, etc.

SCHÜLERZEITSCHRIFT
A school magazine published by the pupils in a particular school or in a group of schools. They are generally published at regular intervals and form a part of the JUGENDPRESSE.

SCHULFERNSEHEN
Television for schools was started up in the BRD in 1964 and is transmitted on the DRITTES PROGRAMM by the LANDESRUNDFUNK-UND FERNSEHANSTALTEN. It provides TV programmes and study materials for schools.

SCHULFUNK
Radio for schools has been broadcast since 1953 in the BRD and is intended to play a support role for the classroom, providing motivation and stimulus. Schools have a say in the kind of material that is transmitted on schools radio.

SCHULGELDFREIHEIT
Free school tuition was introduced into all LÄNDER in 1962 and continues until pupils have finished their formal school career at the latest when they have taken their ABITUR. Private schooling has only marginal importance and carries no special prestige.

SCHULGESUNDHEITSPFLEGE
The system of school health care for maintaining the good health of pupils and teachers. It includes regular, compulsory check-ups by school doctors and dentists.

SCHULJAHR
The school year throughout Germany officially begins on 1 August, but summer holidays vary from LAND to Land principally to relieve overcrowding on the roads during the holiday season. Holidays in BERLIN begin at the end of June and continue through July, while schools in BAYERN have their summer break during August and the first part of September.

SCHULLEISTUNGSTEST
Standardised performance and aptitude testing to determine a pupil's ability for purposes of streaming in various subjects. This is carried out at regular intervals throughout the school career.

SCHULMEDIZIN
Conventional medicine as practised by doctors who have received a training at a medical faculty in a university. There has been quite a reaction against *Schulmedizin* in recent years, and now many alternative forms of medicine can be claimed by patients on their KRANKENVERSICHERUNG. See also: ALTERNA-TIVMEDIZIN

SCHULPFLICHT
Compulsory education in Germany begins at the age of six years, and pupils can leave school after the ninth or tenth year depending on the LAND (ten years in BERLIN and NORDRHEIN-WESTFALEN). All pupils then have the right to attend a BERUFSSCHULE for three years until the end of their 18th year of age or to continue studying at school for the ABITUR. See also: SCHULREIFE

SCHULPFORTA
Famous *Fürstenschule* founded in 1543 by Protestant Elector Moritz of Saxony to give deserving boys a free education. It was attended by the poet Klopstock and the philosophers Fichte and Nietzsche. Today, it is a HUMANISTISCHES GYMNASIUM with INTERNAT in SACHSEN-ANHALT.

SCHULREIFE
The developmental stage at which a child is able to attend the GRUNDSCHULE (normally at the start of the school year following the child's sixth birthday). Every child is seen by a medical prac-

titioner and the head of the school to establish physical and mental fitness for school attendance. These tests are carried out prior to EINSCHULUNG. See also: SCHULPFLICHT

SCHULREIFETEST

The series of tests carried out at the age of six to determine whether a child has reached SCHULREIFE. Medical histories are taken and children are tested for physical and cognitive development before being admitted into the school system. In some LÄNDER the wishes of the parents are taken into account. Roughly 10% of children do not start school until they are seven.

SCHULTE, DIETER (1940–)

Bricklayer who worked in the steel industry and was elected chairman of the BETRIEBSRAT at THYSSEN in 1990. He became a member of the AUFSICHTSRAT at THYSSEN STAHL AG in 1991 and joined the VORSTAND of IG METALL in the same year. He became chairman of the DEUTSCHER GEWERKSCHAFTSBUND in 1994.

SCHUMACHER, MICHAEL (1969–)

Formula 1 racing driver. He has won many Grand Prix and was Formula 1 world champion in 1994 and 1995. He was nominated *Sportler des Jahres* in 1995 and signed up with Ferrari in Italy for 1996 and 1997, reputedly with a contract making him the best-paid racing driver ever.

SCHUPO See: *SCHUTZPOLIZEI*

SCHUTZPOLIZEI (SCHUPO)

The regular, uniformed police force that patrols the streets, controls traffic and deals with petty crime. The *Schutzpolizei* is under the control of the *Ministerium des Innern* in each LAND.

SCHWABEN

Schwaben is situated in BADEN-WÜRTTEMBERG and part of BAYERN, and has a cultural identity that has persisted despite the area having long since lost its importance as a political entity. The people of Swabia embraced the Reformation wholeheartedly and are well known for espousing the Protestant values of hard work and thrift. They are the butt of jokes for concentrating all their efforts on building a house and speak the distinctive dialect of SCHWÄBISCH. The area called Bayerisches Schwaben was part of the original medieval duchy of *Schwaben*, most of which later became *Württemberg*.

SCHWÄBISCH

The dialect spoken in SCHWABEN, one of the *oberdeutsche Mundarten*. A typical feature of this variant of German is the diminutive noun suffix *-le* (instead of *-lein*), which at least solves the gender problem in what Mark Twain called 'the awful German language' by making the nouns neuter. The popular folk ditty *Schaffe schaffe Häusle baue und nit nach de Mädle schaue* not only demonstrates the Swabian work ethic but is also typical of the dialect.

SCHWÄBISCHES MEER See: *BODENSEE*

SCHWANGERSCHAFTSABBRUCH

Termination of pregnancy is permitted in Germany up to the end of the 12th week, with the proviso that the pregnant woman should have received counselling. The issue of abortion regulated by *Paragraph* (§) 218 of the STRAFGESETZBUCH has been a controversial issue in the BRD for many years and took on new significance with reunification. Abortion was legal in the DDR up to 12 weeks without the need to specify grounds (*Fristenlösung*), whereas in the BRD the woman was required to obtain a doctor's certificate showing one of four reasons: risk to the mother's health, risk of genetic disorder, rape, or social hardship (*Indikation*). In 1992, the BUNDESTAG voted to introduce a *Fristenlösung* throughout Germany, but in 1993 the BUNDESVERFASSUNGSGERICHT ruled that the Bundestag had no authority to make abortion legal (unless medical grounds existed), while leaving the government free not to have to impose a penalty for carrying out an abortion. It also ruled that counselling should favour the pregnancy continuing to birth and that claims could only be made against a person's KRANKENVERSICHERUNG in cases of hardship or rape.

SCHWARZER, ALICE (1942–   )

Journalist and prominent feminist who wrote the bestseller *Der kleine Unterschied und seine großen Folgen* (1965). She was a reporter on the satirical magazine *Pardon* until she founded the feminist magazine EMMA in 1977, of which she remains publisher and editor. She is also head of the feminist archive Stiftung Frauenmediaturm in KÖLN.

SCHWARZWALD

The Black Forest, a mountainous region in BADEN-WÜRTTEMBERG, is the land of the cuckoo clock, *Schwarzwälder Kirschtorte* and flamboyant traditional dress. Freiburg im Breisgau is the 'capital' of the Schwarzwald and the atmosphere engendered by the dour trees, plunging valleys and stunning mountain views combine with the homespun culture to give the region a special place in the German psyche. Mining for copper, iron, lead and silver were well-developed in the sixteenth and seventeenth centuries and in addition to clock-making the region has a tradition of producing handmade musical instruments and precision engineering. Today, tourism is a flourishing industry throughout the region.

SCHWARZWALDKLINIK

Popular hospital soap set in the SCHWARZWALD, with 27.5 million viewers.

SCHWEBEBAHN

Suspended monorail public transport system in WUPPERTAL built between 1898 and 1903 by Carl Eugen Langen. This rail system suspended on triangular girders has proved extremely safe, never having had a serious accident in its history.

SCHWERIN

Schwerin is the LANDESHAUPTSTADT of MECKLENBURG-VORPOMMERN and is situated on the Schweriner See (dialling code 03 85, postal area code 19...). Schwerin received its charter in 1160 and was the seat of the dukes of *Mecklenburg* (with a brief interlude between 1764 and 1837) from the end of the fifteenth century until 1918. The importance of the city increased in the mid-nineteenth century when the dukes of *Mecklenburg* returned to Schwerin in 1837 and created the nineteenth-century Paulusstadt and neo-renaissance *Schloß*.

The city has a population of some 115,000 with about 3% foreigners (16% Vietnamese). The SPD runs the city and has been in office since 1990. Industries include food processing, machinery and cables.

SCHWERINER VOLKSZEITUNG
Daily newspaper established in 1946 and published in SCHWERIN, with a circulation of 168,000.

SCHYGULLA, HANNA (1943–   )
Actor who made her reputation in films by R.W. Fassbinder including *Katzelmacher* (1969), *Die Ehe der Maria Braun* (1979) and *Lili Marleen* (1981). She appeared as Eva in Fassbinder's TV series based on Döblin's *Berlin Alexanderplatz* (1980), and her roles in other films include *Eine Liebe in Deutschland* (1983) and *Das Abenteuer der Catherine C.* (1991).

SCORPIONS
A rock group from HANNOVER formed in 1965. The band broke up and reformed in 1968 rising to prominence in the 1970s and gaining an international following during the 1980s. The group's combination of hard rock and ballad style gained popularity in the US and Japan. Their recordings include *Lonesome Crow* (1972), *Virgin Killer* (1976), *Crazy World* (1990) and *Wind of Change* (1991).

SDR See: *SÜDDEUTSCHER RUNDFUNK*

SECURITY (INTERNATIONALE SICHERHEITS-FACHMESSE)
'International Security Exhibition' – a trade fair for security, alarm and surveillance systems, fire protection, crime prevention and vehicle alarms held in ESSEN every two years with around 30,000 visitors.

SED See: *SOZIALISTISCHE EINHEITSPARTEI DEUTSCHLANDS*

SEEHOFER, HORST (1949–   )
Administrator and CSU politician who has been a MITGLIED DES BUNDESTAGES since 1980. He was appointed STAATSSEKRETÄR at the BUNDESMINISTERIUM FÜR ARBEIT UND SOZIALORDNUNG and has been BUNDESMINISTER FÜR GESUNDHEIT since 1992.

SEEKASSE See: *SEESOZIALVERSICHERUNG*

SEESOZIALVERSICHERUNG
A PFLICHTVERSICHERUNG for seamen working on ships registered in Germany providing KRANKENVERSICHERUNG, RENTENVERSICHE-RUNG and UNFALLVERSICHERUNG.

SEITE, BERNDT (1944–   )
Veterinary surgeon and CDU politician. He has been GENERAL-SEKRETÄR of the CDU in MECKLENBURG-VORPOMMERN since 1991 and became MINISTERPRÄSIDENT in 1992.

SEKT
The German answer to champagne – a home-grown sparkling wine that is brought out on all festive occasions worthy of cele-bration, notably SILVESTER. A *deutscher Sekt* has to be produced entirely from grapes harvested in Germany.

SELBER MACHEN
Monthly DIY magazine aimed at all DIY enthusiasts and pub-lished by JAHRESZEITEN VERLAG with a circulation of 230,000. It gives expert advice and suggestions on home improvements.

SELBSTBESTIMMUNGSRECHT
The right of self-determination enshrined in the preamble of the GRUNDGESETZ. The Grundgesetz gives all German citizens a con-stitutional right to hold their own philosophy of life and the free-dom to structure their family life, their property and their wealth in accordance with their own wishes. These rights should not infringe the rights of other individuals and must accord with a citizen's own constitutional obligations.

SELBSTVERWALTUNG
The concept of autonomy guaranteed by the GRUNDGESETZ in local government (as exercised in the GEMEINDE and GEMEINDE-VERBÄNDE) and in other SELBSTVERWALTUNGSKÖRPERSCHAFTEN. The principles behind *Selbstverwaltung* are the decentralisation of administration, bringing decision-making closer to the ground and the individual citizen, and involving individuals in local affairs. See also: KOMMUNALE SELBSTVERWALTUNG

SELBSTVERWALTUNGSANGELEGENHEITEN

Functions that local authorities (GEMEINDEN and GEMEINDEVER-BÄNDE) are empowered to carry out in their own right. These functions include culture (theatres, museums and libraries), hospitals, swimming baths and playgrounds, welfare, water supply, sewage disposal, refuse collection, public transport (buses, trams and suburban rail networks), fire service, roads, construction of schools and provision of educational facilities. See also: AUFTRAGSVERWALTUNG; SELBSTVERWALTUNG

SELBSTVERWALTUNGSKÖRPERSCHAFT See: *KÖRPERSCHAFT DES ÖFFENTLICHEN RECHTS*

SELTEN, REINHARD (1930–)

Mathematician, economist and professor in BONN (RHEINISCHE FRIEDRICH-WILHELMS-UNIVERSITÄT). He was the first German to receive the Nobel Prize for economics in 1994 (with J.C. Harsanyi and J.F. Nash) for his work on equilibrium in non-cooperative Game Theory.

SEMESTER

The division of the academic year in HOCHSCHULEN into two sessions: the *Wintersemester (WS)* normally lasts around four months and the *Sommersemester (SS)* three months. The academic year generally commences with the *Wintersemester* in October/November.

SEMINAR

Autonomous administrative unit within a FAKULTÄT or FACHBEREICH, generally specialising in a particular subject (e.g. *Germanistisches Seminar* within the *Philosophische Fakultät*). Also a type of teaching class usually characterised by the presentation of one or more papers and subsequent discussion. See also: INSTITUT

SEMINARSCHEIN See: *LEISTUNGSNACHWEIS*

SENAT

The official title for the LANDESREGIERUNG in BERLIN, BREMEN and HAMBURG. Senat is also the term for the town council in LÜBECK.

BAYERN is the only BUNDESLAND to have a Senat as a second chamber to the LANDESPARLAMENT. The Senat has 60 members elected by social, economic, cultural and local-government bodies. It has an advisory function and a third of the Senat is newly elected every two years.

In the OBERLANDESGERICHTE and the highest courts (e.g. BUNDESGERICHTSHOF) Senat refers to a panel of judges.

Senat is also a term for the self-governing body in a *wissenschaftliche Hochschule*. It is composed of members of the teaching staff, students and other employees in accordance with the respective institution's constitution.

SENATOR
A member of the LANDESREGIERUNG (SENAT) in BERLIN, BREMEN and HAMBURG. The equivalent of the rank of MINISTER in other LÄNDER. This term also refers to a member of the Senat (STADTRAT) in LÜBECK.

SENATSPRÄSIDENT See: *BÜRGERMEISTER UND SENATSPRÄSIDENT*

SENDER FREIES BERLIN (SFB)
A regional public-service radio and TV broadcasting corporation based in BERLIN and broadcasting to West Berlin until reunification in 1990. Sender Freies Berlin is now a member of the ARD and broadcasts to the LAND of Berlin. See also: LANDESRUNDFUNK-UND FERNSEHANSTALTEN

SENIOREN-SCHUTZ-BUND „GRAUE PANTHER" e.V.
A pressure group founded in 1975 and based in WUPPERTAL to promote the interests of old people. A splinter group later formed a political party entitled DIE GRAUEN to promote the same aims from a political platform rather than through other parties.

SFB See: *SENDER FREIES BERLIN*

SGB See: *SOZIALGESETZBUCH*

sid See: *SPORT-INFORMATIONS-DIENST*

SIEBENGEBIRGE
A range of volcanic mountains in NORDRHEIN-WESTFALEN along-side the Rhine that is rich in legend, reputedly the home of *Schneewittchen und die sieben Zwerge*. It includes the Drachen-fels mountain where the legendary hero Siegfried in the medieval *Nibelungensage* was supposed to have dispatched a ter-rible monster and attained virtual invincibility. The area was declared Germany's first national park in 1889.

SIEGEN, UNIVERSITÄT-GESAMTHOCHSCHULE
University in NORDRHEIN-WESTFALEN founded in 1972 and teaching some 13,000 students. The Universität-Gesamthochschule Siegen has departments of philosophy and religion, history, education and psychology and physical education, languages and literature, art and design, economics, mathematics, physics, chemistry and biology, architecture, construction engineering, mechanical engi-neering, electrical engineering.

SIEGERLAND
Siegerland is a hilly area on the river Sieg in NORDRHEIN-WEST-FALEN. The main town is Siegen. There are large areas of forest, and the area was a coalmining centre for over 2,000 years until the last mine was closed in the early 1960s, but the traditional industries of iron and steel remain in the heavily industrialised valleys. The hills and forests are a popular area for German holi-daymakers. See also: RHEINISCH-WESTFÄLISCHES INDUSTRIEGEBIET

SIEMENS AG
Europe's electronics giant manufacturing electrical and electronic equipment from washing machines to nuclear power stations. Siemens is a world leader in the telecommunications industry and medical technology, and also manufactures PCs, switchgear equipment and automotive electronics. Company headquarters are MÜNCHEN and BERLIN, and Siemens has some 382,000 employ-ees.

SIEMENS NIXDORF INFORMATIONSSYSTEME AG
IT company originally founded in 1952 in Paderborn (BAYERN) and taken over by SIEMENS in 1990. Company headquarters are in MÜNCHEN. Siemens Nixdorf has some 39,000 employees.

SILVESTER

New Year's Eve is celebrated with fireworks and SEKT at midnight, and complete strangers may embrace each other in a frenzy of amiable *bonhomie*. A speech by the BUNDESKANZLER is televised. A popular custom is *Bleigießen*, which involves melting lead charms over a candle, dropping the molten lead into water and drawing dubious conclusions about the coming year from the resulting shapes.

SIMONIS, HEIDE (1943–   )

Economist and SPD politician. She joined the SPD in 1969, and after a period in local politics in KIEL she was a MITGLIED DES BUNDESTAGES in 1976–1988. Simonis was then minister of finance in SCHLESWIG-HOLSTEIN in 1988–1993, and after the resignation of Björn ENGHOLM she was the first woman to become a MINISTERPRÄSIDENT in Germany in 1993.

SITZENBLEIBEN

Repeating a year at school through not having achieved the required results in the current year is very much at the back of all schoolchildren's minds. The stigma of parting with one's friends and staying down is something to be avoided at all costs. The key to moving up into the next class is the annual *Schulzeugnis* with the grades for each subject ranging from 1 (*sehr gut*) to the fail-mark 6 (*mangelhaft*).

SMV See: *SCHÜLERMITVERWALTUNG*

SOLDAT AUF ZEIT

Member of the BUNDESWEHR who has signed up for a fixed period of time.

SOLIDARITÄTSZUSCHLAG

An additional tax deduction levied in 1991/1992 and since January 1995 throughout Germany to finance the economic recovery in east Germany. It is 7.5% of tax payable, although the amount is reduced for low-income families. The government estimated that the *Solidaritätszuschlag* would yield DM 26,500 million to the BUND in 1995. There has been considerable discussion about gradually reducing this somewhat unpopular levy.

SOLINGEN

Solingen is situated on the river Wupper in NORDRHEIN-WESTFALEN (dialling code 02 12, postal area code 42...). The city was granted a charter in 1374 and during the Middle Ages was a centre for armourers making swords. Solingen is now a centre for the ironware industry and has an international reputation for knives and cutlery.

The city has a population of some 165,000 with about 15% foreigners (35% Italian). A coalition between the SPD and BÜNDNIS 90/DIE GRÜNEN has been running the city on a slim majority since 1989. Apart from cutlery, industries include engineering, steel, electrical goods, chemicals and confectionery.

SONDERSCHULEN

Schools for children with special needs. There are *Sonderschulen* for children with physical or mental disabilities and for children who are slow learners, emotionally disturbed or who come from deprived backgrounds. They prepare mentally handicapped children for work in special working environments and provide appropriate schooling for physically handicapped children to enable them to exploit their full potential.

SONNTAG AKTUELL

Sunday paper established in 1979 and published in STUTTGART with a circulation of 869,000.

SORBEN

The Sorbs are Germany's only ethnic Slav minority, numbering about 100,000 and living in the historic area of LAUSITZ. They follow the Catholic faith and have their own customs, music and literature with colourful national dress. The Sorb language is related to Czech and Slovak, and street signs in Sorb add an exotic feel to a fascinating region. The Sorbs have lived in the Lausitz since before the seventh century, and although their lands were taken over as the Germanic tribes moved eastwards, they have retained their own cultural identity to this day. After considerable persecution under the Nazis they were partially rehabilitated under the DDR regime. The town of Bautzen in SACHSEN is the cultural capital of the Sorbs with an institute for ethnic research into Sorb culture, a museum of Sorb history and culture, a Sorb theatre and a publishing house. Cottbus in BRAN-DENBURG is also a centre of Sorb culture.

SOZIALABGABEN

The contributions made by the ARBEITGEBER and ARBEITNEHMER to pay for the SOZIALVERSICHERUNG.

SOZIALAMT

The office in KREISE and KREISFREIE STÄDTE that delivers all the social services prescribed by law under SOZIALHILFE.

SOZIALBEITRAG

In the context of higher education, the contribution collected at EINSCHREIBUNG for the STUDENTENWERK and the ALLGEMEINER STU-DENTENAUSSCHUSS.

SOZIALBEITRÄGE See: *SOZIALABGABEN*

SOZIALDEMOKRATISCHE PARTEI DEUTSCHLANDS (SPD)

Germany's oldest surviving political party dates back to 1890 when it emerged from the *Sozialdemokratische Arbeiterpartei*. During the WEIMARER REPUBLIK the party formed part of a number of coalition governments and Friedrich Ebert (SPD) was the first *Reichspräsident*. The party was dissolved in 1933 and was re-formed in 1945. The SPD in the Soviet zone was merged with the KPD in 1946 to form the SED. In the Western zones the SPD went on to become the second strongest party in the BUNDESTAG and was in opposition between 1949 and 1966. An important step on the road to power was the *Godesberger Grundsatzprogramm* adopted in 1959, which rejected Marxist objectives and realigned the party as a left-of-centre party based on social-democratic principles. The party first came to power in the post-war Bundestag when it formed a GROSSE KOALITION with the CDU/CSU in 1969–1982 to tackle economic problems. In 1969–1982 the SPD was able to form a coalition government with the FDP under the chancellorship of Willy Brandt (SPD) from 1969 to 1974 and then under Helmut SCHMIDT (SPD). A separate SPD party was formed in the DDR in 1989, which then merged with the Western

SPD in September 1990. The party has been in opposition since Helmut Schmidt resigned in 1982. The 1994 elections saw the SPD gain 36.4% of the votes cast with a total of 252 MANDATE in the Bundestag. Oskar LAFONTAINE was elected *Parteivorsitzender* in 1995.

The left-of-centre SPD is committed to social democratic values. It is concerned to promote social justice, advocates an economy with a balance of competition and planning in order to protect the individual from exploitation, and rejects links with Communism.

Parteivorsitzende: Kurt Schumacher (1946–1952), Erich Ollenhauer (1952–1963), Willy Brandt (1964–1987), Hans-Jochen Vogel (1987–1991), Björn ENGHOLM (1991–1993), Rudolf SCHARPING (1993–1995), Oskar Lafontaine (since 1995).

SOZIALE MARKTWIRTSCHAFT

The social market economy was introduced under Ludwig Erhard, the BRD's first BUNDESWIRTSCHAFTSMINISTER and the architect of Germany's WIRTSCHAFTSWUNDER. The policy effectively combined the ethos of the market with liberal principles by creating an economy that allowed free enterprise but permitted limited intervention by the state.

SOZIALER WOHNUNGSBAU

The construction of housing subsidised by public funds to provide low-cost rented accommodation for the socially deprived members of society.

SOZIALGESETZBUCH (SGB)

The body of law that covers the legislation relating to social matters including *Ausbildungsförderung*, SOZIALVERSICHERUNG (KRANKENVERSICHERUNG, UNFALLVERSICHERUNG, RENTENVERSICHERUNG, PFLEGEVERSICHERUNG), WOHNGELD, JUGENDHILFE, SOZIALHILFE, etc.

SOZIALHILFE

The non-contributory social benefits prescribed by law for those in need of welfare. The services are delivered at local level by the SOZIALAMT.

SOZIALISTISCHE EINHEITSPARTEI DEUTSCHLANDS (SED)

The political party that was formed in 1946 under the tutelage of the Soviet Union and went on to rule the DDR until the collapse of Communism. All four zones permitted the KOMMUNISTISCHE PARTEI DEUTSCHLANDS after the end of the Second World War, but in 1946 the 'Socialist Unity Party of Germany' was formed in the Soviet zone by merging the SPD and the KPD. Although other parties were permitted in the DDR to placate the feelings of the bourgeoisie and professional classes, the SED effectively had absolute power and ruled the DDR as a one-party state under the direction of Walter Ulbricht (until 1971) and Erich Honecker (1971–1989).

SOZIALLEISTUNGEN

Social and welfare benefits obtained under SOZIALVERSICHERUNG and SOZIALHILFE and fringe benefits granted by ARBEITGEBER.

SOZIALPARTNER

The two sides of industry comprising ARBEITGEBER and ARBEIT-NEHMER. In the annual payround negotiating a TARIFVERTRAG for a particular sector of industry or commerce, the two sides are generally represented by a GEWERKSCHAFT and an ARBEITGEBERVER-BAND.

SOZIALPLAN

A social plan with a package of compensation measures for a change in circumstances in a business necessitating redundancies. The plan is worked out between the BETRIEBSRAT and the ARBEITGEBER and is intended to reduce the short-term effects of redundancy.

SOZIALVERSICHERUNG

Statutory social-insurance payments for provision of health care and sickness, unemployment, invalidity, accident and pension benefits. See also: ARBEITSLOSENVERSICHERUNG; KRANKENVERSICHE-RUNG; PFLEGEVERSICHERUNG; RENTENVERSICHERUNG; UNFALLVERSI-CHERUNG

SOZIALVERSICHERUNGSAUSWEIS

The social-security card issued to every ARBEITNEHMER since 1991 with the individual's ID number for SOZIALVERSICHERUNG, their surname and forename. This document has to be presented to any ARBEITGEBER before commencement of work and was introduced to stop moonlighting and abuse of the benefits system.

SOZIALWOHNUNGEN

Subsidised housing constructed using public funds that can only be rented out at a rent that simply covers running costs. *Sozialwohnungen* can only be let to tenants who have a certificate of entitlement to low-cost housing. See also: SOZIALER WOH-NUNGSBAU

SPAR HANDELS-AG

Food wholesaler and retailer founded in 1985 with SPAR shops first coming to Germany in 1952. Company headquarters are in HAMBURG. SPAR has some 23,000 employees.

SPARKASSE

Traditionally a savings bank run by a local authority, *Sparkassen* now provide customers with most of the services offered by private banks.

SPARTENKANAL

A TV channel specialising in a particular genre, for example sport, feature films or news as opposed to a channel offering a VOLLPROGRAMM.

SPD See: *SOZIALDEMOKRATISCHE PARTEI DEUTSCHLANDS*

SPEKTRUM DER WISSENSCHAFT

Specialist science magazine established in 1978 and published monthly in Heidelberg (BADEN-WÜRTTEMBERG) with a circulation of 117,000. It is aimed at scientists and anybody with an interest in science, and presents current findings and research.

SPESSART

An upland forest region in HESSEN and BAYERN, much of which is a nature reserve and a popular leisure area for the inhabitants of the RHEIN-MAIN-GEBIET.

SPEYER
The Romanesque cathedral of this former imperial city in RHEIN-LAND-PFALZ has been made a UNESCO world heritage site.

SPIEGEL See: *DER SPIEGEL*

SPIEGEL-AFFÄRE
A test of Germany's democracy in 1962. SPIEGEL journalists produced a critical investigation about NATO forces and defence procurement policy. VERTEIDIGUNGSMINISTER Franz Josef Strauß sent the police in to raid *Der Spiegel*'s offices and arrested Rudolf AUGSTEIN and some of his editors. However, the paper's integrity was rewarded when Strauß was forced to resign. This was a major victory for freedom of the press over heavy-handed government intervention.

SPIEGEL-VERLAG RUDOLF AUGSTEIN GmbH & CO KG
Publishing company founded in 1947 by Rudolf AUGSTEIN. The company runs news-magazine DER SPIEGEL and has some 850 employees.

SPIELPLATZ
Most families have a children's playground close by. Playgrounds are well-equipped with an emphasis on wooden structures and safety. Some *Abenteuerspielplätze* have elaborate structures that offer good scope for older children. German society is ambivalent towards children, and some playgrounds have notices restricting use to certain times of the day to stop noise nuisance for adjoining houses.

SPIO See: *SPITZENORGANISATION DER FILMWIRTSCHAFT e.V.*

SPITZENORGANISATION DER FILMWIRTSCHAFT e.V. (SPIO)
An umbrella organisation founded in 1949 in WIESBADEN to promote and represent the interests of the German film industry. SPIO runs a number of film institutes, compiles a register of

films, produces statistics on the film industry and is also responsible for the classification of films. See also: FREIWILLIGE SELBSTKON-
TROLLE DER FILMWIRTSCHAFT

SPITZENVERBAND
An umbrella organisation (ÜBERREGIONAL) representing the interests of a particular sector of industry, commerce or public life at
the level of the LAND or BUND.

SPORT-BILD
General sports magazine published every week in HAMBURG by
SPRINGER VERLAG with a circulation of 677,000.

SPORT-INFORMATIONS-DIENST (sid)
Sports news service founded in 1945 and based in DÜSSELDORF.

SPORTS LIFE
Up-market general sports magazine published weekly by GRUNER
+ JAHR with a circulation of 146,000.

SPRANGER, CARL-DIETER (1939–   )
Lawyer and CSU politician who has been a member of the BUN-
DESTAG since 1972. In 1982–1991 he was STAATSSEKRETÄR in the
BUNDESINNENMINISTERIUM and he has been BUNDESMINISTER FÜR WIRT-
SCHAFTLICHE ZUSAMMENARBEIT since 1991.

SPREEWALD
The Spreewald in BRANDENBURG is an area of forest around the
river Spree and its tributaries that has been declared a world
biosphere reserve by UNESCO. The area is mostly populated by
the SORBEN (a Slav minority) and apart from market gardening
the main activity here is tourism.

SPRENGEL MUSEUM
An exciting museum of modern art in HANNOVER with a big collection of work by Kurt Schwitters.

SPRINGER VERLAG AG, AXEL
Media company owning a clutch of newspapers including BILD
ZEITUNG and DIE WELT (ÜBERREGIONALE ZEITUNGEN) and a number
of other newspapers including BERLINER MORGENPOST, BZ and HAM-
BURGER ABENDBLATT. A group of magazines and journals also

come from the Springer stable, and the group owns several printing companies and book publisher ULLSTEIN. Company headquarters are in BERLIN. The publishing house was started up after the war by controversial right-wing tycoon Axel Springer who in 1959 built a new, high-rise Springer headquarters next to the BERLINER MAUER in West Berlin with a provocative sign flashing the message eastwards: '*Berlin bleibt frei!*' The company was floated on the stock exchange in 1970. Springer has some 13,000 employees.

SR   See: *SAARLÄNDISCHER RUNDFUNK*

SSD   See: *STAATSSICHERHEITSDIENST*

SSW   See: *SÜDSCHLESWIGSCHER WÄHLERVERBAND*

STAATLICHE KUNSTSAMMLUNGEN DRESDEN

The collections of art and treasures gathered by the Saxon electors and kings are housed in DRESDEN in a number of museums including the Gemäldegalerie Alte Meister, Gemäldegalerie Neue Meister, the Grünes Gewölbe and the Zwinger palace. There are collections of sculpture, porcelain, armour, a superb collection of old masters and one of the world's most impressive collections of gold and silver treasure.

STAATLICHE MUSEEN PREUSSISCHER KULTURBESITZ

The collection of monumental museums in BERLIN under the auspices of the STIFTUNG PREUSSISCHER KULTURBESITZ including the PERGAMONMUSEUM, the Alte Nationalgalerie, the Neue Nationalgalerie and the Bodemuseum, and over a dozen other museums with collections of Egyptian, Greek and Roman antiquities, as well as Islamic, Asian and Byzantine art, Berlin's state art collection and ethnography. See also: MUSEUMSINSEL

STAATLICHE ZENTRALSTELLE FÜR FERNUNTERRICHT (ZFU)

This central authority was founded in 1971 and is based in KÖLN. It is responsible for approving correspondence courses. See also: FERNUNTERRICHT

STAATLICHES MUSEUM
Museum in SCHWERIN holding the art collection built up by the dukes of Schwerin. The heart of the collection is Flemish and Dutch paintings from the 17th and 18th centuries.

STAATSANWALT
Public prosecutor in the STAATSANWALTSCHAFT. See also: RECHTS-ANWALT

STAATSANWALTSCHAFT
The prosecuting authority responsible for carrying out preliminary investigations into criminal cases, presenting the case for the prosecution in court, and making representations regarding the sentence. The *Staatsanwaltschaft* is under the authority of the BUNDESJUSTIZMINISTER. See also: STAATSANWALT

STAATSBIBLIOTHEK ZU BERLIN – PREUSSISCHER KULTURBESITZ
The Prussian state library in BERLIN was founded in 1661. When Germany was divided the library was also split, but following reunification it has been reunited to form a collection of over 8.5 million volumes.

STAATSBÜRGER
A citizen of a state possessing all the political rights and obligations associated with that state.

STAATSEXAMEN
Examinations held by the state for admittance to professions in the *Staatsdienst* (teachers and judges) and professions that are subject to national registration procedures (doctors, lawyers, pharmacists). Generally a theoretical *Erstes Staatsexamen* concludes the course of study at a HOCHSCHULE and a practical *Zweites Staatsexamen* is taken after further training. Doctors and pharmacists additionally require a licence (*Bestallung* for doctors, *Approbation* for pharmacists).

STAATSGALERIE STUTTGART
The gallery housing STUTTGART's magnificent art collection was founded in 1843 and holds a collection of paintings from the Middle Ages to the 20th century including E. Burne-Jones's

cycle *The Legend of Perseus*. The Neue Staatsgalerie is an extension completed in 1984 to house the expanding collection of modern acquisitions.

STAATSMINISTER

In the BUNDESREGIERUNG a junior minister within the BUNDESKANZLERAMT or a BUNDESMINISTERIUM. In the LANDESREGIERUNG in BAYERN, HESSEN and SACHSEN a minister responsible for a ministry. See also: STAATSSEKRETÄR

STAATSPRÜFUNG   See: *STAATSEXAMEN*

STAATSSEKRETÄR

The ministerial rank immediately below that of MINISTER in the BUNDESREGIERUNG and LANDESREGIERUNG. Each BUNDESMINISTERIUM has one or two Parlamentarische Staatssekretäre (who may be STAATSMINISTER and who are MITGLIEDER DES BUNDESTAGES) and one to three Staatssekretäre who are BEAMTE.

STAATSSICHERHEITSDIENST (SSD)

The *Staatssicherheitsdienst* or '*Stasi*' was the sinister East German secret police that penetrated every walk of life in the DDR through up to half a million paid informers. It maintained over 180 km. of files on roughly one in three of their fellow citizens, some going into minute detail of people's personal lives. Former *Stasi*-boss Erich Mielke was jailed in 1993 for six years for the murder of two policemen in 1931 but was released in 1995 after serving two-thirds of the term. He was brought to trial on human-rights charges in the DDR but was declared unfit to stand trial. As former East Germans struggle to come to terms with the new culture, the issue of the *Stasi* and its informers continues to rumble on. See also: GAUCK-BEHÖRDE; STASI-AKTEN

STACHELSCHWEINE, DIE

A cabaret theatre in BERLIN.

STÄDELSCHES KUNSTINSTITUT UND STÄDTISCHE GALERIE

The Städel in FRANKFURT AM MAIN, founded in 1816 by banker Johann Städel, is one of Germany's most prestigious art galleries. It houses an outstanding collection of old masters. The gallery's modern collection is still impressive although it was decimated by the Nazis' purging of '*entartete Kunst*'.

STADT

This term may be used to refer collectively to towns and cities without differentiating between the type of local government that may be in place. A distinction is drawn in Germany between a KREISANGEHÖRIGE STADT and a KREISFREIE STADT.

STADTBEZIRK

Areas within a town which may have local-government offices able to carry out certain functions.

STADTDIREKTOR

The official title of the HAUPTVERWALTUNGSBEAMTER in towns in NORDRHEIN-WESTFALEN. See also: OBERSTADTDIREKTOR

STADTHAUS See: *RATHAUS*

STÄDTISCHE KUNSTHALLE

Founded in 1907, the Städtische Kunsthalle in MANNHEIM has one of Germany's most important collections of painting and sculpture from the nineteenth and twentieth centuries, including exhibits by the Romantics, Manet, Cézanne, and a fine collection of twentieth-century German sculpture with works by Ernst Barlach, Wilhelm Lehmbruck and the avant-garde.

STADTKREIS See: *KREISFREIE STADT*

STADTPRÄSIDENT

Official title of the RATSVORSITZENDER in towns in SCHLESWIG-HOLSTEIN.

STADTRAT

The local council in the STADT elected in local elections. The chairperson of the council is the BÜRGERMEISTER or OBERBÜRGERMEISTER in large towns and cities. The Stadtrat decides all important issues in the town or city and is responsible for drawing up a budget and for passing local by-laws.

The term Stadtrat is also the term for an elected member of the Stadtrat in southern Germany and for an elected member of the MAGISTRAT in HESSEN, NORDRHEIN-WESTFALEN and Bremerhaven

(BREMEN). The position of Stadtrat may be a full-time post in large towns and cities in BAYERN. See also: STADTRATSMITGLIED

STADTRATSMITGLIED
An elected member of the STADTRAT, also known as a Stadtverordneter, Ratsherr or Stadtrat.

STADTSTAAT
A city state which has the status of a LAND in Germany. There are three *Stadtstaaten*: BERLIN, BREMEN and HAMBURG.

STADTVERORDNETENVERSAMMLUNG
The official title for the STADTRAT in HESSEN, Bremerhaven (BREMEN) and some towns in SCHLESWIG-HOLSTEIN.

STADTVERORDNETENVORSTEHER
Official title of the RATSVORSITZENDER in HESSEN.

STADTVERORDNETER See: *STADTRATSMITGLIED*

STADTVERTRETUNG
The official title of the STADTRAT in SCHLESWIG-HOLSTEIN.

STADTVERWALTUNG
The local authority governing a town or city. See also: STADTRAT

STADTWERKE
The public services operated by a town including the suburban transport system and public utilities such as water supply, gas and electricity.

STAECK, KLAUS (1938–   )
Illustrator who trained as a lawyer before turning to graphic design. He became well-known as a designer of satirical political posters.

STAMMTISCH
An integral part of German beer and wine culture is the *Stammtisch*, a prominent table in any self-respecting *Gaststätte* or *Weinstube* where regulars congregate to set the world to rights. It also refers to regular meetings of groups of colleagues or friends for a friendly drink.

STANDESAMT
The local office responsible for the registration of births, deaths and marriages. Only marriages held at a Standesamt have legal status. See also: TRAUUNG

STÄNDIGE KONFERENZ DER KULTUSMINISTER DER LÄNDER IN DER BUNDESREPUBLIK DEUTSCHLAND (KMK)
A standing conference of the cultural ministers of the LÄNDER, based in BONN. The conference is responsible for coordinating policy between the Länder on cultural affairs, particularly in education.

STANDORT DEUTSCHLAND
Term used to describe corporate Germany as an economic and political entity, and as a location for business enterprises.

STARTBAHN-WEST
An additional runway at the RHEIN-MAIN-FLUGHAFEN in FRANKFURT AM MAIN which generated much controversy in the early 1980s. The area was occupied by protesters and there were many eruptions of violence between demonstrators and police. See also: DIE GRÜNEN

STASI See: *STAATSSICHERHEITSDIENST*

STASI-AKTEN
The files kept by the STAATSSICHERHEITSDIENST on around 6 million members of the 17 million population in the DDR. The *Stasi-Unterlagen-Gesetz* passed in 1991 gave citizens the right to apply for access to their personal file. See also: GAUCK-BEHÖRDE

STASI-UNTERLAGEN-GESETZ See: *STASI-AKTEN*

STATISTISCHES BUNDESAMT
The federal statistics office is based in WIESBADEN and is under the auspices of the BUNDESMINISTERIUM DES INNERN. It was founded in 1953 and is responsible for collecting statistics on just about anything of interest. It has a library with nearly half a million volumes and supplies information on request.

STATT-PARTEI-GRUPPE

Conservative party founded in HAMBURG in 1993. The party has some 1,800 members and focuses on solving specific problems. It gained more than five percent of the votes in the 1993 elections for the BÜRGERSCHAFT and formed a coalition with the SPD. The party lost its status as a FRAKTION in the Bürgerschaft when the founder and another SENATOR left the party.

STEIN, HORST (1928–   )

Conductor who became famous with his performances of Wagner operas. He was conductor at the Staatsoper in East BERLIN in 1955–1961, before emigrating to the West where he became opera director at the Nationaltheater MANNHEIM in 1963–1970, musical director at the Staatsoper HAMBURG in 1972–1977 and principal conductor of the Orchestre de la Suisse Romande in Geneva in 1980–1985. Stein was appointed principal conductor with the Bamberger Symphoniker in 1985.

STEIN, PETER (1937–   )

One of a number of German theatre directors who raised German theatre to international standards at the end of the 1960s. He has been director of the Schaubühne in West BERLIN since 1970, *Schauspielregisseur* at the Salzburger Festspiele since 1992, and has worked in film and television. Stein has been an exponent of democratisation in the theatre with all the members of the cast being involved in a production. His drama productions include P. Weiss' *VietNam Diskurs* (1968), B. Brecht's *Die Mutter* (1970) and B. STRAUSS' *Groß und Klein* (1978). His opera productions include R. Wagner's *Rheingold* (1976) and C. Debussy's *Pelléas et Mélisande* (1991).

STERN

Germany's largest-selling weekly news and general-interest magazine with TV listings, published by GRUNER + JAHR in HAMBURG with a circulation of 1.2 million. Publication of the spurious Hitler diaries in 1983 dented the reputation of this competitor to DER SPIEGEL. Establishment of the news magazine FOCUS in 1993 has so far had little impact on sales, although increased competition generally has led to a reduction in recent years.

STEUERBERATER
Tax consultant who advises individuals and companies on their tax affairs. See also: KANZLEI

STEUERLICHER FREIBETRAG See: *FREIBETRAG*

StGB See: *STRAFGESETZBUCH*

STICHWAHL
In an election, a deciding vote held between the two candidates with the most votes cast if an absolute majority was not obtained in the first ballot.

STIFTERVERBAND FÜR DIE DEUTSCHE WISSENSCHAFT e.V.
Association of donors for the promotion of science and humanities in Germany founded in 1920 with around 5,000 members. It aims to raise funds from German business for research and also runs some 220 foundations with assets of over 1,000 million marks. See also: STIFTUNGEN

STIFTUNG DEUTSCHE SPORTHILFE
A foundation based in FRANKFURT AM MAIN dedicated to promoting talented athletes and sportspeople.

STIFTUNG PREUSSISCHER KULTURBESITZ
The foundation for Prussian cultural heritage came into being in 1957 and is based in BERLIN. It had long been recognised that PREUSSEN had created exemplary museums, libraries and archives, and this represented an attempt to preserve a heritage that had been split up by the creation of two Germanys. The reunification of Germany saw the collections once again united under the auspices of the Stiftung Preußischer Kulturbesitz.

STIFTUNG VOLKSWAGENWERK See: *VOLKSWAGEN-STIFTUNG*

STIFTUNG WARENTEST
A testing centre financed by the BUND and based in BERLIN. The centre was founded in 1964 and reports to consumers on the quality of goods and services, testing according to objective

criteria. The centre publishes the monthly magazine *Test* with reports on consumer products and services.

STIFTUNG WEIMARER KLASSIK
Foundation that administers the museums, archives and libraries in and around Weimar (THÜRINGEN) relating to the literary period of Weimar Classicism. See also: GOETHE-NATIONALMUSEUM; KLASSIK

STIFTUNGEN
There are around 13,000 independent foundations in Germany with funds totalling some 4,000 million marks. German business has a strong tradition of promoting research and KULTUR, with such foundations as the Bertelsmann Stiftung, Robert Bosch Stiftung and VOLKSWAGEN-STIFTUNG.

STIMMRECHT See: *WAHLRECHT*

STIMMZETTEL
The ballot paper that has to be completed by voters in an election. See also: BRIEFWAHL; BUNDESTAGSWAHL; LANDTAGSWAHL

STINNES AG
Trading, distribution and transport company with a chain of DIY stores founded in 1902 and now wholly owned by VEBA AG. Company headquarters are in Mülheim (NORDRHEIN-WESTFALEN). Stinnes has some 33,000 employees.

STOCKHAUSEN, KARLHEINZ (1928–   )
Composer and pioneer of electrophonic music who trained in KÖLN and under Milhaud and Messiaen. From 1963 until 1989 he was musical director of the Studio für elektronische Musik at the WESTDEUTSCHER RUNDFUNK, bringing the rigour and precision of scientific method and physics to the composition of music whilst allowing the performer scope for improvisation. He lectures extensively on his music. Works from Stockhausen's prolific output include *Gesang der Jünglinge* (1955/1956), *Gruppen* for three orchestras (1955–1957), *Klavierstück XI* (1956), *Mantra* for two pianists (1970) and *Jubiläum* for orchestra (1977). For the past 20 years he has been working on a seven-part symbolic opera cycle looking at the phenomenon of human existence: *Licht – die sieben Tage der Woche (Teile I-III – Donnerstag* 1981, *Samstag*

1984, *Montag* 1988, and *Teil IV – Dienstag aus Licht*, premiered at LEIPZIG opera house in 1993); the cycle is due to be completed in 2003.

STOIBER, EDMUND (1941–   )

Lawyer and CSU politician. He has been a member of the LANDTAG in BAYERN since 1974 and was GENERALSEKRETÄR of the CSU in 1978–1983. He rose through the LANDESREGIERUNG, occupying the positions of STAATSSEKRETÄR and STAATSMINISTER in the Bayerische Staatskanzlei, and Bavarian Innenminister in 1988–1993. He became MINISTERPRÄSIDENT of Bayern in 1993.

STOLPE, MANFRED (1936–   )

Lawyer and SPD politician. He was head of the administration of the EVANGELISCHE KIRCHE in BERLIN-BRANDENBURG (DDR) in 1982–1990. He became a member of the SPD in 1990 and was elected MINISTERPRÄSIDENT of Brandenburg with an SPD majority in the same year.

STOLTE, DIETER (1934–   )

TV journalist and INTENDANT of ZDF who has made changes in programming to meet competition from commercial TV channels. Stolte has been with ZDF since 1962 and has been Intendant since 1982. In 1984 he started up 3SAT together with ARD, Austrian TV and Swiss TV.

STRABAG AG

Construction company founded in 1923. Company headquarters are in KÖLN. Strabag has some 23,000 employees.

STRAFANZEIGE

A report made by anyone to the police, STAATSANWALTSCHAFT or AMTSGERICHT concerning the suspicion that a criminal offence may have been committed. Motoring offences are an area where reports are frequently made to the police by other motorists.

STRAFGESETZBUCH (StGB)

The criminal code used in the BRD dating from 1871 and applied with amendments and additions in the version of 1987. See also: STRAFRECHT

STRAFRECHT
The body of law relating to criminal law and laid down in the STRAFGESETZBUCH.

STRAFREGISTER See: *BUNDESZENTRALREGISTER*

STRASSENVERKEHRSRECHT
The body of law relating to the use of public highways, tracks and spaces for traffic. It relates to matters such as the registration of vehicles, the issuing of the FÜHRERSCHEIN, motor-vehicle insurance, highway code, etc.

STRAUSS, BOTHO (1944–   )
Writer who started out as editor and critic with theatre periodical *Theater heute* (1967–1970), was appointed *Dramaturg* at the Schaubühne am Halleschen Ufer in BERLIN (1971–1975) and went on to become one of Germany's most widely performed playwrights, being awarded the GEORG-BÜCHNER-PREIS in 1989. His works use lucid language and often surreal situations to depict the absence of creative communication in contemporary society. Plays include *Trilogie des Wiedersehens* (1976), *Besucher* (1988) and *Das Gleichgewicht* (1993). Prose works include *Der junge Mann* (1984), *Über Liebe* (1989) and *Wohnen Dämmern Lügen* (1994). The right-wing views expressed in his essay 'Anschwellender Bocksgesang' (1993) in DER SPIEGEL were the subject of considerable controversy.

STROMVERSORGUNG
Electricity prices in Germany are the highest in the EU and the market is dominated by three companies: RWE, VEBA/PREUSSEN-ELEKTRA and VIAG/BAYERNWERK.

STRUBE, JÜRGEN (1939–   )
Laywer and industrialist who has been with BASF since 1969 and was appointed VORSTANDSMITGLIED in 1986. He has been chairman of the VORSTAND at BASF since 1990.

STUDENTENAUSWEIS
Student ID card requiring a stamp at the beginning of each SEMESTER in order to verify that the student is an *ordentlicher Studierender*. The card entitles students to discounts on a variety

of facilities such as public transport, theatres, concerts, cinemas and museums.

STUDENTENBEWEGUNG

The student movement that manifested itself during the 1960s and formed the focus for the AUSSERPARLAMENTARISCHE OPPOSITION.

STUDENTENPARLAMENT

An autonomous body elected by the STUDENTENSCHAFT which in turn elects the ALLGEMEINER STUDENTENAUSSCHUSS of the UNIVERSITÄT.

STUDENTENSCHAFT

The body of students at an institution of higher education.

STUDENTENWERK

Centre at a HOCHSCHULE responsible for administering grants (BAFÖG) and constructing and running STUDENTENWOHNHEIME and MENSEN. See also: DEUTSCHES STUDENTENWERK E.V.

STUDENTENWOHNHEIM

Hall of residence for university students run by the STUDENTENWERK.

STUDENTISCHE VERBINDUNGEN

Fraternities of almost exclusively male students and alumni (*Alte Herren*) which were originally founded to foster conservative values and a sense of honour and pride in the fatherland. Today, members live, study and drink beer together, and in some of the older universities they can still be seen dressed in brightly coloured sashes and hats in an annual parade. The *Verbindungen* are differentiated into *Burschenschaften*, *Korporationen* and *Landsmannschaften.* Although forbidden by law, some of the *Verbindungen* are reputed to still engage in duelling.

STUDENTISCHE VEREINIGUNGEN

Student associations formed to pursue common aims including political, social, religious and cultural aims and to promote international relations.

STUDIENBERATUNG

Study counselling covering general and specialist issues on the organisation of a particular STUDIENGANG. The question of whether foreign qualifications or courses of study permit attendance on particular courses can very often be solved by the relevant PRÜFUNGSAMT.

STUDIENBRIEF
The main means of instruction in FERNUNTERRICHT, containing the study material and exercises to test knowledge.

STUDIENBUCH
A book given to all students when they first register (EINSCHREIBUNG). All courses attended during the STUDIUM are recorded in this book, which serves as a record that a student has attended all the necessary components of a *Studium* when registering for the ABSCHLUSSPRÜFUNG.

STUDIENFACH
A subject studied at a HOCHSCHULE.

STUDIENGANG
The particular course of studies pursued by a student in their STUDIUM at a HOCHSCHULE, comprising the lectures, assignments and PRAKTIKA leading to the ABSCHLUSSPRÜFUNG. The length of university studies and the time that students can remain at university is a subject perennially under the microscope. Students finish their course of studies on average at the age of 29 and there is growing support for shorter *Studiengänge.*

STUDIENJAHR
A way of organising the academic calendar used particularly at the newer HOCHSCHULEN, in which courses are organised over two consecutive SEMESTER starting with the *Wintersemester.*

STUDIENORDNUNG
The regulations and syllabus relating to a particular STUDIUM at a HOCHSCHULE.

STUDIENSTIFTUNG DES DEUTSCHEN VOLKES
The German scholarship foundation was founded in 1925, dissolved in 1934 and then re-formed in 1948 based in BONN. It

provides some 6,000 scholarships annually to university students of exceptional ability.

STUDIUM
A course of studies leading to a degree at a HOCHSCHULE, also known as a *Hochschulstudium.*

STUDIUM GENERALE
General lectures held on subjects of general interest for students from all faculties.

STUTTGART
Stuttgart is the LANDESHAUPTSTADT of BADEN-WÜRTTEMBERG and is situated on the river Neckar (dialling code 07 11, postal area code 70...). The city was granted rights as a town in 1219 but was long overshadowed by grander neighbours. Then at the beginning of the nineteenth century, Stuttgart was made the royal capital of *Württemberg* and industrialisation came with the railways, Robert Bosch and Gottfried Daimler. Even now, Stuttgart remains proud of its agricultural heritage, and the area around the city is a leading fruit and wine-growing district.

The centre of the city was subject to extensive destruction in the Second World War and most of the city's historic buildings were rebuilt. Today, the city has the highest overall standard of living of any city in Europe, owing success and prosperity to the automobile industry in the form of MERCEDES-BENZ and PORSCHE and electronics giant BOSCH. Stuttgart's ballet company has attained international acclaim and the city hosts an international Musikfest every four years. The city's festivals also include the Canstatter Volksfest at the end of September (the world's second-largest beer festival after the Munich OKTOBERFEST), the Stuttgarter Weindorf wine festival at the end of August, and one of Germany's oldest WEIHNACHTSMÄRKTE.

The city has a population of some 568,000 with a total student population of around 32,000 (2 UNIVERSITÄTEN and 6 other HOCHSCHULEN) and nearly 24% foreigners (32% Yugoslav). The CDU has been running the city since 1974, although lack of an absolute majority has necessitated the support of other parties. More than 80% of Stuttgart's industry revolves around engineering and the manufacture of automobiles. Other industries include publishing, chemicals, textiles and fruit and wine production. Although not a major trade-fair centre, the city hosts a number of international trade fairs including INTERGASTRA and INTERVITIS/INTERFRUCTA. See also: HOHENHEIM, UNIVERSITÄT

STUTTGART, UNIVERSITÄT

University in BADEN-WÜRTTEMBERG founded in 1829 (university status 1967) and teaching some 21,000 students. The Universität Stuttgart has faculties of architecture and town planning, civil engineering and surveying, chemistry, electrical engineering, industrial engineering, biological sciences, geosciences, history and social sciences and economics, aerospace engineering, mathematics, physics, chemical engineering, computer science, philosophy (arts).

STUTTGARTER NACHRICHTEN

Newspaper established in 1946 and published daily including Sunday in STUTTGART, and distributed throughout BADEN-WÜRTTEMBERG. See also: STUTTGARTER ZEITUNG

STUTTGARTER ZEITUNG

Daily established in 1945 and published in STUTTGART. Together with its sister dailies STUTTGARTER NACHRICHTEN, *Nordstuttgarter Rundschau* and *Fellbacher Zeitung* it has a circulation of 217,000. It is a liberal paper distributed in Stuttgart and surrounding areas.

SÜDDEUTSCHE RATSVERFASSUNG

A type of local-authority constitution applicable in BADEN-WÜRTTEMBERG and BAYERN. Under this constitution the BÜRGER-MEISTER (directly elected) is chairperson of the GEMEINDEVERTRE-TUNG (GEMEINDERAT) and is also responsible for administration in the GEMEINDE (*Gemeindeverwaltung*). This type of constitution gives the Bürgermeister both political and executive power.

The Süddeutsche Ratsverfassung has been broadly adopted in the NEUE BUNDESLÄNDER although there are a number of regional variations: for example, the Bürgermeister is elected by the *Gemeindevertretung* in MECKLENBURG-VORPOMMERN, SACHSEN and THÜRINGEN. See also: GEMEINDEVERFASSUNGSRECHT

SÜDDEUTSCHE ZEITUNG (SZ)

A left-of-centre serious national daily established in 1945 and published in MÜNCHEN. The *Süddeutsche* has a circulation of 406,000, the highest circulation of the daily ÜBERREGIONALE ZEITUNGEN. The first edition is published the evening before the date on the paper. It has a number of local editions featuring a section with local news, and relies on BAYERN for two-thirds of its readers. The *Süddeutsche* pursues a liberal agenda and is widely respected for its objective treatment of current affairs.

SÜDDEUTSCHER RUNDFUNK (SDR)

A regional public-service radio and TV broadcasting corporation based in STUTTGART and broadcasting principally to BADEN-WÜRTTEMBERG. Süddeutscher Rundfunk is a member of the ARD. See also: LANDESRUNDFUNK- UND FERNSEHANSTALTEN

SÜDDEUTSCHER VERLAG GmbH

Newspaper publishing company founded in 1945 and based in MÜNCHEN. The company has some 2,500 employees and publishes the SÜDDEUTSCHE ZEITUNG, has holdings in other newspaper publishers and printing companies, and publishes a range of special-interest magazines.

SUDETENDEUTSCHE

A term referring to the roughly 3.5 million ethnic Germans from the former Czechoslovakia who mostly lived in the area known as SUDETENLAND. They were forcibly repatriated at the end of the Second World War in accordance with the POTSDAMER ABKOMMEN.

SUDETENLAND

The area in the former Czechoslovakia (in *Böhmen*, *Mähren* and SCHLESIEN) that had been part of the Austro-Hungarian Empire and had been settled over the centuries by about 3.5 million ethnic Germans. The Sudetenland was occupied by Germany in 1939 following the Munich Agreement, which British Prime Minister Chamberlain hailed as 'peace in our time'. At the end of the Second World War the area was returned to Czechoslovakia and it now forms part of the Czech Republic.

SÜDSCHLESWIGSCHER WÄHLERVERBAND (SSW)
A political party with around 5,000 members, founded in 1948 in SCHLESWIG-HOLSTEIN to represent the interests of the Danish minority there. The FÜNFPROZENTKLAUSEL does not apply to this party because of the historic status of the Danish ethnic minority, which has had one member in the LANDTAG since 1962.

SÜDWEST PRESSE
Daily newspaper published in Ulm with a circulation of 360,000 and distributed throughout BADEN-WÜRTTEMBERG and BAYERN.

SÜDWESTFUNK (SWF)
A regional public-service radio and TV broadcasting corporation based in Baden-Baden and broadcasting to RHEINLAND-PFALZ and BADEN-WÜRTTEMBERG. Südwestfunk is a member of the ARD. See also: LANDESRUNDFUNK- UND FERNSEHANSTALTEN

SÜDZUCKER AG
Food manufacturing company producing sugar, feedstock and agricultural products, founded in 1926. Company headquarters are in MANNHEIM. Südzucker has some 13,000 employees.

SUKOWA, BARBARA (1950–   )
Actress who has gained an international reputation for her film performances in *Die bleierne Zeit* (1981), *Lola* (1982), *Rosa Luxemburg* (1985) and *Homo Faber* (1991). She has performed at theatres throughout Germany and played Mieze in Fassbinder's TV series based on Döblin's *Berlin Alexanderplatz* (1980).

SUPER ILLU
Weekly magazine of current affairs, politics and general interest published by BURDA in BERLIN with a circulation of 541,000.

SÜSKIND, PATRICK (1949–   )
Writer who landed an international bestseller with his first novel *Das Parfum* (1985) about an eighteenth-century Parisian murderer obsessed by olfactory sensations. Süskind has also written *Geschichte von Herrn Sommer* (1991) and the play *Der Kontrabaß* (1984), and he co-scripted TV series *Kir Royal* (1986).

SÜSSMUTH, RITA (1937–   )

Professor of philosophy and CDU politician, she was head of the *Bundesministerium für Jugend, Familie, Frauen und Gesundheit* in 1985–1988. She was elected MITGLIED DES BUNDESTAGES in 1987 and appointed BUNDESTAGSPRÄSIDENTIN in 1988. At the 1995 party conference she spoke for a motion advocating a quota of women candidates (*Frauenquote*) in elections, which was narrowly defeated despite the support of Helmut KOHL.

SWAKOPMUND

Town in the former German colony of Namibia (Africa) where the river Swakop enters the Atlantic. A last bastion of Germany's imperial ambitions, first colonised in 1892, when German settlers attempted to gain a foothold on the coast of Namibia. Today, 30% of the whites in the town are German speakers and the town still boasts the architecture of a Bavarian village and its own brewery producing beer from imported hops and malt.

SWF See: *SÜDWESTFUNK*

SYBERBERG, HANS-JÜRGEN (1935–   )

Film director whose controversial films on Germany include the seven-hour epic *Hitler – Ein Film aus Deutschland* (1977). Other films include *Ludwig – Requiem für einen jungfräulichen König* (1972), *Karl May* (1974), *Winifred Wagner – Die Geschichte des Hauses Wahnfried von 1914–1975* (1975) and *Die Nacht* (1985). Latterly he has also worked as a theatre producer.

SYLT

The biggest and most northerly of the islands off the North Sea coast of Nordfriesland in SCHLESWIG-HOLSTEIN, connected to the mainland by a narrow spit of land. It is a popular tourist resort for well-heeled Germans. There are extensive KUR facilities and the island has long offered the opportunity for FREIKÖRPER-KULTUR.

SYSTEMS

Systems is a trade fair for the IT and communications industries held in MÜNCHEN every two years with around 120,000 visitors.

SZ See: *SÜDDEUTSCHE ZEITUNG*

TAG DER ARBEIT
May Day is the traditional celebration for workers, and it is a public holiday in Germany with union rallies in big cities. More traditional rituals associated with raising the maypole are usual in rural environments. There is intense rivalry between some villages and it is not unusual for a village to wake up one morning with the maypole gone, spirited away to a secret hiding place by the menfolk of a neighbouring village.

TAG DER DEUTSCHEN EINHEIT
Originally, the *Tag der deutschen Einheit* was instituted as a West German public holiday on 17 June in remembrance of the 1953 uprising in East BERLIN (DDR). This public holiday has been moved to 3 October in celebration of the formal reunification of Germany in 1990.

TAGESSCHAU
TV news on ARD, the main *Tagesschau* being at 8 pm.

TAGESSPIEGEL, DER
Newspaper published daily including Sundays in BERLIN with a circulation of 129,000. It has a readership among executives and power brokers in politics and business.

TAGESZEITUNG, DIE (TAZ)
The left-wing daily newspaper *die tageszeitung* (often abbreviated to *taz* in analogy to FAZ) is published in BERLIN with a circulation of 59,000. It was established in 1979 as an alternative national daily and is run on cooperative principles.

TANTE-EMMA-LADEN
The archetypal 'corner shop' present in every village and once typified by the EDEKA chain. However, *Tante-Emma-Läden* have

been closing down at a great rate during the 1980s and 1990s as the mobile population shops further afield and bigger stores move in on the outskirts of towns and villages.

TARIFVERTRAG

A collective agreement generally between ARBEITGEBERVERBAND and the GEWERKSCHAFTEN. The unions are responsible for negotiating centralised *Tarifverträge* with the *Arbeitgeberverband* or ARBEITGEBER, and the annual payround starts well before current wage agreements expire. Such agreements are legally binding, and strikes are illegal while an agreement is in force or negotiations are proceeding. Any strike requires a 75% mandate from a secret ballot of the union membership. As union membership declines and companies desert *Arbeitgeberverbände* to avoid the strait-jacket imposed by *Tarifverträge*, collective agreements covering entire industries are looking increasingly outmoded and under threat.

TATORT

Popular crime series on ARD. See also: GEORGE, GÖTZ

TAUNUS

A range of forested hills in central HESSEN. The Hochtaunus has been turned into a nature reserve where city-dwellers from FRANKFURT AM MAIN unwind over the weekend.

TAZ See: *TAGESZEITUNG, DIE*

TCHIBO-HOLDING AG

Owners of TCHIBO coffee and a chain of coffee shops. Company headquarters are in HAMBURG. TCHIBO has some 13,000 employees.

TECHNISCHE HOCHSCHULE (TH)

A tertiary institution providing degree courses in technical and scientific subjects. Most of the courses are in applied subjects and require a period of practical training before or during the course of study.

TECHNISCHE ÜBERWACHUNGSVEREINE (TÜV)

The technical inspectorates are independent organisations which

are organised regionally with testing centres for carrying out regular tests on cars and for testing all types of technical device.
They also test products for compliance with the GS-ZEICHEN and
award a certificate permitting manufacturers to apply the seal to
the tested product. See also: VERBAND DER TECHNISCHEN ÜBER-
WACHUNGSVEREINE E.V.

TECHNISCHE UNIVERSITÄT (TU)
A technical university generally providing degree courses mainly
in applied science and engineering, though some also include
other subjects, e.g. in the arts.

TECHNO
Youth cult of the 1990s based on American-style *Techno-Musik*
and eschewing a political allegiance. It originated as a subculture
in the strongroom of the former Wertheim-Bank in BERLIN after
the WENDE. Techno is a movement devoted to pleasure, the loud
computer hits of *Techno-Musik*, and consumerism, with big public events, notably the LOVE-PARADE in BERLIN, and the *Munich
Union Move* in MÜNCHEN under the motto '*Music is the only
drug*'. While the use of hippie-drug marijuana is spurned, the
designer-drug Ecstasy has become popular at *Techno Parties*
alongside energy drinks. The Bunker, one of Techno's best-
known clubs in Berlin, was closed at the end of 1995 to make
way for new development while there are moves to make
another club, E-Werk, a listed building.

TELEKOLLEG
A system of further education founded by the BAYERISCHER RUND-
FUNK in 1967 and later joined by other regional TV networks.
Students study for the FACHSCHULREIFE and FACHHOCHSCHULREIFE,
and courses are delivered by a mix of television broadcasts, writ-
ten material and study groups that meet roughly every month.

TELLY See: *D1–NETZ*

TEMPO
Monthly lifestyle magazine established in 1979 and published by
JAHRESZEITEN VERLAG in HAMBURG. It has a circulation of 102,000

and appeals to a younger audience with features, interviews and articles on culture and entertainment.

TENGELMANN-GRUPPE

Supermarket retail group with headquarters in Mülheim (NORD-RHEIN-WESTFALEN). Tengelmann has some 197,000 employees.

TESTAMENTSERÖFFNUNG

Anyone in possession of a will after a person's death is legally obliged to submit it to the NACHLASSGERICHT immediately. The opening of a person's will following their death is carried out by the Nachlaßgericht in the presence of all interested parties.

TEUFEL, ERWIN (1939–)

Administrator and CDU politician. He has been a member of the LANDTAG in BADEN-WÜRTTEMBERG since 1972 and in 1978–1991 he was chairman of the CDU FRAKTION in the Landtag. Teufel has been MINISTERPRÄSIDENT since 1991 and formed a CDU/SPD coalition. He became chairman of the CDU in Baden-Württemberg in 1992.

TEUTOBURGER WALD

An ancient forest in NORDRHEIN-WESTFALEN and NIEDERSACHSEN made famous by Tacitus who recounts how the Romans were beaten by the Germanic tribes at a battle in 9 AD. It also contains the land belonging to the former tiny principality of *Lippe* that maintained its independence throughout the ages until it was swallowed up at the end of the Second World War by Nordrhein-Westfalen.

TH See: *TECHNISCHE HOCHSCHULE*

THEOLOGISCHE HOCHSCHULEN

Germany has 11 HOCHSCHULEN for Catholic theology, four *Hochschulen* for Protestant theology and 1 *Hochschule* for Jewish studies in Heidelberg (BADEN-WÜRTTEMBERG).

THOMA, HELMUT (1939–)

Lawyer, appointed GESCHÄFTSFÜHRER of private TV company RTL in 1991, who brought American-style TV to Germany with gameshows, talkshows, soaps and sitcoms.

THÜRINGEN, FREISTAAT

The 'Free State of Thuringia' is a FLÄCHENSTAAT covering an area of 16,175 sq. km., with a population of some 2.5 million. The LANDTAG (LANDESPARLAMENT) enacts legislation and comprises 88 members elected every four years, with the next election in autumn 1999. The Landtag elects the MINISTERPRÄSIDENT, head of the Landesregierung Thüringen, which holds executive powers. The Ministerpräsident appoints the ministers with responsibility for individual portfolios. Thüringen comprises five KREISFREIE STÄDTE and 35 KREISE, and the LANDESHAUPTSTADT is ERFURT.

Thüringen in the former DDR is a historic region that has been Germanic since the Dark Ages by contrast with the ALTMARK, SACHSEN and the DEUTSCHE OSTGEBIETE which comprised land wrested from the Slavic peoples. Over the years its territorial borders have been buffeted by the fortunes of war and inheritance. The historic town of Weimar – whose roll-call of distinguished citizens includes Goethe, Bach and Nietzsche – saw the drafting of the constitution for the ill-fated WEIMARER REPUBLIK following the relinquishing of political power by Kaiser Wilhelm II and the aristocracy in 1918. The LAND of Thüringen was forged from a patchwork of small states after the First World War but was broken up by the Communist authorities (like all other DDR Länder). Erfurt saw the beginning of post-war German reconciliation when DDR premier Willi Stoph met BUNDESKANZLER Willy Brandt in the first real success of OSTPOLITIK. Thüringen was reinstated in 1990 following reunification. Martin Luther translated the Bible into German at Eisenach's *Wartburg* (fortress), and as in the other eastern Länder, the majority of Christians follow the Protestant faith.

The landscape is mainly rural and the vast Thüringer Wald covers the south-west portion of the Land. This has meant that Germany's *grünes Herz* escaped the worst excesses of East Germany's polluting industry, although the forests have suffered substantial damage. Industrial production is concentrated in and around Eisenach, Erfurt and Jena. Eisenach has long been a centre for automobile production with manufacture of the DDR *Wartburg*, and latterly OPEL and BOSCH have invested in new production facilities here. Erfurt is an important horticultural centre and Jena is historically associated with optics manufacturer Carl Zeiss (CARL-ZEISS-STIFTUNG). Important industries in Thüringen include engineering and metalworking, electrical engineering, textiles, toys and forestry, and the state has Europe's biggest slate quarries. Thüringen's venerable towns, unspoilt scenery and forests also attract tourists in increasing numbers. A CDU/FDP coalition was formed following reunification but since the 1994 elections a coalition between the CDU and SPD has held power. See also: LAND; LANDESREGIERUNG; VOGEL, BERNHARD

THÜRINGER WALD
A hilly area of forest in the south-west of THÜRINGEN that is famous for hiking and includes the Rennsteig, a trail established in the last century running right through the forest. The area thrives on tourism. Glassware, clocks and toys are the local industries.

THYSSEN AG
The holding company of the Thyssen-Gruppe founded in 1953 with the original company dating from 1890. Members of the steel and engineering group are: THYSSEN INDUSTRIE AG, THYSSEN HANDELSUNION AG, and THYSSEN STAHL AG. Company headquarters are in DÜSSELDORF. Thyssen AG has some 132,000 employees.

TIB See: UNIVERSITÄTSBIBLIOTHEK HANNOVER UND TECHNISCHE INFORMATIONSBIBLIOTHEK

TIETMEYER, HANS (1931–   )
President of the DEUTSCHE BUNDESBANK since 1993 and member of the CDU.

TINA
Weekly fashion magazine established in 1975 and published by BAUER VERLAG. It has a circulation of some 1.5 million and carries articles on fashion, cosmetics and lifestyle.

TOEPFER INTERNATIONAL GmbH, ALFRED C.
Grain and feedstock trader founded in 1979. Company head-quarters are in HAMBURG. Toepfer has some 900 employees.

TOP BUSINESS

Monthly business magazine established in 1966 as *Industriemagazin* and targeted at managers in industry and commerce with analysis of successful companies and reports on key areas of politics and business.

TÖPFER, KLAUS (1938–   )

Economist and CDU politician who was minister at the Ministerium für Soziales, Gesundheit und Umwelt in RHEINLAND-PFALZ in 1985–1987. He then went to BONN as BUNDESMINISTER FÜR UMWELT, NATURSCHUTZ UND REAKTORSICHERHEIT in 1987–1992 and has been BUNDESMINISTER FÜR RAUMORDNUNG, BAUWESEN UND STÄDTEBAU since 1994.

TRABI

The *Trabant* was the people's car produced at Zwickau in the DDR. The car has a fibreglass body and a two-stroke engine and citizens had to wait up to 12 years before they received their new model. Spare parts were treated like gold-dust. Today the car has become something of a cult vehicle – particularly following the film *Go, Trabi, go* (1991) – and has outlived the joke that you could double the value of a *Trabi* by filling it with petrol!

TRANSRAPID

A fast rail link between HAMBURG and BERLIN officially due to open in 2005, although delays in construction make this date increasingly unlikely. The magnetic rail system is being built on a reinforced concrete structure five metres high and was estimated to cost around nine billion marks. Revised calculations suggest a price-tag nearer 12 billion. The rail link has been heavily criticised by the SPD and BÜNDNIS 90/DIE GRÜNEN as being an environmental disaster.

TRAUERARBEIT

Term in psychoanalysis used to denote a process of mourning, and particularly applied to atonement for the crimes committed in the DRITTES REICH since Alexander and Margarete Mitscherlich's key work *Die Unfähigkeit zu trauern* (1967) analysed the German people's inability to engage in *Trauerarbeit*. See also: VERGANGENHEITSBEWÄLTIGUNG

TRAUUNG

The marriage ceremony undertaken to join a man and woman in matrimony. In Germany there are two marriage ceremonies: *kirchliche Trauung* and *standesamtliche Trauung.* All marriages have to go through a *standesamtliche Trauung* (civil marriage) at a STANDESAMT in order to have legal validity. The *kirchliche Trauung* is optional.

TREUHANDANSTALT

The Treuhand was the trust body responsible for privatising DDR state enterprises. The trust inherited the bulk of East Germany's industrial facilities comprising around 10,000 large companies with 45,000 factories. The trust was also responsible for returning state assets such as KINDERGÄRTEN and sports facilities to local authorities, and businesses to their former owners. By the time the activities of the trust were wound up on 31 December 1994 around 14,500 enterprises from the former DDR had been returned to the private sector, some 3,661 businesses had been wound up, and 4,300 had been returned to previous owners. Matters previously handled by the Treuhand are now dealt with by the Bundesanstalt für vereinigungsbedingte Sonderaufgaben (BvS) under the auspices of the BUNDESMINISTERIUM DER FINANZEN. The trust left debts totalling DM 300 billion, which were picked up by the taxpayer. See also: KOMBINAT; VOLKSEIGENER BETRIEB

TRIER

The Roman monuments at Trier (RHEINLAND-PFALZ) are the most impressive north of the Alps, and they have been made a UNESCO world heritage site together with the cathedral and the Gothic Liebfrauenkirche.

TRIER, UNIVERSITÄT

University in RHEINLAND-PFALZ originally founded in 1423 (closed in 1798, re-opened in 1970) and teaching some 11,000 students. The Universität Trier has faculties of education and philosophy and psychology, languages and literature, history and politics and classical archaeology, Egyptology and art history and papyrology, economics and sociology and applied mathematics and ethnology, law, geography and geosciences.

TRITTIN, JÜRGEN (1954–)

Politician who joined DIE GRÜNEN in 1980 and has been spokesman for BÜNDNIS 90/DIE GRÜNEN since 1994. He was chairman of this FRAKTION in the LANDTAG in NIEDERSACHSEN in 1985–1986 and 1988–1990.

TROTTA, MARGARETHE VON (1942–)

Actor, film director and script writer who initially won acclaim as an actress in films by Fassbinder, ACHTERNBUSCH, her husband SCHLÖNDORFF and Chabrol, and later turned to directing. Together with Schlöndorff she scripted and directed *Die verlorene Ehre der Katharina Blum* (1975, based on the novel by H. Böll). Other films directed by Trotta include *Das zweite Erwachen der Christa Klages* (1978), *Die bleierne Zeit* (1981), *Rosa Luxemburg* (1986) and *Die Rückkehr* (1990).

TU See: *TECHNISCHE UNIVERSITÄT*

TÜBINGEN, EBERHARD-KARLS-UNIVERSITÄT

One of Germany's oldest universities, founded in 1477. The university is in BADEN-WÜRTTEMBERG and teaches some 26,000 students. The Eberhard-Karls-Universität Tübingen built up a strong reputation in philosophy and theology, and has departments of Protestant theology, Catholic theology, ecumenical theology, law, economics, medicine, philosophy, social sciences and education, languages and literature, history, classics and oriental studies, mathematics, physics, chemistry and pharmacology, biology, geosciences, computer science.

TUTOR

Generally a senior student who organises study groups in particular subject areas for less advanced students at a HOCHSCHULE. The term is also used to refer to a warden of a STUDENTENWOHNHEIM.

TUTORIUM

A group tutorial accompanying a course of study and intended to convey further in-depth knowledge of a subject, often provided during the GRUNDSTUDIUM. This type of teaching is also often organised by the AKADEMISCHES AUSLANDSAMT for foreign students to provide them with tuition to supplement a lecture series.

TÜV See: *TECHNISCHE ÜBERWACHUNGSVEREINE*

TV HÖREN + SEHEN
TV programme guide published weekly that also covers household, fashion, health, music and other general topics of interest to the family. It is published weekly by BAUER VERLAG with a circulation of 2.1 million.

TV KLAR
TV listings magazine published fortnightly by BAUER VERLAG with a circulation of 1.2 million.

TV MOVIE
TV guide established in 1991 and published fortnightly by BAUER VERLAG with a circulation of some 2.3 million. In addition to programme news it has articles on TV, cinema, videos, music and books.

TV NEU
TV guide established in 1992 and published by SPRINGER VERLAG in HAMBURG with a circulation of 861,000. It is aimed at younger viewers who use television day and night for information gathering.

TZ (TAGESZEITUNG)
Daily newspaper established in 1968 and published in MÜNCHEN by the Münchener Zeitungsverlag with a circulation of 152,000.

U-BAHN
The underground railway system in some big cities including BERLIN, MÜNCHEN and FRANKFURT AM MAIN.

ÜBERHANGMANDAT
When a party in a particular LAND gains more *Direktmandate* (ERSTSTIMMEN) in a BUNDESTAGSWAHL than the number of ZWEIT-STIMMEN allows for, the number of ABGEORDNETE in the BUNDESTAG increases beyond the prescribed number of 656. In the 1994 federal elections there was a record number of 16 *Überhangmandate*, partly because an increasing number of voters are casting their *Erststimme* and *Zweitstimme* for different parties (*Stimmensplitting*).

ÜBERREGIONAL
A term used to designate that an audience or group of people is being addressed at a level higher than the LAND, usually at the level of the BUND. It is frequently used of organisations and publications such as newpapers.

ÜBERREGIONALE ZEITUNGEN
The press in Germany is structured on the basis of local allegiances. Some newspapers such as BILD ZEITUNG, FRANKFURTER ALLGEMEINE ZEITUNG, FRANKFURTER RUNDSCHAU, SÜDDEUTSCHE ZEITUNG, DIE WELT are distributed nationally but still retain a strong regional readership and produce local sections for different parts of the region. These newspapers are therefore referred to as the 'supraregional press' rather than the national press. Perhaps the only truly national daily is the SPRINGER VERLAG tabloid *Bild Zeitung*, although this, too, is produced in localised editions. DIE ZEIT is a non-regional weekly broadsheet that is widely read in intellectual circles.

ÜBERSIEDLER
Generally used for citizens of the DDR who left the country during the summer and autum of 1989 before the BERLINER MAUER came down in November of that year. A trickle of emigrants coming through third countries became an exodus when Hungary opened up its border with Austria.

ÜBUNG
Courses provided for students in the GRUNDSTUDIUM which are intended to introduce them to aspects of the subject, academic methods and basic study skills.

UECKER, GÜNTHER (1930–   )
Sculptor and artist who left the DDR in 1955 after studying in BERLIN and continued his studies in DÜSSELDORF. He was a member of the *Gruppe Zero* and is best known for his nail pictures, comprising hundreds of nails driven into panels to form precise geometrical formations, generally white, as in *Nagelobjekt* (1963). He works with the kinetics of light and has created sculptures with light boxes and with fluorescent tubes, as in *Lichtregen* (1966). He has also worked on sculptures with ropes and string, and has been producing *Messerskulpturen* since 1984.

UHSE, BEATE (1919–   )
Founder of the Beate Uhse AG which owns a string of sex shops and blue-movie cinemas across Germany. She started out after the Second World War advising farmers' wives in northern Germany on contraception. In 1996 a Beate Uhse Erotik-Museum opened in BERLIN near Bahnhof Zoo, a similar venture having been foiled in MÜNCHEN.

UKRAINISCHE FREIE UNIVERSITÄT
Private university in MÜNCHEN founded in 1921 and teaching some 500 students. The Ukrainische Freie Universität has faculties of philosophy (arts), law and economics, education, Ukrainian studies. Languages of instruction are Ukrainian, English and German.

ULLSTEIN VERLAG GmbH & CO KG
Publishing company founded in 1887 and owned by SPRINGER

VERLAG in BERLIN. It publishes the widely read dailies BZ and BERLINER MORGENPOST.

ULM, UNIVERSITÄT
University in BADEN-WÜRTTEMBERG founded in 1967 and teaching some 6,000 students. The Universität Ulm has faculties of natural sciences, medicine, engineering, information science, mathematics.

UMSATZSTEUER (USt.)
A turnover tax in Germany (equivalent to value added tax) in which a tax is charged on the turnover of all goods and services supplied by a business. *Umsatzsteuer* is collected by the FINANZ-AMT, and the BUND and LÄNDER are jointly entitled to the revenues from the tax in accordance with federal law. The rate is currently 15%, with some goods and services (e.g. books, newspapers and magazines) attracting a reduced rate of 7%.

UMWELTBELASTUNG
Environmental pollution was driven to the top of the political agenda by the arrival of DIE GRÜNEN at the beginning of the 1980s and their election to the BUNDESTAG. They highlighted the plight of the forests by making the issue of WALDSTERBEN a matter for public debate, and the pressure brought to bear from all sides induced the larger parties to adopt environmental issues, making Germany the most environmentally aware country in Europe. National schemes include the DUALES SYSTEM DEUTSCHLAND, the GRÜNER PUNKT and the local institution of the WERTSTOFFAN-NAHMESTELLE.

UMWELTBUNDESAMT
Federal office for environmental affairs that is based in BERLIN and is part of the BUNDESMINISTERIUM FÜR UMWELT, NATURSCHUTZ UND REAKTORSICHERHEIT.

UMWELTSCHUTZ
Environmental protection is a big issue in Germany, with strict regulations governing the separation of waste in the home, trade and industry to permit recycling and reuse. There are also tough regulations on air pollution, noise, waste disposal and the use of

pesticides. See also: DIE GRÜNEN; DUALES SYSTEM DEUTSCHLAND; GRÜNER PUNKT; LÄRMSCHUTZ; UMWELTBELASTUNG; WERTSTOFFAN-NAHMESTELLE

UNBEDENKLICHKEITSBESCHEINIGUNG

A clearance certificate issued by the FINANZAMT stating that an individual has met all their tax obligations. Such a certificate is required for the award of public contracts and for entry in the GRUNDBUCH when ownership of land is transferred.

UNFALLVERSICHERUNG

Statutory accident insurance (*gesetzliche Unfallversicherung*) is part of SOZIALVERSICHERUNG and funded by contributions from the ARBEITGEBER. It covers employees against industrial accidents and work-related illnesses and provides a number of benefits including treatment, rehabilitation, industrial-injury pension, death benefit and surviving dependant's pension.

UNGARNDEUTSCHE

The ethnic German minority population living in Hungary numbering roughly 240,000. They are Hungary's largest ethnic minority and the remnants of a larger population of over half a million which was deported under the POTSDAMER ABKOMMEN at the end of the Second World War. The remaining Germans were accorded equal rights under Communist rule and underwent a cultural revival during the 1970s and 1980s.

UNGELERNTER ARBEITER

An unskilled worker employed in jobs where the tasks they are required to perform can be learned in a matter of hours or days without the need for sophisticated training. See also: ARBEITER

UNI See: *UNIVERSITÄT*

UNIVERSALBANKEN

Full-service banks carrying out all standard banking transactions. The 'big three' Universalbanken are the DEUTSCHE BANK, the DRESDNER BANK and the COMMERZBANK. *Universalbanken* fall into three main categories: *private Geschäftsbanken*, ÖFFENTLICH-RECHTLICHE KREDITINSTITUTE and KREDITGENOSSENSCHAFTEN.

UNIVERSITÄT

Universitäten (wissenschaftliche Hochschulen) are traditionally the oldest centres of scholarship with the highest academic status. Students at university during the nineteenth century were very much the privileged few and professors enjoyed great respect and prestige within society. The reputation of these seats of learning suffered when they offered little resistance to Hitler and many incumbents lost their posts in the period of denazification after the Second World War. The old institutions proved slow to adapt to change and came under attack in the 1960s, when student unrest challenged established academic precepts. The main challenges to the universities at present are overcrowding and consequent lack of proper supervision, exacerbated by staff shortages and an ageing professorial population. See also: HOCHSCHULEN

UNIVERSITÄTSBIBLIOTHEK HANNOVER UND TECHNISCHE INFORMATIONSBIBLIOTHEK (TIB)

A technical library founded in HANNOVER in 1831 with a collection of 4.1 million volumes and microfiches. It also has a large collection of research reports, patents, standards, conference proceedings and doctoral dissertations, and specialises in scientific and technical literature in Slavonic and Oriental languages. The library is a national centre for the translation of technical and scientific literature.

UNTER DEN LINDEN

The majestic boulevard in BERLIN that was once imperial Berlin's main street starting at the BRANDENBURGER TOR. It has a central island of lime trees and is regaining its place in the city as a premier shopping mall following its 40-year spell as a DDR cul-de-sac ending in the BERLINER MAUER.

UNTERHALTSGELD

Subsistence allowance paid by the BUNDESANSTALT FÜR ARBEIT to individuals during periods of further training or retraining. The maintenance payments made by a father for the upkeep of a child following divorce are sometimes informally referred to as *Unterhaltsgeld.*

USt. See: *UMSATZSTEUER*

VAP See: *VEREIN DER AUSLÄNDISCHEN PRESSE IN DER BRD*

VARTA AG
Holding company with interests in batteries and plastics. Company headquarters are in Bad Homburg (HESSEN). Varta has some 13,000 employees.

VDE See: *VERBAND DEUTSCHER ELEKTRO-TECHNIKER e.V.*

VDE-SICHERHEITSZEICHEN See: *VERBAND DEUTSCHER ELEKTROTECHNIKER e.V.*

VDI See: *VEREIN DEUTSCHER INGENIEURE*

VDI-NACHRICHTEN
Weekly business publication established in 1946 and published by VDI-Verlag in DÜSSELDORF with a circulation of 172,000. It has reports on all areas of business and technology with a readership among middle and senior management. See also: VEREIN DEUTSCHER INGENIEURE

VDI-NACHRICHTEN MAGAZIN
A supplement to VDI-NACHRICHTEN established in 1984 and published monthly. It covers leisure interests and promotes industry as integral to Western culture. See also: VEREIN DEUTSCHER INGENIEURE

VDS See: *VEREINIGTE DEUTSCHE STUDENTEN-SCHAFTEN*

VDZ See: *VERBAND DEUTSCHER ZEITSCHRIFTEN-VERLEGER e.V.*

VEB See: *VOLKSEIGENER BETRIEB*

VEBA AG

Germany's largest energy distributor with interests in oil, gas and nuclear power founded in 1929. VEBA also has a majority stake in Germany's biggest chain of filling stations ARAL and owns STINNES AG. In 1995, VEBA received a licence to link up 10,000 households in the RUHRGEBIET to a multimedia network in the first step of its ambitions to become a telecoms operator to rival privatised DEUTSCHE TELEKOM. Company headquarters are in DÜSSELDORF. VEBA has some 127,000 employees.

VEDES

The Vereinigung der Spielwaren-Fachgeschäfte is a cooperative of Germany's specialist toy retailers. It is based in NÜRNBERG and the original purpose was to enable members to purchase goods at preferential rates. Today the cooperative also offers members an array of services such as bookkeeping, market research and advertising.

VERANLAGTE EINKOMMENSTEUER

Each individual with taxable income (*Einkommen*) is obliged to declare it to the FINANZAMT in the *Einkommensteuererklärung* at or after the end of the fiscal year when this income is assessed (*Einkommensteuerveranlagung*). Individuals whose sole income is from employment are exempt from this obligation provided their income does not exceed a certain amount (1995: DM 27,000 for individuals, DM 54,000 for married couples) unless they have other income exceeding DM 800 annually (or belong to certain other groups). The amount of tax payable is assessed by the Finanzamt according to an *Einkommensteuertabelle* after the end of the fiscal year and quarterly advance payments are determined for the following year.

VERBAND DER TECHNISCHEN ÜBERWACHUNGS-VEREINE e.V. (VdTÜV)

The federation of TECHNISCHE ÜBERWACHUNGSVEREINE promotes the interests of the member associations at the level of the BUND and advises the government and authorities on technical issues affecting legislation. It ensures that technical testing is uniform, and contributes to the compilation of standards and guidelines.

VERBAND DEUTSCHER ELEKTROTECHNIKER e.V. (VDE)

The association of German electrical engineers promotes research and training in electrical engineering, electronics and IT. The VDE also issues safety standards and guidelines relating to these areas and cooperates with the DEUTSCHES INSTITUT FÜR NORMUNG in the compilation of DIN standards. The association tests products for meeting the VDE specifications laid down for the award of the *VDE-Sicherheitszeichen.*

VERBAND DEUTSCHER SCHRIFTSTELLER e.V. FACHGRUPPE LITERATUR (VS)

The association of German writers was founded in 1969 and joined the union *IG Druck und Papier* in 1974 in order to promote the socio-political aims of authors.

VERBAND DEUTSCHER ZEITSCHRIFTENVERLEGER e.V. (VDZ)

The association of German magazine publishers was founded to promote the interests of magazine publishers. There are regional associations that look after the members' interests at LAND level.

VERBANDSGEMEINDE

A group of small GEMEINDEN belonging to a KREIS that join together to form a GROSSGEMEINDE in RHEINLAND-PFALZ.

VEREIN See: *EINGETRAGENER VEREIN*

VEREIN DER AUSLÄNDISCHEN PRESSE IN DER BRD (VAP)

Association representing the interests of the foreign press in Germany.

VEREIN DEUTSCHER INGENIEURE (VDI)

The association of German engineers promotes the exchange of experience between engineers and interdisciplinary information exchange. The VDI publishes guidelines, reference books, reports and other documentation, promotes the interests of engineering and advises at the level of the BUND, is active in holding conferences and seminars, and fosters contacts abroad.

VEREIN FREIWILLIGE SELBSTKONTROLLE FERNSEHEN (FSF)

A self-regulatory watchdog for the burgeoning commercial TV industry. The body was established by the private channels in 1994 and is intended to regulate the broadcasting of violence and erotica.

VEREINIGTE DEUTSCHE STUDENTENSCHAFTEN (VDS)

Voluntary umbrella organisation for STUDENTENSCHAFTEN, which promotes the interests of students and fosters international contacts. See also: JUGENDVERBÄNDE

VEREINIGTE WIRTSCHAFTSDIENSTE (VWD)

A business news agency that publishes around 20 specialist reports on industry each day.

VEREINSREGISTER

The register of non-profit-making *Vereine*. See also: EINGETRAGENER VEREIN

VERFASSTE STUDENTENSCHAFT

Institutional framework for student representation generally constituted in the form of the ALLGEMEINER STUDENTENAUSSCHUSS, STUDENTENPARLAMENT and the FACHSCHAFTEN. This type of autonomous framework for students has been abolished in BADEN-WÜRTTEMBERG and BAYERN by *Landeshochschulgesetze* but partial re-introduction is on the cards and there tend to be unofficial *verfaßte Studentenschaften* in HOCHSCHULEN in those LÄNDER. Students have to become members of the *verfaßte Studentenschaft* and pay their membership dues when they enrol (EINSCHREIBUNG).

VERFASSUNG

The constitution of the BRD is enshrined in the GRUNDGESETZ. The constitutional bodies include the BUNDESTAG, the BUNDESRAT, the BUNDESPRÄSIDENT, the BUNDESREGIERUNG and the BUNDESVERFAS-

SUNGSGERICHT. A commission comprising members of the Bundesrat and Bundestag was set up in 1992 to advise on changes to the Grundgesetz made necessary by the EINI-GUNGSVERTRAG. Each LAND also has a *Verfassung.*

VERFASSUNGSWIDRIGE ORGANISATIONEN
Organisations that have been declared by the BUNDESVERFAS-SUNGSGERICHT to be contrary to the constitution. See also: PARTEIVERBOT

VERGANGENHEITSBEWÄLTIGUNG
The psychological process of coming to terms with the past – usually applied to the National Socialist past. It is a controversial term in that it suggests a definitive resolution of a problem. See also: TRAUERARBEIT

VERGNÜGUNGSSTEUER
A tax on entertainment at dance venues, cinemas and theatres that is collected by GEMEINDEN in some LÄNDER. It is either based on a percentage of the sale of tickets or collected as a lump sum according to the size of the premises.

VERKEHRSSÜNDERKARTEI See:
VERKEHRSZENTRALREGISTER

VERKEHRSWACHT
One of more than 500 local non-profit-making organisations committed to increasing road safety through cooperation with the authorities and heightening a sense of responsibility in all road-users. Individual *Verkehrswachten* are grouped together in a *Landes-Verkehrswacht.* See also: DEUTSCHE VERKEHRSWACHT

VERKEHRSZENTRALREGISTER
The central register of traffic offences maintained by the KRAFTFAHRT-BUNDESAMT. Each serious traffic offence is allocated points on a scale of one to seven and a driver receives a written warning when nine points have been reached. If a driver clocks up 14 points they have to retake the theoretical test and possibly the practical test. The FÜHRERSCHEIN is taken away if a total of 18 points is reached in any two years.

VERLEGER
Publisher – either a publishing firm (*Verlag*) or its legal represen-tative. A newspaper publisher is generally the proprietor of the newspaper. See also: HERAUSGEBER

VERMÖGENSBILDUNG
Benefit provided by ARBEITGEBER which is generally negotiated in the annual payround with the GEWERKSCHAFTEN to encourage lower-paid ARBEITNEHMER to build up assets. The government pays the employee 10% of the amount provided by the *Arbeitgeber* to a maximum of DM 936, provided that the taxable income of the employee does not exceed DM 27,000 in the cal-endar year in question. The money has to be invested for pur-poses of purchasing shares or real property.

VERPACKUNGSVERORDNUNG
A law enacted in 1991 requiring all packaging to be made of recyclable material and requiring manufacturers and distributors to take back packaging and reuse or recycle it. See also: DUALES SYSTEM DEUTSCHLAND; GRÜNER PUNKT; WERTSTOFFANNAHMESTELLE

VERSICHERUNGSPFLICHT
The obligation to be insured and to pay SOZIALVERSICHERUNG laid down in law. All vehicle owners have an obligation to purchase car insurance privately, and certain professions and trades are obliged to take out third-party liability insurance.

VERTEIDIGUNGSMINISTER See: *BUNDESMINISTER DER VERTEIDIGUNG*

VERTRIEBENE
The German citizens from the DEUTSCHE OSTGEBIETE or ethnic Germans living outside the borders of 31 December 1937 who fled the advancing Soviet armies or were forcibly repatriated between 1945 and 1947 west of the ODER-NEISSE-LINIE in accor-dance with the POTSDAMER ABKOMMEN. Over 14 million Germans either fled or were forcibly repatriated in the immediate after-math of the Second World War, with 2 million perishing in the process. See also: LASTENAUSGLEICH

VEW VEREINIGTE ELEKTRIZITÄTSWERKE WESTFALEN AG

Electricity generation and distribution company founded in 1925. Company headquarters are in DORTMUND. VEW has some 14,000 employees.

VIAG AG

Holding company with interests in energy, aluminium, chemicals, glass, packaging, transport and logistics. Company headquarters are in MÜNCHEN. VIAG has some 86,000 employees.

VILLEROY & BOCH AG

Family-owned manufacturer of high-quality china founded in 1748. Company headquarters are in Mettlach (SAARLAND). The group has some 12,700 employees.

VIZEKANZLER

The position of deputy to the BUNDESKANZLER has traditionally been held by the AUSSENMINISTER (a member of the junior coalition partner FDP) since the 1970s.

VOGEL, BERNHARD (1932–   )

Philosopher and CDU politician. He was a member of the BUNDESTAG in 1965–1967 and minister of culture in RHEINLAND-PFALZ in 1967–1976 before being elected MINISTERPRÄSIDENT there in 1976–1988. He has been Ministerpräsident of THÜRINGEN since 1992 and heads a coalition government between the CDU and SPD.

VOGTLAND

A hilly plateau with deep valleys in south-west SACHSEN, named after the Vogts (*Vögte*) – administrators of the Holy Roman Empire. It has had an important textile industry since the sixteenth century, centred on the silk town of Plauen. The Vogtland is a popular tourist destination with a number of spas, and the 'Musikwinkel' is famous for the production of handmade musical instruments.

VOLK

This word denoting 'people' came into disrepute under Hitler, who used it to give the Germans a sense of togetherness so that they could identify with his policies of racial purity. In the post-war BRD its associations made usage problematic whereas in the DDR it was used freely as a socialist concept. During the WENDE the word became prominent in the slogans '*Wir sind das Volk*' and '*Wir sind ein Volk*'.

VÖLKISCH
A term used to denote the concept of a 'national' identity and used by the Nazis in particular to refer to a nationalism that came to be associated with ethnic purity and anti-Semitism. The term is particularly associated with the newspaper *Völkischer Beobachter*, the mouthpiece of Hitler's NSDAP (*National-sozialistische Deutsche Arbeiterpartei*).

VÖLKLINGEN
The nineteenth-century ironworks in Völklingen (SAARLAND) were the first industrial site to be made a UNESCO world heritage site.

VOLKSABSTIMMUNG
At the level of the BUND, the GRUNDGESETZ only provides for a referendum in the case of territorial changes, whereas some LÄNDER offer greater scope in their constitutions. In May 1996, a referendum proved decisive in rejecting the proposed merger between the Länder of BERLIN and BRANDENBURG. See also: BÜRGERENTSCHEID

VOLKSBANKEN
Cooperative banks traditionally serving the MITTELSTAND with a full range of banking services. In 1972 they joined forces with the RAIFFEISENBANKEN in the BUNDESVERBAND DER DEUTSCHEN VOLKS-BANKEN UND RAIFFEISENBANKEN E.V. See also: KREDITGENOSSEN-SCHAFTEN

VOLKSDEUTSCHE
A term used by the Nazi regime to refer to ethnic Germans living outside the 1937 borders of Germany and Austria in eastern and south-eastern Europe. Many were forcibly repatriated between 1945 and 1947 in accordance with the POTSDAMER ABKOM-MEN. See also: VERTRIEBENE

VOLKSEIGENER BETRIEB (VEB)
A nationalised enterprise in the former DDR. In 1990 all the

VEBs were converted to GMBHS or AGS and sold off or wound up by the TREUHANDANSTALT.

VOLKSENTSCHEID See: *VOLKSABSTIMMUNG*

VOLKSFEST
A local festival often related to the tradition of church festivals and associated with an annual market. In the summer and autumn Germany abounds with a plethora of *Volksfeste* celebrating new beer or wine.

VOLKSHOCHSCHULE
An adult education centre run by the local authorities to provide evening courses for adult learners. They provide a wide variety of courses ranging from foreign languages to art.

VOLKSKAMMER
The national assembly of the DDR, which was housed in the PALAST DER REPUBLIK.

VOLKSMARSCH
An organised walk when people get together to go on a long hike through the country. Distances can be anything up to 40 km., although there are usually two routes – a longer one, and a shorter one for the less robust.

VOLKSVERHETZUNG
Incitement to racial hatred is a criminal offence punishable by a prison sentence of between three months and five years. Anybody promoting violence or hatred against a particular section of the population is liable to be arrested for disturbing the peace or infringing MENSCHENWÜRDE.

VOLKSWAGEN AG
Manufacturer of the famous 'people's car', founded in 1936 as a state enterprise. The 'Beetle' (*Käfer*) was first produced before the Second World War (conceived as a mass-produced car for the ordinary person), and Volkswagen forged ahead in the 1950s and 1960s to become a symbol of the WIRTSCHAFTSWUNDER as the distinctive design and price captured the spirit of the times. New models and robots revitalised the company in the 1970s and

1980s. Privatisation started in the 1960s when the BUND sold half its stake-holding, and now NIEDERSACHSEN has a 20% shareholding. The company owns AUDI, Seat in Spain and Skoda in the Czech Republic. Company headquarters are in Wolfsburg (Niedersachsen). Volkswagen has some 244,000 employees.

VOLKSWAGEN-STIFTUNG
Foundation created in 1961 and based in HANNOVER. It has capital of over three billion marks derived from its right to dividends on shares held by the BUND and NIEDERSACHSEN in VOLKSWAGEN. The foundation gives grants to promote research and training in science, technology and the humanities.

VOLLAUSBILDUNG
The training following the GRUNDAUSBILDUNG in the BUNDESWEHR. It is mainly carried out at the squad and platoon level.

VOLLPROGRAMM
A full programme schedule for TV including news, features, sport and culture.

VON DER HEYDT-MUSEUM
A collection of French Impressionists and German painting from the 19th and 20th centuries in WUPPERTAL.

VORDIPLOM
An intermediate examination, especially in the sciences, taken after a minimum of four SEMESTER of study (GRUNDSTUDIUM) at HOCHSCHULEN. The *Vordiplom* does not have the status of a full qualification.

VORLESUNGSVERZEICHNIS
The handbook of lectures produced each SEMESTER by a HOCHSCHULE, giving the timetable for all lectures and classes scheduled for that *Semester.* It normally includes a list of the teaching staff at the *Hochschule.*

VORRUHESTAND
Early retirement has been used as a way of reducing unemployment by means of subsidies provided by the BUNDESANSTALT FÜR ARBEIT.

VORRUHESTANDSGELD
Money paid by the BUNDESANSTALT FÜR ARBEIT to individuals taking early retirement.

VORSCHULERZIEHUNG
Pre-school education in nursery schools for children aged three to six. See also: KINDERGARTEN

VORSPRUNG DURCH TECHNIK
A trail-blazing advertising slogan meaning 'progress through technology' originated in the early 1980s for VOLKSWAGEN as the centre of an advertising campaign to promote their AUDI range as an up-market competitor to BMW. The slogan has endured to represent the excellent qualities of German engineering.

VORSTAND
The board of management of a company with executive responsibility for the day-to-day running of the company. The *Vorstand* is appointed by the AUFSICHTSRAT and consists of VORSTANDSMIT-GLIEDER.

The term *Vorstand* is also applied generally to the executive body of other organisations.

VORSTANDSMITGLIED
A member of the VORSTAND of a company, appointed by the AUF-SICHTSRAT.

VOSCHERAU, HENNING (1941–   )
Lawyer and SPD politician. He has been a member of the BÜRGER-SCHAFT in HAMBURG since 1974 and was chairman of the SPD-FRAKTION in 1982–1987 before becoming Erster Bürgermeister of Hamburg with an SPD majority in 1988. See also: BÜRGERMEISTER, ERSTER

VOSTELL, WOLF (1932–   )
Artist who set a Cadillac in a wall of concrete on the KURFÜRSTEN-DAMM to celebrate BERLIN'S 750th anniversary in 1987. He studied in KÖLN, WUPPERTAL, Paris and DÜSSELDORF, and started by making collages which he called décollages because they consisted of parts of torn-down posters. He established his reputation with the Fluxus group in the 1960s, which he joined together with

J. Beuys, and by organising happenings in Germany, Paris and New York. He has continued making political statements in his art since then.

VOX

A commercial TV channel with a majority stake held by media mogul Rupert Murdoch and a substantial stake by UFA, a subsidiary of BERTELSMANN, transmitting news, films, sport and talkshows.

VS See: *VERBAND DEUTSCHER SCHRIFTSTELLER e.V.*

VWD See: *VEREINIGTE WIRTSCHAFTSDIENSTE*

WACKER-CHEMIE GmbH
Chemicals company founded in 1914, manufacturing and distributing a range of plastics and chemical products with a 50% shareholding being owned by HOECHST. Company headquarters are in MÜNCHEN. Wacker-Chemie has some 13,000 employees.

WAECHTER, FRIEDRICH KARL (1937–   )
Cartoonist and writer famous for his satirical cartoons in *Pardon, Zeitmagazin* and *Titanic*. He has also written and illustrated many children's books including *Der Anti-Struwwelpeter* (1970), *Wir können noch viel zusammen machen* (1973) and *Wahrscheinlich guckt wieder kein Schwein* (1978). He was awarded the Deutscher Jugendbuchpreis (DEUTSCHER JUGENDLITERATURPREIS) in 1975.

WAHL See: *BUNDESTAGSWAHL*

WAHLBEAMTER
A full-time local-government official who is directly elected in southern Germany or appointed by the council for a fixed term of office.

WAHLBERECHTIGTER
Anybody entitled to vote, in KOMMUNALWAHLEN, LANDTAGSWAHLEN, BUNDESTAGSWAHLEN and other (e.g. European) elections.

WAHLKREIS
A constituency in which a representative is elected. See also: BUNDESTAGSWAHL; LANDTAGSWAHL

WAHLLEITER
The official in charge of an election with responsibility for overseeing that the election is properly carried out and that the votes are counted correctly.

WAHLLISTE
The list of candidates putting themselves forward, for KOMMUNAL-WAHLEN, LANDTAGSWAHLEN and BUNDESTAGSWAHLEN.

WAHLPERIODE
The length of time for which the GEMEINDEVERTRETUNG, LANDTAG or BUNDESTAG is elected. The Bundestag and the Landtage in most of the LÄNDER are elected for a legislative period of four years.

WAHLPFLICHTVERANSTALTUNGEN
A group of elective courses from which students have to select. It is necessary to attend a prescribed number, which is laid down in the STUDIENORDNUNG or PRÜFUNGSORDNUNG.

WAHLRECHT
Aktives Wahlrecht constitutes the right of an individual to vote in KOMMUNALWAHLEN, LANDTAGSWAHLEN, BUNDESTAGSWAHLEN and other (e.g. European) elections. *Passives Wahlrecht* constitutes the eligibility of an individual to stand in such elections.

WAHLSCHEIN
The polling card that has to be presented at the polling station or sent in to the election officer in the case of a BRIEFWAHL.

WÄHRUNGSREFORM
The currency reform was introduced by the Western Allies on 20 June 1948 and replaced the old *Reichsmark* with the DEUTSCHE MARK (DM). This eliminated inflation at a stroke and paved the way for the BRD'S WIRTSCHAFTSWUNDER but was the first step in the separation of east and west Germany. See also: BUNDESREPUBLIK DEUTSCHLAND; DEUTSCHE DEMOKRATISCHE REPUBLIK

WAIGEL, THEO (1939–   )
Lawyer and CSU politician who has been chairman of the CSU since 1988. He was appointed BUNDESMINISTER DER FINANZEN in 1989.

WALDECK
An independent state for seven centuries, the Waldeck is now part of HESSEN and NIEDERSACHSEN. Waldeck-Frankenberg is a

KREIS in Hessen and the area is a quiet rural district around the medieval towns of Waldeck and Frankenberg. The Edersee is a massive reservoir created at the end of the nineteenth century in the middle of the region by damming the river Eder.

WALDORFSCHULEN
Private schools, the first of which was started in 1919 in STUTTGART by the head of the Waldorf-Astoria-Zigarettenfabrik for his workers. Philosopher and scientist Rudolf Steiner was the first headmaster and he organised the school based on anthroposophical principles. The schools were banned by the Nazis but many schools started up again after the Second World War and many were founded abroad. Teaching at the schools centres on art, music and handicrafts and the same teacher takes a class up to the eighth year at school. Class 12 is the final year of the Waldorf education but pupils normally choose to stay on for the 13th year to prepare for the ABITUR.

WALDSTERBEN
Forest decline in which trees become sick and die as a result of pollution from cars, power stations, industry and agriculture. This phenomenon came to prominence in the early 1980s and provided a focus for the Green movement in Germany.

Acidic compounds cause the crowns of the trees to shed needles and leaves, and restrict the development of root systems and thus the uptake of nutrients. A survey carried out in 1994 estimated that 25% of trees were significantly damaged and some 40% of the tree stand had sustained some damage. THÜRINGEN was the LAND in which trees had sustained the greatest damage. See also: DIE GRÜNEN

WALLRAF-RICHARTZ-MUSEUM
Museum in KÖLN founded in 1824 and holding an important collection of the works of the fifteenth-century *Altkölner Malerschule*, as well as galleries with European painting, sculpture and prints up to the Impressionists. The modern galleries of the Museum Ludwig present a collection of twentieth-century art including German Expressionists and Pop Art including Andy Warhol. See also: LUDWIG, PETER

WALLRAFF, GÜNTER (1942–   )

Investigative journalist whose books have caused sensation and uproar. *Der Aufmacher* (1977), based on his exeriences of working incognito for BILD ZEITUNG, was an indictment of the scurrilous journalistic techniques used by the newspaper. His exposé of German industry *Ganz unten* (1985), written after posing as a Turkish worker for two years, revealed exploitation of foreign workers in big companies and gained international publicity. His other works include *Akteneinsicht. Bericht zur Gesinnungslage des Staatsschutzes* (1987) and *Mein Tagebuch aus der Bundeswehr* (1992).

WALSER, MARTIN (1927–   )

Writer who initially worked as a radio and TV editor for the SÜD-DEUTSCHER RUNDFUNK before becoming one of Germany's most successful and prolific post-war novelists. His writing presents a critical picture of life in the BRD and constantly returns to the theme of the individual struggling in vain to achieve fulfilment. Conflicts in relationships form the basis of much of his writing, which includes *Ehen in Philippsburg* (1957), *Halbzeit* (1960), *Seelenarbeit* (1979), *Die Verteidigung der Kindheit* (1991) and *Ohne einander* (1993). Walser has also written numerous short stories, essays, plays and radio plays, and was awarded the GEORG-BÜCHNER-PREIS in 1981.

WALTER BAU AG

Construction company founded in 1876. Company headquarters are in AUGSBURG. Walter has some 13,000 employees.

WARENKORB

'Basket of goods' – the combination of goods and services used to define the LEBENSHALTUNGSKOSTEN.

WASMEIER, MARKUS (1963–   )

Alpine skier and gold medalist at the 1994 Winter Olympics in Norway. He was world champion for the giant slalom in 1985, and retired in 1994 after being voted *Sportler des Jahres.*

WASSERSCHUTZPOLIZEI

The river police are responsible for policing commercial traffic and leisure craft on inland waterways, lakes etc. They also supervise the transport of dangerous goods.

WATT
The coastal mud flats along the *Nordseeküste* reaching up to 30 km. in places, where flats beyond the sea barriers protecting inland areas are only above sea level when the tide is out. Trips across the *Watt* in high horse-drawn carts are a popular tourist attraction.

WAZ See: *WESTDEUTSCHE ALLGEMEINE ZEITUNG*

WBO See: *WEHRBESCHWERDEORDNUNG*

WdB See: *WEHRBEAUFTRAGTER DES DEUTSCHEN BUNDESTAGES*

WDR See: *WESTDEUTSCHER RUNDFUNK*

WECKER, KONSTANTIN (1947–   )
Political song writer and poet who trained as a pianist and studied philosophy and psychology in MÜNCHEN. His anarchical songs brought him popularity in the 1970s and he formed a band in 1974. Wecker recorded his first LP in 1972 (*Die sadopoetischen Gesänge des Konstantin Amadeus Wecker*) and has produced numerous recordings since then including *Liebesflug* (1981), *Konzert '90* (1990) and *Uferlos* (1992, also a novel). He has also performed as an opera singer and jazz pianist.

WEHRBEAUFTRAGTER DES DEUTSCHEN BUNDESTAGES (WdB)
The commissioner for the armed forces is responsible for protecting the constitutional rights of service personnel and assisting the BUNDESTAG in supervising the BUNDESWEHR. The *Wehrbeauftragter* is elected by the Bundestag and serves for a term of five years. Under the GRUNDGESETZ members of the Bundeswehr have the right to take their complaints directly to the *Wehrbeauftragter* without going through their immediate superiors. The commissioner can demand access to papers and records to assist in settling any complaints.

WEHRBESCHWERDEORDNUNG (WBO)
The regulations governing the handling of complaints by members of the armed forces. See: WEHRBEAUFTRAGTER DES DEUTSCHEN BUNDESTAGES

WEHRDIENST
The basic military service of 10 months that has to be served by all conscripts. Military service generally begins in the year in which a male individual attains the age of 19 years. A person can generally not be called up for military service after the age of 28 except in certain cases where eligibility continues until 32.

Individuals unfit for military service on physical or mental grounds, and certain classes of convicted criminals, are excluded from military service. Ordained priests and the disabled are exempt from military service as are certain WEHRPFLICHTIGE who have lost close relatives in military action or in war. Individuals who undertake to serve for a minimum of eight years in civil defence or two years in voluntary service overseas are released from their obligation to do military service. Conscientious objectors (KRIEGSDIENSTVERWEIGERER) are obliged to do ZIVILDIENST which is one third longer.

WEHRPFLICHT
The obligation of a German citizen fit for military service to serve in the BUNDESWEHR. See also: WEHRDIENST

WEHRPFLICHTIGER
An individual eligible to be called up for WEHRDIENST.

WEIHNACHTEN
Heiliger Abend (Christmas Eve) is not an official public holiday but most offices and companies are closed to allow employees to do last-minute shopping before the shops close at lunchtime. The WEIHNACHTSBAUM is set up in the late afternoon and the presents are distributed around the tree in the evening. The *1. Weihnachtstag* (Christmas Day) and the *2. Weihnachtstag* (Boxing Day) are public holidays throughout Germany. If Christmas falls at a weekend, days are not granted in lieu and any time off must be taken as holiday.

WEIHNACHTSBAUM

The traditional Christmas tree without which no German Christmas would be complete. The beginning of Advent marks a burgeoning of Christmas trees in public places. However, in family homes children have to wait with bated breath for the *Weihnachtsbaum* or *Christbaum* to go up on Christmas Eve. It is decked out with baubles, *Engelshaar*, *Lametta* and all manner of other decorations and sometimes still lit with genuine candles. On 6 January (HEILIGE DREI KÖNIGE) the tree comes down again and is religiously recycled in line with the country's strict recycling laws. In some rural districts the tree stays up until Candlemas on 2 February (*Lichtmeß*).

WEIHNACHTSGRATIFIKATION

A Christmas bonus paid by ARBEITGEBER to ARBEITNEHMER. See also: DREIZEHNTES MONATSGEHALT

WEIHNACHTSMARKT

A Christmas market held in many German cities during the four weeks of Advent. Traditionally Christmas decorations are sold including toys, wooden crib figures, decorations from the ERZGEBIRGE, glassware, and of course traditional gingerbread (*Lebkuchen*) and other delicacies. Mulled wine (*Glühwein*) is also sold at stands. The most famous *Weihnachtsmarkt* (*Christkindlmarkt*) has been held at NÜRNBERG for more than 400 years. This particular Christmas market is characterised by the abundance of traditional wooden carved crib figures on display.

WEIMAR, HOCHSCHULE FÜR ARCHITEKTUR UND BAUWESEN

School of architecture in THÜRINGEN founded in 1860 and teaching some 3,000 students.

WEIMARER KLASSIK See: *KLASSIK*; *STIFTUNG WEIMARER KLASSIK*

WEIMARER REPUBLIK

The democratic republic formed in Germany in 1919 after the end of the First World War. It collapsed after Hitler came to power in 1933. The political system in the BRD after the Second

World War sought to avoid repeating features that permitted Hitler's rise to power. A notable example is the FÜNFPROZENT-KLAUSEL, designed to prevent the plethora of *Splitterparteien* that fragmented the Weimar parliament.

WEINFEST
A wine festival held at the time of the grape harvest in many wine-growing areas such as FRANKEN and the RHEINLAND.

WEISSWURSTÄQUATOR
A hypothetical line along the river Main that separates the Bavarians from what are affectionately termed the *Saupreußen* to the north.

WEITERBILDUNG See: *ERWACHSENENBILDUNG*

WEIZSÄCKER, CARL FRIEDRICH FREIHERR VON (1912–   )
Physicist and philosopher who worked on theoretical nuclear physics, astrophysics and cosmology. He was professor of philosophy at HAMBURG (UNIVERSITÄT) from 1957 to 1969 and director of the Max-Planck-Institut for research into living conditions in the industrial world at Starnberg (BAYERN). He has made significant contributions to the understanding of contemporary problems in physics, the philosophy of science and scientific theory, and in particular to research in the area of peace studies. His publications include *Die Wissenschaft im Atomzeitalter* (1957), *Die Einheit der Natur* (1971), *Der bedrohte Frieden. Politische Aufsätze 1945–1981* (1981), *Aufbau der Physik* (1985) and *Der Mensch in seiner Geschichte* (1991).

WEIZSÄCKER, RICHARD FREIHERR VON (1920–   )
Lawyer and CDU politician who was BUNDESPRÄSIDENT in 1984–1994. He studied at Oxford, Grenoble and GÖTTINGEN (GEORG-AUGUST-UNIVERSITÄT) before working in industry and then as a commercial lawyer and RECHTSANWALT in 1967–1970 and in 1979–1981, and was president of the Deutscher Evangelischer Kirchentag in 1969–1984. Weizsäcker joined the CDU in 1954. He was MITGLIED DES BUNDESTAGES in 1969–1981 and Vizepräsident des Bundestages in 1979–1981. He was a member of

the ABGEORDNETENHAUS in BERLIN in 1979–1984, and was REGIEREN-DER BÜRGERMEISTER of West Berlin in 1981–1984. In 1984 he was elected BUNDESPRÄSIDENT, being reelected in 1989 across party lines. Weizsäcker worked for reconciliation with eastern Europe and enjoys great respect in Germany and internationally as a man of high moral principles.

WELLA AG
Cosmetics, health and household products company founded in 1880. Company headquarters are in Darmstadt (HESSEN). Wella has some 16,000 employees.

WELT See: *DIE WELT*

WELT AM SONNTAG
A serious Sunday newspaper established in 1948 and published by right-wing SPRINGER VERLAG with a circulation of 401,000. The paper is mainly distributed in HAMBURG and NORDRHEIN-WESTFALEN and is geared to the affluent business community. It also has a supplement covering travel and culture.

WELT-CENTRUM BÜRO, INFORMATION, TELEKOMMUNIKATION See: *CeBIT*

WELTMESSE DER HAUSGERÄTETECHNIK See: *DOMOTECHNICA*

WELTMESSE DES PFERDESPORTS See: *EQUITANA*

WELTMESSE FÜR TEPPICHE UND BODEN-BELÄGE See: *DOMOTEX HANNOVER*

WENDE
Meaning 'change' or 'turning-point', *Wende* has particularly come to refer to the fall of Communism signified by the breaching of the BERLINER MAUER on 9 November 1989. This now marks the major turning-point in post-war German history.

WENDERS, WIM (1945–)
Film director with an international reputation and exponent of the *Neuer deutscher Film*. His films explore modern German society and the effect of American culture on Europe, and he

has worked extensively with author Peter Handke. His films include *Die Angst des Tormanns beim Elfmeter* (1971, after a novel by Handke), *Falsche Bewegung* (1975, scripted by Handke based on Goethe's *Wilhelm Meisters Lehrjahre*), *Der Stand der Dinge* (1982), *Der Himmel über Berlin* (1987, script by Handke) and the sequel *In weiter Ferne, so nah!* (1993).

WERBUNGSKOSTEN

The expenses incurred by an individual in seeking and maintaining a source of income. These are deductible from EINKOMMEN-STEUER. See also: ARBEITNEHMERPAUSCHBETRAG

WERTSTOFFANNAHMESTELLE

The '*Wertstoffhof*' is a collection point in most villages for the inhabitants to return pre-sorted recyclable materials. These are then sorted further into different categories. See also: DUALES SYSTEM DEUTSCHLAND; GRÜNER PUNKT; VERPACKUNGSVERORDNUNG

WESER KURIER

Daily newspaper distributed in and around BREMEN. Together with its sister newspaper *Bremer Nachrichten* it has a circulation of 207,000.

WESSI

Wessis is used colloquially for west Germans as opposed to east Germans (OSSIS). Particularly applied by east Germans to people from west Germany who represent the slick, flashy face of consumerism and materialism. '*Besserwessi*' is a pun derived from '*Besserwisser*' (know-all).

WESTDEUTSCHE ALLGEMEINE ZEITUNG (WAZ)

Daily newspaper established in 1948 and published in ESSEN by Zeitungs-Gruppe WAZ. This is Germany's biggest selling broadsheet with a circulation of around 624,000.

WESTDEUTSCHE LANDESBANK GIROZENTRALE

The biggest of the LANDESBANKEN and Germany's biggest public-sector bank. It is the central financial institution for NORDRHEIN-WESTFALEN and Germany's third largest bank. See also: ÖFFENTLICH-RECHTLICHE KREDITINSTITUTE

WESTDEUTSCHER RUNDFUNK (WDR)

A regional public-service radio and TV broadcasting corporation based in KÖLN and broadcasting to NORDRHEIN-WESTFALEN. Westdeutscher Rundfunk is a member of the ARD. See also: LANDESRUNDFUNK- UND FERNSEHANSTALTEN

WESTFALEN-BLATT

Daily newspaper published in BIELEFELD with a circulation of 145,000.

WESTFÄLISCHE NACHRICHTEN

Daily newspaper published in MÜNSTER with a circulation of 229,000.

WESTPREUSSEN

A former province of PREUSSEN with Danzig (Gdansk) as its capital, now part of modern-day Poland. See also: ZWEI-PLUS-VIER-VERTRAG

WETTEN, DASS ...?

Popular Saturday-evening live star show on ZDF involving dares and sums of money, with moderator Thomas GOTTSCHALK attracting huge audiences.

WETTERDIENST See: *DEUTSCHER WETTERDIENST*

WIDERSTANDSRECHT

The GRUNDGESETZ grants every German citizen the right to resist anybody or any authority acting contrary to the constitution. The offence against the constitution must be obvious, resistance should be the only available means of restoring law and order, and it may only be offered in an emergency until the rule of law is restored.

WIEDERVEREINIGUNG

The reunification of Germany was triggered by the economic crisis of the Eastern bloc and massive demonstrations in the former DDR. On 3 October 1990 the DDR was reunited within the BRD under *Artikel* 23 of the GRUNDGESETZ.

WIESBADEN

Wiesbaden is the LANDESHAUPTSTADT of HESSEN and is situated on

the Rhine at the foot of the TAUNUS mountains (dialling code 06
11, postal area code 65...). The city was well-known as a spa
during Roman times, and the city's heyday was during the nineteenth century when Europe's aristocrats took the waters and
gambled at the city's casino. The tradition of using the curative
powers of the hot salt springs for medicinal purposes has persisted to the present day. The umbrella organisation for the film
industry (SPITZENORGANISATION DER FILMWIRTSCHAFT E.V.) is based
in Wiesbaden, and the Rheingau Musik Festival is held there
every year.

The city has a population of some 264,000 with a student population of around 8,000 (1 HOCHSCHULE) and about 18% foreigners (25% Turkish). A coalition between the SPD, CDU and FDP has
been running the city since 1993. Wiesbaden is now an administrative centre and home to the BUNDESKRIMINALAMT and the STA-
TISTISCHES BUNDESAMT. Industries include construction materials,
chemicals, machinery and sparkling wine (SEKT) with tourism
also playing an important role. See also: KUR; RHEINGAU

WIESKIRCHE, DIE

This 'Meadow Church' at Steingaden in the Voralpenland of
BAYERN is a church of pilgrimage and was made a UNESCO
world heritage site in recognition of its baroque glory.

WILHELM-LEHMBRUCK-MUSEUM

Museum of twentieth-century sculpture and painting in DUISBURG
opened in 1964 to celebrate the Duisburg sculptor Wilhelm
Lehmbruck (1881–1919) and housing a large collection of his
works.

WIRTSCHAFTS- UND WÄHRUNGSUNION

The currency union between the DDR and the BRD was introduced
on 1 July 1990 in conjunction with economic and social union.
This was the first step towards reunification and introduced the
DM throughout German territory. Private savings accounts were
exchanged at a rate of 1 to 1 up to a limit of DM 4,000, when a
rate of 2 to 1 came into force. The KOHL government was heavily
criticised for allowing a rate that was too generous, but this

proved an astute political move that won the CDU the 1990 BUN-
DESTAGSWAHLEN.

WIRTSCHAFTSGYMNASIUM
A GYMNASIUM where the LEHRPLAN includes economics, business
studies, law and accounting in addition to the usual general subjects.

WIRTSCHAFTSPRÜFER
An auditor who is qualified to audit large companies. In the past
the profession was highly élitist, but the 4th EC directive (1978)
designed to harmonise accounting rules in the EC required
medium-sized and large GMBHS to have an annual audit and publish accounts. This has meant the profession has had to open up
in order to provide the people to deal with the increased work-
load. See also: ABSCHLUSSPRÜFUNG; MITTELSTAND

WIRTSCHAFTSVERBÄNDE
Associations of entrepreneurs and companies from the same sector formed to pursue common economic goals and to promote
their interest to the public and to the authorities.

WIRTSCHAFTSWOCHE (WiWo)
Weekly business magazine with a circulation of 163,000. Its readership comprises top managers and decision-makers and it
reports on economics, finance and management.

WIRTSCHAFTSWUNDER
The 'economic miracle' engineered by BUNDESWIRTSCHAFTSMINIS-
TER Ludwig Erhard during the 1950s. The catalyst for the
Wirtschaftswunder was the WÄHRUNGSREFORM introduced in 1948,
combined with massive aid under the Marshall Plan and hard
work that got industrial production up and running in record
time, resulting in a stable, thriving economic climate.

WISMAR, TECHNISCHE HOCHSCHULE
University in MECKLENBURG-VORPOMMERN founded in 1969 and
teaching some 1,700 students. The Technische Hochschule
Wismar has faculties of civil engineering, electrical engineering,
mechanical engineering, economics.

WISSENSCHAFTLICHE HILFSKRAFT
Part-time teaching/research assistant at a HOCHSCHULE, normally a student (*studentische Hilfskraft*) who has completed the ZWISCHENPRÜFUNG or VORDIPLOM, also known as *Hiwi* (*Hilfswissenschaftler*).

WISSENSCHAFTLICHE HOCHSCHULEN See:
HOCHSCHULEN

WISSENSCHAFTLICHER ASSISTENT
A postgraduate carrying out teaching and research assignments under the guidance of a PROFESSOR and who must at the same time be engaged in independent research. *Wissenschaftliche Assistenten* are expected to work towards their PROMOTION or HABILITATION. Appointments are typically for three years in the first instance with the possibility of extension for a further two/three years; the precise length of service will vary according to the LAND and prevailing financial conditions. This is often the first rung on the academic ladder. See also: HOCHSCHULASSISTENT

WISSENSCHAFTLICHER MITARBEITER
Research assistant at a HOCHSCHULE on a fixed-term contract without the status of BEAMTER. *Wissenschaftliche Mitarbeiter* are often financed by external funding.

WISSENSCHAFTSFREIHEIT
The GRUNDGESETZ guarantees the freedom of scholarship, research and teaching.

WISSENSCHAFTSRAT
An advisory body founded in 1957 as a result of an agreement between BUND and LÄNDER to promote the HOCHSCHULEN, arts, science and research. The *Wissenschaftsrat* is based in KÖLN and makes recommendations on changes in these areas.

WISSMANN, MATTHIAS (1949–)
CDU politician who was briefly BUNDESMINISTER FÜR BILDUNG, WISSENSCHAFT, FORSCHUNG UND TECHNOLOGIE in 1993 and was then appointed BUNDESMINISTER FÜR VERKEHR in 1993.

WITTELSBACH
The dynasty that ruled BAYERN from the twelfth century until 1918. The *Wittelsbacher* still enjoy considerable respect among tradition-conscious Bavarians.

WiWo See: *WIRTSCHAFTSWOCHE*

WOCHENEND
Weekly magazine established in 1976 and published in HAMBURG by BAUER VERLAG with a circulation of 275,000. Its main readership is workers and their families, and it provides a mix of factual information and entertainment.

WOCHENPOST
Weekly newspaper published in BERLIN with a circulation of 102,000. The readership is centred on east Germany among top managers and administrators, and the newspaper covers politics, culture and business.

WOHNGELD
A housing allowance paid by the government to benefit low-income families. Eligibility for *Wohngeld* depends on the size of the family, level of income and the amount of rent payable.

WOHNSITZ
The place of habitual residence of a German citizen that has to be registered with the GEMEINDE or EINWOHNERMELDEAMT. This is the place where a person carries on all their usual activities of living and working and is where any official business with the authorities is conducted. A citizen is permitted to have a second *Wohnsitz* which may be in Germany or abroad.

WOLF, CHRISTA (1929–   )
An author who emerged in the DDR in the 1960s. She considered it a writer's duty to remain in the DDR as a critical socialist rather than emigrate to the affluent West. Her work projects a humanist view of society and centres on individual experience. It includes the novels *Der geteilte Himmel* (1963), *Nachdenken über Christa T.* (1968), *Kindheitsmuster* (1976), *Kassandra* (1983) and *Medea. Stimmen* (1996). Her reputation was tarnished when she published *Was bleibt* (1990), an autobiographical account of her

surveillance by the infamous STAATSSICHERHEITSDIENST in 1979, and it subsequently emerged that she herself had briefly acted as an informer in 1959. The work promoted a wide-ranging public debate on East German literature, and the aesthetic worth of politically committed literature in general. Wolf remains one of the most widely respected contemporary German writers.

WULF-MATHIES, MONIKA (1942–)

Trade unionist, philosopher and member of the SPD since 1965. She was head of the ÖTV in 1982–1994 and has been an EU commissioner since 1995.

WUPPERTAL

Wuppertal is situated on the river Wupper in NORDRHEIN-WESTFALEN (dialling code 02 02, postal area code 42...). The town of Barmen-Elberfeld was formed in 1929 by the amalgamation of the towns of Barmen, Elberfeld, Ronsdorf, Vohwinkel and Cronenberg, and the name was changed to Wuppertal in 1930. The city boasts a unique suspended monorail public transport system known as the SCHWEBEBAHN. The town of Barmen was home to Friedrich Engels, collaborator with Karl Marx, and in 1934 the town witnessed a synod of Protestant opponents of Hitler who declared that the Church was independent of state control. Wuppertal's Schauspielhaus houses Germany's leading modern dance company, the Wuppertaler Tanztheater.

The city has a population of some 387,000 with a total student population of around 18,000 (1 UNIVERSITÄT and 3 other HOCH-SCHULEN) and about 14% foreigners (30% Turkish). A coalition between the SPD and BÜNDNIS 90/DIE GRÜNEN has been running the city since 1994. Wuppertal is one of a number of industrial cities in the BERGISCHES LAND and is the centre for the region's textile industry. Other industries include machinery, chemicals, pharmaceuticals and printing.

WUPPERTAL, BERGISCHE UNIVERSITÄT-GESAMTHOCHSCHULE

University in NORDRHEIN-WESTFALEN founded in 1972 and teaching some 18,000 students. The Bergische Universität-Gesamthochschule Wuppertal has faculties of sociology, philosophy and theology, education, languages and literature, art and design, music, economics, mathematics, physics, chemistry and biology, architecture, construction engineering, mechanical engineering, electrical engineering, safety and accident prevention.

WÜRZBURG

The *Residenz* in Würzburg (BAYERN) has been made a UNESCO world heritage site. This was the palace the archbishops of Würzburg built to rival the palaces of the great European courts. It was painstakingly reconstructed after being badly bombed during the Second World War. The unsupported vaulted roof over the staircase, brilliantly constructed by Balthasar Neumann in 1720–1744, miraculously survived, with the world's largest fresco by Tiepolo intact.

WÜRZBURG, BAYERISCHE JULIUS-MAXIMILIANS-UNIVERSITÄT

University in BAYERN founded in 1582 and teaching some 21,000 students. The Bayerische Julius-Maximilians-Universität Würzburg has faculties of Catholic theology, law, medicine, philosophy (arts), biology, chemistry and pharmacology, geosciences, mathematics and computer science, physics and astronomy, economics.

ZADEK, PETER (1926–)

Theatre producer and film director who has shocked and excited his audiences. After leaving Germany in 1933 he spent the years of the DRITTES REICH in exile in London, returning to the BRD in 1958. He was Schauspieldirektor in BREMEN in 1962–1967, GENERALINTENDANT in BOCHUM in 1972–1977 and INTENDANT at the Deutsches Schauspielhaus in HAMBURG in 1985–1988. His theatre productions include Shakespeare's *Othello* (1977), Wedekind's *Lulu* (1988) and Chekhov's *Iwanow* (1990) as well as numerous films and TV productions.

ZAPF, HERMANN (1918–)

Calligrapher and book designer who has designed and exhibited more than 175 typographical fonts. Among them is the widely used *Palatino*, which Zapf designed in 1950. He has lectured extensively in the US and at DARMSTADT (TECHNISCHE HOCHSCHULE).

ZDF See: *ZWEITES DEUTSCHES FERNSEHEN*

ZDH See: *ZENTRALVERBAND DES DEUTSCHEN HANDWERKS*

ZEIT See: *DIE ZEIT*

ZEITUNGSENTE

A canard or false report, rumour or hoax published in a newspaper. The SÜDDEUTSCHE ZEITUNG publishes a false report as a joke (*Aprilscherz*) each April Fool's Day.

ZENDER, HANS (1936–)

Composer and conductor whose work was influenced by B. A. Zimmermann and includes *Hölderlin lesen* for string quartet and narrator (1979), the opera *Stephen Climax* (1986) and *Memorial* for piano (1990).

ZENTRALRAT DER JUDEN IN DEUTSCHLAND

The central council of Jews in Germany is based in DÜSSELDORF and was formed in 1950 as the SPITZENVERBAND of Jewish communities in Germany. It advises the government on legislation relating to compensation and promotes the culture and religion of the Jewish community in Germany. See also: BUBIS, IGNATZ

ZENTRALSTELLE FÜR DIE VERGABE VON STUDIENPLÄTZEN (ZVS)

The central clearing organisation in DORTMUND for distributing places at HOCHSCHULEN. It allocates places on courses with a restricted number of places according to strict criteria applied throughout the country. See also: NUMERUS CLAUSUS

ZENTRALVERBAND DES DEUTSCHEN HANDWERKS (ZDH)

The umbrella organisation for craft trades in Germany is based in BONN. It lobbies for the interests of craft trades to authorities at the level of the BUND and to the European Union, as well as representing German craft trades internationally.

ZEUGNISVERWEIGERUNGSRECHT

The right of journalists under German law whereby they cannot be compelled to divulge the identity of sources who have provided information in confidence for an article they have written.

ZF FRIEDRICHSHAFEN AG

Power engineering company manufacturing gearboxes, transmissions and components, founded in 1915. Company headquarters are in Friedrichshafen (BADEN-WÜRTTEMBERG). ZF Friedrichshafen has some 31,000 employees.

ZFU See: *STAATLICHE ZENTRALSTELLE FÜR FERNUNTERRICHT*

ZIVILDIENST

Community service carried out by recognised KRIEGSDIENSTVER-WEIGERER instead of military service. The *Zivildienst* of 13 months is overseen by the Bundesamt für Frauen und Jugend and the tasks assigned in this service are generally jobs of a social nature such as ambulance driver or assistant in a hospital or KINDERGARTEN.

ZUGSPITZE See: *BAYERISCHE ALPEN*

ZULASSUNGSANTRAG
Application for admission to a HOCHSCHULE that has to be submitted by all applicants for a place at a *Hochschule*. Foreign students can obtain an application form and a copy of the admission regulations from individual *Hochschulen*, from German embassies or from offices of the DAAD.

ZULASSUNGSBESCHEID
Acceptance for admission to a HOCHSCHULE.

ZUSAMMENSCHLUSS
The amalgamation of a number of GEMEINDEN or GEMEINDEVERBÄNDE.

ZVS See: *ZENTRALSTELLE FÜR DIE VERGABE VON STUDIENPLÄTZEN*

ZWECKVERBAND
An association of GEMEINDEN and GEMEINDEVERBÄNDE formed for the purpose of delivering certain services that are best provided on a larger scale. It is a local-government body provided with the legal status necessary for it to carry out the function or functions for which it was created.

ZWEI-PLUS-VIER-VERHANDLUNGEN
The negotiations commenced on 5 May 1990 between the four Allied powers (France, Soviet Union, United Kingdom, United States) and the BRD and the DDR to resolve the questions posed by German reunification. The negotiations ended with the signing of the ZWEI-PLUS-VIER-VERTRAG on 12 September 1990.

ZWEI-PLUS-VIER-VERTRAG
The treaty signed by the four Allied powers and the BRD and DDR on 12 September 1990 regulating the conditions for German reunification. The treaty defined the territory of the united Germany, the strength of the BUNDESWEHR and the withdrawal of

Soviet troops, and confirmed that Germany's membership of NATO remained unaffected.

ZWEITER BILDUNGSWEG

Secondary education for adult learners who did not gain the qualifications they wish to obtain at school. Learners can study during the day or in the evening, and courses lead to the REALSCHULABSCHLUSS or the ABITUR. Institutions offering these courses include the ABENDGYMNASIUM, VOLKSHOCHSCHULE and ABENDREALSCHULE.

ZWEITES DEUTSCHES FERNSEHEN (ZDF)

The second terrestrial channel in Germany set up by the LÄNDER as a public-service broadcasting corporation (ÖFFENTLICH-RECHTLICHE RUNDFUNKANSTALT). It was established in 1961 and is based in MAINZ and started broadcasting the ZWEITES PROGRAMM in 1963. ZDF is financed by licence fees and advertising. Two-thirds of the viewers are in the over-fifties bracket, and in the first half of 1995 the station trailed in fourth place in the ratings behind RTL, SAT 1 and ARD.

ZWEITES PROGRAMM

The second German public TV channel, operated by ZDF.

ZWEITSTIMME

The second vote in an election in Germany, used to vote for a particular party according to proportional representation. The *Zweitstimmen* hold the key to final percentages and therefore to the number of MANDATE for each party in the BUNDESTAG or LAND-TAG. See also: BUNDESTAGSWAHL; LANDESLISTE; LANDTAGSWAHL

ZWISCHENPRÜFUNG

An intermediate examination, especially in the arts, taken after a minimum of four SEMESTER of study (GRUNDSTUDIUM) at HOCHSCHULEN. Passing the *Zwischenprüfung* does not confer the status of a full qualification.

Bibliography

The listed books give further detail on the areas covered by this dictionary. Most are in English and do not presuppose a detailed knowledge of the German context.

The most up-to-date information on current affairs is of course found in the mass media, which are not included in this bibliography, though the dictionary contains entries for major newspapers, news magazines and TV channels. Increasingly, news publications are available on CD-ROM, and German news is accessible via satellite/cable television or the Internet. The *Spiegel TV Jahresrückblick* videos offer visual highlights. The following annual publications are mostly international in scope, but offer extensive information on Germany (the volumes listed are the most recent ones consulted in the compilation of this dictionary):

Aktuell '96. Harenberg Lexikon der Gegenwart (Harenberg Lexikon Verlag, 1995)

Chronik 1995. Der vollständige Jahresrückblick in Wort und Bild, Übersichten und Vergleichen (Chronik Verlag/Bertelsmann, 1996)

Der Fischer Weltalmanach 1996 (Fischer Taschenbuch Verlag, 1995)

Jahrbuch der Bundesrepublik Deutschland 1993/94, ed. by E. Hübner and H.-H. Rohlfs (Deutscher Taschenbuch Verlag, 1993)

Fischer also issue an annual volume on cinema, video and TV:

Fischer Film-Almanach 1995. Filme, Festivals, Tendenzen (Fischer Taschenbuch Verlag, 1995)

General publications on Germany are listed below:

Ardagh, J., *Germany and the Germans*, 2nd ed. (Penguin, 1991)

Jones, A., *The New Germany. A Human Geography* (Wiley, 1994)

Tatsachen über Deutschland (translated as *Facts about Germany*) (Societäts-Verlag, 1993) (regularly updated; available from the German Embassy, London, as well as from bookshops)

The following books give an insight into specific aspects of contemporary Germany:

Beyme, K. von, *Das politische System der Bundesrepublik Deutschland nach der Vereinigung*, 2nd ed. (Piper, 1991)

Foster, N., *German Law and Legal System* (Blackstone, 1993)

Greiffenhagen, M., and others (eds), *Die neuen Bundesländer* (Kohlhammer, 1994)

Head, D., *Made in Germany. The Corporate Identity of a Nation* (Hodder & Stoughton, 1992)

Humphreys, P. J., *Media and Media Policy in Germany. The Press and Broadcasting since 1945*, 2nd ed. (Berg, 1994)

Kolinsky, Eva, *Women in Contemporary Germany. Life, Work and Politics*, 2nd ed. (Berg, 1993)

Marsh, D., *Germany and Europe. The Crisis of Unity* (Heinemann, 1994)

Randlesome, C., *The Business Culture in Germany* (Butterworth-Heinemann, 1994)

Scharf, T., *The German Greens. Challenging the Consensus* (Berg, 1994)

For a highly readable history of Germany from the Weimar Republic up to reunification see:

Fulbrook, M., *The Fontana History of Germany 1918-1990: The Divided Nation* (Fontana, 1991)

A useful supplement to a general bilingual dictionary when reading the German press is:

Good, C., *Newspaper German. A Vocabulary of Administrative and Commercial Idiom* (University of Wales Press, 1995)